Boycott

The Life Behind the Word

BOYCOTT

The Life Behind the Word

The Life and Times in England and in Ireland
and
The Unusual Family Background
of
CHARLES CUNNINGHAM BOYCOTT

by

Charles Arthur Boycott

Carbonel Press

A Carbonel Press Book

First published in Great Britain in 1997
by Carbonel Press

A CIP catalogue record for this book
is available from the British Library

ISBN: 0 9531407 0 9

Typeset by Palimpsest Book Production Limited,
Polmont, Stirlingshire
Printed and bound in Great Britain by
Creative Print & Design (Wales), Ebbw Vale

Carbonel Press (UK)
Tinkers Hill
Ludlow
Shropshire
SY8 4BW

IRELAND

'No man can know Ireland by inspiration'*
(Robert Ross to Lord Downshire, 9th July 1798)

ENGLAND

If England was what England seems,
An' not the England of our dreams,
But only putty, brass, an' paint,
'Ow quick we'd drop 'er! But she ain't.

Rudyard Kipling

* Quoted by A.P.W. Malcomson in John Foster, *The Politics of the Anglo-Irish Ascendancy.*

Contents

PART THREE: AN 'UNSOUGHT INTERVAL'*

PART FOUR: AUGUST 1881 – JUNE 1897

* (includes Charles Cunningham Boycott's dispute with the Prime Minister [W.E. Gladstone] and his visit to the U.S.A.)

ACKNOWLEDGEMENTS

My thanks are given to the following:

Organisations

Burgh-St-Peter Church Registers
Cambridge University Library
Church Missions Library, Dublin
Colindale Library, London
Essex County Council Library
Gonville & Caius College, Cambridge
Mayo County Library
National Library, Dublin
Norfolk Record Office
Norwich Diocesan Registry
Racing Museum, Newmarket
R.C.B. Library, Dublin
Royal Irish Academy Library, Dublin
Royal Naval Museum Library, Greenwich
Queens University Library, Belfast
Suffolk County Council Library
Valuation Office, Dublin

Individuals

Dr W.O. Attlee; Mr Dominic Beddow; (The late) Mr C.T.A. Beevor; Mr J. Benest; General Sir Cecil Blacker; Mr Henry Blosse-Lynch; Mr Charles Boycott (not the author); Ms Rosie Boycott; Mr Hugh Boycott-Brown; The Reverend John Browne; Mr Stephen Browne; Mr Josh Bullen (Asset Retrieval U.S.A.); Mrs Anne Chadwicke; Mrs Brigid Chesham; The Church of Jesus Christ of Latter-Day Saints; (The late) Mrs Coley; (The late) Mr Charles Collier; Mr T.H. Corke; Dr Fergus D'Arcy; Dr Geoffrey Daw; Lord Erne; Mrs A.G. Evershed; Mr G.R. Fenwick; Ms Sally Fricker; (The late) Mr Maurice Gandy; Mr Goodwin (of Beccles); (The late) Mr Grey (of Dugort, Achill Island); Mr Alan Havsteen-Mikkelsen; Mr Richard Hawkins; Miss Lizzie Henderson; Mr Hilson; Professor John Hudson; Mr T. Huleatt-James; Agher H. Jolland; Mrs Killen; Lord Kilmaine; Mr David Leitch; Mr & Mrs Llewelyn; Mrs Macartney; Mr A.P.W. Malcomson; Mr M. Masterson; Dr H.C.G. Matthew; Mr John Mayock; Mr & Mrs McConnaughey (U.S.A.); Mr James McHugh; Mr A.H. Miles; Colonel Frank Nangle; Mr John O'Shea; Dr W. O'Sullivan; Dr John Pope; (The late) Dr Sandy Pringle; Dr Anne Ralph; Mr Robert Robinson; Mr G.S. Rose; Mr Donald Scott; Rev. Thomas South; Mr Leslie Stewart; Mr J.D.T. Tatham; Miss Trimble (Mrs Gant); Mr Robin Turner; Mr Charlie Viney; Mr Nigel Viney; Mr Jarlett Waldron; Mr S.J. Watson; (The late) Miss Leah Weekes; Air Commodore C.M. White-Boycott; and three *excellent* typists: Mrs Jenny Nash, Mrs Carole Perks and Mrs P.M.S. Rooney (who also lent me reference books).

INTRODUCTION

By Sir Leonard Figg (sometime H.M. Ambassador to Eire)

Charles Boycott has done some impressive research in Ireland and England to produce this story of his famous ancestor. He covers one of the many difficult periods in Anglo-Irish history, including England's appalling failure to cope with the Irish famine. His story of the Boycott family starts in East Anglia, where a succession of Boycotts were rectors in Norfolk. In Ireland the author shows us his ancestor living happily for years on Achill Island and then working as the agent of Lord Erne in County Mayo. His becoming victim of the activities of the Land League is so well described that we must have great sympathy for him.

Charles Boycott's aim has been to show Captain Boycott in a truer and fairer light than popular history has allowed. He has succeeded very well; and readers on both sides of the Irish Sea will find much here to interest them.

By the Author

Who *was* 'Boycott'? Why does the verb 'to boycott' appear in almost every dictionary? Why write about him?

First. Charles Cunningham Boycott came from an unusual family background in which moral rectitude was jealously guarded. Misconduct was frowned upon. Boycott's great-grandfather, grandfather, father, younger brother and nephew (all bearing the Boycott surname) became consecutive Protestant Rectors of the same small South Norfolk parish.*

Second. Because most of the existing portraits of 'Boycott' himself are less than fair. The film *Captain Boycott* (released early

* Boycott himself was the second son of the third Rector.

in 1947) is misleading; Joyce Marlow's book *Captain Boycott and the Irish* omits material; Philip Rooney's book *Captain Boycott* is little more than a novel. Over the years the reputation of Charles Cunningham Boycott has been subject to much ignorant criticism; Alexander Pope's lines are to the point:

> Words are like leaves; and where they most abound
> Much fruit of sense beneath is rarely found.

Third. Because Charles loved Ireland. He married an Irish girl. He became a 'Co. Mayo man'. He farmed well and successfully on Achill Island for eighteen years and for about twelve years equally well on the shore of Lough Mask near Ballinrobe.

Fourth. Toward the end of the nineteenth century the population of Co. Mayo was about 95% Catholic. Despite the fact that Charles always worshipped, publicly, as a Protestant he was never criticised (as far as is known) on account of his religious beliefs.

The French Revolution started in 1789, and later European revolutions followed but the Irish 'revolution' – or Land War – did not start until 1879. That an Irish revolution did not occur earlier was due to the famine, to a post-famine agricultural prosperity and to the curious 'love-hate' relationship which existed between England and Ireland.

This book is able to present no more than an incomplete portrait of a man who died in 1897 at the age of 65; but who left behind him a word in world use. It may be true that '. . . what you are told is threefold; shaped by the teller, reshaped by the listener, concealed from both by the dead man of the tale.' The *details* of history are, almost always, uncertain. Perceptions change. Memories are not infallible. Boycott had no children; a son, or a daughter, might have been able to write something better than that which has been done by his great-great-nephew.*

* Ireland, during Charles's years, was one country forming part of the United Kingdom. Since 1922 Ireland has been divided both geographically and politically. Six counties in Northern Ireland (whose loyalty, for the most part, is to England) make up 'Northern Ireland'; the remainding counties make up Eire which is now an independent sovereign state.

It is difficult to foretell the future and even more difficult to see how Ireland can be re-united into one geographical whole. Many people, living in the north of Ireland, see clear economic advantages in remaining part of England. No one should overlook the fact that the English are a courageous, resilient, inventive and resourceful people; and that England presently stands high in the list of successful manufacturing countries of the world.

BOYCOTT FAMILY TREE

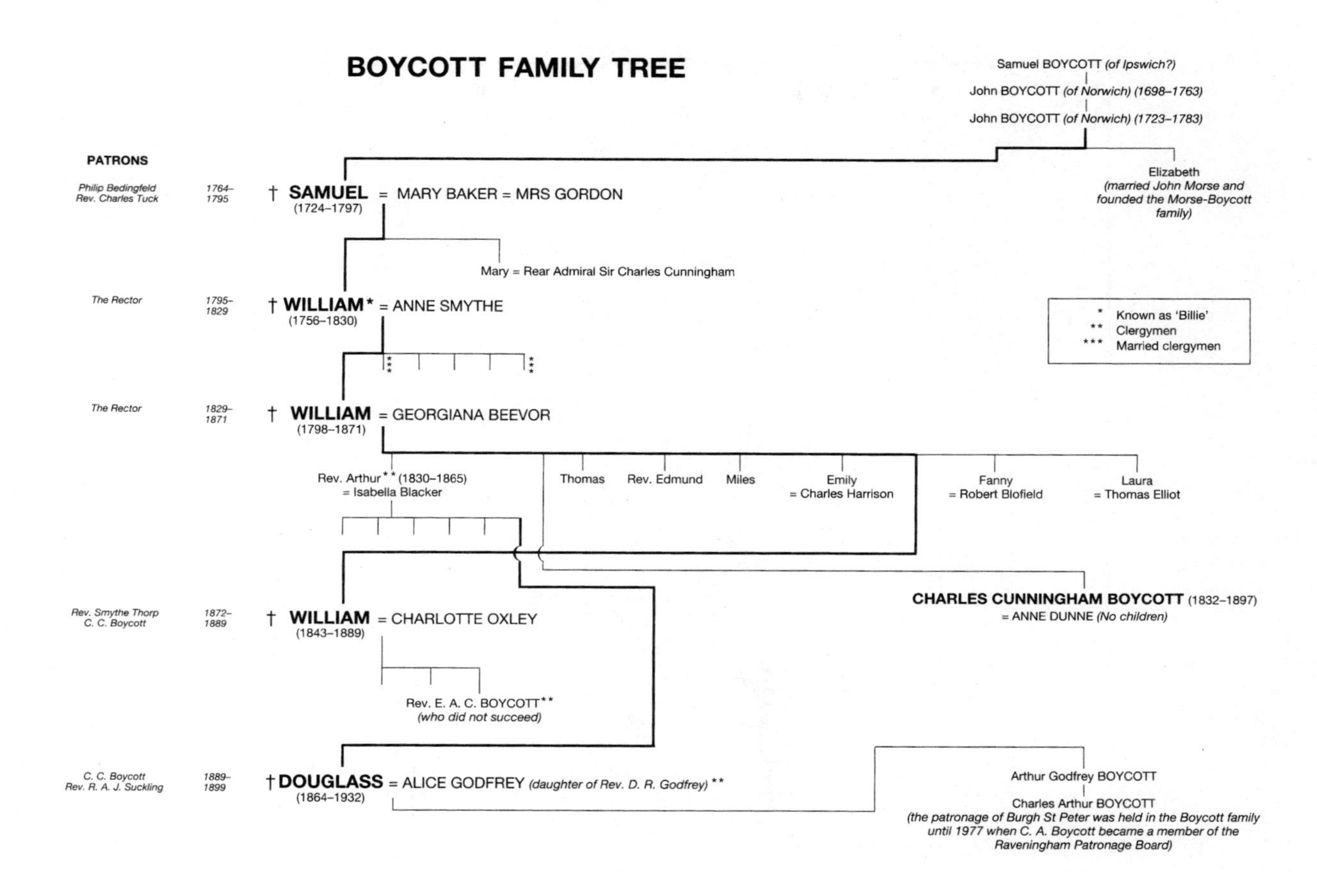

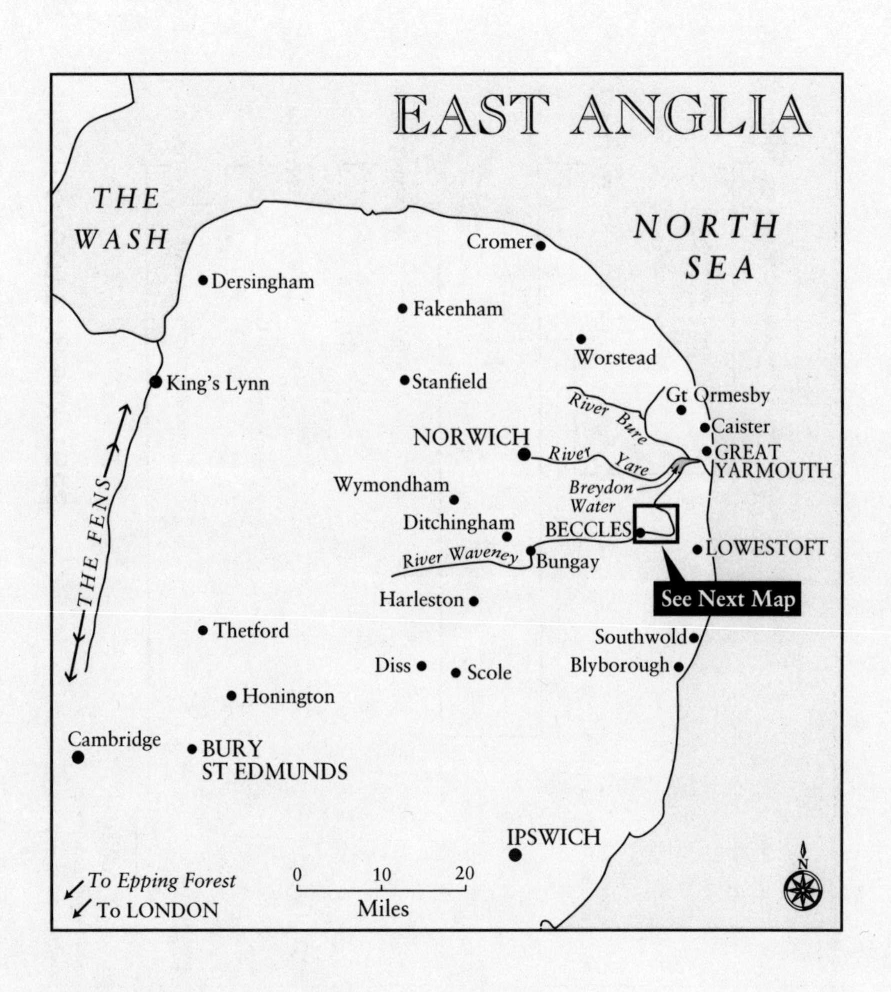
EAST ANGLIA
THE WASH
NORTH SEA
Cromer
Dersingham
Fakenham
Worstead
King's Lynn
Stanfield
Gt Ormesby
River Bure
Caister
NORWICH
River Yare
GREAT YARMOUTH
Breydon Water
Wymondham
Ditchingham
BECCLES
LOWESTOFT
River Waveney
Bungay
THE FENS
Harleston
See Next Map
Thetford
Southwold
Blyborough
Diss
Scole
Honington
Cambridge
BURY ST EDMUNDS
IPSWICH
To Epping Forest
To LONDON
0
10
20
Miles
N

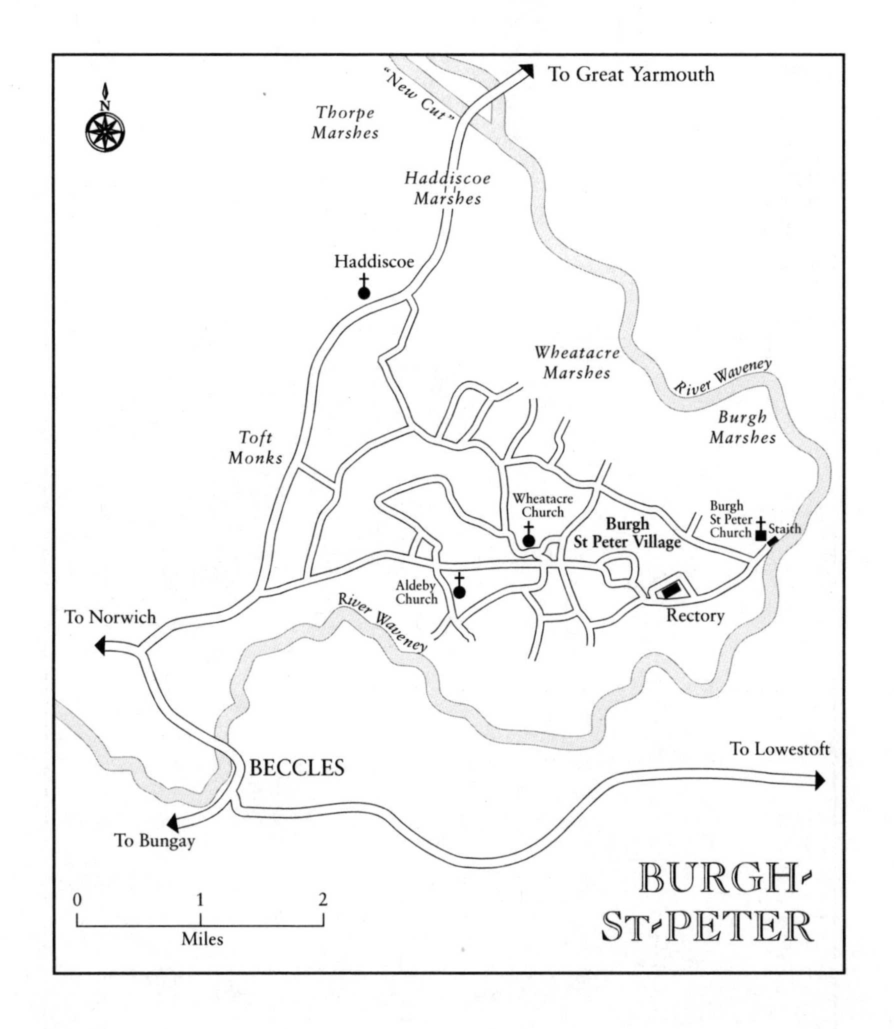
To Great Yarmouth
"New Cut"
Thorpe Marshes
Haddiscoe Marshes
Haddiscoe
Wheatacre Marshes
River Waveney
Burgh Marshes
Toft Monks
Wheatacre Church
Burgh St Peter Village
Burgh St Peter Church
Staith
Aldeby Church
River Waveney
Rectory
To Norwich
BECCLES
To Lowestoft
To Bungay
0
1
2
Miles
BURGH-ST-PETER

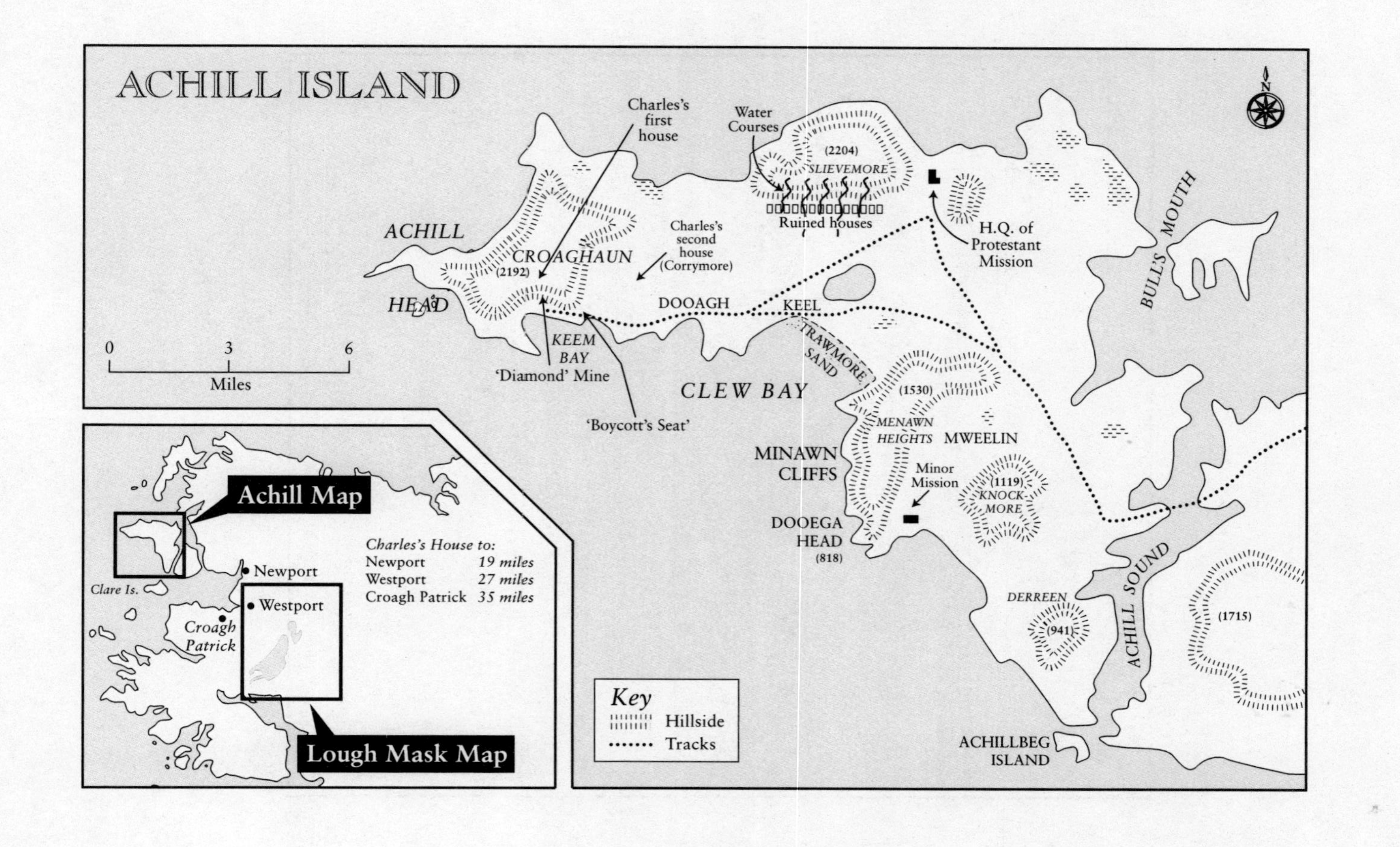
ACHILL ISLAND
Charles's first house
Water Courses
(2204)
SLIEVEMORE
Ruined houses
H.Q. of Protestant Mission
ACHILL
CROAGHAUN
(2192)
HEAD
Charles's second house (Corrymore)
DOOAGH
KEEL
KEEM BAY
'Diamond' Mine
'Boycott's Seat'
TRAWMORE SAND
CLEW BAY
BULL'S MOUTH
0
3
6
Miles
(1530)
MENAWN HEIGHTS
MWEELIN
MINAWN CLIFFS
Minor Mission
(1119)
KNOCK-MORE
DOOEGA HEAD
(818)
ACHILL SOUND
DERREEN
(941)
(1715)
ACHILLBEG ISLAND
Key
Hillside
Tracks
Achill Map
Lough Mask Map
Newport
Westport
Clare Is.
Croagh Patrick
Charles's House to:
Newport 19 miles
Westport 27 miles
Croagh Patrick 35 miles
N

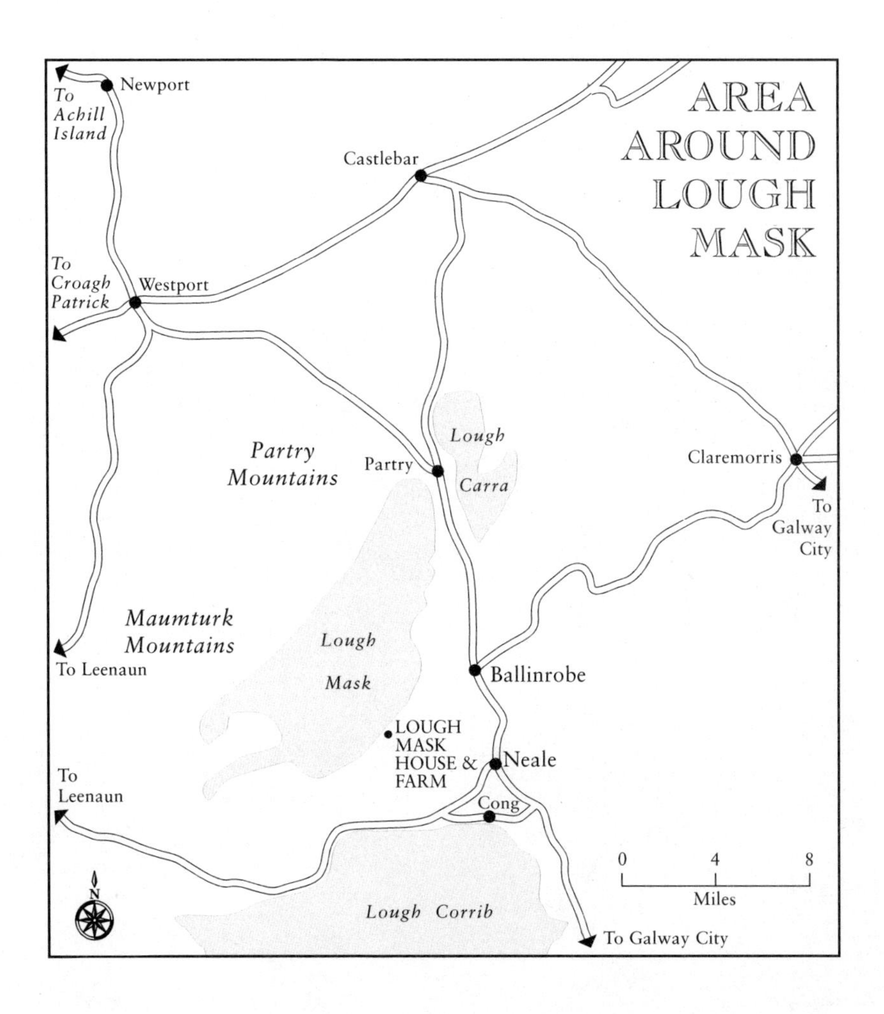
AREA AROUND LOUGH MASK
Newport
To Achill Island
Castlebar
To Croagh Patrick
Westport
Partry Mountains
Partry
Lough Carra
Claremorris
To Galway City
Maumturk Mountains
To Leenaun
Lough Mask
Ballinrobe
LOUGH MASK HOUSE & FARM
Neale
To Leenaun
Cong
0
4
8
Miles
N
Lough Corrib
To Galway City

PART ONE

ENGLAND – IRELAND

ca 1750 – *ca* 1850

CHAPTER ONE

ON THE 12TH MARCH 1832 a second son was born to the Reverend William Boycatt, Rector of Burgh-St-Peter in the county of Norfolk, and his wife Georgiana. The day was quiet and foggy. A few catspaws of wind came southerly but they warmed the air only at midday; the early morning and evening were cold and raw. The long isolated rectory building where the boy had been born lay wrapped, that day, in that stillness and privacy which only fog brings to old buildings. Inside lay warmth and happiness; and a due thankfulness for another safe delivery from 'the great pain and peril of childbirth.'[1]

Four days later the baby was taken down the mile-long lane to within a stone's throw of the River Waveney – bridgeless for miles both up and down stream – and into the even lonelier and isolated church which stands unique as the south-easternmost building in Norfolk. There he was baptised by his father and given the christian names of Charles Cunningham. Both names were new to the Boycatts. As will be seen the names were nicely calculated to fire any boy of the family who turned out well, and who knew and understood their origin and significance, with youthful ambition; and, later, to inspire the man with courage and a sense of obligation and duty.

Like the blind, amongst whom the one-eyed is king, the long grey thatched church stands 'high' at the end of a low promontory itself only a few feet above the 'zero' contour line. The encircling Waveney and its marshes – many of them 'salt' – lay below this line. The river – broad, sinuous and deep – makes its sluggish way northerly past the church to mingle first with the Yare from Norwich, then with the brackish mixtures of Breydon Water – into which the tide floods – and, finally, with the Bure before everything discharges into the sea at Yarmouth. To stand by the church was to stand and look out over a great emptiness of marsh and water.

Unlike so much of its low and wet-under-foot seaward surroundings, the Burgh-St-Peter promontory is sound enduring land. In the days of Christ, salt water, rising and falling with every tide, lapped its zero contour line. The Romans, concerned to defend themselves and their conquered territory against a seaborne counter invasion from the north, built their main fortifications of Burgh Castle[2] and Caistor Castle on two sandy offshore islands; between them and the mainland lay the bay Gariensis Ostium. To Roman eyes the Burgh-St-Peter promontory was *terra firma*; a mainland position of strategic and tactical importance. The Romans moored their boats under Burgh-St-Peter cliff and in them brought ashore great catches of fish. They made bricks and built barracks, stables and houses. Almost nothing of their occupation now remains except for a few Roman bricks buried in the walls of the church.

In 1832 Burgh-St-Peter, lying within its great bend of the Waveney, was a strange remote little place tucked away in a far corner of a county itself renowned for its isolation. There was nothing much to be seen in any direction: nowhere was close; no through traffic was possible. Lowestoft – in Suffolk – was obscured by land rising gently on the far side of the river. As a duck might fly Lowestoft was no more than three miles from the Rectory; but, via Beccles, which was the only route short of boating for all or part of the way, the distance was fifteen miles. Great Yarmouth lying over and beyond Breydon Water was no more, even on a clear day, than a dim smudge on a far horizon. Lake Lothing and Oulton Broad, the Flixton and Fritton Lakes, Breydon Water, the Waveney, the Yare and the Bure which drained the main broads lying further north, the coastal marshes and all their connecting dykes (together with the Fens and the Wash) constituted one of the great natural wet areas of Western Europe. River and marsh, open water and endless reed beds, all rich in food, were home and haunt to otters and hares, to fish in an astonishing abundance, to marsh and other wild flowers and to butterflies and birds; but, above all, to birds. Thousands upon thousands of native and migratory birds came and went by day and by night. Their cries and their clamour assailed every home and every ear.

Perhaps Charles on that sixteenth day of March when he first went to church took something of wind and sky and emptiness into his unconscious being? For the whole of his life he was to be at one with animals. He chose always to live amongst wild remote surroundings never far from the sea and over which the raven croaked and the eagle soared. The windows of the three houses in which he lived in Ireland all opened upon views – clear, clean and sharp as any diamond or softly shrouded in Ireland's western lights – as beautiful as any to be found anywhere.

Charles was born into a family at a period in its history when it had become secure and established; it was by no means poor. Charles grew up in a family much influenced by a sense of continuity and dominated by a sense of social responsibility. Most of the reasons lying behind the sense of 'long belonging' would have been shared with any other well-to-do family which had lived for three generations in the same comfortable house, had married consistently within their county and which found itself living as part of a small community almost entirely dependent upon agriculture for its livelihood. One reason, however, whilst not unique, was unusual.

This peculiar constituent of the family's position in society and outlook on the world was the fact that they had turned the holding of the office of Rector of Burgh-St-Peter into what was beginning to look like a simple matter of heredity. Charles's father, who held the Rectorship from 1829 to 1871, was the third eldest son of the family to hold the office in succession and to occupy the same parsonage house. He should have been followed by his eldest son Arthur had fate not intervened; in the event he was succeeded by the youngest son who, in turn, was succeeded by a son of Arthur's. By the end of the century, and the close of Charles's life, five generations of the family had held the living of Burgh-St-Peter in unbroken succession. The five Rectors were:

1764–1795	Samuel Boycatt (1724–1797)
1795–1829	William Boycatt (1756–1830) (William I, known as Billie)
1829–1871	William Boycatt/Boycott (1798–1871) (William II, the father of Charles Cunningham Boycott)

1872–1889 William Boycott (1843–1889) (William III)
1889–1899 William Douglass Boycott (1864–1932) (Douglass)

(Samuel Boycatt started his ministry in 1748, sixteen years before he went to Burgh-St-Peter, and William Douglass Boycott continued his elsewhere in Norfolk for thirty-three years after he left Burgh. If these two periods are added to the 135 years in Burgh itself then the family ministry may be said to have lasted for 184 consecutive years.[3])

It may be asked how the family were enabled to establish themselves as 'hereditary' rectors of one particular parish. The reason lies in two of the provisions under which the Church of England was then governed. The first related to the method of selecting a candidate for a vacant living and the second to the nature of the tenure under which he subsequently held it. The owner of a (presentative) advowson of a parish, who thereby became its 'patron', possessed the right to nominate a man of his choice to the Bishop for institution as its incumbent. This right was governed by English civil law. Whilst the Bishop had power to reject a nominee for due cause, the patron had power to challenge any such rejection in the Courts. An advowson was a chattel capable of being bought and sold like a horse, a house, or anything else. If not mentioned specifically in an owner's will an advowson was deemed, in law, to be part of the 'residue' of a deceased person's estate so that no advowson ever found itself without an owner.

After acceptance by his future Diocesan Bishop the nominee 'came into possession' of his new living by virtue of two distinct ceremonies. At the first, conducted by the Bishop at a convenient place (frequently the Cathedral of his diocese), he was instituted into the spiritual care and responsibilities of his new parish; the duty and responsibility which he then accepted were described often as 'the cure of souls.' At the second, conducted usually by the Archdeacon, but always, and essentially, in the parish church in the presence of the parishioners, he was inducted into its temporalities; his hand was laid on the key of the church door and he tolled the bell. The temporalities which he then received included the free-holds of the Church itself, the Churchyard, the Parsonage House, and the Glebe[4]; and, because all were held freehold the new incumbent was irremovable, virtually, for life. It was ownership of the advowson (by the family) which 'did the trick' and ensured the succession for as long as there were sons of the Boycott family ready and willing to accept the Rectorship.[5] (Advowsons, then, were valuable. They could be, and were, bought and sold privately. When the Burgh-St-Peter advowson was acquired in 1754 it may have cost Samuel's father something between £5,000 and £6,000.)

The succession of Boycott Rectors of Burgh-St-Peter found themselves occupying an unusual position. Had it ever been said, then 'The Rector is dead: Long live the Rector' would have expressed only what had become a familiar aspect of parish life. Charles himself, his grandfather and father, their wives and children had all either been born into, or been admitted into, a dynasty exclusive to themselves. Such a prerogative exacted its own standards of personal responsibility, of personal family rectitude and magnanimity. As Charles grew up he would have found violation of the dynasty rules discouraged by two, ever present, facts of rectory life. In the first place his father would have argued that a priest's ministry is to be judged only on its quality; and that the behaviour and example of his family is part of his ministry. In the second place Charles could not fail to become aware of the whole body of Norwich diocesan clergy by whom he was surrounded, and the influence which, as a group, they possessed. Most, like his father, were educated, cultured men living quietly in their parishes whose only interest in misconduct was to frown upon it. Between them the diocesan clergy probably knew, personally, nearly every man, woman and child who lived in a diocese which then included Suffolk and contained over 1,000 parishes. There was a strong and natural leaning towards close friendships between clergy families; they were birds of a feather. Many clergy wives were the daughters of clergy and many clergy sons – lay and clerical – found themselves wives from the same source. First and second clergy cousins abounded. That the Boycotts swam strongly in this particular stream is evident from their family tree. The whole clergy pot and boiling was neither a caste nor a club and it possessed no collective voice; but most of its members understood each other and knew that they could trust and rely upon each other. The clergy pond may have been a placid one; there was nothing to be gained, but much to be lost, by dropping bricks into it.

The five Boycott Rectors, naturally, had much in common. They all lived in the same comfortable parsonage house. All were landowners. All married and had families. Each gave his son and successor as Rector a good education which included being sent to Cambridge. Each served his primary ministry amongst a population of about 330 people living in 65 houses. All walked or rode the mile to the church and the other, much longer, distances which separated them from the scattered farms and houses of their parishioners. For none of them was there ever an easy straight-forward means of crossing the Waveney. Whilst a parish of 330 people was around the average in late eighteenth- and nineteenth-century Norfolk, its Rector can scarcely be described as professionally overworked. All had a duty, as priests of the established church, to minister to anyone and everyone who lived in, or entered, their parish boundaries whether alive or dead. No one – on earth – had the power, or the right, to command any of them to do anything. All held the reins of a not easily defined authority. On the one hand they taught and spoke the Word of God in an age of faith and they conducted and shared in the great moments in the lives of most of their parishioners; on the other they occupied the position – but never the title – of a 'Squire' who was resident in the parish. Both were sanctions which kept them, always and to some degree, at arm's length from the people they served. This fact of life had to be squared, also, with the peculiar loyalty and affection which each new young Rector of the family felt towards parishioners amongst whom he had grown up, whom he knew so well and who knew him so well.

The five consecutive rectorships spanned a period of 135 years from 1764 to 1899. These years saw the war of American Independence and the loss of the American Colonies; the French Revolution; the Napoleonic Wars from which England emerged not only triumphant but in possession of a navy so large that it exceeded all the other navies in the world put together; the Repeal of the Corn Laws; the flowering of the industrial revolution and the massive increase in the population of England; Queen Victoria's reign over an Empire upon which the sun could not set and over an England which dominated the world; and the steady growth of democracy and two-party politics. These years saw, also, the turmoil in Ireland of the 1790s; the Union of Ireland with England; a population growth in Ireland which may have exceeded that of England; the Great Irish Famine and its melancholy entanglement with the, essentially English, issue of Corn Law repeal. These years saw also 'the 1880 revolution' in Ireland which brought the name of Charles Cunningham Boycott into common use.

Chapter Two

In 1775, as the first Boycott rector settled himself into the parsonage house in Burgh-St-Peter, England was engaged in the painful business of losing its American Colonies. Ten years later the loss had been shrugged off under a gathering prosperity. The arts flourished. Jane Austen was growing up as a member of that self-assured upper-middle-class society which her mind penetrated so brilliantly; her 'society' seems forever poised in its cocoon of mannered – almost stilted – conversation and exaggerated politeness. It was a sort of springtime; London was its magnet and reflecting glass. To it men with brains and wit were compelled by ambition; from it radiated books and ideas, the first copies of *The Times* newspaper, and toy mannequins exquisitely dressed in the latest fashions so that the ladies of Bath and of the great houses might dress as beautifully as those in London. It was the age of the dilettante: the young men who travelled to Paris, Florence and Rome for the idling pleasure of doing so. It was an age in which wars and hard fighting were the concern, not of the nation at large, but of the military. It was a period, also, in which its own prosperity concealed its own complacency. Those who could afford it ate too much, smoked too much, drank too much and died early. The streets of London were filthy beyond modern comprehension. Lunatics were chained and men hanged for paltry offences. There were no police; drunkenness, crime and brutality went unchecked. Fast decisive good government from the centre was virtually impossible; there was no civil service; such legal and political institutions as existed were corroded by corruption.

Upon this easy tranquillity the French Revolution erupted, in 1789, as if it had been molten lava. The fires it started were unquenchable. Tranquillity was replaced by storms of argument, by long confused years of war and by endless political upheavals.

Slowly men came to see the almost limitless extent of the revolution; that in defining the political duties and rights of Frenchmen it had redefined the rights of all men everywhere.

To most Englishmen the French Revolution was an extraordinary phenomenon. They felt, with justice, that the world and the way it thought and behaved could never be the same again. The ideas which inspired it were all-pervasive. As a Whig lawyer wrote: '. . . everything was connected with the revolution in France . . . not this thing or that thing, but literally everything, was soaked in this one event.' In the early years of euphoria it was not difficult to see much to applaud as the news flooded in from Paris; there were those in England who wished, fervently, not to criticise the French but to emulate them. For the majority, however, it was easy to nod the head and agree that the French were only setting about, in their own way and in their own time, what England had achieved one hundred years earlier by her own 'glorious revolution.'

Within two or three years the outlook of most Englishmen changed *dramatically*. The comfort and prosperity still so generally evident in England compared most favourably with 'liberty' as the French then found themselves experiencing it. Social chaos in Paris, the homicidal Parisian mobs, the persecutions of the French Church and the destruction of property came to be seen in most – but not all – eyes as undesirable models of national conduct. What had happened in Paris might happen in London. Thomas Paine's[6] *The Rights of Man* with its pro-French, anti-monarchy and anti-aristocracy bias frightened the English governing classes as badly as did Edmund Burke's outright condemnation of France in his *Reflections on the Revolution in France*. By 1793, only four years after the Revolution, France and England were at war; as Pitt had remarked the revolution 'soon overflowed the boundaries of France . . . with *armed opinions*.' Simple patriotism and a reluctance to be thought treasonable cooled still further the ardour for things French. Repression became inevitable. Habeas Corpus was suspended in May 1794; two acts of 1795 made it possible to speak and write treason in addition to acting it; large public meetings held without permission were proscribed; government intelligence services, already efficient, were strengthened. The black curtain of war had descended.

* * *

Irish eyes were as dazzled as anyone else's by the flame burning so brightly in France.

Ireland was then governed, in name, by an autonomous parliament. The King of England was, also, King of Ireland; he was represented in Ireland by a Lord Lieutenant who, appointed in London, exercised control over public appointments and the nomination of candidates for parliament through his powers of patronage. It was unsatisfactory, two-handed, government; that it was also new did little to enhance it. What was new about it had been more or less forced out of England by the strategic pressures of her war with America and a closely related wish to placate the much disadvantaged, but very large, Catholic majority in Ireland. Nothing significant was achieved; the Protestant *minority* continued in its so-called Irish 'ascendancy' and the massive Catholic *majority* continued, much as it had always done, in its impotence. Nonetheless the flame radiating so brilliantly from France found combustible material in plenty in Ireland; Ireland and France were *old* friends.

Most, but not all, Irishmen – and this deep cleavage in Irish society cannot be over-emphasised – had reached a point of disaffection such that they felt neither loyalty to their own government nor sympathy for England in her war with France. Many, but not all, Catholics, and some, but not all, Protestants were inspired by the intoxication of events into a belief that their hour of successful revolt against England had struck. Early in the 1790s the 'Society of United Irishmen' was formed; the word 'United' signified an improbable, but nonetheless significant, union of Catholic with Protestant. 'What prevents you' asked a Catholic 'from coalescing with your Protestant brethren? . . . It is the spirit of the present times to let religion make its own way by its own merits . . . Let us lay down the little character of a sect and take up the character of a people.' Insurrectionary groups and committees were formed, but, throughout its history, this revolutionary movement lacked leaders of quality; Wolfe Tone, a passionate but historically ineffective young Dublin Protestant, is typical and probably the best remembered. But, unable to command the support of the entire population, lacking sufficient arms and faced by a resident British army, the United Irishmen could do little to win independence for themselves. Their question became this: would the French help?

For the French the issues raised by this idea were anything but straightforward. Since the Revolution Paris had been thronged by representatives of disaffected European political minorities pleading for help. In principle – and wisely – the French sought to avoid ideological and revolutionary entanglements with their neighbours. But Ireland! An old friend and ripe for rebellion! Lying athwart *England's* western approaches! If Ireland was *England's* backdoor, could that door be forced? If they sent an expedition to Ireland could they *rely* upon sufficient support from the United Irishmen to turn the enterprise into a major threat to England? As it would affect either option, how was the Royal Navy to be countered? These questions were easier to ask than to answer.

Early in 1796 Wolfe Tone went to Paris to negotiate French help. Tone had little tactical or strategical military or naval knowledge. French enthusiasm waxed and waned as government personalities changed and wavered. On all sides the fog of war – the lack of certainty, the spying, the guessing – had already, of course, descended. It descended over London, over Paris and over Dublin; but over nowhere was it denser than over Dublin. United Irishmen waited, expectantly, for news and even more expectantly for orders; orders to rise, to embrace the French and to build a new Ireland without interference from England. (What might, or might not, happen to England in the process was, to most Irish eyes, a matter of small importance.)

Despite their hesitation the French *did* act. In December 1796 (without, overtly, abandoning their threat of a direct cross-channel invasion of England) they mounted a not insignificant expedition to Ireland. This, almost immediately, found itself beset by difficulties so intractable that, without direct orders from its commander so to do, it had to be abandoned. No landing, or contact with the United Irishmen, was made.[7] When the facts became known, early in 1797, the Irish, surprisingly, were not downcast; on the contrary they were elated by the proof of French enthusiasm and willingness to fight on their behalf. Despite the activities of the British Army – which set about the savage ill-disciplined disarming of every United Irishman upon whom it could lay hands – the Irish awaited, with confidence, the despatch of a second expedition.

For England 1797 was a year of fear and great anxiety. The country continued at war with France; daily reports and hourly rumour spoke of French and Dutch invasion fleets assembled in Brest and the Texel. Ireland continued in ferment. Bonaparte's military genius, hitherto not clearly recognised, was becoming all too apparent. Secret Societies, revolutionary in their aims and intent upon overthrowing everything, flourished in and outside London. For a time the Bank of England suspended cash payments. The British Army had distinguished itself only by its incompetence in Europe and its indiscipline and brutality in Ireland. One bulwark – which had never yet failed the nation – remained. When, in the spring of 1797, both the Channel and North Sea fleets, assembled and positioned to repulse the expected invasions, mutinied, England standing alone faced a formidable crisis; she was to wait 143 years for its like.

That the sailors had ample reason for discontent is certain but most of the evidence concerning the incitements to mutiny were either concealed or destroyed deliberately by the mutiny leaders. At the time about one tenth of the Navy's sailors and one fifth of its marines were Irishmen. Wolfe Tone, in the year before, had written to at least some Irishmen serving in the navy that 'Ireland is now at war with England in defence of her liberties; France is the ally of Ireland and England is the common enemy of both nations'. This was sedition at its most naked but it was not out of keeping with the aims and activities of the United Irishmen; there is little doubt that the latter had some part in promoting disaffectation in the navy.

Reaction to the mutinies was swift. After ten weeks of acute anxiety the grievances were sufficiently settled, the ringleaders taken and the sailors returned – most of them thankfully – to their allegiance. No enemy exploited either mutiny. In returning to their duties the sailors took with them a gleaning from the bloody streets of Paris. They had learnt that the awful conditions which they had endured for so long – the food, the pay never adjusted for inflation, the punishments – were not, in themselves, necessary to the fighting efficiency of ships at sea. On the contrary, they were simple human grievances about which any man, whoever he might be, had a right to protest. 'We will be treated as men,' they said.

In the early spring of 1798 the Irish, tired of waiting for the French to help again, dispirited by rumours that the French were breaking up their cross-channel army and were preparing to employ part of it in Egypt (a country of whose existence most Irishmen had never heard and whose strategic importance they could scarcely comprehend), and afraid that the British Army might soon overwhelm them if they did not strike quickly, broke into what is remembered as the 'Irish Rebellion'. It was an unhappy business. English intelligence had penetrated many of the United Irishmen's committees; these had been severely handled by the army and they lacked leaders of stature. The engagements – the Irish 'battles' – were bloody but ill co-ordinated. Nonetheless news of them quickly reached Paris and no less than three supporting operations were mounted by France. All were too late and too hastily put together to affect the outcome of the rebellion. One, commanded by a General Humbert,[8] made its mark; another was still-born; the third was rounded up at sea. (The last carried Wolfe Tone – again in French uniform – who, before he could be executed, committed suicide.) Throughout the rebellion the British Army held fast to the 'strategic high ground.' Slowly, for want of sinew and leadership, the rebellion petered out.

Pitt, his hands overflowing with the responsibility for the conduct of a great war against a powerful enemy and one of the greatest of all military commanders, proposed, and forced through, a union of the Irish and English parliaments and people. The Act of Union came into force on 1st January 1801; it abolished the two Houses of Parliament which, before, had sat in Dublin. It changed, decisively, part of the United Kingdom's political scenery but *not* the play itself; France and Napoleon had, still, to be defeated; Ireland, still, had to be controlled and governed. Throughout the nineteenth century, and for the whole of Charles Cunningham's lifetime, England – 'the Imperial House of Commons at Westminster' – carried the ultimate responsibility for the government of Ireland.

By the union Pitt had intended two things. First, to safeguard better the whole realm. Second, to invert the imbalance in size between the Irish Catholic and Protestant communities by making both part of a much larger population in which Protestants would predominate. By this means Irish and English Catholics combined would be no more than a minority within the new Union and so might be more acceptably 'emancipated.'

So ended a roughly cut, and intensely formative, decade in Anglo-Irish history. In England confidence in her ability to carry on the war had been restored.[9] A major defeat at sea had been inflicted on the French by Nelson at the Battle of the Nile in August 1798. New life, slowly, was being breathed into the British

Army.[10] Earlier fears had, at least partly, disappeared. The Irish distraction had been – for the time being – resolved; all had not been lost. England became free to put forth one of the greatest war efforts in her history; in which, as Pitt later said, 'she had saved herself by her exertions and Europe by her example'. In Ireland it was otherwise; lassitude gripped her:

> Demonstrations seem to have almost ceased, and there were absolutely none of the signs which are invariably found when a nation struggles passionately against what it deems an impending tyranny, or rallies around some institution which it really loves. The country had begun to look with indifference – or with a languid curiosity – to the opening of a new Chapter of Irish history . . .

England and France fought from 1793 to 1815; twenty-two years of confusing conflict into which, at one time or another, many countries in Europe found themselves drawn. By the end of 1805 a curious stalemate had come to exist between the two principal contestants. Napoleon ruled the land and countries of continental Europe; England, as a consequence of her final naval defeat of the French at Trafalgar in October of that year, had become the absolute ruler of the seas and oceans. For lack of conventionally more warlike opportunities of inflicting damage upon each other England and France resorted to economic warfare. Napoleon closed the ports of Europe to whatever goods he chose to list as contraband, whilst England blockaded by sea. Such attrition was immensely damaging; not only to both principals but also to third parties, who, on the one hand, were incapable of challenging England's power at sea and, on the other, had no alternative but submission to Napoleon's contraband orders.[11]

It became apparent to English eyes that, sooner or later, somewhere or somehow, Napoleon and the French would have to be brought to battle and defeated in their own element on land. It became equally apparent, because of her strength and the leading part she played already in financing, supporting and encouraging her various European allies to resist Napoleon, that England herself must play a leading part in any land campaign intended to bring this about. It is now a matter of history that the military power of France was first drained by Wellington's long-drawn-out and brilliantly conducted campaign in the Iberian Peninsula from

1809 to 1813; and later crushed by his final victory at Waterloo in 1815. Both were made possible only by the overwhelming naval superiority which had been won by Nelson between 1798 and 1805; he was the *architect* of victory. (It is not for nothing that he still stands, in lonely eminence, high above London; or that the Royal Navy still drinks to the toast of 'The Immortal Memory'.)

With the consummation of a long, dangerous and uncertain war dependent upon continuing, and assured, supremacy at sea the navy was expanded after Trafalgar to a size never before seen. When peace came finally, in 1815,

> Britain's sea power was supreme in all its elements. In ships of war it was superior to the combined fleets of the world, with over 200 ships of the line, nearly 300 frigates and corvettes, and a flotilla of smaller craft numbering over 400. Bases had been acquired in all the principal oceans . . . British mercantile shipping carried the bulk of the world's trade; its crews . . . were composed of British seamen. Behind the shipping there was a healthy and expanding shipbuilding.

British naval supremacy, and the prestige that went with it, survived the changes from sail to steam and from oak to steel; it was to last for well over a hundred years and throughout Charles Cunningham's life.

Seapower, exercised by an island nation occupying a position of sea centrality in the world[12] was, indeed, ubiquitous. Throughout Charles's lifetime no Englishman could leave England except by sea; and, when he did, so he fell, to some additional and small degree, under the Navy's protection. The Navy's ability to support and protect was, virtually, without limit; its shadow – light or heavy as circumstances might demand – fell across all the ocean routes which connected England to Canada, Africa, India, China, Australia and New Zealand. Its shadow fell, also, across one much shorter sea passage; that from England to Ireland.

CHAPTER THREE

FOR CENTURIES PHYSICAL ISOLATION FROM the rest of England had marked the county of Norfolk as being an almost unknown place. To its north and east Norfolk was confined within a low, empty, dangerous coastline. To the west a traveller found himself obstructed by the watery inhospitable Fens and their three slow, and constantly flooding, rivers.[13] The 100 miles which separated Norwich from London, superficially, were flatter and easier; but this was to forget Epping Forest and its highwaymen. Nonetheless the people of Norfolk were seldom to be confined to their own county. From Great Yarmouth to the Hook of Holland was no further than from Norwich to London; many Norfolk people *preferred* to take a boat to the one than to face the difficulties and dangers presented by the other.

A thousand years ago the bulging coastline which constituted so abrupt an end to so much of the land of Norfolk was an open inviting landfall for the Vikings and Danes in their marauding expeditions across the North Sea; Norfolk's slow easy rivers became arteries up which they continued their penetrations. They settled. They bequeathed to their posterity words and place names from their own language and, quite often, their own fair hair and blue eyes; and a spirit as vigorous as it was independent. In the Middle Ages Norfolk gave asylum to Flemings and Huguenots; from both they acquired skills in spinning and weaving which were to make 'Norwich cloth' the finest in the world. Trade between Norfolk and the continent flourished. Returning businessmen and travellers brought home with them new ideas and perceptions; about art and architecture; about agriculture and drainage; about fishing; about how to snare wild fowl; about printing; and even about the breeding of canaries for which Norfolk has long been famous. Constricted as it was by fen and sea, Norfolk resembled the cut of a trouser pocket; and like the pocket of any proud, hardworking and enterprising man it became well lined. Norfolk became heavily populated and wealthy; its men and women fiercely loyal to their flat landscapes and slowly winding waterways.

In the second half of the eighteenth century Norwich was the beautiful capital of a countryside thriving on the production of grain and wool. Bales of cloth, made-up garments, and grain were shipped far and wide down the rivers of Norfolk and through its ports. Foreign businessmen flocked to the city. Norwich merchants and bankers built fine offices, fine houses and laid out fine tree-lined gardens. The theatre and the arts flourished.[14] At the end of the seventeenth century the city had claimed to be '. . . the chief seat of the chief manufacture of the realm' and 'next to London . . . the most rich and potent city in England.' It was far famed for 'the wealth of its citizens, the number of its inhabitants, the great confluence of foreigners, the stately structures and beautiful churches.' Norwich, indeed, was 'A Fine City'; set in the middle of a county which became renowned, also, for the vigour and enterprise of its farmers.

Charles II is said to have remarked that Norfolk soils were so poor as to be fit only to make roads for the rest of his kingdom; a twelfth-century poet said that 'Satan on the road to hell, ruined Norfolk as he fell.' What happened to turn such an unpromising part of England into the bread-basket it was to become? The 'Agricultural Revolution', which found its centre in Norfolk, is the answer but the word 'Revolution' – in the sense of sudden unheralded change – is misleading. As always in farming innovation was *slow*.

Since settled farming began the difficulty had been the loss of soil fertility by continuous cropping. The only known remedy for this was to let land lie fallow – or idle – for one year in every three or four. The modern science of soil fertility was unknown but, slowly, certain crop sequences were chanced upon which, in themselves, reduced fertility losses. Gradually these sequences were refined into different crop 'rotation' systems in which new crops such as turnips, lucerne and clover performed a critical function in preserving, and even enhancing fertility. Productivity was increased also – at a cost – by adding marl or lime to soils deficient in it. Of crucial significance within a rotation was the ability to keep and over-winter more animals; more livestock increased grain yields by the additional manure obtained and the animals themselves consumed the new fodder crops upon which the rotation itself depended for its success. These developments transformed farming. In the old days of fallow a man, in effect, was unable to use 25–30% of his land in each year; employing a suitable rotation he used it all and from it he took more than he had ever done before.[15]

Several factors brought Norfolk into prominence within the universal wish to eradicate the difficulty of retaining soil fertility. First was the spur of the market; by 1769, according to Defoe, Yarmouth was exporting more grain and malt per annum than any other port in England, London not excepted. Secondly Norfolk seemed to have farming in its blood; farms were larger and better managed than elsewhere because more land in Norfolk had been held privately for longer than in most other counties. (William Cobbett, himself a countryman and farmer, went to Norfolk in 1821 and took home with him 'a great admiration of, and respect for, this county of *excellent farmers* and hearty open and spirited men. They are diligent and make the most of everything. Their management of all sorts of stock is most judicious; they are careful about manure; their teams move quickly and, in short, it is a county of most excellent cultivators.'[16]) Third was the influence of the Dutch. Skills in drainage, a light-weight plough, new crops like turnips, clover and new grasses, and Friesian cattle all transported themselves easily and naturally over the sea from low-lying Holland to the flat countryside of Norfolk.[17] Last, but certainly not least, came Norfolk leadership in publicising the new methods. This happened at a time when an expanding population needed to be fed and was the achievement, largely, of three Norfolk families; the Walpoles at Houghton, the Townshends at Raynham and, most famous of all, Thomas Coke[18] at Holkham.

Thomas Coke is remembered, principally, for his 'Sheep Shearings' which he held every summer at Holkham for forty-five years. What started in 1778 as domestic gatherings ended in 1821 as prestigious affairs at which as many as 600 people were entertained from all over England and the Continent (and, even, from America). The 'shearings' amounted, in effect, to modern agricultural shows. Talks were given, discussions encouraged, and visitors were free to ride around Coke's great estate and to inspect his crops and animals and the operation of his Norfolk rotations on what had become his model home farm of 3,000 acres. When Coke was a young man Horace Walpole described Holkham as a place so barren that two rabbits might be seen fighting for one blade of grass; when he died Holkham was fertile and its tenants rich and happy to pay higher rentals for their land.

The great wool industry of Norwich and its surrounding villages possessed – not surprisingly – a large appetite for its basic raw material. In the language of economic theory wool, mutton and – since the new agricultural rotations and the wish to have more of it – sheep manure are products in 'joint supply'; that is, it is impossible to create more of the one without also creating more of the others. In an age lacking refrigeration the product which governed the total quantity of sheep which Norfolk could maintain profitably was mutton. For centuries Norfolk had bred its own 'Norfolk' sheep but these were narrow backed and their wool, although fine, was short-fibred when good Norwich worsted[19] required a long-fibre wool. By 1800 Coke himself had changed to 'South Downs', his animals being '. . . remarkably good, of the largest size, fine woolled, clean'. Other Norfolk farmers soon followed. But, despite the fact that 30,000 Norfolk sheep were driven annually to the London meat market, Norfolk itself could *not* satisfy the voracious appetite of its own wool industry.

About one sixth of England's total wool requirement came in from Ireland. Like England, Ireland had acquired the necessary weaving skills though emigrant Huguenots who had settled in Dublin as they had settled in Norwich; and where, for a time, they became 'brawny weavers and traders'. But serious competition in so important a national industry was not something which England could tolerate. By means of various 'trade acts' of around the year 1700 imports of finished woollen goods were controlled. In consequence, in Dublin, 'hundreds of Huguenot weavers' became destitute. 'Their cries can scarcely be out of your ears . . . it is impossible to have a just idea of this calamity unless you have been an eye witness to it.' An Irish wool manufacturing industry which, inspired by the vigour and drive of the Huguenots, might have become a significant part of the Irish economy was stifled before it had any chance of reaching maturity.

* * *

The Reverend Samuel Boycott (1724–1797) founded the Boycott clerical 'dynasty' in Burgh-St-Peter. He was son and brother to two John Boycotts; both owned and ran a dying business in Norwich. Samuel's father John I died in 1763 as a very comfortably off, if not wealthy man; John II died twenty-two years later as a very wealthy man. Dyeing was ancillary to the wool industry but crucial to it; the family is said to have possessed the twin secrets of a process to make dyes fast and of a special, perhaps beautiful, blue dye. A memorial to John I, erected by his children in St Edmund's Church in Norwich, records their 'gratitude to . . . so worthy and indulgent a parent.' At John II's death in 1785 the *Norwich Mercury* wrote that he had been 'for many years an eminent dyer in this city, in which business he acquired a large fortune with unblemished reputation.' Cynics hold reservations about such posthumous declarations of integrity and moral worth. Whatever the truth about these aspects of the two Johns their wills provide evidence that both had clear thoughtful heads on their shoulders and suggest that both had been excellent businessmen.

John II, as he executed his will in 1783, was faced by a serious difficulty. The document makes plain that his eldest child and only son John (John III) was a 'weakling' incapable of inheriting either his Father's dyeing business or his Father's wealth in any active continuing sense. Luckily for everyone concerned John II's only surviving daughter (Elizabeth) had married John Morse; and, before her own death in 1778 (at age twenty-four) had given birth to two sons. Morse was a Norwich brewer and a man of *exceptional* quality. In effect John II bequeathed his business, his estate (including, almost certainly, Sprowston Hall) and the bulk of his wealth to John Morse and his two Morse grandsons. He had little alternative; nonetheless his will makes clear his confidence in John Morse.[20]

Deliberately John II tied no strings to, and fastened no tapes round, his dyeing business; he just left the whole thing in Morse's hands. (What ultimately happened to it is not known, but a firm of dyers in Norwich named 'Morse and Hall' appeared in a city directory in 1811.)

John II's death in 1785 marked the end of the family's direct concern with business. It marked also, if less precisely, the decline of Norwich as the centre of a manufacturing region of international importance. Both John Boycotts, and Samuel in his early years, had been part and parcel of the affluent and cosmopolitan city. They had gossiped and done business with bankers and friends whose own businesses took them so often to the continent; they had pushed their way through the crowded streets scarcely conscious, above the hubbub, of the rattle and clack of the looms upon which so much depended; they met and talked with visitors from France and Germany and the Low Countries and from the Baltic and Mediterranean. In its heyday the flavour of Norwich had been unique; its pungency not quickly forgotten by those who, however briefly, had known it.

John I had three sons. The eldest, John II, went into the dyeing business as did William, the youngest (little is known of him; he died aged twenty-seven). Samuel, the second son, chose the church. It was a decision of significance to later generations of the Boycott family.

Their are still threads of evidence which suggest that both John I and John II and their families were religiously inclined church-going people. Both may have been church wardens of St Edmund's, their family church, in Norwich; William left his History of the Bible ('in three volumes folio') not to Samuel but to John II. Drawn together these slender threads probably constituted a web of sincere family support for Samuel in his eventual choice of a career in the church; but nothing suggests that any aspect of family support was either inspirational or compelling. Even if three sons in the family dyeing business were thought to be one too many, Samuel had no need 'to look for a job'. He was intelligent and energetic and possessed of considerable strength of character. With his father's money and influence behind him he could have been entered almost anywhere in the prosperous Norwich wool industry of the mid 1740s. What – or who, in addition, perhaps, to God – blew the trumpet which cleared Samuel's mind for him and of which a curious resonance was to ring for 184 years? The finger points, with some assurance, to the Reverend Charles Tuck.

Tuck was a Beccles man; he was schooled there, and, in due course, he went up to Caius College, Cambridge, where he did well. He was a resident Fellow of his College from 1726 to 1741. He was ordained in 1727. At a date prior to the spring of 1754 he, with Philip Bedingfeld of Ditchingham, jointly acquired the advowson of Burgh-St-Peter; it is likely that Tuck had it in mind to present *himself* to the Burgh living at the next vacancy. In the event his life took a different turn; in 1741 Caius presented him to their two linked Norwich livings of Great Melton and St Michael Coslany (the livings were linked to provide a reasonable income for one man; Great Melton lies five miles west of Norwich; St Michael's Coslany was a city church standing in a street named Coslany). John I and Charles Tuck were contemporaries; St Michael's Coslany and the Boycott family church of St Edmund's were not far apart. It seems almost certain that John I and Charles Tuck and their families become friends; and that Charles Tuck took an interest in Samuel if, as perhaps was the case, he was unable to decide upon a career.

After being educated privately in Norwich Samuel, in 1744, went up to Caius College where he became a scholar. The decision that he should go to Caius may well owe something to Tuck. After ordination in 1749 Samuel served two curacies. He did his first (and normal one) at Bardwell (a village in south Norfolk then much engaged in the wool trade and having a lovely church) and his second as Tuck's curate in Melton. On 1st May 1754 Samuel married Mary Baker, the daughter of the Reverend William Baker, the Vicar of Hedenham (close to Ditchingham). Samuel and Mary were married in Hedenham not by Mary's father – as might have been expected – but by Charles Tuck. A few weeks earlier Tuck and Philip Bedingfeld had been 'parties of the third part' to John I's marriage settlement upon Samuel; under which they were to present him as the Rector of Burgh-St-Peter at the next vacancy; and, at the same time, to make over the advowson to him. Two presumptions seem reasonable. First, that Tuck having settled himself comfortably in Norwich was content to surrender whatever right he had to Burgh; secondly, that Tuck needed help in Melton and was happy to let Samuel and his young wife live in its country rectory in exchange for the work Samuel did there until such time as the living at Burgh should fall vacant. (Such evidence as exists suggests that Samuel lived rent free; the 'Rev. Mr Tuck' certainly paid the parish poor rate.)

As matters turned out Samuel did not take up the first opportunity of moving to Burgh; in 1758 the Reverend Christopher Smear took the living from the Reverend Thomas Page[21] and held it for six years. However, on 2nd February 1764 Charles Tuck and Philip Bedingfeld (as, no doubt, they had undertaken to do in Samuel's marriage settlement) were able to present Samuel to the

Rectorship of Burgh-St-Pater. Simultaneously the advowson – the right of *future* presentation – passed into Samuel's hand. The stage on which the family was to stand for so long had been erected.

When Samuel took over Burgh in 1764 he was aged forty; it is still possible to part a few of those 'rags of time' which then were his. Samuel was a well-educated man; the house he rebuilt still stands; we know something of his friends; there is a portrait[22] which, although not a particularly good one, is probably a good likeness as his appearance is an unusual one; and we have the evidence of his handwriting which, for a man of his day and age, is remarkably distinctive and revealing.

Samuel's early married life was short. His and Mary's three children were all – no doubt happily – born and baptised in Melton but, in October 1759, Mary died there aged thirty-three. Samuel was then thirty-five; one can only grieve for so young a widower and his three, now motherless, children. When Mary died she left William (William I, who become the second Boycott Rector of Burgh) aged three, Samuel aged two and Mary aged nine months. Samuel's mother-in-law, Mrs Baker, had been dead for some time and his only sister-in-law had already died, aged twenty (in Rotterdam); inevitably much depended upon Samuel's own family and, in particular, upon his own mother. (Several years later the second Boycott Rector was to commemorate 'his Grandmother Anne' in Burgh-St-Peter church; perhaps in grateful acknowledgement of the affection he had for her.)

Samuel had been brought up comfortably. His Melton rectory had been a 'commodious residence'. He had become accustomed to living well. The parsonage house he acquired in Burgh was too small and he set about enlarging and improving it. In the first of a long succession of Burgh-St-Peter terriers[23] signed by members of the family, Samuel in 1770 described the Georgian house he had rebuilt (at his own expense): '. . . the Rectory or Parsonage House is on the north side of Burgh . . . it hath two parlours,[24] a kitchen pantry and cellar, eight lodging rooms . . . also a bake house, coal and other houses, a Barn with stables or Chaise House etc'. Outside his 'yards, orchard, gardens with two hemplands, or small pightles' comprised two acres and his Glebe lands of ten or eleven acres were close at hand. A few years later the *History of Antiquities of Norfolk* remarked that Samuel had created 'a handsome parsonage house, ornamented in much taste with plantations etc.'. Samuel's handwriting reveals that he was unostentatious and not devoid of artistic ability; the parsonage house he constructed is not grand but it is comfortable; his rooms are light and well proportioned and his stair is a graceful one. What he achieved was the construction of a pleasant, but not too large, family house and home which has stood the test of time. (The house was sold recently by the Church Commissioners and is now divided into two; even so Samuel would have little difficulty in recognising what he had created.)

Charles Tuck and Samuel were friends for twenty years at least. When Tuck moved from his Cambridge fellowship to the wealthy Cathedral city of Norwich he exchanged one robust and stimulating society for another. His friendship with Samuel, it seemed, did not falter; Tuck surely must have valued it. Philip Bedingfeld (a member of a large and well known Norfolk landowning family much involved with church patronage) must have formed a good opinion of Samuel, otherwise he would not have acted as he did. But of greater significance in any assessment of Samuel was his intimate friendship with the Reverend Peter Routh who, as Samuel went to Burgh, became the Rector of Beccles. By an odd chance a random collection of letters written by Peter Routh to his son Martin at Magdalen College, Oxford, and by Samuel's son William to Martin, have survived in Magdalen. Peter's kindness and learning, his fatherly concern for his children and for his friends shine through his letters. Occasionally a letter, or parts of it, are in Latin or Greek. (One contains a sharp scholastic admonition upon a piece of Martin's work of which his father did *not* approve!) Peter's biographer wrote of him: 'Had not [he] been drawn into the thorny wilderness of a busie world, into those corroding cares which attend a married priest and a country parsonage . . . he might have been as great a scholar as his son'. To the eyes of the onlooking 'busie world' this was a considerable compliment; the son, Martin, was to be described by his biographer as 'the last of a race of giants in theology . . .'

The Magdalen letters establish, beyond doubt, that a close friendship existed between Samuel and Peter and their families. Samuel had the permanent loan of Peter's portrait; Peter stayed at Burgh (and, by chance, wrote one of his Magdalen letters from there); Martin's letters to his father are full of 'kind regards' to the Boycotts and, especially to Samuel; Samuel's daughter Mary may, at one time, have joined three of Peter's daughters in running a girls' school in Norwich; Samuel lent his Yarmouth home to a son of Peter's; and Samuel entrusted Peter with the education of his son William.

At first sight Samuel's portrait is unattractive; it is as if suet had been used to mould his cheeks and his jowl. But an awareness of his character, as this is disclosed by his handwriting, compels a second look. His eyes are not two plain plums in a dull pudding; they are wide open and intelligent and a quirky elusive humour plays around them. Napoleon said 'Give me a man with a nose' – Samuel had a splendid one! His chin is firm. He has an air of authority. He is a man who, having adopted a position, adheres to it.

As a widower of forty, Samuel, no doubt, was often lonely. But, as his handwriting reveals, he was a dignified man and one not given to wearing his heart on his sleeve. There can be little doubt that he could be good company. A cheerful – if ugly – face, complete integrity, an ability to take infinite pains, and an entire lack of ostentation are, in any man, a good recommendation; add originality of mind and some artistic appreciation and the possessor becomes someone who makes his friends and keeps them.

Samuel, probably, finished the house when he was forty-two or three. For the next quarter century he appears to have jogged along the path of what can only have been an easy duty comfortably enough. He became a Director of the nearby 'House of Industry' at Heckingham; fifty years later surviving records show that 'the poor', in Burgh, were noticeable by their almost *total* absence. As the years passed he was blessed by a steady flow of inheritances as members of his well-to-do family died and remembered him and his motherless children in their wills. He owned land and property in Norfolk and Suffolk; he was a careful man and, no doubt, he saw to these responsibilities as he should have done. He bought a second house in one of the fashionable Yarmouth Rows, to which he and his children could escape from the isolation of Burgh and in which he could enjoy society and the company of people of his own sort. He had time to travel – accompanied by his own manservant[25] – whilst attending to family business. In March 1781 he went 'to London with Mr and Mrs Mapes to attend upon a Committee of Parliament about a Bill for the exchange of a settled Estate for one more convenient lately Purchased'; and 'if they find time the two gentlemen intend spending a day at Oxford'. In 1785 Samuel had the pleasure of marrying his only daughter Mary in his own church to a satisfactory young officer in the Royal Navy named Charles Cunningham.[26] In due course Mary became the mother of two little girls; one feels Samuel was well suited to the position of grandfather. Later on – late in the lives of both men – Samuel saw his only surviving son marry (but he did not live to see any of William's children).

Superimposed on these years of Samuel's life is the important fact that, during them, he married again. His second wife was a Mrs Gordon. When and where she and Samuel married and her then age cannot be discovered.[27] One assumption may be justified; Samuel had been thirty-five when his first wife died but he had no more children. If he and 'Mrs Gordon' were near contemporaries then either they married when she was past child-bearing or she was barren; of the two possibilities the first seems the more likely. This being so they might have married between 1765 and 1775. By the Magdalen letters Peter Routh was staying with Samuel in January 1777. In a letter to his son Martin he wrote 'Mr Boycott, in whose house I write this, is in very good health and spirits'. An agreeable new wife might have induced both; and made entertaining easier!

In 1793, at the surprising age of sixty-nine, Samuel set about the reconstruction of his own church tower. Over the years criticisms and witticisms have been lavished upon what he then created. 'Absurd', 'a huge telescope set on end', 'a monstrosity', 'an edifice a child might construct out of a box of bricks', 'an endearing parody of a Mesopotamian Ziggurat on the tip of Norfolk' have all been written descriptions of a unique church structure of which, certainly, it is true to say 'once seen never quite forgotten'. Nevertheless there is more to Samuel's 'folly' than meets the casual passing eye; as he constructed his tomb and raised his tower he did so at a time when originality of mind, innovation, and intellectual freedom were much admired. If anyone had told him that, in 200 years, his tower would be regarded as 'absurd' he would have been surprised; and as much by the vagaries of fashion as by anything else.

In June 1793, at the instigation, obviously, of Samuel himself, the Churchwarden and the four principal inhabitants of Burgh received notice of a diocesan faculty 'to repair and build up the steeple which has long been in a ruinous condition . . . entirely at the charge of the Rev. Mr. Boycott'. No drawing or description of the old steeple has survived but, in Norfolk, 'steeple' usually means 'tower'. Samuel's new tower stands on a substantial square 'base unit' which has been reliably dated to the early sixteenth century. Because of its position in relation to the nave it can only have been – more of less – the same base which supported the earlier tower. The faculty also referred to two bells. Because of these the floor area underneath the old tower must – presumably – have been accessible, failing which the bells could not have been rung. (Almost certainly the same space would have served as a vestry.)

What Samuel *actually* did, by way of 'repairing and building up the steeple', was to build into the western end of the church three new features which altered it very considerably, both internally and externally. All still exist. In the first place he dispensed with the old 'bellringing vestry' space under the tower. In its place he constructed a massively built and enclosed empty space which he intended should become – and it did so become – a family tomb. (Because of the weight this structure bears and because its upper and still visible surface is of solid brickwork it must, internally, include a number of vaulted arches). This done, Samuel proceeded to add, on top of this reconstructed base unit, four steadily diminishing cube-like brick and stone 'boxes'. On top of the topmost he placed a capstone and finial (both have since fallen). Finally, he appropriated the lowest and largest of the boxes as a vestry (its visible and solid brick floor being the top of the tomb). Samuel's vestry is reached through an inconspicuous narrow door and staircase. There is now no visible means of entry to the tomb.

The questions fall over themselves. Why, so late in life, did Samuel build his 'Mesopotamian Ziggurat on the tip of Norfolk'? Was it his own idea or someone else's? Of definitive answers none, as yet, have emerged. The possibilities and the legend press forward, of necessity, into the life of Samuel's son William (known as Billie), the second Rector. As he watched his capstone and finial being hauled to the top of his most enduring monument, Samuel had reached retirement. And he did so – as England fought France and Ireland boiled over into rebellion – to his house by the sea in Yarmouth.

It is easy to think of Samuel as a 'well endowed clergyman of the old school, round, indolent and rubicund . . . regular and exact in his conduct . . . charitable in word and deed . . .'. But to do so is to diminish Samuel; he was more than that. The professional graphologist who analysed his handwriting – himself a retired canon of the Church of England – wrote, at the beginning of his report, that it was 'a privilege to see such a remarkable script'. He signed it with the words 'I bow before him'. There can be little doubt that Samuel was a well educated man of considerable ability and of sterling character.

Of Samuel's qualities as a man it has been possible to learn something; of his qualities as a priest nothing is known or remembered beyond the probably irrelevant fact that he was 'a benefactor'. Did Samuel – in a phrase of John Buchan's – 'want to live face to face with God?' To assume that he did – and he died before the geologists started to upset all the old ideas – would be unwarranted. Nonetheless, when he chose the Church and happened upon Burgh, he chose and made a bed. As a man he was too well constructed not to lie upon it. His ministry in Burgh lasted for thirty-one years. During them he became deeply familiar with a great solitude of sky and marsh through which only the Waveney meandered. Four-footed creatures, fish, butterflies and moths, and birds in their endless migrations, were his endless companions. He may never, himself, have been inspired to live 'face to face' with God; but as he looked out and about himself he was confronted with a serenely wonderful manifestation of the creation.

Samuel, of course, could not have known it, but he had founded a strange clerical dynasty which was to give, on the whole, a good account of itself. He was a worthy founder.

CHAPTER FOUR

ABOUT THE YEAR 1800 – AS England fought France and Ireland became part of the United Kingdom – a fiercely radical and outward-looking City of Norwich, and its county of Norfolk, fell upon leaner, harder times. Both city and county found themselves obliged to compete against machine-made woollen materials from Yorkshire and Lancashire at the same time as war had closed so many of their old continental markets. Their jealously guarded municipal independence from central Government served only to emphasise the fact that Norwich and Norfolk found so much to admire in revolutionary France. Pitt, overburdened with responsibility for the conduct of the war as a whole, came to look upon Norwich with suspicion; and, after the Jacobin Club had been founded in Paris in 1789, he called her the 'Jacobin City'.[28]

Two men, father and son and both named Sir Thomas Beevor, became prominent in the radical political life of Norwich. The elder Sir Thomas (uncle to Charles's mother) became part of the oligarchy of Norwich and, when the French Revolution broke out in 1789, proposed a warmly received toast to 'the Friends of Freedom all over the world and success to the third Estate of France in their noble struggle for Liberty'. Some years later the younger Sir Thomas (cousin to Charles's mother) held equally strong political opinions but he was, also, a member of the 'United Friars' who loved learning and who counted among their Honorary Members a varied group of men; these included the eccentric Earl of Orford, who sold his father's famous collection of pictures at Houghton to the Empress of Russia; Humphrey Repton, the landscape gardener; and Luke Hansard, who printed the journals of the House of Commons until his death in 1828 (when he was succeeded by his sons).

Charles's father and the younger Sir Thomas Beevor were both aged seventeen at the time of Waterloo. Both young men emerged into an England their fathers can scarcely have recognised; inflamed by the revolutionary example of France and with sections of her economy exhausted by war she was, nevertheless, being driven by a population explosion and her own 'revolutions' in agriculture and industry. For agriculture the summer of 1815 was a watershed; peace, combined with a good harvest, brought a collapse in the price of corn and bankruptcy to thousands of farmers accustomed only to high wartime prices. Unemployment – much aggravated by an uncontrolled influx of 350,000 discharged and soon-to-be-disillusioned soldiers and sailors – soared. A new Corn Law intended to limit the importation of grains (and so to support the home production of grain) nonetheless kept the price of bread too high in relation to a labouring wage which was too low and which had not been adjusted for inflation. To the largely bread-eating labourer and his hungry family his inadequate wage and the simple necessaries it could not buy seemed as incomprehensible as it was humiliating.

The 1815 Corn Law was introduced at a time when the quality and quantity of the annual United Kingdom harvest was a matter of major importance. For the first time census returns were beginning to put government in possession of statistical evidence concerning the total number of people for whose lives it carried a responsibility. It was evident that the population of the United Kingdom was growing fast. Agriculture continued to be, by far, the largest industry and still employed 25% of all Englishmen aged twenty and over. In a continent still seething with ideas of 'freedom' – and how revolution might secure it – the possible consequences of serious food shortages were to be avoided at all cost. That government chose, broadly, to keep the farmers in business is not surprising, but what accompanied the decision was unfortunate. Inevitably the major beneficiaries of government policy could only be the owners of the great estates – who dominated the House of Lords – and the country landowners who still formed the most powerful body in the Commons.

The 1815 Corn Law prohibited the import of grains until the price at home exceeded 80/- the quarter, but its mechanism was sluggish. Despite modifications it failed to produce either cheap bread or satisfactory support to the farming industry. The poor suffered severely. Throughout the 1820s and 1830s farming continued in the doldrums and the 'Hungry Forties' were worse. Social unrest, some of it violent, spread throughout East Anglia and, eventually, to London. The government of the day had reason to fear that the laws and constitution of the country were 'in jeopardy'.[29]

The younger Thomas Beevor – as radical as any earlier member of his family – succeeded to the baronetcy in 1820. Three years later he met William Cobbett. Cobbett – the 'poor man's friend' – was the most charismatic figure on the national stage. Born a peasant, he had educated himself. Essentially he was a political journalist. Using vivid, extravagant language he taught the great mass of his fellow citizens, the 'underfed, overworked, uneducated . . . voiceless, voteless and hopeless' Englishmen of the day, what politics was all about. The *Political Register* – Cobbett's weekly political paper – was 'read in every cottage where the march of intellect has enabled them to do so'. He was provocative and no respector of persons; people either detested him or loved him. Those who loved him found a great 'John Bull' of a man; he stood 6ft 4in. He wrote a score of books; his lifetime's output of the written word was prodigious; he was an enthusiastic farmer, arborist and agriculturist; he knew his Bible; he loved England and the English countryside *passionately*; and he wrote about these things with a charm and sympathy at surprising odds with his abrasive political life.

By the early 1820s the wool trade of Norwich was in serious decline. Cobbett was too astute a sailing master not to recognise combustible political material when he saw it. In January 1823 he addressed a huge meeting in Norwich at which he proposed large reductions in unpopular taxation. His enormous audience – ignorant of the humdrum necessities of government to raise money – applauded him wildly. The speech reverberated round England and a translation appeared in Paris. Despite the marked difference in their ages the second Sir Thomas became a fervent admirer of Cobbett; and the self-appointed champion of all those in England who 'wished to see Mr Cobbett placed in the House of Commons'.[30]

Supported by Beevor in person, Cobbett fought – and lost – Preston in the general election of 1826. (Afterwards the Editor of the *Morning Herald* described Cobbett as 'an old man'; incensed,

Cobbett replied that he was young enough to catch the editor 'by one of those things he calls legs, and toss him over the fence from Piccadilly into Green Park'.) Apart from this one incident Cobbett took his election defeat with equanimity. Four years later, after the shock of the French uprising in July 1830, he wrote that he was 'glad that no borough monger would let me have a seat. I shall now have one in a reasonable time, or there will be *no seats for anybody.*' In 1832 Cobbett was tried at the Guildhall on a charge of seditious libel. Supported in court by Beevor he defended himself and won. Afterwards an evening paper remarked that 'The proceedings at Guildhall may be regarded either as a trial of Mr Cobbett instituted by the Whig administration, or as a trial of the Whig Administration conducted by Mr Cobbett.' The comment was good journalism made at a time when newspapers were being read more widely, when society and government were, inevitably, becoming more complicated and when 'a public opinion' – which might be manipulated – was beginning to emerge.

Cobbett died in 1835, having given the greatest efforts of his life to the cause of social and political reform. The great Reform Bill became law in May 1832, when he was aged seventy, after eighteen months of political turmoil, riot, bloodshed, the burning of central Bristol, against the collective opinion of the Bishops and whilst everyone was living in fear of cholera. The Act abolished most of the rotten boroughs and extended the franchise significantly but not dramatically. As Cobbett himself said, 'it does not extend so far as my wishes would go; but . . . every sensible man takes what he can get'. Charles was only two months old when the Bill became law; incapable of understanding either the reason for the bonfires or why the Duke of Wellington thought the end of the world had come. The rejoicing marked not so much the Act itself as the fact that Englishmen as a whole had won a victory; that the sovereignty of the people had been established; and that the immense power wielded by the House of Lords had been, at last, pierced.

Cobbett stood for much that was well regarded in Norfolk. The Beevors were by no means the only local family in sympathy with the hardships endured by the poor and, in their hearts, fearful of what might happen if grievances, all too obvious to those willing to see them, were not put right. When Cobbett had written, in a private letter, that he would soon get a seat in parliament or there would be 'no seat for anybody', he was only expressing what many feared. Young Lord Suffield of Gunton, a large Norfolk landowner, wrote in December 1830, '. . . every day's observation tends to confirm my entire belief that if some steps be not speedily taken to employ and provide for the redundant population, the finest estate in England will not a short time hence be worth six months purchase'.

R.M. Bacon, a well-known editor of the *Norwich Mercury* and an ardent supporter of the English aristocracy, argued strenuously that the poor must be relieved from their distress. John Wayland (an M.P. and a Fellow of the Royal Society) stated that labourers were in a state 'of great degradation, moral and temporal' and said of Norfolk that he knew no county 'where a better disposition pervades all classes to act with equity and humanity to others'. Sir Robert Gooch (a Suffolk man), after declaring that he would never yield to intimidation, went on to speak of '. . . his determination . . . to arrest the evil which seemed to threaten us . . . the landlord, the titheholder and the farmer were equally called upon to take an active part in ameliorating the distress in this country'.

Samuel Boycott was succeeded, in 1795, by his only son William Boycott; known to everyone as Billie. Billie, in worldly terms, was the most talented, but also the most controversial, of the five Boycott Rectors.

Billie was small and suffered from ill health. He became a man not well suited to a life of rural isolation but rather to the cut and thrust of the common rooms of Oxford and Cambridge, to the company of his influential friends in Norwich and London, and to the life of a clever enquiring student and traveller in Europe. At Cambridge he was the seventh Wrangler of his year. Many of his friends might have remarked that Billie had earned 'Fortune's Smiles' by his good manners and charm, by his loyalty to them, by his wit, his knowledge of the world and by his own cleverness and scholarship; others that his style and his wit could be too curt, and too pointed, for comfort and that he was a man too full of promise and too empty of achievement. Billie was a man of sensitivity and moods; a man whose servant remembered him as a good master but a hot-tempered one; a man who, as his own death approached thirty years later, found himself unreasonably out of sympathy – the impression is intuitive – with his own son as the latter approached the third of the five family ministries in a world turned upside-down by revolution and war.

Billie's mother died when he was aged three and a half; except that she was the daughter of a clergyman and the mother who could no longer love, cherish and support a not very strong, highly strung and exceptionally clever and intelligent little boy, nothing is known of her. The immediate sorrow of her death passed but the consequences endured. When Billie was eight his younger and only brother Samuel died.[31] Much of the business of looking after and caring for his sister Mary, the youngest of the family, fell, inevitably, upon Billie. There is evidence to suggest that the surviving brother and sister became devoted to each other; it would have been surprising, perhaps, if their relationship had turned out in any other way.

About 1760, when Billie was six, Samuel and Peter Routh, the Rector of Beccles, came to an understanding that Peter would teach Billie and his own eldest son Martin together. This arrangement lasted for nine years. (During these years Peter gave up the Rectorship of Beccles and became the Headmaster of the Fauconberg School in that town.) In due course Billie followed Samuel to Caius College, Cambridge, but Martin went up to Magdalen College, Oxford. This parting of the ways never affected the lifelong friendship between Billie and Martin but, in retrospect, it came to reflect a striking difference in their chosen ways of life.

Martin took a Doctorate and lived in Magdalen as a Fellow and bachelor until, in 1791, at the age of thirty-six, he was elected to the Presidency[32] of Magdalen. Thereafter he continued his immense investigation into the history of the early Christian Church to the aid of which his friends ransacked the continental libraries; amongst the ransackers Billie was the most notable and the most industrious.

Eventually Martin published, in Latin and in four volumes, his *Reliquiae Sacrae*; Volume II contains his thanks for the help of his friend 'Guillelm Boycott'. Outliving all his contemporaries Martin continued in the Presidential Rooms until he died a few months short of his hundredth birthday.[33] He became a great figure in Oxford; he had innumerable friends and a vast acquaintance. Like his father before him he was kindly and courteous to everyone but he was no respecter of persons; he said and did only what he thought was right. He possessed a marked sense of humour and 'gave an anecdote all the benefit of good telling'. He bequeathed his private library of over 16,000 books to Durham University. At the age of sixty-five he married a lady of thirty-two who, 'with her strongly marked features, her abundance of grey hair and her luxuriant moustache' became as well known in Oxford as her husband. He loved dogs; one, Romulus, was brought up by a strong-willed cat in consequence of which the dog washed his face with his paws and refused to allow his feet to get wet. Almost deliberately, it seems, Martin declined to live with the times; he became 'venerable' at forty. In a 1954 *Times* correspondence a Mr Jonathan Routh recalled that Martin, a hundred years earlier, had been unable to see any reason for 'the installation of baths in the college since the young men were up for only eight weeks at a stretch'. Neither did Martin ever believe in the existence of railways; he dismissed undergraduates who told him they had travelled from London to Oxford in two hours 'as conspirators bent on making him take leave of his senses'.

Having become the seventh Wrangler of his year[34] Billie decided to take Holy Orders. Caius gave him a junior Fellowship intended, probably, to tide him over while he switched his mind from mathematics to theology. He was ordained deacon in 1778 at the age of twenty-two. In June 1779 Samuel was obliged to rush to Cambridge where Billie was in a fever so severe 'as to expect his death every hour'; the fever subsided but was followed by 'drowsiness and stupor . . . removed by proper applications'. Clearly Billie had no wish to launch himself, prematurely, into the church; instead he chose to travel. Samuel, his father, apparently raised no objections. Like his own father before him Samuel had become, probably, an 'indulgent parent'; reluctant to cross his clever and delicate – and sometimes difficult and impatient – son.

Billie's only surviving travelling journal is, almost certainly, his first. This opens on 14th February 1784 as he leaves London for Paris by stagecoach with Charles Harvey[35] at four o'clock in the morning and ends in mid sentence fourteen days later in Paris (its no doubt – numerous – successors have all disappeared). At first reading Billie's journal lacks sparkle. At second reading it improves; one can only admire his power of observation, his interest in everything he sees, his knowledge of architecture and his clear English.

The journal includes a Preface. In it Billie explains that the journal is addressed to his sister Mary and is for the information of himself and his intimate friends only. He does not refer to any overriding reason lying behind his travelling intentions nor to their cost. The most likely explanation for this period of Billie's life is the simple one that, toward the end of 1783 – rising twenty-eight and unmarried – he did not know what to do with his intelligent, and by nature enquiring, self. It was too soon to take over Burgh from his father – even if he had wanted to bury himself there – and, apparently, he had no wish to take up some other, even temporary, ecclesiastical employment. He was very well off and legacies were to be expected. To travel in Europe, to enjoy its pictures and architecture, its fashionable and welcoming societies and – what young men then supposed to be its universally unvirtuous – women was already the fulfilled ambition of many of Billie's friends and acquaintances. He would have been drawn, also, to the continent by another motive; a sincere wish to help his oldest friend Martin Routh discover and present to the world the ancient, and largely forgotten, sources of the religion into which both had been ordained.

Billie's relations with his father appear to be still good. He writes home immediately he is 'safe on Gaelic sands' using his returning ship's captain as postman; and, later, he is 'very much disappointed at not hearing from England'.

Between them Billie and Charles Harvey do not lack for friends and introductions into Parisian society; they are well wined, well dined, and well looked after. They manage three theatres even though Billie's French, it seems, is then barely adequate to such tests. They deliver the letters 'which Mr Pitt had supplied us' to the British Ambassador, the Duke of Dorset. (The Duke, however, 'would not be seen'. A few days later they receive 'an invitation to dine with him tomorrow, but we are elsewhere engaged'.) Billie inspects, and then writes, a clear description of a one-man-operated flying machine 'in which Blanchard has elevated himself sixteen feet from the ground'. He is full of comment upon the buildings he sees. Not all are admired. On one occasion he sees a 'magnificent open staircase' which 'to bring the matter more home to you' – that is to Mary – 'is somewhat like that . . . at Holkham[36] . . .'

More interesting for the light they throw on Billie's complex personality are his journal observations about the poor of France and the glaring imbalances between the classes which he saw as he drove along the coaching road to Paris. 'I passed through Abbeville,' he writes, 'when in it I saw symptoms of depopulation, houses *very old* falling into decay, and Poverty much like that which is the truly descriptive characteristic of every village, thinly scattered as they are, that I have passed through'. Between Calais and Amiens he 'saw not more than two or three what may be called good houses, I mean Gentlemen's Houses (which the French call Chateaux) standing singly in the country; tho' observable however it is not a matter of wonder, for the French are too fond of fluttering in a court to bear the quietness of a country life and too volatile to feel any compunction for the miseries of rustic poverty which their continual absences is *at least one* cause of. These Chateaux however become more frequent as I proceed from Amiens towards the Capital, but Village Poverty remains the same, for the Chateaux tho' more frequent are not, I believe, more frequented.'

He passed a night at Chantilly and went, early next morning, to see what he could of 'the Palace of the Prince de Condé'. He discovered 'many new buildings contiguous to the palace which . . . were necessary to supply the wants of modern luxury, but the greatest . . . is the Prince's Stables. What an immense front is this when you hear that the height is in proportion to the length, and that the length contains twenty-six large windows besides those of the Bow; it is built with . . . very good stone, every arch is ornamented in bas relief; and every centre arch and building magnificently ornamented with emblematic figures.' He was sufficiently struck by what he saw to add the only sketch the journal contains; this shows that the stable block included a large coach house, a blacksmith's shop, a circular exercise yard and kennels for the Prince's staghounds ('fine dogs' he notes on his sketch).

Between Paris in 1784 and his reappearance in Dresden in August 1793 (in the form of a letter to Martin Routh) little is now certain about Billie's life. He is believed to have 'lived in' – rather than visited – Holland, Rheims, Vienna, Ratisbon (now Regensburg) and Italy; this belief owes its origin, probably, to the fact that Billie's travelling journals were kept in the family for many years. He was back (temporarily) in Caius for Easter 1791 on which day he wrote to Martin Routh asking, in affectionate agitation, for news of the Magdalen Presidential Election. Later that year he was 'to be found in Cambridge or Yarmouth'. Three years earlier Samuel had begun to have second thoughts about Billie's long absences. At about the same time Martin Routh had, himself, contemplated travel on the continent but had reckoned without his father, Peter Routh. 'To part with you . . . would bring yet more home to me what I sympathise in with my friend Mr Boycott, who, I hear, is again likely to endure the same pang.'

On 3rd August 1793 Billie, in Dresden, wrote a surviving letter to Martin Routh; this divides, strikingly, into two parts. In the first, and longer, part he is a 'Jack of Hearts', writing to his most intimate friend about his continuing research work in a Dresden library; he is articulate, businesslike, light-hearted, agreeable and very much a 'Mr Fixit'. In the shorter part he has, chameleon-like, transformed himself into something suspiciously like a black Knave of 'Clubs and Tantrums'. 'For nothing' he writes 'seems less clear than that I shall come any more to England . . . I have received here a most unaccountable letter from my Father. I have answered it and told him flatly my mind – I go to Hanover to meet his reply; if it is an angry one I renounce my country; I meet with nothing there but griefs, and so the sacrifice cannot well cost me much. I have not yet determin'd where I shall set up my staff, but if I can get a safe conveyance from Hanover to England I will send over the copies of the MSS from thence. Adieu, God bless you: believe me to be ever most gratefully and affectionately yours. W Boycott.'

Strong words; strong by a son of his father and by one priest of another.

In the event Billie *did* come home in mid-October; as Peter Routh reported to Martin in Oxford: 'He landed [in Southwold] . . . came thither, and the next day upon receiving an answer to a Note sent to his Father proceeded to Yarmouth, where, if he finds a comfortable lodgement, he is to bathe for a time in sea water warmed, and then go to Bath, having suffered much pain from a disorder in the liver. In his passage to, or return from, Bath you are to see him . . .'.

That Autumn Billie had reached a point in his life when he was in need of cures more drastic than 'sea water warmed' or a few weeks in Bath. On the one hand he had become an exceptionally cultured man; he was a brilliant – if rusty – mathematician, a classical scholar, an experienced and well-travelled connoisseur of the arts – which included a special interest in architecture – a man with distinguished friends in the academic world and a man who possessed an intimate knowledge of the continental libraries and centres of learning. On the other hand he was aged thirty-eight; entries in his Paris journal make clear that he had a sharp eye for a pretty girl but he had found himself no wife; his health was not robust; he had been ordained for fifteen years but he had served no ministry; he had spent a great deal of money with nothing to show for it except the perfunctory gratitude of a few friends; as far as can be discovered he had, himself, undertaken no great personal endeavour which might, when accomplished, have reflected his talents; certainly he had published nothing.

Billie's handwriting is less individualistic than his father's but it is sufficiently distinctive to make an analysis possible. Some of his personal qualities are not surprising; he wrote with a 'high degree of regularity'; he was well organised and thorough; his writing shows, and his portrait confirms, that he was a man of intellectual ambition and great mental activity; he was enthusiastic, energetic and reluctant to waste time or space; he had determination (although it must be doubted if this matched his father's!). Like most people of his day he was much influenced by the lives and traditions of his forebears; and, in Billie's particular case, by the respect he had for Peter Routh who had taught him for nine years and who he once described as 'my dear old master'. There were, however, other sides to Billie's character.

First, his writing lacks 'simplifications'. By this is meant a script which is both naturally connected and which uses letter combinations to save time. This suggests a lack of imagination, originality of mind and of humour, all of which characteristics are confirmed by almost everything else still known about Billie. Wit is not humour. He was a precise and highly intelligent man who could be a witty participant in any number of university debates, but not the life and soul of some unbridled party. Second, the middle zone of his writing tends to dominate the whole. This suggests a not unhealthy, but nonetheless strong, regard for money, possessions and sex. Third, his upper zone is comparatively weak. This confirms the well organised and precise side of his nature, but suggests, also, that he was not a philosophically minded man and that he lacked *personal* ability as a musician or as an artist. (The Condé stables sketch in his Paris journal is crystal clear but not 'artistically' drawn.) Lastly, his dated and surviving written material spans thirty-nine years from age eighteen to fifty-seven. During them his writing 'changed' very little. This is unusual. It suggests that he developed early – under the inspiration of Peter Routh, the example of Martin and his personal success as a mathematician? – but that, thereafter, he made no strong personal effort in any direction and that he underwent no serious emotional stress, either of which should have found their reflection in a 'changing' hand.

It seems most likely that the quarrel between Billie and his father – as aired but not illuminated by the Dresden letter – centred on the question of who was to succeed Samuel as Rector. Three years earlier Samuel had appointed a curate named Page. If, as is likely, this Page was related to the Reverend Thomas Page, an earlier Rector of Burgh, then his appointment had been a clear warning shot across Billie's bows. In 1793 Samuel was aged sixty-nine. Samuel himself, his Churchwarden, Page the curate, conceivably the Bishop, the parish as a whole – and, for that matter, Billie himself – had all needed, for some time, to know what the future held. Dryden has a line: 'Beware the fury of a patient man'; Samuel may have run out of it. Would Billie, or would he not, come home, settle himself in the rectory and take over as Rector? To Samuel the question was entirely reasonable; for Billie acceptance meant the end of an extravagant but agreeable life, the loss of friends, the carrying of a responsibility for which he had not prepared himself and the loneliness of living as a bachelor in an isolated rural parish. These private considerations did not, in 1793, end Billie's difficulties. In August of that year Europe was in ferment. Billie's Dresden letter was written about the middle of that period of the French Revolution remembered as the 'Reign of Terror'. Over a period of eighteen months Louis XVI, Marie Antoinette and thousands of other cultured French men and women (including, no doubt, several of Billie's friends) had been guillotined[37]; and, six months before the Dresden letter, France and England had declared war. Tension and foreboding stalked Europe. Friends and families split and changed political sides; it was difficult for any two men – including a father and son – to see the same events in the same way. If, earlier, Billie had found himself in sympathy with the Revolution, it is entirely possible that, by August 1793, he had changed his mind; on the other hand Samuel, born and bred in Norwich, may have continued to be in broad sympathy with the revolution.

(That, eventually, Samuel's wishes should have prevailed should surprise no one; Samuel, by far, was the stronger character.)

In November of the following year and two months short of her thirty-sixth birthday, his sister Mary, of whom Billie had been so fond, died. The place and cause of her death are unknown. Her funeral took place in Burgh and she became the first, and unexpected, occupant of the family tomb. Charles Cunningham, her husband, had been back in England for only a few weeks before her death; it seems certain that he was with her when she died.[38] It was an age when death flew in, unannounced and overnight, to many a household, but for Samuel and Billie the shock of her death must have been overwhelming. For Samuel it was the beginning of the end. For Billie it was, with dramatic finality, the end of his beginning, the end of his bohemian and extravagant continental touring and the end of his years as a man of 'no fixed abode'.

On the 16th November 1794, and only nine days after Mary's funeral, Samuel executed what was to be his last will. On 7th April following, and upon the presentation of Samuel, Billie was instituted as the second Boycott Rector of Burgh-St-Peter. In his 16th November will Samuel left almost everything he possessed, including the advowson, to Billie. Something had knocked two heads together. It is possible that father and son both knew that Mary had set her heart upon this outcome to the family disagreement. She had spent her childhood in Burgh, she alone among all the Boycott daughters had chosen to be married there, and she had brought both her own daughters to be baptised there. No portrait of Mary can now be traced but, by family legend, she was a strikingly beautiful red-haired woman of great character.

After a year of rectorial solitude Billie determined upon matrimony with a lady young enough to be his daughter. When he married Anne Smythe[39] in East Dereham church on 3rd March 1796, he was forty and she nineteen. On the day before his wedding Billie wrote to the physician who had saved his life in Cambridge: 'Dear Dr Glynn – I owe my health to you therefore ultimately owe the happiness to which tomorrow I am to be consecrated. W.B.' To his old friend Thomas Kerrich he wrote an even more abrupt note: 'My dear Kerrich – I am to be married tomorrow. W.B.'

Of Billie's married life little is known except that it did not last long. Anne presented him with a first-born son named William in 1798 (William II, the third Rector) and five daughters who were all born between 1800 and 1806. As has been noted Billie's handwriting shows that his sexual instincts were strong; much as he needed Anne's company in the parlour and her management in the kitchen he may have needed her in the master bedroom even more. There is evidence that he did up the house for her; an 'upholsterer' named 'E.J. Smith' signed his name on some plaster in one of the parlours in 1797 and 'J. Musk', probably a carpenter, signed a floorboard in the same room in 1808. In the summer of 1810, and within three months of each other, Anne and her second daughter both died. Both were laid in the family tomb. Poor Billie was plunged, once again, into a loneliness which must have been hard to bear. He was then aged fifty-four. His son William was twelve. His four surviving daughters ranged from ten down to four. (His fourth daughter was to die in 1818 aged thirteen.)

In July 1797 Samuel died in Yarmouth. Rightly, his body lies beside that of his daughter in the vault he had constructed and beneath the curious tower by which he is remembered. The year of his death was that year of war during which little went right for England; his last months were shadowed by fears of invasion. In May he and the people of Yarmouth had watched helplessly as Admiral Duncan's North Sea fleet – assembled to protect London and the east coast – melted away; ship by ship, they struck their colours, cleared Yarmouth roads and sailed to join the most dangerous of the naval mutinies at the Nore. Duncan's command was reduced to his flagship and one other; with these he stood off the Dutch coast sending out a stream of signals to an imaginary fleet.

Under his uncle John's will (John II, who died in 1785) Billie inherited the advowson of Beeston-St-Andrew, a hamlet not far from Norwich. Beeston consisted of one large house and sixty-five people but – because it had fallen down around 1730 – no church. Lacking church and parsonage house, and having only a small population, Beeston was a more than usually reprehensible plurality but, in 1806, Billie became free to appoint himself its Rector and to draw an annual tithe income of £220 until he died.

Nothing suggests that he ever felt any obligation to 'put in an appearance' at Beeston; nothing, certainly, would have compelled him to do so.

Billie's ministry lasted for thirty-four years and, for over half of it, England was at war. As Bonaparte prepared to invade England in 1803 it fell to Billie to read out, in church, a stirring governmental precursor to those equally stirring exhortations that came into English homes by wireless during Hitler's war in 1940. The tyrant Bonaparte had 'erected a despotism the most oppressive, the most capricious, the most cruel . . . we must not remain free lest they should learn lessons of freedom; we must destroy . . . our ancient monarchy . . . lest they should sigh for a lawful and merciful King; . . . we must not breathe, we must cease to exist, because our existence gives umbrage to a man, who, from the Walls of Accra, fled, in shame and disgrace, before a handful of Britons'. It ended in an even finer roll of 'Churchillian rhetoric'. 'Singly engaged against the tyrants of the earth, Britain now attracts the eyes and the hearts of mankind; groaning nations look to her for deliverance; justice, liberty, and religion are inscribed on her banners; her success will be hailed with the shouts of the Universe . . .'

On taking over the parish Billie had examined the church registers. He may, or may not, have had sound reason to suspect the efficiency of the unfortunate Mr Page – his father's curate – but Billie records that while Page had kept the books he had found 'so many mistakes' that he, Billie, 'thought it better to cut out the page than transmit the mistakes to posterity'. Several mistakes seem to have concerned illegitimate children, but whether or not the curate ought to have known of these 'merry begotten' infants it is impossible now to say; nor is it possible to discover how many mistakes went to make up 'so many'. Billie became aware, also, of an incorrect baptismal entry made in 1749 by Thomas Page, Samuel's predecessor as Rector; the baptism of Bridget Willson had been recorded but the watering had related to *Roger* Willson. In the spring of 1808 something most unpleasant happened to Billie himself; he was, evidently, bamboozled into conducting a bigamous marriage. Affronted, he added explanatory notes in both the Banns Book and the Marriage Register; from the latter it appears that the 'bridegroom' had 'told the Parish Clerk that he had a wife alive'. This was disgraceful conduct by the clerk, and, no doubt, by a number of other parishioners as well. Billie had every right to be *extremely* angry!

Thomas Kerrich – the son of a Norfolk clergyman and the recipient of that curtest of wedding announcement notes – was a close friend of Billie's for forty years. Within Cambridge University he was as distinguished a figure as was Martin Routh in Oxford. Martin became President of Magdalen; Thomas President of Magdalene[40] and, in 1793, the Cambridge University Librarian. As a young man Kerrich studied in the Low Countries and in France and Italy before returning to Cambridge and becoming a Fellow of Magdalene. He was ordained at the age of thirty-six when he succeeded his father as vicar of Dersingham in North Norfolk. He was an antiquarian, his absorbing interests being architecture and illustration; he was a fine draughtsman, a distinguished etcher and one of the earliest lithographers; he was also a painter and a miniaturist (his portraits include that of Billie which is reproduced in the plate section). A copy of Kerrich's own portrait hangs in Magdalene. His face is that of a handsome and strong, rather forbidding man. He is remembered as someone of the highest personal standards, of the most severe judgements and from whom the merest crumb of praise was never forgotten. (The face, in the Magdalene portrait, is softened, curiously, by an elusive smile.)

When Thomas Kerrich died in 1828 he left a large collection of coins, books, architectural drawings, illustrations and paintings which, variously, found their way into the British Museum, the Society of Antiquaries and the Fitzwilliam Museum in Cambridge. Many items in the collections had a continental provenance. As Kerrich himself (as far as is known) only lived on the continent for four years as a young man, the inference must be that he received help in making his collections, failing which he could not have accomplished all that he did. In the Scott papers an (undated) manuscript note reads: '[Billie's] letters to Thomas Kerrich date from 1784 to 1824. All those from the Continent are full of information and appreciation of pictures, statues and other works of art . . .'. The probability is that Billie gave the same intelligent and investigative help to Thomas Kerrich as he gave to Martin Routh.

One 'note' from Billie to Kerrich has – somehow! – survived. It is undated but was written almost certainly from Burgh soon after Anne's death in 1810.

Dear Kerrich

I know not whether you are tolerant of comments – but if I interest myself at all – I must enter into the thing . . . In truth I have so lost what little interest my idleness ever permitted to me in classics, that I was very near sending back your book unlooked at.

But the remarks on Agricola's virtues seemed to me to have been written by you with an especial feeling – and that gave me an interest . . . – but I stop at about half way. Where I have read – I have commented. You may disagree – but as you have encouraged by sending it, you must bear it with patience.

I shall – I believe – bring this myself and in case of seeing no one – beg my regards to the ladies.

Ever yours

W. Boycatt

Kerrich did not, with a grunt of irritation, throw Billie's note into his grate! Both men, of course, were academics; both understood why 'the merciless persecution of one mind by another' led, so often, to good academic work. And, of course, Kerrich knew Billie; they had not been friends for half a century for nothing.

The local legend – the 'story' – to explain Samuel's extraordinary tower runs something like this. Samuel receives from Billie (in Italy?) sketches or descriptions of a stepped tower and of a path leading up to a church porch having cypress trees on each side of it. Samuel, to please his son, goes to work. Billie comes home. Samuel, in some excitement, walks him down the lane until the new church tower comes into view. A flabbergasted silence follows. Billie says, 'But Father, where are the cypresses?' (he had had in mind a small cypress avenue).

Is anything, now, to be sifted out of this odd tale? Or otherwise to be brought into a more distinct focus?

The evidence is clear that, over ten or more years, Billie sent home a stream of information from the continent; letters on the early history of Christianity to Martin Routh in Oxford; letters on artistic and, probably, architectural matters to Thomas Kerrich in Cambridge; and, by journals addressed to his family, general accounts of what he had seen and done. It is perfectly possible that, somewhere in these writings, Billie *did* describe a stepped tower and cypresses which had taken his fancy – but, sadly, little of what he wrote is still available to be consulted. The Routh

Sacrae archive was pruned of all supporting material many years ago. Billie's letters to Kerrich were kept and they may have come to light, briefly, forty to fifty years ago, but they have since disappeared. Only one of Billie's travelling journals has survived and this, whilst emphasising his interest in architecture, sheds no light whatever on the tower.

The Diocesan faculty authorising the rebuilding of the tower is dated 4th June 1793. Samuel was not the man to accept ideas as to what he should, or should not, do without giving them careful thought; and particularly so if they concerned his *own* church and how he should spend his *own* money. Billie, for his part, was a precise and careful man; it is difficult to imagine that he ever sent home confusing sketches or imprecise descriptions of anything. Nothing now suggests why Samuel did not start his church reconstruction earlier in life; but, at age sixty-nine, it seems unlikely that he would have embarked upon his expensive project, and agreed to pay for it himself, without the willing consent of both his children. (Billie's Dresden letter of 3rd August 1793 makes no reference to the tower as being the cause of his quarrel with his father.)

Circumstances suggest that Kerrich may have become involved in the tower's reconstruction. There is no evidence that he ever went to Burgh, but his friendship with Billie was such as to make it certain that he did; and, as a clergyman himself, he must have been reasonably familiar with the original church and its fallen tower. Kerrich's surviving manuscripts show that he knew at least five of the neighbouring churches, that he possessed a wide knowledge of English and Continental church buildings, and that his technical interest in architecture gave him a sound knowledge of their construction. Who better than Kerrich with whom to discuss ideas about the building of a new tower and tomb? And from whom to get advice about the technical considerations and the likely cost?[41]

One other possibility exists: Samuel took no marriages, baptisms or burials in Burgh between August 1779 and the end of March 1780. Illness may have stopped him but, on the other hand, he may just have married Mrs Gordon. Did he, on his honeymoon, see something – in the Low Countries? – that made him think of his own church? And of how his tower might be reconstructed?

Age now has softened the outlines of Samuel's extraordinary

tower; here and there plants have taken root in its crevices. At close range the stone and brick of the tower growls at the long low unbroken line of reed thatch under which lies the flintwork of the combined nave and chancel; the contrast between colours and textures is too great for it to be otherwise. But, from a more distant lengthwise viewpoint – and, in the later twentieth century this is not easily found – tower and thatch marry well enough. The disparate colours and textures fuse and fade into the isolation and emptiness of the place in which they exist. The whole becomes what it is; a plain country church standing, silently, where it has stood for 800 years.

In 1816 Billie put a new pulpit into the church. At first thought a plain dark oak pulpit cannot rival, in curiosity, the tower erected by his father but, over the years, it has come to distinguish the interior of the church as remarkably as Samuel's tower distinguishes its exterior. To his pulpit Billie secured three copper plates. These record the fact that he installed the pulpit and that it was dedicated to the memory – in the order of their deaths – of his brother Samuel (whose grave lies *under* the new pulpit), his grandmother Anne, his sister Mary, and his father Samuel. Later generations of the family have added their own and plates now cover almost the whole of the pulpit's visible surface. The plates are kept polished; they twinkle and shine and, on a drab day, they bring an always surprising dash of colour into what, otherwise, would be a long narrow and austere interior which has been described as 'more like a corridor or cloister than the nave of a parish church'.[42] Billie, invited back to preach again from his own pulpit, would approve of what he saw. He had respect for the past and a sharp eye for the unusual.

Today, in the summer months, the church is much visited. The old staithe has been transformed into a broadlands marina. Visitors from their holiday boats walk up to the church they have seen across the water. They stretch their legs and write their names in the visitors' book. 'My birthday. A tower like a cake. Thank you.' A visitor from Western Australia – oblivious of the busy marina and the boats cruising up and down the Waveney – writes 'Peaceful old England'. Almost every visitor gazes up at the tower. 'Who built it?' 'When?' 'Why?' To the 'who' and the 'when' there are answers. The answer to the 'why' – the precise origin of an idea in the mind of a man who died 200 years ago – seems, at least for the time being, to have slipped away. But – it is still possible that

Billie's long series of letters to Thomas Kerrich and the remainder of his travelling journals lie forgotten in some drawer or attic. For 150 years both were thought to be well worth keeping! Has anyone got them?

Of Billie's life between Waterloo in 1815 and his death in 1830 at the age of seventy-four, little is known. By the evidence of his own entries in the church registers he was regular in his parish duties. In 1824 he suffered from an attack of angina and other agonising attacks may well have followed. These, coupled with other infirmities, may have reduced him, from 1824, to being a semi-invalid; coincidental or not, this year marked the end of his forty-year-long correspondence with Thomas Kerrich. Toward the end of his life Billie sold the Yarmouth house and, in its place, he bought the Manor House in the village of Great Ormesby; this became the family's second home for most of the nineteenth century.

Billie executed his last will in the year he retired. He died in Ormesby on 6th November 1830. To his only son William (William II) he left the Burgh advowson, his land and property in Burgh and his land and property in Mendlesham in Suffolk and Stratton in Norfolk. His three surviving daughters, Frances, Emily and Harriet, were still unmarried; they shared the remainder of their father's estate. This included what remained of what, at one time, must have been large holdings of 'investment stock' and probably the Manor House and its, no doubt, valuable contents. He appointed the three girls as his joint executrixes. The impression is that he was very grateful to all three of them; they probably looked after him lovingly and well during his last years.

Billie's was an odd, rather sad, life. He was denied the love, sympathy and support of a mother; his only sister – who perhaps replaced the mother he never really knew – died when he was still young. The devil served him ill – as devils will – when, as a young man, he gave him too much money but took away ambition. He lived alone, and pleased himself alone, for too long. In truth he was a dilettante; no books, no manuscripts, no treatises on any subject, survived his death; he seems never to have set his mind to anything which demanded long grinding hours of hard work. As the Rector of Burgh-St-Peter he was, with little doubt, a misfit; he was insufficiently earthy for the simple, mostly illiterate, people who became his parishioners. One wonders about his sermons?

And of the words and expressions he used in them? And of how he managed when he visited his people? They understood the land and the slow rhythms of the seasons and the work which each season brought, but of higher mathematics and the architecture and artefacts of Paris and Pisa and Padua they had no comprehension.

If the question be asked, 'Did Billie *want* to live face to face with God?' the answer must be, 'No'.

CHAPTER FIVE

THE SLOW RIVERS OF EAST Anglia, kept bare of trees to catch every breeze, and the wherries and keels which served them, provided an internal transport system which was second to none. The smooth level water surfaces were the local highways and byways of the age. The Yare, the Bure and the Waveney and their tributaries, linked at Breydon Water, connected, in one way or another, almost every town, village and farm over a wide area. Norwich – with its city docks on a tributary of the Yare – was joined by water with all its overseas markets on the Continent and round the Mediterranean; an immense commercial advantage marred only by the twin necessities of transhipment from river to ocean-going vessels at Yarmouth and the charges, delays and pilferings which thereby arose. After Waterloo, when the city's manufacturers were fighting for survival, these constraints could be tolerated no longer. As a simple commercial resolve to improve distribution and reduce delivery costs, the initiative taken by Norwich was commonplace; but, in this instance, the decision to force change was to bring considerable consequences.

The commercial interests of Yarmouth differed from those of Norwich. Much of Yarmouth's transhipment trade depended on the fortunes of Norwich, but Yarmouth, in addition and literally, had 'other fish to fry'. The town had grown from a few summer huts on a sand bank in the days when salt water lapped the Burgh peninsula into what many judged to be one of the finest ports in Europe; largely on the ever-growing importance of its fishing industry. In the 1820s the supply of herrings out of the North Sea appeared to be as limitless as was people's liking for them. Yarmouth and Norwich, therefore, held only *some* trading interests in common.

Norwich, to relieve itself of the Yarmouth annoyances, floated the idea of dredging and straightening the Yare sufficiently to allow ocean-going vessels to sail *directly* up to the city. Accordingly 'overtures were made to the Corporation of Yarmouth for a friendly conference' and, given goodwill, a new arrangement satisfactory to both sides might well have been reached. But Yarmouth would have none of it. They 'refused all co-operation in such a measure [and] declared that they would oppose every effort to carry the same into effect'. Predictably the merchants and bankers and manufacturers of Norwich declined to allow their intentions to be frustrated and put forward a startling alternative. This involved major 'geographical surgery' – by shovel and wheelbarrow – which had, as its object, the entire elimination of Yarmouth as a factor in the shipping affairs of Norwich. Even today their proposal commands respect for its audacity and for its ruthless concentration upon essentials as these were then perceived.

As with the earlier proposal the River Yare's difficult bends were to be straightened and the river dredged to twelve feet. Where the Yare and the Waveney began to converge, south-east of Reedham, the two rivers were to be joined by a straight seventy-foot-wide and two-and-a-half-mile long 'New Cut' (it is still so described on modern maps) beyond which the Waveney would be followed until its junction with the old Oulton Dyke. Oulton Dyke was to be made navigable and connected, via Oulton Broad and Lake Lothing, to the sea at the then small town of Lowestoft (in Suffolk). Lowestoft, inevitably, would grow; if, in growing, it became a thorn in the side of Yarmouth, then the planners in Norwich doubtless considered that any such eventuality would be no concern of theirs.

The necessary 'Norwich and Lowestoft Navigation' Act (of Parliament) was obtained in 1827 and was the cause of much rejoicing in Norwich. (Some of the celebrators got out of hand and were gaoled.) The work was completed in 1833 and the first sea-going vessel – a collier – to reach Norwich did so a few days later. For a year or two things went tolerably well but, sadly, the city's export trade in cloth never really recovered; and, in addition, two matters had been either misjudged or overlooked. First, Yarmouth – still having the advantage of the shorter route to the sea – put its house in order; and, secondly, the exit to the sea at Lowestoft was found to be subject to frequent, and serious, silting.

From Burgh-St-Peter church to the junction between the Waveney and Oulton Dyke is not far. It was not every day of the week that isolated Burgh-St-Peter found itself holding free grandstand seats from which to watch scene-shifting on such a scale! What better for Charles's father and mother than to take a boat and a family picnic and inspect the new work in person? Perhaps the most exciting moment arrived in 1831 when, before a large crowd, Lake Lothing was opened, finally, to the sea. One who witnessed this unusual event described an unexpected aspect of it:

> The salt water entered the lake with a strong undercurrent, the fresh water running out at the same time to the sea upon the surface . . . Lake Lothing was thickly studded with the bodies of pike, carp, tench, bream, roach and dace, multitudes of which were carried into the ocean . . . it is a singular fact that a pike of about twenty lbs weight was taken up dead near the Mutford end of the lake; and, on opening the stomach, a herring was found in it entire.

Whilst the 'Norwich to Lowestoft Navigation', as such, was never much more than a watery white elephant, the old local heavy goods carriers, which had worked the three rivers system for so long, demonstrated a fine resilience to competition from the new railway system. They continued to be cheap and they could be uniquely convenient. A farmer possessing his own dyke might have his grain collected from, and his marl delivered to, his own land; and any family wanting a ton of coal could be almost as fortunate. (In the days of poor lanes and heavy cumbersome carts these were significant advantages.)

Most of 'The Navigation' excavations and constructions soon greened over and were forgotten about. But for Lowestoft and its 'beautiful and spacious Lake Lothing' the bell had tolled; neither place could ever be the same again. For hundreds of years the people of old Lowestoft had fished their lake, its lovers had strayed away from its paths, and men and women had stood back on Normanston Hill to gaze over its tranquillity to the restless ocean beyond. As a wild flower is seized and destroyed so was Lake Lothing seized by salt water and tides. Within a few years, and under the powerful influence of Samuel Moreton Peto and his railways, it became Lowestoft Harbour. For the little town of Lowestoft itself the change was equally dramatic. In 1831 it had been a sleepy but attractive market, sea-fishing, fine china manufacturing and small watering resort of 4,238 people; by 1881, on the back of its thriving harbour, it had become *much* larger.

The wherry was the heavy commercial carrier – and the undisputed Queen – of the Norfolk waterways. The sight of a majestic black sail gliding, ravenlike, across the open flats and marshes – attached, apparently, to nothing – was commonplace. A heavily laden boat, moving fast under its huge sail in a stiff breeze in a narrow waterway was a fine – and sometimes frightening – sight; it was more or less unstoppable and smaller craft – which meant everything else – made haste to make themselves scarce. Wherries were owned by merchants and manufacturers as part of their businesses and by individuals who crewed them themselves and picked up their freights as and where they could. All kept their boats as smart and trim as paint, tar, and loving care could keep them.[43] The wherrymen knew every inch of the waterways; every reach and every wind, every set of the tide, every mooring, every staithe and who kept it, and every pub where they could meet their friends and, perhaps, pick up a freight or two. Each boat flew, from its masthead, its own house flag. Any small boy of Burgh, sighting a light green pennant with yellow and blue bands flying high above a wherry cutting viciously into the stream and showing barely an inch of free board, knew, as well as he knew his own name, that it was a W.D. & A.E. Walker boat; grain merchants and maltsters of Bungay and a firm of considerable importance to the agricultural neighbourhood. (Wherry spotting in Norfolk came long before train spotting!)

The Burgh-St-Peter staithe – or small harbour – lay close to the church and at the only place where river, sound land and hard lanes converged. As the ports of the world go it was not large; but, to the otherwise isolated households and farms, it was a Godsend. Through it passed all manner of freight; bricks[44]; marl and lime; cement; timber (the wherry mast serving as a derrick); sand from Yarmouth for scouring kitchen floors; sacked and labelled grain; coal from Kent or the North still measured by the 'chaldron' (which meant one quantity in London but another in Newcastle); olives and olive oil and oranges from the Mediterranean; mails every now and then; and – no one will ever know how much –

contraband. (Squire, parson and everyone else who could manage it preferred to pay less rather than more for their tea, their 'hollands', their wine and their tobacco.[45]) Every town, village, farm and factory within the area connected itself into the three rivers transport system if it could do so. The wherries underpinned the East Anglian economy; it was no wonder that local advertisers made the point that their wares were 'very convenient for water carriage'.

The East Anglian system of 'water carriage' operated in a still clean and unpolluted environment. The system itself caused no pollution; neither did any of the crop rotation systems which had been adopted as part of the agricultural revolution. Although, by the early nineteenth century, land drainage, especially in the fens, was beginning to limit the wetland areas, and birds and their eggs were beginning to be taken for sale, the waterways and reed beds, the swamps and marshes remained, generally, as they had always been. These supported food chains which, in turn, supported vast quantities of animals, birds and fish. Wild flowers and butterflies and moths abounded. The food chains were infinitely complex in their structures but ferociously simple in the manner in which they were utilised. Everything was interdependent and held in balance. Much of the wild animal kingdom of the Norfolk waterways – ruled by instinct – still strode, as it were, centre stage and unafraid. Mankind, thinly distributed and still lacking any fast reliable means of long distance transport, stood in the wings. The air was sweet.

Instinct drew sea and migrant birds in vast numbers to the Norfolk coast and waterways and to their seclusion and food. They joined as many native birds. These included countless small birds which, unlike those on the continent, enjoyed a comparative immunity throughout England. Most, particularly the perching birds, preferred the margins of the marshes which were closer to higher ground and its woodland and thick hedgerow cover. The number of varieties to be seen during the summer months was as astonishing as the multitude itself.

Breydon Water, lying west of Yarmouth and its surrounding marshes, were pre-eminent in the hospitality they offered to birds. Into Breydon flowed the Bure, the Yare and the Waveney which, combined, scoured a two-mile channel to the sea, so creating the quays and harbour of Yarmouth. Each flood tide brought salt water into Breydon where it mixed with fresh water still pouring in from the rivers. Each ebb left channels of clear water and laid bare treacherous mud-flats upon which the birds congregated but across which a man could not walk except with mud pattens. The birds gorged themselves on small red worms and sea centipedes which flourished in the saline water. A Norfolk clergyman, writing in 1845, said of it: 'Though last, perhaps pre-eminent over all, Breydon Water . . . which has furnished at different times as many objects of interest to the naturalist as any locality in Britain . . . something new was perpetually presenting itself.'

It occurred to no one that the multitude of birds might, one day, be reduced so dramatically. Some writers of the day looked back to the pre-drainage days and even greater numbers, but few extrapolated any such awareness forward into concern for the future; birds and their eggs seemed to have been regarded as an ever renewable resource. The cornucopia engendered its own human activities and attitudes of mind.

Gentlemen made collections of birds for their halls, studies, and gunrooms but few took any serious interest in ornithology. Some walked and looked and hoped they might make some interesting discovery; others thought only of their stomachs. Golden Plover, Dotterel, Woodcock, the Ruff and the Reeve, and the Black Tailed Godwit ('the 12th of May is Godwit Day') were all excellent eating. Not many people, then, wrote articles or books on birds, but one exception, whilst Charles was growing up, was Edward Stanley, the new Bishop of Norwich; he published his *Familiar History of Birds, Their Nature, Habits and Instincts* in two volumes in 1836.

A good water-dog, not afraid of Breydon, was, to a 'Breydoner', a pearl of great price. Richard Lubbock has left this account of how one Yarmouth dog served his master:

> In the winter his favourite pursuit was to go out by himself and search in the rough stones which face Breedon Wall for wounded wild foul; these always, if possible, creep into some nook or corner . . . he sometimes carried home eight or nine fowl . . . in the same morning. After leaving one with his master, he returned on his own accord to the place where he took it, proceeding regularly in his search, and every time recommencing exactly where he left off. As he travelled to and fro upon the marsh wall, he would, if unloaded, wag his tail and acknowledge the notice of anyone who spoke to him; but no sooner had he obtained booty than

> he seemed to consider himself the guardian of a Treasure and to distrust everyone. As soon as a man appeared coming towards him he left the wall, and crossing a wide dyke, betook himself to the marshes and went the longest way home.

Immature gulls were taken in quantities unknown and their soft feathers used for pillow making.

Some migrants came to breed in large colonies. Their sudden arrival on a spring day, and the clamour and excitement they brought with them, were notable events. Black Terns, the slender darting sea swallows of the waves, came in every year to an alder carr[46] near Acle 'in myriads' until the 1820s. The existence of such large nesting colonies made the task of 'eggers' hopelessly easy. The London markets usually wanted 'plovers' eggs but they got mixtures; any egg which looked about right would be sent off. In 1821 one man took nearly 2,000 'plovers eggs' from around Potter Heigham; in 1829 a merchant sent 6–700 eggs, mostly 'plovers', to London every week during the season; at Scoulton Mere a 'normal season' was said to produce 30,000 Blacked Headed Gulls' eggs[47]; (these charming birds were known also as 'Scoulton Pies', probably because their young were netted at Scoulton Mere and sold as food). In 1845 a Leadenhall Market dealer admitted that he might sell, each year, 60–100,000 game bird eggs to estates for hatching out; he supposed *all* had been poached.

An ancient method of taking duck in large numbers throughout the winter was in decoys. (Method and word are of Dutch origin: *kooi* – a cage.) Decoys were common along the East Anglian coast on sheltered waters to which duck flew in regularly. Although easily frightened, duck, when they feel themselves secure, are inquisitive little creatures; the decoy was both sanctuary and killing ground. Fritton lake, midway between Burgh and Breydon, had been a famous one for centuries. Towards the end of the eighteenth century someone wrote of Fritton: 'The duck, mallard and teal, are in such plenty as is scarce to be conceived. They are taken in prodigious flocks . . . They send these fowl to London twice a week, on horseback, from Michaelmas to Lady Day . . .' A few decoys still exist but now they only catch, tag and release duck for research purposes. (Pubs named 'The Decoy' are still to be found; there is one at St Olaves, not far from Fritton.[48])

The first legislation to protect wild birds was not passed until 1880. This – more or less – stopped the wholesale taking of wild birds eggs but was incapable of re-creating the *immense* quantity of birds which, previously, had either lived in, or which had visited, East Anglia.

Norfolk was astonishing, also, for the number of salt water fish which lived in its North Sea and for the number of fresh water fish which lived in its many waterways. For many years the quantities of both defied either calculation or conjecture. An author, in an 1875 *Blackwoods Magazine*, remarked that 'any attempt to estimate the quantity of fish in the North Sea can only produce a state of utter bewilderment'.

The North Sea had been fished – in moderation because human populations had been so small – by all comers for centuries. These included the Dutch who, in their 'Holland-toads, crab skuits, walnut shells and great and small yeures' sold their catches in Yarmouth so allowing themselves to take home 'a great sum of money which ought to have stayed in Yarmouth'. As the centuries passed it seemed that nothing could limit the quantity of fish which might be taken, with impunity, from the North Sea; it was thought of as being 'an inexhaustible storehouse' which was maintained 'at a constant quantity'. In 1873 the catch of herrings, by Yarmouth and Lowestoft combined, amounted to 49,649 tons or approximately 422 million fish. This was slaughter on a prodigious scale; no stock of anything, anywhere, could withstand such depletions.

Like the fish in the North Sea the coarse fish of the inland waters were taken in very large – if not often recorded – quantities. There was no close season. The catch to one rod in a day was reckoned usually, not by the brace or the pound, but by the bushel or stone. It was said that poachers, using nets, could take seven or eight tons of fish from Fritton, as famous for its fish as it was for its duck. Bream, roach and rudd were often fed to pigs and poultry and to any dog which would touch such food; anything left over would be thrown on the ground to rot as manure. Perch were less common because they preferred gravelly bottoms, but to catch a good one of two pounds or more was an event; they fought well and their flesh was firm and clean. But the pike – the invisible freshwater shark, Izaak Walton's 'mighty luce' – was king; not only because of his size and because he ate everything else but also because he was, himself, good eating if properly prepared and cooked. Fritton and the Waveney from Bungay to the 'New Cut' were renowned for the number of pike they held.

With good fishing so close to rectory and pulpit it is not surprising that several Boycotts have been keen fishermen. There is a story that, during the best of the pike fishing season, the days of the week on which christenings might be performed in Burgh church were restricted on account of the font being required for the Rector's live bait. Charles as a boy, using a home-made hazel rod, strong gut and a weighted hook, an old cork pierced by a goose quill and some worms or bread paste, could catch more fish in a morning than he could stagger home with. Luke, one of his great nephews, over a long angling career, continued to use, if he could, a home-collected and home-made horsehair cast; it was the give and stretch of horsehair, he said, that made it so pleasant to use.

Last, but certainly not least, in the story of birds and fish in Norfolk, was Breydon Water. Dominated turn and turn about by salt and fresh water its brackish and ever changing saline mixtures allowed sea and fresh water fish *to swim together.* They also died together. An odd collection of recognisable corpses, stranded on the Breydon mud, was once found; this consisted of a large skate, some brill, a cod, two eels together weighing nine pounds, a conger of twelve pounds and a large pike which, perhaps, had frightened and disoriented the group at the critical moment on a falling tide. Perch, after swimming through Breydon and the port area were occasionally taken at sea, close inshore, in the nets of shrimpers. Shoals of grey mullet were caught in nets in Breydon and could be seen splashing. Flounders came in and so did the cucumber scented smelts. In October great hauls of whiting and codling were made. To the Breydon 'fraternity' it was the sea fish in Breydon which were valuable and about which most has been remembered. Nonetheless fresh water fish drifted downstream constantly and pike 'were everywhere'. So also, were eels; like all anadromous fish these were excellent eating; they commanded a good price and were 'caught by the hundred weight'.

The 'Breydoners' of Charles's young days shot and fished their way through rough, hard-drinking lives. Illiterate and unschooled, their boats were leaky and their guns dangerous[49] but they knew Breydon as they knew the backs of their hands. They had need to; Breydon was a paradise for birds but for a man it could be wild, lonely and bitterly cold. By definition rare birds did not come in either often or in sizeable parties. A parcel of two or three spoonbills, spotted preening and resting themselves and beginning to feed as the tide went out and dusk drew on might be left until dawn. Then, dead, they fetched a good price; one Yarmouth dealer was said to 'pay up like a banker'. Valuable specimens were sold to museums and rich collectors; handsome birds were taken alive and sold to the owners of ornamental ponds and lakes.

Most 'Breydoners' lived in old houseboats; some in 'houses' strung together under old boats. Their crude scarecrow lives possessed an element of timelessness. Theocritus, the Greek poet of the countryside, who lived in Syracuse in the third century BC, would have recognised a 'Breydoner' instantly:

> Two ancient fishers in a straw-thatched shed,
> Leaves were their walls, and seaweed was their bed,
> Reclined their weary limbs; hard by were laid
> Baskets and all their implements of trade.
> Rods, hooks, and lines composed of stout horse-hairs,
> And nets of various sorts, and various snares,
> The seine, the cast-net, and the wicker maze,
> To waste the watery tribe a thousand ways.
> Hats were their pillow, wove of osiers dank –
> Skins, caps, and coats, a rugged covering made;
> This was their wealth, their labour and their trade.
> No pot to boil, no watch-dog to defend,
> Yet blessed they lived with penury their friend.
> None visited their shed, save, every tide,
> The wanton waves that washed its tottering side.

If anyone, at the time, had proposed the creation of a 'European School of Nature Studies' and asked where such a place might be established, then 'somewhere near Breydon' would have been high on any list. As Charles knew it in his boyhood it was a marvellous – if often intimidating – place; the natural order was *overwhelmingly apparent.* The comings and goings of its teeming multitudes of native and migratory birds and sea and freshwater fish set standards and examples of variety and quantity and interest which few other places could equal. For Charles the wild life of Breydon and the East Anglian waterways – but especially Breydon – became a kind of benchmark against which the many immeasurable aspects of nature could, nevertheless, be measured.

Chapter Six

Most Englishmen, in the 1820s, were simple, uncomplicated people; untouched by newspapers, radio or television. Almost everyone believed in the existence of an all-seeing, but still merciful, God. Most people worshipped him not only because they believed he cared for them as individuals, but also because God carried scales; the wicked, in due course, would be weighed. Almost everyone believed in some form of life after death. By today's standards church attendances were high; many people thought they could not live their lives *without* the church. Nonetheless the church, in the 1820s, found itself in some disarray; it was out of focus with the march of events. Its shortcomings brought it into contempt at a time when no one could forget the fate of a worldly and avaricious church in revolutionary France.

No ship possessed of an apparently eternal buoyancy could be sunk. Nonetheless it was something of a miracle that, from within itself, the church was able to find not only the men, but also the will, to put its house in order. Several matters needed urgent attention.

The first and second Rectors of Burgh-St-Peter believed that the world had been created in six days as described in Genesis. (Some bibles added to the feeling of certainty about the creation by dating the event, precisely, to 4004 BC.[50]) The significance of the fact that, according to Genesis, God had created the grass and herb bearing seed 'before he had created the greater light to rule the day' was usually ignored; that other civilisations held different opinions concerning the likely age of the physical world was disregarded.

The first shock to so faulty an understanding of the nature of the creation was administered by the geologists. These began to assert – about 1830 – with a scientific assurance which soon overwhelmed the assurances of Genesis that rock formations existed in England of an immeasurable antiquity. Astronomers and biologists soon pointed in similar directions. Charles Darwin, aged twenty-three, and sitting in his cabin in the *Beagle* off South America a month before Charles had been born, wrote home to his father that he had 'strolled in the forests of the new world'. Thirty years later he proclaimed his epoch-making hypothesis of 'natural selection'. Suddenly it became necessary to seek God, not through the miracles of Genesis, but through the constantly evolving mysteries of nature; but it was impossible to perform this somersault quickly. As usual nothing was gained without cost. Every new fact learnt about the sun, the moon and the stars, the oceans, the weather, the soils and their crops added immeasurably to human knowledge but detracted from, and eventually destroyed, the old wonder and mysticism. A world created in six days had been a deeply mysterious conception; long traditional belief in so awesome an occurrence could not be thrown off either lightly or quickly.

The diocese of Norwich, then containing over 1,000 parishes[51] and more churches (many of surpassing beauty) than anywhere else of comparable size in the whole of Christendom, represented all that was wrong with the established church. Its Bishop ought to have been one of the best and busiest on the bench, but when Charles came into the world in 1832 its Bishop was aged eighty-eight. He then received emoluments amounting to £5,395 p.a., which compared with the £323 p.a. received, on average, by the clergy in his diocese. Bishop Bathurst survived – still enthroned as Bishop of the 'Dead See' – until his death in April 1837 at the age of ninety-three. Such a state of affairs could not continue. New men – new leaders – had to be found capable of breathing new life into the great establishment which, in their hearts, many people still knew they could not live without.

Edward Stanley resembled his predecessor as Bishop of Norwich in one respect only; he, too, was a Whig. At his installation in August 1837 he was aged fifty-eight. He had been a parish priest for thirty-two years. He knew his business. He understood duty and discipline. He was, himself, a man of great courage. He proceeded to sweep his new – and overlarge – diocese with the strong stiff broom it so badly needed. Amongst other interests far removed from the church he was a passionate admirer of the Royal Navy; his eldest son wrote of him that his parish 'had been his ship'; his See became likewise.

During his short bishopric Stanley erected no less than 173 parsonage houses; he appointed seventy rural deans (to keep him in touch with every corner of church life in his enormous diocese); he did much for the poor; he increased the number of church services; he was stern with clerical wrong-doers (at his own expense he prosecuted those clergy, who, by misconduct, had brought themselves into conflict with the law); he was the author of two pamphlets intended to reduce the continuing distrust between Protestant and Catholic; he was keenly interested in the new scientific thinking; he was a great lover of birds and published a book on them, in two volumes, in 1836. (It was no more than fitting that, a year later, he should become the diocesan to such multitudes!)

Stanley died in 1849; the Bishop of a See which was not dead but which had come alive again. The great west window of the Cathedral commemorates him and he lies buried in the centre of the nave. Several of those who attended his funeral must have recalled his installation twelve years earlier; and the anxious text, taken from 2 Corinthians, which he had then chosen for his sermon – 'And who is sufficient for these things?'.

According to his son Arthur,[52] Edward Stanley left behind him 'carefully . . . laid up in chests' the whole of his correspondence with his diocesan clergy. Had this survived (which now seems most doubtful) it would constitute a unique day-by-day record of the rebirth of a great diocese.

Stanley left, also, in the heart of one of his clergy, the memory of a visit: 'I felt as if a sunbeam had passed through my parish.'

Because, for centuries, England had been almost wholly rural and its wealth had resided primarily in land, the clergy had been remunerated by the actual 'fruits of the land.' An incumbent of a living – by virtue of his office – had been entitled to a tithe, in kind, of one tenth part of everything produced from the land lying within the boundary of the parish he served. In theory tithing was simple;

in practice it had become impossibly difficult. How, for example, was a litter of seven piglets to be divided both amicably and fairly? Practical and vexatious difficulties without number and the costs of collection had, gradually, forced most tithe holders into making 'compositions'; that is to say they accepted payment in cash instead of kind. (As a matter of history compositions were never popular in Cambridgeshire and Suffolk, nor, probably, in South Norfolk; in 1832 Charles's father, when making a tithe return, noted that his father '. . . had for many years taken *nearly* all his tithe in kind.')

Precedent, respect for the church of God, the occasional resort to law, and far more goodwill than bad had, over the centuries, buttressed a system of paying the clergy which had small hope of survival in the post-Waterloo age. Old compositions had been eroded in real value by war and inflation.

The agricultural revolution had introduced 'new' crops. Some farmers, struggling against post-war economic depression, argued that, for example, a crop new to them, like turnips, could not be tithed because there was no local precedent for tithing turnips; the incumbent argued – with more justice – that it was a share of the *fruit* of the land, whatever that might be, which was his by right. To the farmer tithes were an onerous unfair tax in an increasingly 'modern' world; why should he, only, bear it? If the clergyman might help himself to one tenth part of everything produced on a farm why did he not, also, fund one tenth of the cost, say, of marling, by which the yield, and so the tithe, was increased? To the progressive farmer tithe was a stupid tax upon enterprise and investment. The clergy were no less caught up in the toils; they, like everyone else, had to eat, meet their expenses, and pay their taxes. Most loathed the almost degrading business of demanding their tithes but none were free to consult only their own inclinations. Because of the power of precedent most incumbents felt bound to fight, not so much for themselves, as for their successors. This obligation was particularly relevant in the case of a clergy family like the Boycotts; in their case successor meant son.

Billie – Charles's grandfather – had been rector during the most difficult tithing years. In 1820 he had contemplated taking a farmer to court over what he regarded as a derisory tithe payment upon a piece of marshland, but, eventually, he decided not to proceed. 'I intended to contest this, but the certain expense . . . and the uncertain issue, induced me to refrain . . .'. In the same year, and on account of tithe differences, he and his principal parishioners were unable to agree upon the wording of the terrier (a periodical 'inventory of church property'); two terriers, one signed by the Rector, and one by the leading parishioners, were sent to Norwich. About 1838 Charles's father recalled that, during his father's time, 'the taking of tithe in kind' had been 'conducted on the mutual-injury principle; the farmer opposing and resorting to every shift to annoy the clergyman and the latter leaving the tithes in kind to rot in his yard in defiance'. (Even easy-going Parson Woodforde – living not far from Burgh – had his tithe troubles. At one of his annual 'Tithe Feasts' one of his farmers 'behaved so insolent towards me that I don't intend to have him ever again at my Frolick'.)

It is difficult to imagine a more unpleasant wedge being driven between an incumbent clergyman and those who should have been his farming friends, neighbours and supporters. The quarrels in Burgh were matched up and down the county and the country. The disagreements were not about nothing; livelihoods and the honourable discharge of obligations were at stake. Few individuals were to blame. The truth was that the church had acquiesced for far too long in a system of paying a clergy which had become totally outmoded and, as has been observed, 'incredible'.

To universal sighs of amazement that the church had, for the first time, consented to parliamentary interference in its affairs a Tithe Commutation Bill became law in 1836. The act abolished tithe in kind and substituted a 'rent charge' payable by all land owners (based on the price of corn). The detailed work involved in the commutation of tithes took many years.[53] Over 63% of all local commutation agreements were reached voluntarily; the Burgh agreement, negotiated by Charles's father, was one. In consequence the family's annual tithe income was reduced by almost 25%; from about £500 to £374. There is no evidence to show that Charles's father thought this too high a price to pay for piece of mind and the burying of old hatchets.

(The 1836 Tithe Act applied only to England. The Irish Tithe Act of 1838 is discussed at page 109.)

There were as many different opinions about the 'individual clergyman at work' as there were shifting hues to a rainbow. The country parson, the Bishop himself, and any other man in Holy Orders, became a hotchpotch of different opinions about a loosely tied and independently minded group of men who, together, made up 'the church'. A pertinent dimension of the hotchpotch was time itself; wars, revolutions and periods of peace brought changing expectations of the church and of clergymen. Like the members of any other army the clergy suffered severely when – as had occurred particularly in the Diocese of Norwich under Bishop Bathurst – they were so badly misdirected.

Oliver Goldsmith saw a clergyman who was

> . . . . . .to all the country dear,
> . . . .
> More skilled to raise the wretched than to rise . .
> But in his duty prompt at every call.
> He watched and wept, he prayed and felt, for all . .
> His house was known to all the vagrant train,
> He chid their wanderings, but reliev'd their pain.

John Wesley, the founder of Methodism (and a frequent visitor to East Anglia) spoke out against 'indolent clergymen, pleasure taking clergymen, money loving clergymen, praise loving clergymen, preferment seeking clergymen . . .'. Some people saw only the 'bloated parson clutching his tithe pig'. William Cobbett – never short of some axe to grind – held that parsons and their wives did not advance their cause with God or their parishioners when they shone 'at balls and in pumprooms'. Benjamin Rogers (Rector of a parish in Bedfordshire) farmed his own land and was a keen businessman as to rents, crops, pigs and horses; a man who believed that good living and high thinking should go hand in hand; and a man who treasured his books but who loudly condemned 'the tricks and foul practices of the Whigs'. Baring-Gould, on the one hand, admitted to the continuing existence of the 'well endowed clergyman of the old school', but, on the other, he wrote of the rector who, as Charles's father so nearly did, held his country living for forty-seven years:

> I have heard some people speak as if the care of a few hundred souls were insufficient employment for the zeal and energy of a clergyman of mark. What God had charged him with was the

> care of those 5–600 people for whom there was no-one else to care; among whom there was no praise to be won, no distinction to be attained, no ambition to be gratified. He was content with this, and sought nothing more. The people he loved and willingly served, wisely also and discretely, as a spiritual father and friend, who understood them, and was able to speak to them in a way which they could understand. There was not one, young or old, whom he did not observe and study. His interest in individuals was not capricious or transitory but patient and persevering. It was long before he despaired (if he ever did despair) even of those who went astray.

The Clergy of the Church of England have *always* defied classification. It was never possible to *command* any of them to do anything. Most had a conscience; in addition, and of course, they were educated, intelligent and independently minded men. Most – but not all in the nineteenth century – did what they could, for as long as they could, as well as they could.

As reform took hold, the Church of England produced its own leaders of outstanding quality at every level. By the end of the century the Bench of Bishops had become a brilliant group of men; who led, not only by their precept, but also by their example.

Chapter Seven

When Charles was aged nineteen, at the time of the 1851 census, the population of England was a little under 18 million, divided equally between urban and rural dwellers. Of the 8,936,000 people who lived in the country nearly half worked on the land and lived in 'isolated' villages. As Charles grew into an understanding of the intensely rural and agricultural society by which he was surrounded he saw that leadership, influence and control of *local* affairs lay in the hands of *local* 'gentlemen'. To Charles the difference between one man who was a gentleman and another who was not was obvious. (The word 'snob' then described, only, a shoemaker.) Gentlemen became officers in the army and navy, clergymen (and so Bishops), Members of Parliament, diplomats, lawyers, overseas administrators, progressive farmers, and connoisseurs and patrons of painting, sculpture, architecture and music; but they were seldom to be found 'in trade'. Most possessed, in themselves, something more than the mere trappings of gentility. They were healthy and vigorous, self-confident and high-spirited; for the most part they treated all comers alike; most possessed the ability to study and to think.

Almost by definition the gentleman was a landowner. He lived in the 'big house'. He was an educated man. Tradition and a sense of public duty had, with few exceptions, persuaded him to become an unpaid Justice of the Peace. As a Justice he was required to administer the law from day to day; and, in emergency, to get on his horse and administer it, in person, on the ground, regardless of the inconveniences, and sometimes the dangers, involved. As a local Justice he carried, also, a general responsibility for the administration of his parish. Usually in conjunction with its clergyman, he appointed its officers; these maintained the church, kept the peace, repressed vagrancy, relieved destitution, mended roads, suppressed nuisances, destroyed vermin, supervised the game laws and, from time to time, supplied recruits to the army and navy.

Above all else the English country gentleman – whether he was Lord of the Manor or Squire – was to be seen. He was seen out shooting, out hunting and walking his dogs; he was seen, with his family, in church, almost every Sunday; he was seen visiting and talking to his neighbours in the parish, whom he had known all his life and who had known him all their lives. His wife was usually as well known by her care for the poor, the sick and the aged. His children were as much the children of the village, and the subject of its chatter, as were the children of anyone else. Lord George Bentinck expressed it all in one sentence: 'I believe the first ingredient in the happiness of a people is that the gentry should reside on their native soil and spend their rents among those from whom they receive them.'

It was a cheap system of local government which produced an extraordinary social stability in a world being turned upside-down by European revolutions. The country gentlemen of England lived where they did and became the public servants they were because they wanted to; no one compelled them. They, and the people they served, were divided by a class distinction which could neither be removed nor glossed over but which could be, and was, bridged. It was bridged easily and comfortably by civility and kindness on both sides and by an almost privately shared love for the same fields, the same pastures and woodlands, the same animals and birds, and the same church. All felt themselves to be members of the same 'local family'. To this family they gave their loyalty and from it they knew they could count on help when that was needed; or a fair hearing from someone they knew, and who knew them, when *that* was needed. There was a common awareness of misfortune and trouble. Dimly and dumbly everyone knew that they were heirs to something greater than themselves; and that they held a freehold in:

> This other Eden, demi-paradise
> This fortress built by nature for herself
> Against the envy of less happier lands . . .

Farming, in the early years of the nineteenth century, was of crucial importance to England; the nation still either fed itself – more or less – or starved. To be a *Norfolk* farmer was still something of which to be proud.

Conveniently the farms of Burgh-St-Peter were reported on in 1838. The Boycott family farm then consisted of about ninety acres. Five others in the parish were larger. Most included 'upland' (that is land lying along the centre of the Burgh peninsula) and marshland. The upland soil was 'a freeworking lightish loam' which required manuring. It was described as 'good wheatland' and, in 1838, was growing wheat, barley, turnips and clover. Such a mix was typical of a Norfolk rotation; turnips fed the animals which supplied the manure whilst clover prepared the land for a following cereal crop. The quality of the marshland varied. Some was 'cold and wet'; some flooded in winter; the best was 'unequal to the fattening of bullocks'; but, even so, almost all was capable of producing 'litter for the yards in winter'; (and so, later on, cartable manure).

Farming the Burgh land was never easy. Charles's boyhood experience of it taught him two things. First, that even the poorest of wet land (of which there was to be no lack in the west of Ireland) could be made to yield something when handled correctly. Secondly, that the amount of work done regularly by Norfolk farm labour could not be matched elsewhere; and, most certainly, not in Co. Mayo. The contrast between the daily output of work achieved by farm labour in Norfolk and the standards accepted in Ireland was to cause Charles irritation. (Neither Charles, nor anyone else at that time, understood that far too many poor potato eating Irishmen were *seriously* undernourished; and *incapable* of long hours of physical work.)

The 'Swing' Riots of 1830, as they showed themselves in Norfolk and as they affected Burgh-St-Peter and Charles's father personally, provide an example of local government 'in an emergency'. The riots started in Kent in late August, spread over the south and up the Midlands and then down through Norfolk and Suffolk; they reached Burgh-St-Peter in early December. Riots, and news of them, spread nationally along the coaching roads and were diffused locally through local markets. Norwich held a Saturday market in late November and this instigated, probably, the trouble in Burgh a few days later. The rioters consisted principally of farm labourers protesting against low wages and high food prices. Unrest was heightened by disturbances in France and Belgium, by two preceding bad harvests and by pressure for political reform. Rioting took the forms of arson, the destruction of threshing machines, threatening letters from a mythical 'Captain Swing' and by attacks on Justices and Clergy. Higher wages were demanded from employers but many of these avoided becoming worse off themselves by forcing the clergy to accept lower tithes. It was a period when the principles of *Laissez-faire* – the belief that each man could, and should, stand independently and fight his own corner for himself – were generally held to be correct; it was a period, also, when those in authority knew that, whilst the war against Napoleon had been won, it was still quite possible to lose the peace.

Taken as a whole the Justices of Norfolk had much sympathy for the rioters. Many Justices were Whigs. Almost all were farming landowners who knew, only too well, how little food a man's wages would buy. Some dragged their feet when their duty as Justices demanded swift action; others did their duty. In North Norfolk, on 20th November 1830, three Justices, including John Boileau, came upon a riotous assembly in Hindolverstone. They read the Riot Act and 'the ring leaders being pointed out, the gentlemen instantly rode into the midst of the crowd and seized them . . . so spirited and determined was the conduct of the magistrates . . . that they succeeded in apprehending seven or eight persons'. Boileau was a resolute, courageous man, who always did his duty whatever it might be. During the riots his wife wrote regularly to her sister: 'Mr B begins to feel alarm . . . with the *real grievances* we *know* the lower classes of England have to bring forward, and the frightful carelessness there seems to be among clergymen and magistrates for the interests of the poor.' And again: 'I have never seen Mr Boileau so disheartened as last night . . . no weapons have been used as yet except stones which were flying about yesterday at a terrible rate . . . I wish the magistrates on the other side of the county may prove as active as some of ours on this side.' Later, when things became quieter, she wrote, 'Mr Boileau . . . fears it is only a crust formed over the volcano.' But throughout, the Boileaus had no personal fears; 'I still feel free of fear as to ourselves and so does Mr Boileau.'[54]

The two ringleaders of the Burgh protest, Joseph Godbolt and George Turner, were tried in Norwich in January 1831. The charges against them included unlawful and riotous assembly and an attempt 'to extort' from the Reverend William Boycott a certain sum of money through fear and terror. Charles's father was the principal witness. He was then aged thirty-two and had been Rector for a year.

About 150 men, some with sticks and Turner with a billhook (which he swung threateningly) and almost all the farmers of the parish had assembled in early December and demanded to see the Rector. The farmers claimed to be 'oppressed' by tithe and said that 'whatever Mr Boycott refunded to them would be given to the men'. The Rector stated that he already paid a good wage to his own farm labour (which he substantiated), that the 1830 crops had been good, that corn prices were high and that he would not refund. Eventually, after much, often violent, argument the Rector agreed to refund 'under intimidation, thinking it better to sacrifice part of my property than the whole of it and my life'. Throughout he showed common sense and presence of mind; at one stage it appears that he bought them all a drink. The defence called no witnesses and appears to have been content to rely on what the Rector had said of Godbolt (a resident of Burgh) during his prosecution evidence. He had then told the court that Godbolt had said he 'would not hurt a hair of my head', that he (the Rector) 'had known Godbolt since a boy' and that he was 'decidedly a good character'. On this evidence, the jury acquitted both defendants.[55]

Clearly the system of local government was by no means perfect. There were, as yet, no effective rural police; the army was thin on the ground; individual Justices held different political and private opinions. Charles's father found himself obliged to fight his own 'laissez-faire' corner more or less alone. As he faced the angry crowd assembled against him he did so as Rector; and, in effect, as squire. The future serenity of his parish and the success of his own ministry depended, crucially, on how he conducted himself. Central to the outcome was the fact that almost everyone involved knew everyone else; both sides, in a sense and to some degree, protected the other. Nothing *disastrous* occurred; Metternich's remark that the English were 'prodigiously sensible' was proved true once again. When it was all over the young Rector was as pleased, no doubt, to have Joseph Godbolt safely home again – and proved innocent in a court of law! – as were Godbolt's family and friends.

Charles must have heard his father's 'swing' story several times; and, perhaps, have contrasted it with the experiences of two lands less happy than England. In the France which preceded the Revolution, and by the evidence of his own grandfather's journal, the gulf which separated rich and poor had been unbridgeable; they did not, and could not, know and respect each other. In Ireland, far too many landlords who should have known, cared about and protected their poor tenants were 'absentee'; these did not, as Lord George Bentinck said they should, 'spend their rents among those from whom they received them'. The landed aristocracy of France had, already, met its fate in the French Revolution; many Irish landlords began to meet theirs seventy years later in the same Irish 'Land War' which brought Charles into his notoriety. As Charles then faced his own crisis he must, sometimes, have recalled his father's 'Swing experience'; and the quiet manner in which his father had then conducted himself.

In November 1849 Norfolk was electrified by the murder, by close-quarter shooting, of Isaac Preston Jermy (aged fifty-nine and a former Recorder of Norwich) and his son Isaac Jermy Jermy (aged twenty-seven) at Stanfield Hall, near Wymondham.[56] During the shooting the murderer fired at (and severely wounded) Isaac Jermy Jermy's young and pregnant wife Sophia and at a housemaid (also severely wounded) who he may have mistaken for Isaac Preston Jermy's teenage daughter Ellen. The shooting took place after dark on a dark night. The Hall was dimly lit. The murderer was masked. It is possible that nothing more substantial than 'bad light' prevented the extermination of five members of the Jermy family (including a Jermy baby as yet unborn). Deservedly, 'The Trial of James Blomfield Rush' for the killing of the Jermy father and son is included in the *Notable British Trials* series.

James Rush was illegitimate, being the son of 'a gentleman farmer'. He was aged 'about 46'. He was poorly educated and, generally, immoral. He farmed, as a Jermy tenant, near Stanfield

Hall. He was well known to the Jermy family and their servants and he knew the Hall intimately. Relations between Isaac Preston Jermy and Rush were seldom other than bad; if any other relationship of significance existed between the two men the Court never learnt of it.[57]

Of Isaac Jermy Jermy (the son) nothing is known. His father, the Recorder, was described as 'a capable blunt-mannered man who was not greatly liked'. The father had been born as Isaac Preston, the son of the Reverend George Preston, then the owner of Stanfield Hall. The Prestons and Jermys had been connected by marriage; a feud had existed for many years as to whether the Stanfield Estate was, properly, a Preston or a Jermy property. When the Reverend George Preston died in 1837 his son Isaac Preston took possession of the Stanfield estate; and, a year later, he assumed the end surname of Jermy, so becoming the Isaac Preston Jermy who was murdered. His possession of Stanfield was disputed; in this dispute Rush took an active part.

At his trial Rush chose to defend himself. He failed to exploit several weaknesses in the prosecution's case. Despite his closing address (which rambled on for fourteen hours) and his unwavering and defiant demeanour, Rush was found guilty of murder and sentenced to death. The first excitement created by the murders carried over, with a vengeance, to Rush's public execution in Norwich. Crowds came in on foot, in carriages and carts and in – still novel excitements in themselves – excursion trains. One man walked a round trip of sixty miles to see Rush die.

The actual murders, the other murders which may have been intended, the evidence given, the evidence which Rush, for some inscrutable reason, may have withheld and the, perhaps crucial, evidence not available to the Court because the Jermy father and son were not alive to give it, made up at the time, and continue to make up, a mysterious web of doubt and wrongdoing. What might have been the *true* motive for such a crime? Was Rush the murderer? The trial judge, apparently, satisfied himself that Rush had sufficient motive for the killings. (The Judge later became Lord Chancellor with the reputation of being 'A man of high personal character and strong common sense . . . a sound lawyer and an acute and patient Judge'.) John Boileau (who had been prominent in Norfolk during the Swing Riots in 1830) was one of the examining magistrates and was present throughout the trial; he became convinced of Rush's guilt.

The murdered, and the surviving, members of the Jermy family, and the Boycott family, were connected by marriages and by a later friendship. Isaac Jermy, the Recorder, was married twice. His first wife and the mother of the (to be murdered) son Isaac Jermy Jermy had been a first cousin and near contemporary of Georgiana (Charles's mother). Sophia (Isaac Jermy Jermy's widow, who lost her right arm as the result of her wound but who, in due time, gave birth to a Jermy daughter) married again. Her second husband was Thomas Beevor, Georgiana's cousin and, eventually, the fourth Beevor baronet. (Sophia, by Thomas Beevor, had eleven more children; all were Georgiana's nephews and nieces and Charles's cousins.[58])

At the time of the double murder Charles was at the impressionable age of sixteen and, almost certainly, away from home. His mother was connected to both the murdered Jermys; Charles, probably, knew them both. Although no motive for the murders ever became wholly apparent the murders actually committed (and those almost certainly intended) had been planned with care. Neither was something that Charles was ever likely to forget. As, no doubt, Charles later discovered for himself, they bore some resemblance to 'political' murders in Ireland; it was difficult, sometimes, to see *why* they had been committed.

In 1785 Charles's great-aunt Mary – by repute a beautiful red-haired woman – had married a sailor from Eye named Charles Cunningham. Twelve years later, in 1797, Captain Cunningham (later Rear-Admiral Sir Charles) took command of a thirty-eight-gun frigate named *Clyde*. Cunningham died in 1834; two years after Charles had, at his christening, been given the custody of the Admiral's two names.

Frigates were the fast, lightly built – but heavily armed – 'Knight Errants' of the Navy. Their Captains were chosen accordingly; they seldom became rich from prize money but they often became well-known – even in those days – for their dash, their leadership, their ability to fight their ships and for their personal gallantry. Frigates often operated independently of the fleet or squadron to which, nominally, they belonged. The story of

Cunningham's adventures in *Clyde*, over six years of almost continuous seakeeping, is as good an example as is likely to be found of what the exercise of seapower in the Revolutionary and Napoleonic Wars actually meant for those doing the hard work at the business end. (It was, in Mahon's words, the story of 'that far-off line of storm-beaten ships on which the eyes of [Napoleon's] Grand Army never looked'; and which 'stood between it and the Dominion of the World'.)

Charles Cunningham deserves to be better remembered than he is for one unique service which he gave to his country. That he was able, when the moment came, to perform it was the direct consequence of his own powers of leadership, the force of his personality and the personal devotion which his qualities as a man inspired amongst his crew. It was Cunningham who, in May 1797, did more than any other man to bring about the collapse of the Nore mutiny; which, in the circumstances of that dreadful year, constituted a threat to England which might have been catastrophic.[59]

As England's luck would have it *Clyde* was refitting in the Thames when the Nore mutiny broke out. Virtually all the ships which, for one reason or another, found themselves at the Nore (and which were later to be augmented by the bulk of the North Sea fleet which had assembled at Yarmouth under Admiral Duncan to defend London and the east coast against a Dutch invasion), fell under the control of mutineers. Cunningham, however, was never 'absolutely dispossessed' of his command. Parker, the mutiny leader, went on board the *Clyde* in Cunningham's temporary absence and found the attitude of the First Lieutenant and the ship's company not to his liking: 'You and your damned Captain have too much the confidence of the ship's company; and I will take you both and hang you', he is said to have shouted as he left (in the event it was Parker who would hang). What eventually happened has been described in Marshall's Naval Biography (Vol II pt I):

> On the 29th May, seventeen days after the first symptoms of mutiny had appeared, Captain Cunningham gave orders that the signal from Parker, the rebel chief, for all delegates to repair to him, should not be answered by the *Clyde*. Her fore-sail being unbent at the time, and it being known that she was unprovided

> with a pilot, the rest of the fleet did not suspect that this was the prelude to her secession from their cause. At 9pm Captain Cunningham assembled his crew and made known to them his intention of working the ship into Sheerness harbour in the course of that night. Soon after midnight the cables were slipped, and by sunrise on the morning of the 30th, the *Clyde* was safely anchored in Sheerness harbour, thus giving the first blow to a most diabolical conspiracy, which while it lasted, was terrifying to the whole country, and, but for the promptitude and activity displayed by Captain Cunningham, his officers and loyal crew, might have spread into a serious extent of mischief to the State.

Cunningham's service had been distinguished both before, and after, the 1797 Mutiny. When the war started again in 1803 he was aged forty-eight. In September of that year he was nominated a commissioner of the Navy's Victualling Board by Earl St Vincent; not because he knew much about buying in food for the Navy but because he was incorruptible. Three years later he became 'Commissioner' of the Deptford and Woolwich naval dockyards and a member of the 'Navy Board'; in 1823 he became 'Commissioner' of the great yard at Chatham. At Chatham he lived in the splendid 'Commissioner's House' which still stands as 'the oldest intact naval building in the country'. Charles Cunningham retired in 1829 with the rank of Rear-Admiral, having served for fifty-four years. During the twelve years of war which followed 1803 Cunningham played his part in creating the greatest navy the world had ever known; and, for the last fourteen years, he helped run it down.[60]

In October 1832 Cunningham was created Knight Commander of the Royal Hanovarian Guelphic Order by William IV, the 'Sailor King'. Although he married again he was cared for, during his retirement, by the two daughters that Mary had given him. Sir Charles Cunningham died on 11th March 1834 in Suffolk, not far from Burgh-St-Peter; two years, almost to the day, since his small 'great nephew-in-law' had been entrusted with the custody of his two names.[61]

CHAPTER EIGHT

THE FAMILY IN WHICH CHARLES grew up was a good example of that nineteenth-century English phenomenon, 'the Rectory Family'. All over England, in their comfortable houses and large gardens, clerical parents produced their well brought up, well educated, hard working and resourceful children; their sons convinced that the first thing to do in life was to prepare for it; their daughters convinced that 'if you educate a woman you educate a family'. Clergy children were to be found everywhere. Throughout the nineteenth century they graced the schools and universities, the services, the professions and the arts; they moved up the structure of command and control in government at home and in the Empire overseas. Almost all owed almost everything to their parents; to the frugality of rectory lives and to the sense of disciplined endeavour which had been imposed upon them.

At her marriage[62] to William Boycott Georgiana Beevor had been slim and graceful. Wide open and wide-set eyes and a long nose only sharpened the narrowness of a face which suggested strength and character. She was the second of the two daughters of Captain Arthur Beevor, a soldier and cousin to the Sir Thomas Beevor who had supported Cobbett. Her paternal grandfather had married a daughter of Miles Branthwayt and her father had married into the same wealthy family; there is no doubt that Georgiana brought money into her marriage.

William and Georgiana became the parents of the largest of the five Boycott rectorial families. Arthur William ('Willie'), Charles Cunningham, Thomas Edward Branthwayt ('Tom'), Edmund and Miles (who died as an infant) were born between 1830 and 1838. Emily, William and Fanny followed between 1840 and 1845, accompanied, perhaps, by a sigh of satisfaction from their mother that her principal service had been accomplished. If so, she was mistaken. In 1852, at the age of forty-six, she gave birth to Laura, the last of her children. At Laura's birth Willie was aged twenty-two and Charles twenty; both had left home.

Like most children Charles learnt as much at home as he ever learnt away from it. He was born and brought up in the house of a gentleman and scholar. Willie, Charles, Tom and Edmund – and later William – knitted themselves into a strong group of boys in which any failure to run, ride, swim or climb with as much vigour and courage as each possessed would have been as roundly condemned by their mother – that formidable woman – as by their father and themselves. The boys led a 'Rectory Life' of endeavour in all things; their disgrace was to be called 'a slacker'.

The Parsonage House was not only home to the Rector and Georgiana and their children; it was, also, an institution to which more or less anyone could claim access. From it the third Rector conducted much of the business of his parish and from which he ran his farm. To it his parishioners brought a thousand problems. He prescribed and weighed out simple medicines from his medicine chest and did his best to cure their illnesses. He buried those secrets which were better buried. He walked, or rode, in his black gown, to succour the sick, the bereaved and the poor; to care for those for whom no one else cared; and just to talk. Georgiana did much the same; to her sympathy and the warmth of her kitchen (heated by a great stove into which a gardener or a farmhand threw a scuttle of coal every few hours) might come a sick child and a frightened mother; and from it Charles would take his turn in carrying out a hot dinner to a family he had known all his life, and for whom the weariness of undernourishment and cold had, at last, proved too great. The contrast between the two houses and homes, and the children in each, was great. The contrast could be, and was, relieved by duty and kindness but it could not be removed. No one – on either side – supposed that it could be.

The rustle of a stiffly starched petticoat down the elegant staircase announced the daily arrival of Mother, of morning prayers and of breakfast. Prayers and meals re-established, each day, that it was the Rector who – at least in public – ruled the household. When, as happened to a visitor in July 1847, 'All their boys are at home . . . I daresay there is a fine stir for 5 boys must make a house lively and during the holidays it is the system at Burgh to give up everything to the boys that they may enjoy them to the full – provided only they have satisfied their Papa in their progress at school! He does not care what he does for them when at home . . . They have three horses kept up for them to hunt and every other fun and amusement is promoted.'

There were more things to do in and around Burgh than for which any one day could provide hours. Riding, sailing, rowing, bird's nesting, shooting, walking the dogs, coursing, fishing, archery, skating and jobs on the farm or in the garden were all there for the taking. There were trips to Lowestoft, Beccles and Norwich; or a day out to the gay spa of Bungay[63] (which had been so much liked by the boy's grandfather) and its new playhouse. In the evenings, round candlelit tables, the family played whist, loo, cribbage, spillikins and 'up Jenkins'; they wrote their long, and carefully composed, letters; they rehearsed and played out their well dressed charades; they read to themselves or to each other the latest novel – or serial – from Charles Dickens; they argued a topic stood up for them by their father; they studied their languages and their history and even their mathematics. When, at last, the soft sea-laden summer air of Burgh proved too heavy a burden to be carried any longer, they went to bed; to sleep amidst the purring of nightjars through darkened windows.

As William and Georgiana faced the question of how to educate five sons a reforming wind of penetrating intensity – inspired by Dr Thomas Arnold of Rugby – was forcing its way through the schools and universities of England. Until Dr Arnold took over Rugby in 1828, it, and the eight other public schools like it, were disgraceful establishments. Arnold stood Rugby on its head. He was – if only just – a man of his time. He, and other reforming headmasters, perceived that England and her emerging Empire required men who had been well educated and who were Christians of high moral worth; and that these were the qualities which intelligent caring parents wanted for their children. (What Arnold did *not* perceive was the unstoppable progress of scientific thought; he once remarked that 'Rather than have science the principal thing in my son's mind, I would gladly have him think the sun went around the earth, and that the stars were so many spangles set in the bright blue firmament.')

Charles's elder brother Arthur was sent, like his father before him, to Winchester; he found it transformed from the school his father remembered by the 'inexhaustible vigour' and the 'sparkling brightness' of George Moberly, a deeply religious Headmaster and a future Bishop of Salisbury. A lady visitor to Burgh during the Christmas holidays, when Arthur was aged sixteen, described him as 'a very gentlemanly, promising boy'. The same visitor also remarked that the other boys 'are dispersed at different schools'. Edmund, the fourth son, who entered the world as a tiny seven-month baby and continued, all his life, to be delicate, went to the Fauconberg School at Beccles (and stayed there until he was nineteen). William, the fifth and youngest son (and eventually the fourth Rector), went to Shrewsbury and Cambridge. Of the education given to Tom, the third son, and the three girls nothing is now known except that, in 1855, the Rector and Georgiana had it in mind to leave the parish in the care of Arthur (who, after going on to Cambridge, had been ordained in 1854) and to go 'abroad for a year or two for the education of their daughter'. (Negative evidence suggests they did not, in the event, do so.)

This leaves Charles. It is clear that he had declared himself for the Army at an early age. In March 1846 his father wrote to the Military Secretary[64] asking that Charles should be noted for a Commission in the Line by purchase as the boy 'though only fourteen is so entirely bent on a military life . . .'. Three years later, his father revealed those personal qualities which made a career in one of the services so understandable a choice. 'Suspicious as a Father's testimony must appear, I cannot refrain from adding that my son has, from his earliest years, shown a hardihood and boldness of character, coupled with a manly submission to lawful authority, which seem to fit him for a soldier's duty and also a passion for the profession which unfits him for anything else . . .'

Charles went, probably, to two schools. One source states that he went to a school in Blackheath which may well have had military associations. Another[65] remembers him as a boy at a private school at Roughton in Norfolk, and an affair which confirms his father's assertion regarding 'boldness of character'. Charles and a boy named Philip Shepheard liked climbing church towers. 'One morning both of them scrambled up the stairway at Hanworth . . . and dared each other to swing round the flagstaff, feet over the parapet. He [Philip] did it first but when his companion's turn came there was a terrible crack and the flagstaff splintered right through. Luckily, Philip was able to seize his friend by the knees and drag him down on to the leads. If he had not done so Parnell and his lot would have been cheated out of their first victim and, come to that, all of them out of a new word.'[66]

Although, in the end, Charles did obtain exactly that for which his father had first asked (a commission in the line by purchase) something arose to turn his mind away, *not* from the army, but from service in the line. Good reports from school, a marked ability in mathematics – inherited, no doubt, from his grandfather – drew him towards 'The Scientific Corps' of Engineers and Artillery. Commissions in this Corps were then granted, not by purchase, but only after training at the Royal Military Academy in Woolwich. In January 1848, Charles, and fifty-five other cadets, joined the Academy. Woolwich, then, was a particularly rough and tough and badly conducted establishment; and one which offered to any boy passing through it an experience he was never likely to forget.

Prior to his becoming a cadet Charles had been required to pass an entrance examination 'of a searching character'. In practice exacting standards of entry and patronage did not mix, and the examination had been whittled down 'to meet the views of influential complainants'. Nonetheless the examination Charles did pass probably bore some relation to the Academy syllabus which then included Mathematics, English and French Grammar, the Classics, Geography, History and Drawing. Instruction was not well given, text books were scarce, the cadets, as a whole, were idle and any of them 'manifesting a desire to work' came in for very rough treatment. Six to nine cadets shared a room with beds hinged to the walls, sanded floors, and grills over their windows. The occupants of each room were not of an age but of all ages; this led to bullying of an intensity to challenge any found in any public school. Occasionally a cadet could be expelled for bullying but, not infrequently, parental influence obtained his re-instatement when he 'boasted of having gained a victory over the Academy authorities'. An 'outdoor gym', a bathing pond (which doubled, in winter, as a skating rink) and a racquets court existed but no athletics or organised games took place. The food was 'plain and insufficient'. The mother of a cadet had, a year or two earlier, complained that smoking and drinking prevailed so generally; she also enquired why the cadets were permitted to breakfast 'on gin and water'.

Early in 1849, after a year as a cadet, Charles failed a periodical examination and, on the 7th February, he was discharged. (The same thing happened to ten cadets, on average, each year.) His father reacted quickly. On 22nd February he wrote again to the Military Secretary reminding him that, three years earlier, Charles *had* been noted for a commission in the line by purchase. He also offered the following explanation of his son's poor performance at Woolwich: '. . . his failure was principally owing to over-anxiety and illness; but I may be permitted to say that it was not from want of general diligence and zeal in his pursuits and further that I am honoured with testimonials, from General Parker, under his own hand, of my son's good conduct'.[67] (The testimonials have not survived.)

It is evident that, in February 1849, an anxious father was doing his best to preserve his second son's chosen career. Charles was too intelligent, too hard working and too conscientious to allow himself to fail an examination without good cause; something impeded him. The Rector's letter to the Military Secretary contains the word 'illness'; and it was this, almost certainly, that forced Charles to abandon his hopes of a career in the Army. It is the fact that, in September 1849, the Academy at Woolwich suffered a serious outbreak of scarlet fever from which one cadet died; the strong probability is that Charles, also, contracted it. Scarlet fever, in 1848, was a *serious* illness; it could be followed, all too often, by complications; these could be both slow to declare themselves and be capable of lasting a lifetime.

After his forced departure from Woolwich Charles – still true to his ambitions – was sent to a cadet school on the continent. There he improved his French and German and studied military tactics. In the meanwhile, nothing had been heard about any commission by purchase. By the end of 1849, the Rector and his wife had become sufficiently concerned to seek help from Lord Stradbroke (a neighbour). Stradbroke then wrote, crisply, to the Military Secretary. 'His parents are very anxious about him and wish to see his appointment to some Regiment as the best hope of preserving him from temptation to idle habits.' This did the trick. In January 1850 the Rector remitted £450, this then being the cost of an Ensign's commission by purchase[68]; and, on the 15th

February 1850, Charles Cunningham Boycott was commissioned, as Ensign, in the 39th Foot.

Charles could not, immediately, have known it but the 39th, although serving at home, were under orders to proceed overseas. They were required to help keep the peace in Ireland.

Part Two

Ireland – England

1820–1886

CHAPTER NINE

CHARLES, AGED EIGHTEEN, JOINED THE 39th Foot in Preston on 30th April 1850. Almost the next day the Regiment sailed to Belfast.

Anyone greeting Charles on board – and the arrival of a new officer, however young, ignorant and presently insignificant, is always a matter of importance within a regiment – would have found a clean-shaven, spare young man (he stood 5′ 8″) not given to loquacity when answering questions. If Charles had given an opinion about anything it was likely to have been about horses. As a young man his hair was dark, touched, probably, with auburn; in middle age it was to be remembered – somewhat oddly – as being 'yellow-red'. His nose was prominent. His eyes were of that strange quality which made them appear grey to some people but blue to others; one later observer remembered those 'widest-opened, fiercest blue eyes' but another those 'small grey eyes in which firmness and determination were visible.' His dress would have been as clean as standing on the – perhaps heaving – deck of an early coal-fired paddle – or screw-driven – ship would have allowed; he was later to be remembered as being 'well tailored' and as a man of fastidious habits. He carried himself well. A lifelong passion for horses and for racing them himself obliged him to stay, always, a 'thin man'; he was to be recalled as standing 'upright as a dart'. His voice and mannerisms would have reflected the twin facts that he had received a good education and that he had come from an easy, cultured home. His gaze could be uncomfortably direct. Few would have taken him for a fool. For an eighteen-year-old the new ensign was a not unconfident figure; if, knowing no one, he stood alone, he was content to do so.

Less apparent were those influences which had weighted him, this way and that, from his cradle and beyond. He was the son, grandson and great-grandson of clergymen of the established Church of England. He believed in God. He knew what it was to live as an entirely accepted part of a small and isolated – almost island – parish. He was at home with animals and they with him. He understood hard physical work, particularly as he knew it on the farms of Burgh-St-Peter and in its neighbouring Norfolk and Suffolk parishes. He knew wealth and comfort but he knew poverty also; he had learnt at least something of the obligations due from those who possessed money and influence towards those who did not. He had an inherited eye for business. His rectory upbringing had taught him to waste nothing. He had learnt what it was to be unwell in an age when medicine had few effective cures for anything. A particularly unpleasant and close-to-home example of murder had illustrated vividly the range through which human wickedness could pass; 'wickedness' may have become, already, something for which Charles could find little patience. He had been brought up in a family which, broadly, held liberal Whig opinions. He had seen the vital part played in rural society by landowners and gentlemen in the ordering of local affairs in England; and, from his father's personal experience, he had learnt of the unpleasantness which could, and sometimes did, arise when it became necessary for a man of position to face a hostile assembly and a hostile popular opinion. And, in the afterglow, which he carried personally, of the life of Admiral Sir Charles Cunningham, Charles carried an example of what character endurance and leadership could achieve.

The 39th Foot[1] had long associations with Ireland; it had been raised there in 1701. Under Clive of India it had won its first battle honour at Plassey and its motto 'Primus in Indis.' It fought under Wellington in the Peninsula. In the year of Charles's birth it returned to India and, in 1843, was 'conspicuously engaged' in the decisive battle of Maharajpore (sometimes called the 'one-day war'). Between times the 39th returned, again and again, to Ireland and the trials and tribulations – and the pleasures – of soldiering in that wild and troubled, but lovely, country.

Lieutenant Colonel Thomas Wright C.B. commanded the 39th when Charles joined; he was aged fifty-six. He had fought round the world and had been wounded, severely, twice. At Maharajpore he had commanded a Brigade. Most of his officers had seen active service overseas. As Charles became surrounded by these new brother officers he became acquainted with professionals who had lived through the heats and monsoons of India; who knew hard living and hard fighting; who understood the *true* meaning and purpose of military discipline: and who regarded the Regiment as their home and serving it their purpose in life. The medals and scars, the inside stories of faraway campaigns and the tales of long exhausting marches and longer sea journeys were all meat and drink to Charles's eager young mind.

'Tis Ireland gives England her soldiers; her Generals too' was, in the nineteenth century, an incontestable fact of life. (Percy French wrote about 'The Killyran Wreckers': 'Says Bonaparte . . . It's not that Sepoy General who spoilt my finest plan – it's that regiment of ruffians from the town of Killyran!') As the 39th crossed to Belfast in 1850 more than half of its soldiers were Irishmen. With the assurance of hindsight we know that, by 1850, the Great Famine was over; but we know also, with a similar assurance, that in the following year no less than 250,000 young Irish men and women were destined to flee Ireland. What Charles then saw and heard left its own marks upon him.

After six months in Belfast Charles and the 39th set out on a typical foot soldiering tour of Ireland: they marched south, for forty-five miles, to Newry. Military units, serving in the United Kingdom, were kept on the move to reduce boredom and the number of friendships between soldiers and local women. Newry, then, was a small town of some importance; it was linked by canal to the linen industry round Lough Neagh and by salt water to Ireland's principal linen markets in England. Linen, of the finest quality, was still an important Irish product; the 39th found themselves quartered in 'barracks' which, earlier, had been halls for the display of fine linens.

After Newry Charles and the 39th marched on south for sixty miles to Dublin. Parts of that capital city, as Charles first saw it, were like a beautiful woman who had been robbed of her legitimate partner in marriage – Parliament; its authority and its trappings of wealth had been carried off to London fifty years earlier. For the rest of it Dublin was sombre, filthy, overcrowded, diseased and rebellious, but a city shot through and through by cynical Dublin wit and laughter. The city's markets were crowded but its wealth-producing manufactures were limited to whiskey and ale and a little poplin. Dublin's army of ragged beggars made their weary jokes; its girls ogled the soldiers in scarlet who strolled its pavements; endless funerals, led by white plumed horses, wound through its twisting streets; and the *blind* ballad singer sang that he lived

> . . . in Faddle Alley,
> Off Blackpits near the Coombe
> With my poor wife, Sally,
> In a narrow dirty room.

The 39th were stationed in this city of decayed dignity and dirt from August 1851 to August 1852. During his year in Dublin Charles took two major decisions. First, he decided to marry. Second, he decided that intermittent ill health – from which he was unlikely, ever, to be relieved – left him with no choice but to abandon his boyhood dream of a splendid career in the British Army. Nothing suggests that the two decisions were connected directly, but both forced their way into his mind at much the same time.

Charles and Anne Dunne – Annie – were married in St Paul's Church, Arran Quay, Dublin on 17th July 1852. Charles was then eight months short of his twenty-first birthday; Annie, almost certainly, was equally young. Their marriage was witnessed by a Doctor William Vaughan Donovan and by Maria Nevin. Annie gave her address as 21 Arran Quay, which was the home of Dr Donovan and next door to St Paul's. Charles gave his address as 20 Arran Quay; it was, probably, an accommodation address.

The monthly returns of the 39th, whilst the Regiment was in Dublin, show that Charles was 'sick' for about seven continuous months from August 1851 to February 1852. Between August and Christmas 1851 he was present with his Regiment but marked 'sick in quarters'; during January and February 1852 he was absent under a medical certificate. In August 1852 Charles and the 39th continued their foot soldiering tour of Ireland by marching south, for about 100 miles, to the small town of Clonmel lying on the northern bank of the River Suir in Co. Tipperary. There, on 17th December 1852, still an Ensign and still four months short of his twenty-first birthday, Charles sold his commission and left the army. Being sick in barracks, or absent under medical certificates, was one thing; the abandonment of a career upon which Charles had been 'so entirely bent' and for which his 'hardihood and boldness of character' and 'his passion for the profession' had, apparently, so well suited him, was very much another. What had happened? Three important considerations, which Charles himself could not ignore, probably bore down on him.

First, young as he was, he had taken a wife; he had acquired a new responsibility.

The second reason may well have been the condition of the British infantry which, certainly at home and in the years preceding the Crimea, was *not* at its best. For the soldier, life in barracks was dreadful. The drills he was required to learn were dull, senseless and stupidly complicated; his barrack rooms were bare, cold and overcrowded; he was ill clothed, ill paid, ill fed and, as often as not, unheeded by his officers. Not infrequently he found himself engaged in expiating infringements of a draconian code of discipline; fifty days' 'hard labour' could be meted out for next to nothing. To go drinking in the evening was the soldier's only solace. For a young officer life in the Officers' Mess was more comfortable but, otherwise, was dull and unchallenging because infantry weapons and battlefield drills were dull and unchallenging; they made few demands on the brains, abilities and enthusiasms of ambitious young officers. Any young Ensign daring to offer an opinion about anything was liable to be met with the rejoinder, from a more senior officer, 'And who gave you leave to think?' A new Ensign performed a few weeks' recruit drill, did a few supernumerary guards and, accompanied by a more senior orderly officer, did a few ration, barrack and kit inspections. By late morning the day's work was done. Ahead stretched nothing – no organised games, no discussion of military tactics or history, no intelligent conversation – until it was time to dine, and like the soldiers, start the evening's drinking.

The third reason which persuaded Charles to leave the army, almost certainly, was the fact that he had caught scarlet fever at Woolwich. Scarlet fever, then, carried the threat of future relapses into rheumatic fever. Such relapses led, in turn, to progressive damage to the heart muscle, to increasing breathlessness and to pain in, and swelling of, the joints. Relapses, then, were treatable only by rest and warmth. (The condition had been feared for centuries; Shakespeare wrote of 'fever weakened joints, like strengthless hinges'.[2])

Charles started his 'retirement' in Clonmel; the *Tercentenary Record* of that charming place records that 'Captain Boycott, who added a new word to the English language, served as a soldier in Clonmel and later owned a farm near "Landscape", Kilsheelan'. Kilsheelan stands on the River Suir six miles east of Clonmel, on the Waterford Road. The position of Charles's farm is no longer known, nor is it known whether he owned or rented it. The Suir Valley contains some of Ireland's best agricultural land. For centuries this rolling countryside has been one of Ireland's bread-baskets; from it, down the Suir to Waterford, floated grain, meat and dairy products most of which were on-shipped to England. The Suir itself is broad, clear and swift; it was full of salmon, white trout (as the Irish know seatrout) and brown trout. The region grows good grass. Clonmel horse fairs were celebrated. Charles Bianconi, owner and manager of Ireland's only efficient coaching service, had his headquarters nearby.[3] Clonmel also had literary associations: Lawrence Sterne had been born there; Anthony Trollope, in his capacity as an official of the Post Office, lived there in the 1840s; and, perhaps of more interest to Charles, George Borrow – a Burgh-St-Peter over-the-marsh neighbour – had been to school there. (George Borrow learnt Irish because he liked 'the strangeness and singularity of its tones'.)

Charles's decision to leave the army closed a book which had barely been opened. As he stepped out, at Christmas 1852, on to those wider terraces of life which lay beyond the artificial confines of the 39th, he had become a not uninteresting young man to meet. Two years of what may have been disappointing soldiering, uncertain health, and an early marriage had removed a layer of youthful optimism; what remained was easier to see. Any intelligent girl who glanced twice at him was tempted to glance again because of those deeper qualities that lay within. Charles was never to be much of a man 'to make hay whilst the sun shone'; he took life – as it, suddenly, had taken him – if not too seriously then, at least, responsibly. The graphologist who analysed his handwriting saw two unusual qualities in Charles. First, that he was the possessor of an almost 'stoical' courage which allowed him to face any risk when and if – but only if – it was necessary to do so; and, secondly, that he could become a *formidable* opponent to anyone who challenged his standards and beliefs.

Whether or not Charles and Annie ever thought of settling down and farming near Clonmel is not known but, in the event, Kilsheelan was to be no more than a trial run into farming. In the spring of 1854 they packed their bags and moved to Achill Island in County Mayo. Charles was to farm there, initially in partnership with Murray MacGregor Blacker, an Irishman who was eight years Charles's senior but who had learnt his farming in Norfolk.

Clonmel had been soft, like honey; Achill was to be hard, like adamant.

Chapter Ten

IRELAND HAS *NEVER* BEEN CONQUERED *completely*. (The Romans never crossed the Irish Sea and so never imposed their own perceptions of law and authority upon Ireland. Ireland was never conquered, completely, by England.)

In 1169 the Anglo-Norman invasion of Ireland was of insufficient resolution to subdue a country such as Ireland. Ireland was not, then, a centrally-controlled sovereign power the destruction of whose army would have signalled the collapse of resistance; on the contrary, she was a tribal land without central control and without a national army capable of being defeated. Many tribal 'fortresses', particularly in the west, were never engaged, let alone conquered. For over 200 years after the invasion, Ireland continued in anarchy and a half-subdued dependency upon England. (By about the year 1500 English law was paramount, but ideas of enforcing English law 'Beyond the Pale' had been abandoned.) In Charles's day Ireland was not homogeneous. The Scots predominated in Counties Antrim and Armagh; the survivors of the Anglo-Norman invasion lived in the east; the descendants of Cromwell's army still lived in Counties Cavan and Fermanagh, where they had been given land in lieu of pay; several ships of the Spanish Armada were wrecked along the west coast where their survivors took up a new life; a hardworking colony of Germans lived around the centre of Ireland.

Despite the fact that a number of 'foreigners' had become part and parcel of Ireland, and despite centuries of English 'occupation', those generations of Irishmen who lived in the early years of the nineteenth century were still, largely, *Celts*. Their Celtic language and their ancient customs were still virtually intact. These had been kept alive by daily use, by legend, by literature, and by Ireland's ancient, and still just surviving, Bardic schools whose students sang of Ireland's beauty and learning, of the valour of her sons, and of her eventual deliverance; *and* of an ancient rule of law *and* of ancient rights to the *land* of Ireland.

Ireland's ancient Brehon Law was not so much a system of law as a guide to living. The Brehon himself was an expounder of the law and its arbitrator; but he was not a judge. Brehon criminal law discountenanced revenge and retaliation. Under Brehon law, certainty was not impossible but it *was* elusive. In tribal Ireland the political, genealogical and geographical unit had been the *Tuath*.[4] Each *Tuath* contained four classes, or degrees, of men of which the lowest was *Fuidir*. *Fuidir* were serfs and unable, as such, to claim membership of the *Tuath*. Nevertheless descendants of a *Fuidir* (in the third generation) became *Saer*, or free, and so members of the *Tuath* with a right of domicile. A *Saer-Fuidir* had no right to own land but, even as a tenant-at-will, he had some rights in the land he was allowed to use. For example, if he had manured, he was permitted to take the benefit; if evicted without cause he was entitled to his buildings and he paid no rent; and he acquired some rights to the actual piece of land upon which he had erected any building. Promotion above *Saer-Fuidir* – including to the ultimate position of Tribal Chief – was possible.

Land descended by 'tanistry' or 'gavelkind'. Tanistry governed succession of the land of the Tribal Chief which descended to his Tanist, or Successor (who was usually the most vigorous male of his kin and who was elected during the Chief's lifetime). Under gavelkind the land of lesser members of the *Tuath* was added, at their death, to the tribal stock and the whole redivided. Both methods of inheritance conveyed a strong sense of continuity; and an assurance that *tribal* lands would remain *tribal*. Tanistry and gavelkind continued in general use until 1605; neither were ever completely forgotten. The absence of overwhelming military defeat and subjection, either by Rome or by England, left, in Celtic hearts and minds, a vague awareness of a past which was both Celtic and congenial; *and* an awareness of an ancient freedom.

Throughout the nineteenth century some poor families, particularly in the west, still possessed an inherited gentility. Natural good manners, natural courtesy and an easy hospitality distinguished them. Shan F. Bullock, in his *After Sixty Years*, said that a man he knew '. . . was of another breed . . . had softer ways and speech, better manners somehow, knew more about the country and its life and the things that mattered . . . they . . . had a sense of humour all their own . . . were very poor and somehow rich . . . they were real Irish.' Paul Henry – an artist – in his *An Irish Portrait* wrote: 'Swathed round his slight figure was a whole sheepskin. He wore a black velvet jockey's cap. He had a long grey beard parted in the middle; his long grey hair fell in ringlets on his shoulders . . . a refined ascetic face, a beautifully modelled aristocratic nose, and gentle brooding grey-green eyes, the colour of the sea, under a thick thatch of eyebrow. At first he was very shy and distant but with an invariable courtesy and charm of manner; he was an artist . . . An artist he was, of the vague kind one meets occasionally in Ireland, inchoate and purposeless.' Carey and Rhodes, in their *View of the Irish Peasantry* remarked: 'In an intercourse with the common people a day, an hour, cannot pass without being struck by some mark of talent, some display of an imagination at once flowing and enthusiastic, or some touch of tender and delicate feeling'. Paul Henry also wrote that: 'My old friend Brian O'Malley . . . died . . . up to the last he had ridden his horse with the same free poise . . . and his gesture in touching his hat – his battered bowler – with his whip had an elegance of style that was inimitable. Whenever I had been away . . . and he came to meet me, he dismounted . . . and kissed my hand with an eighteenth-century grace and courtliness which had to be seen to be believed . . . it was not servility . . . it was just his way of welcoming an old friend. As I have said Brian was a sort of under bailiff to Captain Boycott . . .' W.S. Trench described an Irish girl in his *Realities of Irish Life*: 'She was a pure Celt. Her hair was black as jet, her eyes dark and flashing and as rapid as lightning in their motion; her nose . . . had . . . a tendency upwards; and her short upper lip and small chin [had] a similar inclination. There was nothing of the peasant in her appearance.'

Many poor Irishmen – particularly the very poor, whose land grew the food on which they existed – felt, in their hearts, that they had a right to 'the land of their fathers'. To 'possess' land in such a way did not, of course, mean legal and enforceable ownership; but it did mean that they farmed 'their' land in a 'morally just way'. (This equated, very approximately, to the way land had been held under the old Brehon system.) Instinctive feelings of injustice hovered round the head of a peasant father compelled to move himself and his family out of, and away from, a piece of land to which he felt he had a long established *right*. Dim recollections of a bygone age may explain the often heard complaint: 'My fathers held under your fathers; we have committed no crime; what right have you to turn us off our land?' G.M. Trevelyan in his *English Social History* had much the same thing to say when he wrote that the Irish peasant 'loved the plot of earth from which he wrung the food of his family and which he regarded, as by right, as his own'. (The legal distinction between 'ownership' and 'possession' was not easy for an uneducated mind to grasp. Eviction sometimes meant that the previous 'occupier', literally, had nowhere else to go.)

For centuries individual Irishmen, at all levels, have made their own way in the world. As individuals they have graced many offices. During the nineteenth century Irishmen worked with distinction in London and throughout the British Empire in many, and varied, capacities. Irishmen became splendid – if sometimes ill-disciplined – soldiers and distinguished commanders. But the hard fact is that Ireland is not a rich country. She has no coal and few minerals; she lacks a sound industrial base. Some of her land is good, but much is not. Her western coast has no ports of value and her more sheltered eastern coast opens only upon England. Comparative poverty had made it impossible for Ireland to sustain great national enterprises; as a nation the Irish seldom produce collective brilliance. But – as individuals – the Irish are *most* talented. They are highly intelligent, courageous, vivacious, witty and generous; artistic and amongst the world's best playwrights. Providence indeed has 'balanced, very lightly, the airy Irish nature. It swings to a touch . . . the Celtic temperament leaps to the weight of a feather.'

A poor nineteenth-century Irish peasant family possessed its cabin, its tiny plot of land, a few clothes, a stick or two of furniture, a pot for its potatoes and a pig but not much else – which could be seen or touched – to grace its life. Such poverty was a cold and heavy stone to carry. The Devon Commission said that the suffering of the poor Irish 'was greater than the people of any other country in Europe'; but it said, also, that they bore their sufferings 'with an exemplary patience'. A surprising tact, a love of music and of dancing, and a willingness to share a last morsel of food with a neighbour helped bear the cold stone's weight. The Irishman must talk; somehow he must shatter the mystery which separates him from his neighbour and from his eternity. He must forget that he lives in a world of infinite indifference. To converse, to smile, to laugh, to sing – and perhaps to dance – were the greatest pleasures the day could bring. To gaze at the heather, to look upon a beetle, to admire the wild yellow flags in their June splendour, to shelter from the tempest were all one thing; but to talk about them, to ask the beetle why it burrowed and the storm why it blew was to come alive. Conversation was the coin of life. A few lilting lines written by Percy French catch the beauty of Ireland:

Or were you that Francis Farrelly I knew so long ago,
In the bogs below Belmullet, in the County of Mayo?
That long legged freckled Francis, with the deep set wistful eyes,
That seemed to get their colours from the ever changing skies.

Many Irishmen during the nineteenth century were compelled to flee Ireland. John Locke wrote, in *The Exiles Return*, of an Irishman who found himself in Texas:

. . . Then it is
The dawn on the Hills of Ireland!
God's angels lifting the night's black veil
From the fair, sweet face of my sireland!
O Ireland isn't it grand you look –
Like a bride in her rich adornin'?
And with all the pent-up love of my heart
I bid you the top o' the mornin'!

Oh! often upon the Texan plains,
When the day and the chase were over,
My thoughts would fly o'er the weary wave,
And around this coast-line hover;
And the prayer would rise that some future day
All danger and doubting scornin' –
I'd help to win for my native land
The light of Young Liberty's mornin'!

Locke's lines were not unlike the petals of an old musk rose; long plucked but *still* coloured and *still* scented.

CHAPTER ELEVEN

ENGLAND AND IRELAND WERE UNITED, into one country, on 1st January 1801. Ireland then became governed by the House of Commons in Westminster; at the same moment Ireland's own Parliament, in Dublin, ceased to exist.

In 1800 both England and Ireland were in difficulties. England had been at war with revolutionary France for some time but, in 1800, had no continental allies; the British Army was inefficient and badly led; Ireland's love affair with revolutionary France continued to pose a threat to England; the Royal Navy stood supreme but the French had been brought to battle only once. England herself was indecisive about the wisdom of continuing to fight the French. Ireland – not surprisingly – was dispirited. Liberty and Equality, as the French proposed them, appealed only fitfully to those Irishmen who saw their future as lying with England. The three French expeditions to Ireland in 1796 and the so-called Irish rebellion of 1798 had all failed. At the Union William Pitt (the first Prime Minister of an enlarged United Kingdom) hoped, genuinely, to placate Ireland. He intended to emancipate all Catholics, but in this he was to be disappointed: the King, and much influential English opinion, were opposed to it.

England's long war against revolutionary France was not decided until Wellington's defeat of Napoleon at Waterloo in 1815. When the fighting ceased, England – through her dedication and her financial, military and naval skills – had become, in effect, mistress of the world; Ireland the mistress of nothing. It is true that, in 1798, parts of Ireland had risen for a cause; for freedom from England. But the fact was that England had been fighting for a more worthy cause; not merely to save herself but also 'to save Europe by her example'.

Peace, after years of exhausting war, brought with it time for reflection both in England and Ireland. Had the wartime 'union' between them been of hearts or of parchment? England had begun to look upwards and outwards over wide horizons; Ireland had nowhere to look except inwards. The pressures of war had forced England and Ireland together; in what directions would peace force them? England – rightly – had proceeded to invest much in Ireland but, prior to 1845, Irish circumstances became increasingly difficult; not only did her population increase at a *startling* rate – even faster than England's – but she suffered, also, under a series of minor, but nevertheless serious, famines. As the century wore on it seemed increasingly difficult for Irish hearts and minds to unite, genuinely, with English hearts and minds. Who *were* the Irish? Who were the English? To answer the question 'where lay the truth?' was not easy; particularly for an England whose ever widening imperial influence could scarcely be enhanced by dissension so close to home.

The Irish were, for the most part, Celts; an *ancient* people of western Europe. The English were Anglo-Saxon and of later origin. The Irish were, almost entirely, Roman Catholics; as Catholics they owed allegiance to the Pope at Rome. The English, predominantly, were Protestant; as such they owed allegiance to a Protestant King who, at his coronation, had sworn to protect the Protestant religion. As the nineteenth century got into its stride more prosaic difficulties came to the fore. The difficulties involved in governing a Catholic country by a Protestant 'Ascendancy' became clear. The number of Catholic church buildings in Ireland was inadequate. The Irish were compelled to pay tithes towards the upkeep of Protestant churches. Nonetheless the 39th Foot did not carry Charles to a country then thought of as being 'foreign'; what it did was to carry him to a country which was different from England and which was virtually unknown to almost all Englishmen. Since the end of the famine little had been heard from Ireland; Englishmen, vaguely, hoped that the great emigration was solving Ireland's obscure problems. Charles started to learn about the differences which separated Ireland from England as he marched south from Belfast to Newry, to Dublin, and to Clonmel; in the company of so many young Irishmen who found themselves serving in the British Army.

* * *

'The Administration of Ireland' (in Ireland) was located in Dublin; it was known, colloquially, as 'The Castle'.

The Union of Ireland with England was seldom as mutually advantageous as the Unions between England with Scotland and Wales had become. For the most part it tossed upon a sea of storms. For many Irishmen and Englishmen the 'union' between them was a sham – a misnomer, a nothing, a union not of hearts but of parchment: others – those few Englishmen who knew and loved Ireland and those Irishmen who loved and admired England – saw only pathos.

Under the terms of the Union Ireland became represented, immediately, at Westminster. Twenty-eight Irish peers and four Bishops sat in the House of Lords and 100 elected Members sat in the House of Commons; all were Protestant. The 100 Irish Members of the Commons represented only 15.4% of the total Commons membership. At this turning point in its existence Ireland required much from its Members of Parliament but these were a disappointment; probably because they had been recruited only from such a narrow Protestant base. Lacking either the will or the ability to unite amongst themselves the new Irish members allied themselves to one or other of the English parties in the hope that, thereby, some beneficial Irish legislation would result. The times, however, were stirring ones; the Commons did the work that the United Kingdom's national wartime circumstances compelled it to do. And, when peace came, it became of over-riding importance not to lose it to economic depression and internal revolution and bloodshed on the French model. Later, the Irish Members of the Commons were to be described as 'a humdrum lack-lustre crew'; Richard Cobden later wrote, 'hardly a man of business among them; and not three who are prepared cordially to co-operate together for any one common object'.

To modern eyes an astonishing feature of the Union was the lack of attention given to its interacting consequences upon the existing machines of government in London and Dublin. London Parliamentary and other debates had ranged over the constitutional, religious, and economic issues involved; but not over the question of how the day-to-day affairs of the two countries were to be meshed. The Lord Lieutenant, the holder of a great and historic office, became an immediately obvious symbol of ambiguity in the chain of command and control. He 'represented' the Sovereign; . . . in a *united* Kingdom?

At the Union twenty-two Irish government departments existed together with the three 'institutions' of the law, the army and the established – that is the Protestant – church. Most departmental heads were politicians. Senior positions in the Departments were filled by the Lord Lieutenant as matters of patronage. Little new life was forced into the system before 1817, when the Irish and British Treasury *Boards* were united (a further twenty years were to elapse before the two Treasuries themselves were united). Henceforth London became responsible for the financial affairs of Ireland; she planned the collection of all Irish revenue and controlled all Irish expenditure. At about the same time the position of the army in Ireland changed; any unit serving in Ireland did so as a unit of the British Army.

At the summit of Irish affairs stood *two* figures: the Lord Lieutenant and the Irish Secretary. Both were political appointments. The first was normally (until 1829 and the emancipation of Catholics) a Protestant peer; and, usually, a wealthy one, as the cost of doing the job properly considerably exceeded its salary. The Irish Secretary was always a member of the House of Commons. Between the Union and 1880 twenty-seven peers filled the appointment of Lord Lieutenant but only ten of them held it for four years or longer. In the same period thirty-eight politicians held the appointment of Irish Secretary; but only ten held it for four years or longer.[5] The Lord Lieutenant – referred to, usually, as 'H.E.' or 'His Excellency' – in addition to representing the Sovereign and acting as the leader of Irish society, possessed wide statutory powers. He was responsible for the peace and security of Ireland. He appointed to numerous offices, he exercised the prerogative of mercy and, in a general way, he supervised the government machine in Dublin. He was, usually, the man on the spot and often the immediate authority behind urgent government action. Prior to the Union the Irish Secretary had been, in effect, the Lord Lieutenant's assistant. After it they became partners; two horses – in want of a driver – hauling a single coach. During the nineteenth century the Irish Secretary customarily spent the Westminster Parliamentary recess at his desk in Dublin – where an overwhelming volume of work constantly awaited him – and the Parliamentary sessions in London dealing with Irish Parliamentary business. The Irish Secretary's position within the Government of the day was always important and his job seldom less than 'the most troublesome office in the British Empire'.

Two, significant, Government 'appendages' existed. First, an Under Secretary (who did not change as governments in London changed) was resident permanently in Dublin. If (as frequently happened) the Irish Secretary went to London, then the Under Secretary acted as the principal adviser to the Lord Lieutenant. Secondly, Irish Secretaries found it convenient to maintain their own small department, styled 'The Irish Secretary's office', in Dublin. The work of this office could be, and frequently was, wide; its opinions were influential; its decisions, usually, significant.

Proposals to rationalise the control of Irish affairs were made constantly. In 1850 Lord John Russell, Prime Minister of a Whig Government, introduced a 'Lord Lieutenancy Abolition (Ireland)' Bill. This proposed that Ireland should be run by a Secretary of State and an Under Secretary. It secured a large majority at its second reading but was then abandoned because the Commons had more business than it could handle. There were, however, other opinions as to how Ireland ought to be governed. Sir Robert Peel (who understood Ireland as well as anyone) declared himself in favour of the existing arrangements; Ireland required, he said, 'the protecting care of some official organ of Government residing upon the spot.' About 1860 a distinguished Irish official named Larcom agreed that the system would have to be changed, but thought that the time to do so had not yet arrived: Ireland was 'an old country with new institutions.' Later, discussion centred round the question of how often the Queen ought to visit Ireland in person; could the Lord Lieutenant be replaced, as it were, by 'an Irish Balmoral' and a Secretary of State? From about 1885 the issue became submerged within the (then burning) issue of 'Home Rule' for Ireland.

For better for worse nothing was done. Two 'political' horses continued to trundle the Irish coach as best they could. As someone put it, 'the Lord Lieutenant governed without ruling and the Chief Secretary ruled without governing'. Percy French took a hand in the muddle when he wrote his 'Queen's Advice to a new Lord Lieutenant (As Overheard and Reported by Larry Flyn, waiter)':

"See here my Lord
You'll find it hard,
To play yer card." sez she

"You'll be met with ovations
And grand orations
So have yer reply
All cut and dry" sez she

"Take a party down
To Punchestown
And give a ball
In St Patrick's Hall
Or maybe two
For one mightn't do." sez she

"I know what you mean
betwixt and between" sez he
"Up wid the Green
And God save the Queen".

Between the Union in 1800 and the last pre-famine census in 1841 the population of Ireland *doubled*. In the 1840s only one fifth of the population of Ireland lived in towns; the remainder lived where land was available. Of the latter about three million people grew only potatoes and lived solely upon them. The seemingly ever-increasing population forced the sub-division of many land holdings. The Devon Commission (which reported in 1845 in the first year of the Great Famine) described the struggle for land as resembling 'that of a dying man for water in a desert.' Many of the poorest Irish gave their labour in exchange for their tiny plots of 'potato land'. Land rentals, of necessity, were low. For this reason many families had been able to live on the same land for generations. A number of landowners in Ireland owned very large estates. Most – but not all – had little incentive either to improve, or to invest in, their properties. By any standard in the then known world peasant 'farming' in Ireland was grossly inefficient and hopelessly under-capitalised; cultivations were dominated by ancient custom, superstition and ignorance. In consequence, 'the poor Irishman' lived in an almost unimaginable squalor; the gulf which separated him from his – often 'absentee' – landlord was overwhelming. Neither side of this terrible equation ever made any real contact with the other.

Dissatisfaction with the system and customs of land ownership in Ireland tended to lie dormant when agriculture and the potato crops were good; but to erupt in discontent when times became bad.

From 1826 the English 'statute acre' became the official unit of land measurement in Ireland.

Prior to 1826 land in most of Ireland had been measured in 'Irish acres'[6] (or its exact equivalent termed 'Plantation Measure'). Because the statute linear perch measured five and a half yards whilst the Irish perch measured seven yards the difference between one acre 'statute' and one acre 'Irish' was considerable. From 1826 official documents were expressed always, and unambiguously, in 'English Statute acres'; but this was not always so in 'other' writings or in conversation when people used the word 'acre' but had in mind the particular unit of land measurement with which they were familiar. Throughout the nineteenth century Irish farmers continued to reckon land in 'Irish acres'.

People studying the 'small print' of nineteenth-century Irish history – for example when attempting to calculate the average yield of potatoes 'per acre' – can all too often find themselves baffled when faced by some casually recorded 'number of acres'.

In Ireland *two* languages were spoken. English was the language of government, of law, of most literature and of most business. Gaelic – 'The Irish' – was the day-to-day language of poor communities and of some literature.

Any person speaking English only, and whose work or interest took him amongst peasant families, was obliged to learn Gaelic. (Gaelic itself is a strange language. Some people consider it to be related more closely to Urdu than to any European language.)

The north-east corner of Ireland, round Belfast, bore some resemblance, in economic terms, to a mistletoe, verdant on the far bough of a leafless tree.

Belfast and its immediate hinterland was capitalised, industrialised and commercially buoyant. It was a 'new town'. It had a 'new look'. Prosperity stemmed from religious customs in regard to the holding of land,[7] from the profitable growing of flax and the manufacture of linen; and, later, from heavy engineering and shipbuilding. *Many* of its people were of Scottish and English descent. Prosperity allowed it to buy in coal from England. The area played a small, but innovative and important, part in England's own industrial revolution.

Elsewhere in Ireland the position was different. Ireland was not given the powerful industrial 'sinews' of coal and minerals which were given to England. Her ancient forests had been destroyed. The *immense* quantities of fish in her seas, rivers and loughs were exploited hardly at all; and then *not* by Irishmen. There was local warmth but no further utility (then) to be had from her vast reserves of peat. Land laws and customs did not encourage thrift, hard work and pride in possessions. In consequence Ireland (excluding Belfast) lacked capital. A traveller in 1839 remarked that there was 'a general conviction among moneyed men that Ireland is, as yet, an insecure place . . . for capital'.

Considerable efforts were made, through the Irish Board of Works, to improve the Irish infrastructure by digging canals, by extensive drainage works, by improving the Shannon Estuary and river and by assistance to Irish railways (and fisheries). But, unfortunately, there is a difference between private capital which moves of its own volition to wherever it can earn a satisfactory return and government funding intended to improve an infrastructure which, it is hoped, will then attract private capital. (That those improvements to the infrastructure did not attract the anticipated volume of private risk capital is the measure of the opinion which private capital held of Ireland as an acceptable risk.)

For most of the nineteenth century Ireland had *two* churches; an *established* Protestant church which served the influential *minority* and a comparatively small Roman Catholic Church which served the Catholic *majority*.

The 'influential Protestant minority' was known, collectively, as the 'Protestant Ascendancy'. (The term originated in the seventeenth century; not by the elevation of Protestants but by a 'de-scendancy' – or penalisation – of Catholics as part of England's hostility to the Church of Rome.) The Ascendancy became prominent in government; in law; in politics; in architecture by the creation of beautiful buildings, many of which still adorn its memory; by the wit, the wisdom and the writings of such men as Swift, Goldsmith, Sheridan and Burke; and in its undisputed leadership of Irish society. Patronage was its tramcar. It had been possible for the United Irishmen of the rebellion days to be 'united' only because they included many Protestants in whose eyes the charms of France then outweighed those of England. As Protestants, the Ascendancy had a natural sympathy with Protestant England but this did not make them Englishmen; the Ascendancy mind was not the English mind; the Ascendancy were Irishmen before they were anything else.

The arguments which preceded the Union brought to the Ascendancy the twin prospects of additional security and heightened anxiety. When it came the Union strengthened the Ascendancy; its position, as it were, had been underwritten by the British Government. Conversely, Pitt's half-promise of Catholic Emancipation contained a serious threat; religious equality could lead only to the loss of Ascendancy superiority. In the event Catholic emancipation was delayed until 1829; Ascendancy fears of it were placated in their increased influence and authority. The Union between England and Ireland resulted, therefore, in a sharpening of the complex gulf which elevated Protestants on the one side but which oppressed Catholics on the other. The Ascendancy supported the growing world-wide power and influence of England; the Catholics looked, with more interest, to the future of Ireland.

When the excitement of the 1829 Emancipation had died down many Catholics were left with a sense of disappointment; a political victory had been won but no balm had been laid on the long standing sore of Irish tithe or on the difficulty surrounding the religious education of children. Because the Protestant church was an established one, the Catholic majority had been obliged to pay tithe, not to their own clergy and such churches as they possessed, but to the upkeep of Protestant churches and their clergy. This unreasonable tax – for that is what Irish tithe was – was not removed until 1838 when an Act, similar to the English Tithe Act, was introduced. (The nine years between emancipation and tithe reform are remembered as the 'tithe war'.) The difficulty surrounding the education of children took longer to resolve. Catholics regarded Protestant teaching, and Protestants regarded Catholic teaching, as heresy. 'United' teaching pleased no one. Both sides wanted their own children to be taught their *own* religion.

Emancipation and tithe reform removed the immediate causes of bitterness between the two churches but could not remove the underlying distrust between them. Few Protestant clergy in Ireland could bring themselves either to cross the bridge of reconciliation with Catholicism or to accept that what emancipation had done could not be undone. Even a measure of tolerance between the two churches was a long time in coming.

England, for some time, had been structured in permeable social layers. A transitional layer, in the form of an intelligent, educated and ambitious middle class, had been growing in size and significance. The large number of successful manufacturing and commercial enterprises of which the British 'industrial revolution' consisted depended on the brains and characters of individuals. There was no lack, in England, of socially aspiring upward – and outward into rural England – movement. Cobbett cursed the 'damned aristocracy of money' but it was not only money that went upwards; so did hard common sense, the self-confidence of success, and a wish to leave a good inheritance. Most of the 'nouveau riche' – or at any rate their sons or grandsons – soon joined, and took their cue from, the old landed gentry of England; and from the tolerant and sensible way in which they themselves had been received.

The population of Ireland was constructed quite *differently*. On the one hand it contained a numerically small Protestant aristocracy and gentry and, on the other, a much larger mass of Catholics. The latter embraced two elements; the whole of the, mostly illiterate, Gaelic-speaking peasant population and a small but educated and prosperous group, which might have become an effective middle class had it not been denied (until 1829) some, at least, of the usual rights of citizenship.

In Ireland the upper and the lower layers of society, divided as they were by privilege and wealth and by an almost unimaginable poverty, did not 'mix' in any ordinary meaning of that word. No transitional middle-class sponge and lubricant, of significance, existed; its absence was one of the most divisive crosses under the burden of which Ireland laboured.

In August 1845, after several exceptionally cold and wet weeks, the first chill warnings of what was to become an appalling human tragedy began to fret their way into a few perceptive minds in England and in Ireland; that of Sir Robert Peel, the Prime Minister of a Conservative Government and a man with an intimate knowledge of Ireland, was one. The poor Irish were all too familiar with food shortages but, in the autumn of 1845, fear of the future was compounded by a fearful mystery concerning the present. Sound potatoes were being converted, literally overnight, into a putrid stinking mass by an agency of which the only thing known was that no one understood what it was, from whence it had come, or how it might be avoided or contained.

The English Corn[8] Laws (under which the amount of grain imported into the United Kingdom was controlled by a price mechanism) had been introduced, in a collapsing grain market, after Waterloo. The consequence had been to keep the price of grain high to the advantage of the landed, conservative and wheat-growing interest but to the disadvantage of the poor, bread-eating, interest. The Corn Laws (and surviving Navigation Acts) had turned the United Kingdom economy into a *protected* one at a time when it was the strongest, the fastest-growing, the most enterprising and the most competitive economy in the world. As the urban manufacturing population increased, so too did the demand for the free import of food and raw materials. Understandably, manufacturers asked 'How can other nations buy from us if we do not, first, buy from them?' At the same time, therefore, as famine threatened in Ireland, 'protection' or 'free trade' became the major impending political issue in England; its resolution of the greatest importance to England herself, to an anxiously waiting world outside (clamorous to trade freely with the world's strongest economy) and, *suddenly*, to Ireland for whom cheap food in sufficient quantity could not be brought in, openly, until the Corn Laws had been repealed.

To his other qualities Sir Robert Peel added an extraordinary openness of mind; he had demonstrated already that he was never afraid to change it. By 1845 he had, almost certainly, completed the mental processes of changing his mind yet again. Despite his Conservative and wheat-growing party's total allegiance to protection, as enshrined in the Corn Laws, he had become convinced that 'protection' was now holding back economic growth. In his mind, but not yet in any public utterance, Peel had become converted to the principle of free trade; and to the glittering economic future which it promised for England.

It was into this tense political situation that the wet summer months of 1845 intruded themselves so peremptorily. As Prime Minister, Peel was well informed. He knew that all European harvests had suffered severely and that potatoes were rotting in England and Scotland; and, by the middle of November, he knew that most of the Irish potato crop had been lost. Peel *knew* Ireland; he judged, because of the diversity of their agriculture, that England and Scotland could survive but that Ireland, with its weak economy and sharply increasing population, could not. He was acutely aware, also, that if he and his government did not take immediate steps to provide for Ireland they would be held responsible for what might occur. He was well aware, also, that it would be impossible to import grain regularly without first repealing the Corn Laws; but that for the leader of the Conservative party to attempt repeal – for whatever reason – might well be to attempt the impossible. Driven by an extraneous event which he could not control, by his knowledge of Ireland, and by the obligation imposed by his personal conversion to free trade, Peel found himself, suddenly, facing the greatest political crisis of his career. He was driven to it at a time not of his own choosing and upon a ground of the most confusing complexity.

In June 1846, after seven months of political turmoil, the Corn Laws, and with them 'protection', were jettisoned. Repeal destroyed the old Conservative party and led to a long period of Whig government. Sir Robert Peel never again held office. Free to trade as they chose, the business men of England marched outward all over the world with immense vigour. A new union between labour and capital was forged. Agriculture which, for centuries, had dominated the English economy found itself supplanted by trade and industry. The United Kingdom (in effect England, Scotland and Wales) became not only the 'workshop of the world,' but the carriers, in their own ships, of the world's goods.

Repeal of the Corn Laws has been described as 'perhaps the most significant event in the history of the British Empire'. At the same moment as Peel and his Conservative government fell *Ireland* found itself in *major* crisis; not the threat of famine but famine itself. As the spring of 1846 turned to summer, large numbers of Irish men women and children starved. There were no potatoes.

'Tis around us and about us,
'Tis with us everywhere.
We can feel its dark wings beating
on the still and frightened air.[9]

Ireland, in her long history, has suffered many 'famines'. Three are known to have occurred prior to the year 1000 and no less than seventy-four occurred between 1011 and 1845.

The Irish nation was marked, indelibly, by the Great Famine of 1845–49. The suffering which it caused was so great, and its consequences were so complex, that no account of nineteenth-century Irish history, however incomplete it may be, can ignore it. The great Irish Famine remains unique in the history of world famines; it was bought about by the sudden, and virtually total, failure of a single crop; the potato.

The Whig Government – whose responsibility the famine became from June 1846 – was conditioned, in its early stages, by two principles of conduct which were then believed to be correct. First, Englishmen believed in 'laissez-faire'; that is the doctrine that starving individuals should, somehow, be able to 'help themselves'. Secondly, the Government believed that market forces of demand and supply were by far the best controllers of physical supply and that artificial interference with these forces should be avoided. In consequence it was believed by the Whigs that 'free trade' would respond to the imperative call for food in Ireland. It did *not* do so. Its failure was not so much a failure of 'market forces' as a failure of understanding, by those who ought to have been wiser, of the physical, social and economic conditions which prevailed in Ireland; and which made operation of the principle impossible. Within so vast a tragedy it is difficult to say where lay its heart; but these unjustified expectations were not far from it. The risk that private enterprise might prove to be ineffective, in a situation where the consequences of failure were so exceptionally grave, was very great.

By late 1846 the situation in Ireland had become very serious. 'Autumn was now passing into winter. The nettles and blackberries, the edible roots and cabbage leaves . . . had . . . disappeared. Children began to die . . . The winter . . . of 1846–47 was "the most severe in living memory and the longest". Snow fell early in November; the wind came from the north-east; . . . in

England, by the middle of December, the Thames was a mass of floating ice . . .'

Saving seed for the next harvest became a matter of overriding importance; but, faced with the choice of eating his seed or dying before the next harvest, the poor Irishman usually chose to eat. In the early months of 1847, 'Though urged to buy and distribute seed, the Government refused to do so for a variety of reasons the most myopic of which was that people would thereby be discouraged from preserving their own.' (It is a bitter fact of famine history that the 1847 crop of potatoes might have been a good one; in fact it was reduced to about one seventh of normal for lack of seed.[10])

Disease followed famine as the night does day. It was believed, universally, that starvation itself was the cause of fever. Famine fevers were two; typhus and relapsing fever. Both are transmitted by lice which almost all the poor Irish carried on themselves as a matter of course. Most of the fever patients collapsed into a welter of misery and died. Also present was dysentery and its even more distressing associated disease, called bacillary dysentery, or the 'bloody flux'. So also was scurvy which, although not infectious, manifested itself rapidly as soon as the vitamin C in potatoes was withheld. And, as if these afflictions were not enough, Asiatic cholera[11] broke out in 1848; it was probably 'imported' on a ship.

Especially distressing was the plight of children. Modern knowledge of famine demonstrates that, when adequate food becomes available again, adults usually recover but that children may never do so completely either mentally or physically. In Ireland starvation appears to have affected the children's bones; the jawbones became fragile and some children's jaws became so distended that they could not speak. Many children were reduced to a deathlike stupor; some looked like little old men and women; 'even the babies were aged'.

In 1847 the Government in London turned to prayer. The 24th March was proclaimed a day of intercession for those 'who in many parts of the United Kingdom are suffering extreme famine and sickness'; and, using a prepared service sheet, those who could get to church on a Wednesday prayed 'For the removal of those heavenly judgements which our manifold sins and provocations have most justly deserved, and with which Almighty God is pleased to visit the iniquities of the land by a grievous scarcity and dearth of diverse articles of sustenance . . .' That humanity should, in extreme circumstances, allow the Almighty to accomplish his ends was then the sustaining admission of last resort. Prayer, no doubt, was of more comfort to the people of England than it was to those in Ireland; the Irish might have preferred more soup kitchens and thicker, less watery soup; or copies of the curious prayer offered by John Tyler Pettee:

> Pray for peace and grace and spiritual food,
> For wisdom and guidance, for all these are good,
> But don't forget the potatoes.

The number of people who died of starvation or disease between 1845 and 1849 can never be known accurately. No record was kept of deaths; many who died could only be buried in fields and ditches. Such calculations as are possible depend, principally, on the two census returns of 1841 and 1851. That of 1841 shows that 8,175,124 people then lived in Ireland, but this figure may well have understated the true position because the existence of many families, particularly in the west, was unknown. That of 1851 records a population of 6,552,385 people. Whilst this figure is likely to have been closer to the truth the *bare* 1841 and 1851 total population figures are misleading; neither figure includes those who were born after 1841 and who died before 1851.

In the five years which started in 1850 well over a million, mostly young, Irish men and women fled Ireland. These were determined, it was said, to undergo any misery 'save that of remaining in Ireland'. Nothing was done by the British Government to control the exodus. Most emigrant ships were dangerously overcrowded and inadequately victualled. Those who died at sea were, without ceremony, thrown overboard. Those who reached their 'farther shore' did so, despite their homesickness, with feelings of deliverance akin to waking from a nightmare. About 850,000 people, or 77% of all emigrants, went to the U.S.A. The early years of these young people were hard indeed. It was said that they 'work like horses, drink like fish, fight like tigers, die like rotten sheep, and are buried like dogs in the mounds of railways and banks of canals without priest or minister.' Eventually a new breed of Irish-Americans prospered and became a loyal and hardworking community in their adopted country; and, despite the fighting and drinking, they never forgot their families still in Ireland. A steady stream of dirty, but generous, dollar notes flowed eastward either to support a parent or to pay the passage money of a new family emigrant.

Volume V of the *New History of Ireland* (published in 1989) contains the following description of the behaviour of Irish men and women during the Famine:

> . . . the records . . . are replete with anti-social behaviour and acts of gross inhumanity – committed by wealthy farmers and shopkeepers against the poor, by the poor against others of their own class, by parents against their children, and by sons and daughters against their parents. By their very nature prolonged famine and epidemics of fatal disease lead to the large-scale erosion or collapse of traditional moral restraints and communal sanctions. For many of the survivors of the great famine of the late 1840s the recollection of their anti-social conduct against neighbours and even close relatives was a heavy psychological burden crying out for release and displacement. What made the displacement of this guilt on to Albion's shoulders so compelling was not only that England represented the ancient oppressor but also that its government during the famine had such a damning record in Ireland. Who today should be surprised that many of 'Erin's boys' wanted 'revenge' . . . ?

It is true that England did represent the 'ancient oppressor'. It is true, also, that the quality of help actually given to Ireland by England was not only inadequate and ungenerous; it was also inappropriate as between two sister nations. Ireland *was* part and parcel of 'the United Kingdom'. What went wrong?

Sir Robert Peel and his Conservative party fell from power in June 1846 (the Great Famine having declared itself nine months earlier), through the obduracy of the English landed, and corn-growing, classes and their short-sighted fear of repeal of the Corn Laws. Had these men not so conducted themselves Peel would have continued, with little doubt, to lead his party and his country from an almost unassailable position of power and *personal* authority.

Lord John Russell and his Whigs did not replace Sir Robert Peel and his Conservatives in June 1846 upon some surge of public enthusiasm; rather it was recognised generally that 'the present position was owing to accident and not to any general wish . . . to see [the Whigs] in power'. Russell, personally, was not a warm and attractive figure; people doing business with him were obliged to make what they could of his 'cold, short, abrupt, indifferent manner'.[12] Robert Kee, in his *Ireland*, records a letter written from Ballinrobe in Co. Mayo in April 1847 containing these words: 'The curse of Russell, more terrible than the curse of Cromwell, is upon us . . .' Charles Trevelyan, who controlled the purse strings and much of the policy of famine relief at the Treasury in London, had no personal knowledge of Ireland; he seldom displayed other than an unemotional efficiency as he discharged his heavy responsibilities.

In 1846 Peel was aged fifty-eight. He was a man of compassion and integrity. He possessed a fine intellect. He was a man of independent judgement. He had proved himself to be a courageous innovator. He possessed a comprehensive and detailed grasp of the whole machinery of government; he knew what government could do, and more importantly, what it could *not* do. He did not much like Ireland but he had known it, as a young man, between 1812 and 1818 when he had been resident in Dublin as the Irish Secretary. He had then experienced, on the spot and for himself, the then inexplicable weather of 1816 and 1817 which had led to *serious* (if localised) food shortages. These had a surprising cause. Both 1816 and 1817 were years 'without summer'; and, in many parts of the world, of poor plant growth. The cause of this phenomenon is now known to have been an immense volcanic eruption in Indonesia in April 1815; this blew 5,000 feet off the top of Mount Tambura, so leaving a crater some four miles in diameter and nearly one mile in depth. The haze (or 'darkness') forming agent of such an eruption is understood now to have been 'not fine dust, but an aerosol of tiny sulphuric acid droplets'.

In June 1816 Byron – not, fortunately, lost for words – wrote his poem 'Darkness'. His opening lines constitute a chilling foretaste of how he thought the world was about to end:

> I had a dream, which was not all a dream.
> The bright sun was extinguished, and the stars
> Did wander darkling in the eternal space.
> Rayless, and pathless, and the icy earth

> Swung blind and blackening in the moonless air;
> Morn came and went – and came, and brought no day,
> And men forgot their passions in the dread
> Of this their desolation.

Peel, still under thirty and living in Dublin as the Irish Secretary, can only have found the weather of 1816 and 1817 as perplexing as did everyone else. Nevertheless, his reaction to a shortage of food in Ireland was clear. On 8th March 1817, 'There was a general disposition to admit the pressures of the case to be so strong as to put all considerations of general policy and principle aside, and to resort to any measures which, whether wise or not under ordinary circumstances, could be shown to be applicable to the present emergency.' Peel, of course, *knew* Ireland. Hard experience had already taught him that the summer months were always months of food shortages. He had learnt that '. . . the poor in Ireland . . . are not buyers of food but growers of it and have no money to purchase if what they usually grow fails them.' Experience had already *warned* him of those extreme measures which might be necessary if Ireland was to be governed, effectively, in crisis. 'If there were within the reach of government a number of persons actually starving . . . I would overleap every difficulty and buy food for them at public expense.'

In 1829 Peel had spoken of ministerial responsibilities. 'As a minister of the Crown I reserve to myself, distinctly and unequivocally, the right of adapting my conduct to the exigency of the moment, and to the wants of the country.'

A few days before he fell from power in June 1846 Peel received a letter from Richard Cobden, leader of the parliamentary Free Trade Movement. It included these words:

> It is said you are to resign . . . Are you aware of the strength of your position? . . . I will not speak of the populace, which, to a man is with you; but of the active and intelligent middle classes, with whom you have engrossed a sympathy and interest greater than was ever before possessed by a Minister . . . Now, the whole interest centres on yourself. You represent the IDEA of the age, and it has no other representative amongst statesmen . . . I need not tell you that the only way in which the soul of a great nation can be stirred is by appealing to its sympathies . . . it is necessary for the concentration of a

people's mind that an individual should become the incarnation of its principle . . ..

(The letter, in fact, addressed the Repeal of the Corn Laws; but it illustrated, vividly, Peel's position in England.)

The facts of the matter are that England and Ireland had been united in 1801 into one nation by the pressures of war; and that famine, on so terrible a scale, had softened Ireland. What the Irish needed, during their long ordeal, was help given by every means which the ingenuity, the resourcefulness and the *generosity* of their powerful English 'brothers and sisters' could devise. Such a reaction required a controlling – and an inspiring – architect; Sir Robert Peel (and he is, not infrequently, described as the greatest of all British Prime Ministers) would, with little doubt, have been that architect. After the dark cloud of famine had lifted, the Irish, a warm-hearted and impulsive people, might have been enduringly grateful for the generous way in which they had been *helped.* Death and emigration – inevitably on the largest scale – would in time, have been forgotten; what would have been *remembered* was generosity.

What, during those four long years of dreadful famine, might Sir Robert Peel have achieved?[13]

CHAPTER TWELVE

As, IN 1854, CHARLES FIRST went to Achill its 5,000 inhabitants were emerging from an abandoned isolation which had been almost total; for centuries it had been unmapped, unlit at night and almost unknown.[14] Achill is the largest, and nearly the most western, of Ireland's islands. It thrusts out into deep water. It is mountainous and, when Charles knew it, still accessible only with difficulty. Its heather, its peat bogs and its towering rockfaces were the haunt of ravens and eagles[15] and wild goats; its caves the lonely haunt of men fleeing from justice. To some, when streaming rain and flying cloud tore in from the Atlantic, Achill was Ultima Thule; not only the last outpost of Europe but the end and boundary of all things. To others – like Charles, who had been brought up at the eastern and low lying edge of all things – it was a place of majestic beauty. It was – and is – treeless. A windless day is uncommon; violent and tremendous winter gales are not. Its beaches – few and far between – were golden in the sunlight of summer; its ozone-laden air the most pungent of draughts.[16] Its seas teemed with fish; its ocean salmon fisheries were famous. Its amethysts – its 'Irish diamonds' – rose from quartz of the purest white from a spot on Charles's land. At its western extremity a great curved finger of rock pointed as an index – and as a challenge to starving Irishmen – over the Atlantic to America. Beside it the soaring cliffs of Croaghan are the highest in Western Europe. The Minaun rock-fall is scarcely less forbidding. The bare and beautiful cone of Slievemore fills the eye.

Achill, as Charles knew it, was separated by a long, narrow and unbridged sound – through which the tides race violently – from a mountainous and empty coastal mainland by the equally empty and mountainous peninsula of Carraun. Although, by the time

Charles first went there, getting on to Achill had become – very slightly – easier, a traveller of only a few years earlier had faced formidable obstacles. First, following a track only, he had to get himself to the best, but still empty and deserted, crossing place; this was about nineteen miles from Newport and twenty-seven from Westport. When he reached it nothing awaited him except the 'ruined walls' of an old building, and 'the rippling of the water on the beach or the scream of the curlew.' Somehow, he had to cross the 225 yard obstacle; either by a ferry boat whose owner, all too often, was either absent or blind to entreaty, or by a dangerous combination of swimming, wading and underwater rock clambering which was possible only at a fleeting low water. Lastly, he had to find his way, through yet another empty wilderness, to wherever he thought his destination might be. For Charles and Annie crossing the sound did not mean they were home; neither of their two houses on Achill were much less than about fourteen English miles from the crossing place. For the people of Achill, as a whole, the difficulties were too great; they stayed where they were. The surprise is not that Achill had been so isolated and its people so abandoned but that it ever became drawn into any regular contact with the mainland. (Achill Sound was not to be bridged until after Charles and Annie had left the island.)

A confusing factor within the confused years of Irish rebellion in the 1790s had been the 'union' between Irish Roman Catholics and Irish Protestants. At the time it had created the 'United Irishman' but this, as a marriage of convenience for a political purpose, was short-lived; by the 1820s mutual tolerance had worn thin again. Not surprisingly Irish Catholics became strongly influenced by ideas of liberty and equality which were sweeping Europe in the wake of the French Revolution; and, in the wake of Catholic emancipation, by an exalted awareness of, and respect for, the absolute authority of the Pope in matters of faith and religious discipline. Protestants – that is the Protestant Ascendancy who, as always, were Irishmen before they were Englishmen but who, in consequence of the Union of 1801, had become more than usually sympathetic to English opinion – were influenced by events occurring across an even wider canvas. Englishmen had begun to think that the Imperial Authority of the British Crown was as limitless as was its obligation to bring good government, civilisation and the blessings of Christianity – by which they meant the Protestant Religion – to the world at large. As Charles came into the world in 1832 the revitalised Protestant churches of England and Ireland could not fail to endorse such a clarion call to their evangelism. Missionaries – ardent crusading men funded by public subscription – went out world-wide; 'world-wide' *included* going to Ireland. Most took the Protestant religion to people who had no recognisable religion, but those who went to Ireland took – or endeavoured to take – the Protestant religion to Roman Catholics. A society for Irish Church missions to the Catholics of Ireland was formed. Amongst these the mission to Achill Island became, by far, the best known and the most explosive. Its founder and leader was the Reverend Edward Nangle. A visit to his Mission became almost an obligatory pilgrimage for militant evangelicals.

There is, always, a world of difference between the priest who blazons his faith by living a godly and quiet life amongst his own people, and a man such as Edward Nangle who endeavoured to do so by a publicly waged campaign to change the faith of a whole community. Nangle was a man of good family; intelligent, imaginative, hard working, resourceful and determined; a man likely to achieve some prominence in any walk of life. He was, by his cloth, a priest. As such, duty obliged him to carry bibles and school books wherever he went but Achill presented unique difficulties; its size, its inaccessibility and the number and backwardness of its people demanded more than bibles and school books. Nangle needed money, friends in high places, and specialised help; he needed knowledge of how the world worked and who made it work as much as he needed his own vision of what ought to be attempted. The Achill Protestant Mission was Nangle's own creation; he became, inevitably, its 'Chief Executive'. As an adventure in Protestantism by an uncompromising man who resented criticism and who could comprehend, in matters of religion, no viewpoint except his own, Edward Nangle's enterprise never really succeeded; and, ultimately, it failed. Of his secular work it is impossible to say either that it failed or that it succeeded; parts failed; parts had their day and then failed; parts endured whilst their begetter became forgotten. But that he had 'created' much of the Achill which Charles and Annie were to know, and love, there is no doubt.

* * *

The religious faith of the 5,000 inhabitants of Achill before Edward Nangle went there in 1834 was, nominally, Roman Catholic. Such evidence as exists suggests that the people depended more upon habit and superstition to guide their lives than they did upon God and the Roman Catholic religion.[17] Collectively they were what might be described as a 'plain pudding'; but one having a bias toward, and some knowledge of, Catholicism. Edward Nangle, wielding a stern unbending spoon, set about stirring the pudding against the bias. Predictably, the mainland Catholics, incensed at this interference with their island flock – which, of course, they had neglected – counter-attacked with vigour; and, with an equally unbending spoon, began not only to stir the pudding back again, but to give their religion an active life in Achill itself. Both sides were supported by outspoken Bishops. Robert Daly, the Protestant Bishop of Cashel – a wealthy man and a good friend of Edward Nangle – 'assumed the position and bearing of a Protestant Pope'. His opinions were said to be those of 'Irish Toryism, pure and simple, hatred of popery which nothing could mollify, hostility to all sorts of liberalism which nothing could conciliate, invincible dislike of any man, especially any clergyman, who dissented from his opinions.' Dr McHale, the Roman Catholic Archbishop of Tuam, has been quoted as saying, 'There is no place outside of hell which more enrages the Protestant Colony.' Had the affair been a military one a correspondent might have remarked that 'No quarter was asked or given.'

Edward Nangle first saw Achill in the summer of 1831. He was then aged thirty-one. He had gone to the west to investigate the famine of that year. He stayed with the Reverend William Stoney, the Rector of Newport and, himself, a controversial figure in the Protestant Church of Ireland.[18] He then 'set out on his first visit to Achill. It took him a day's ride to reach Achill Sound which he forded at low tide the following morning . . . He was an object of curiosity to the local people who flocked around him . . . He spoke to many of them in Irish . . . he saw for himself the appalling destitution and ignorance of most of the people . . . the area without roads, schools or medical facilities, and with only hovels for houses. He also noted that the spiritual welfare of the people was neglected by the churches both Protestant and

Catholic'. And, as the biography of Edward Nangle continues: 'By the time he had returned to Newport he had decided that Achill would be the place where he would devote himself to missionary work . . . The first step was then taken when Mr Stoney introduced him to Sir Richard O'Donnell, the owner of the land of Achill . . . and, from whom, he later obtained the lease of some one hundred and thirty acres of uncultivated land near the village of Dugort.'

It took Edward Nangle three years to get ready. In August 1834 he and his wife and young family moved, permanently, to Dugort on the northern coast of the island. Deliberately he cut himself off from the 'civilised' world; he had no friends, and, initially, no doctor; Achill offered no food of the kind to which he and his wife and his children had been accustomed. It was the start of a missionary and social enterprise which was to attract an extraordinary publicity; to live in Achill, in the Mission's heyday, was, at times, to live in a floodlit room. Edward Nangle created the 'lived in' island which Charles and Annie were to know and to love. He moved it from an isolation which had been almost total into the mainstream of Irish life.[19]

Edward Nangle and his Mission were to be tested to their limit during the Great Famine. By 1845 an appreciable number of 'Catholics' had been converted to the Protestant religion. Such evidence as has survived suggests that Edward Nangle and his Mission subordinates – pitched headlong into a crisis of survival for which they were as unprepared as anyone else – worked devotedly to bring what help they could to wherever it was most needed. The fifteenth Annual report of the Mission – (covering the period July 1848–May 1849) – stated that the famine had continued 'in unmitigated severity during the past year.' Jaundice, dropsy, diarrhoea, dysentery, gastric fever, acute rheumatism, scarlatina and night blindness had all been 'most prevalent'. (N.B. It is curious, and perhaps an oversight, that the list did not specifically include scurvy.) In the same report it transpired that a cargo of Indian maize had been imported. The Mission had hoped to receive this on credit but, in the event, payment before landing had been demanded. In consequence, Edward Nangle had been compelled to go begging in London and Bath, but the maize 'saved many lives'.[20] From the sixteenth Report (1849) it appears that between 1,800–2,000 'poor children received daily a supply of food which sufficed to satisfy the cravings of hunger. The equable distribution of this food in such a way as to prevent fraud was attended with difficulties which none but those immediately concerned could imagine.' Charge and countercharge of dishonesty and of 'taking the soup' resounded. ('Souperism'[21] meant the giving of food to those who surrendered their faith for it; or, as the jingle put it, 'Souper, souper ring the bell, souper, souper, go to Hell'.) It is improbable, in the highest degree, that a clergyman of Edward Nangle's stature would have withheld food deliberately from any starving person; but the charge of 'souperism' against him may have some justification in so far as he created new employments in Achill which he may have been inclined to give to Protestants when he could.

In the spring of 1852 (and two years before Charles went to Achill) Edward Nangle had been transferred to the large mainland parish of Skreen in County Sligo. Some saw this move as a clerical promotion; others as its reverse. Nangle was not to be separated, however, by a mere posting from the Mission he had created and the island he loved. He continued to be an active Mission Trustee and member of the Mission Committee, to edit the monthly Mission newspaper, and to spend three of the summer months of each year in Achill. At the age of fifty-five – when Charles first saw him – Edward Nangle had become a striking figure. He spoke of a – Protestant – God in whom he professed total belief; he did so, frequently, in fluent flowing Gaelic. He was tall, dark and well built; his nose was large; his eyes were those of a fanatic; his dark hair and fine beard – flecked with grey – threw some sort of halo round the head of a man who, in the imagination, resembled nothing so much as one of the biblical prophets. If he had a sense of humour it did not, often, emerge. Someone wrote of him that he seldom smiled but that when he did he could be transformed. Gentleness and warmth (reflecting his love of the violin and of painting) was capable of driving out – banishing for a moment – the stern commanding priest. Edward Nangle was not easy to know; few accomplished that difficult task.

There is no doubt that Charles and Edward Nangle were, at least, acquainted. Both were gentlemen in a closed island community. Charles's father and Nangle were both Protestant clergymen and – within a year – contemporaries. Like priests the world over both answered their calling in their own way. Charles might have understood, more easily than most, what might have driven Edward Nangle; not only into his religious crusade in Achill but, also, in his secular 'interventions' in the island's economy and society. Both men loved horses; both were good shots and keen fishermen. Edward Nangle did a small water colour of a spirited horse and its rider crossing the arched bridged below Charles's Keem Bay house, which has survived in the Nangle family. It is possible that the rider is a representation of Charles.[22]

Edward Nangle could not have decided upon Dugort as the headquarters and centrepiece of his Mission solely upon the evidence of what he saw of so large an island during his first fleeting visit in 1831; he must have returned several times. His eventual choice of Dugort was an excellent one. His essential requirement boiled down to a need for communications. First, he needed to be able to reach out spiritually, inspirationally, educationally and medically to the people of Achill and they, in turn, to him. Secondly, he could not create an enduring mission, capable of doing the work and providing the services he intended, without attracting in other people who would have to be housed and looked after. As these considerations became apparent it became equally clear that the existing overland link with the mainland was inadequate, and that the only practicable link was by sea with Westport. Dugort was then seen to have advantages. It stood at the north-east end of Achill's low-lying 'waist' so giving access to most of its population; it possessed a shelving, and partly sheltered, beach of hard sand off which laden carts could be driven; a satisfactory building site existed close by and at which water was available; and, as the gradient from beach to site was not severe, a road, up which heavy stores could be hauled, could be constructed. As Achill existed in the 1830s Dugort was a carefully calculated choice.

Achill's new 'port' at Dugort may have been simplicity itself but shipping in a considerable quantity of materials and stores was not straightforward. In 1834 there was need of a controlled ordering, marking, and despatch organisation at Westport – and *strict* instructions regarding the maximum package weights and dimensions – and a similar receiving system at Dugort. Sweating men and straining animals – Catholic at Westport? – made the whole operation possible but neither men, animals nor carts appeared out of thin air at either, well-separated, end. No telegraph or telephone existed. No doubt Edward Nangle delegated this particular responsibility but much depended on a smooth running system; he was bound to take a close interest in it.

From its earliest days the Mission owned its own hooker. These, typically Irish, single-masted boats varied in size but a common burden was ten to twelve tons; or – as one was reported as carrying – '112 migrant workers.' Two – one owned and one hired – may have been needed in the Mission's early days. A visitor in 1838 described how he became a passenger in one of three hookers which raced each other through Achill Sound; this was, he wrote, 'a fine scene'. (The visitor was right! Racing through and between the Sound's shifting shallows and constantly moving sand-banks, and in the grip of violent tidal currents and fluky winds, *was* exciting!) In 1842 the Mission's hooker was sunk by collision in deep water. The boatmen maintained that this was *not* accidental and that the parties to 'the outrage' were known. (A replacement vessel, costing £46, went into service in 1844.)

As the requirement for building materials slackened so the Mission's hooker seems to have taken on outside business; and, after the famine, it made at least two annual profits. There was a demand in Westport for Achill peat and the hooker may have won some of this business. The overland route to Newport and Westport remained unimproved for some time and, even then, its capacity was limited; Achill people may have been glad of an alternative way to the mainland for themselves and their parcels and freights. As a way of leaving Achill it was reasonably reliable; and, on a fine day, as lovely a way of doing so as can be easily imagined.

Virtually all of what Nangle built at Dugort still stands. Most of his buildings face east and look out over Blacksod Bay and the beach; all lie comfortably in the lee of Slievemore. It is obvious that a competent architect was employed. Everything was built of stone, Welsh slate and sound timber and was put up to stay up. Today the place is still very much alive but it has a cloistered faded air; the old bustle and enthusiasms have moved on; hedges and gardens, and even a few trees, shroud and soften everything.

Nangle obtained his stone locally but, otherwise, he was obliged to ship in everything he needed. Achill possessed unskilled – and sadly undernourished – labour but neither stonemasons nor carpenters, tilers, plumbers, plasterers, painters nor, as far as is known, tradesmen of any other kind. The island possessed no building tools, wheelbarrows, or scaffolding poles or rope. The skilled men required had to be discovered in and around Westport, persuaded to leave their families, and to take themselves and their tools off to Achill's wild mountains and into the employment of a man about whom they can have known little. Were the skilled tradesmen Protestants? Hardly! At Dugort what did they find? Nothing! As they stumbled ashore was it *pouring* with rain? Very possibly! No one, imagining Edward Nangle aged thirty-four, and standing on Dugort beach to welcome his first party of skilled responsible workmen, should under-estimate either his magnetism or his clear-headed, articulate and determined leadership. His was the irresistible force which set out to move a mountain; which, in a way, he did.

The Colony buildings were divided into two groups; 'The Square' (which contained sixteen houses laid out in the form of an 'L'); and 'Rock Lane' (which contained eight, more loosely separated, houses). In addition the Colony needed, about itself, other buildings. These included – round Rock Lane and so closer to the beach, through which several obtained supplies – a carpenter's shop, stores and stables, a piggery, a tuck mill (which made a heavy waterproof material called freize, and which, in 1844, was converted into a blacksmith's shop), a grain mill, the Mission shop and later a small hospital. The foundation stone of St Thomas's Church had been laid in 1835 but completion had been much delayed, almost certainly, by the famine. It was opened, eventually, in March 1855 before five hundred people, which may have included Charles. Two houses, one large and one small, were built apart from both 'The Square' and the church; the larger became Edward Nangle's rectory. A line of thirty low thatched cottages ran behind the long arm of 'The Square'; these housed domestic servants and Mission employees. (New building was not confined to Dugort. For example, what amounted to a subsidiary mission was built in the Mweelin Valley. This contained a school house, a teacher training school, a chapel, a house for the missionary and twelve cottages.)

In one way and another a large number of people lived in the colony at Dugort and at Mweelin. All were held together by their Protestant religion and a sense of mission. They constituted a more diverse – and so, no doubt, more interesting – group than might have been expected. Most were educated. Some came from the upper classes of society. Why some of them lived where they did is no longer apparent. The whole colony was kept on its toes by visitors, all of whom were intelligent and enquiring and some of whom were distinguished. Several went home to praise, or to criticise in print, what they had seen. Those who criticised, and of whom Edward Nangle heard, received in return more than they had reckoned upon; he was a touchy man.

Number 1, The Square (at its northerly and highest 'Rock Lane' end) was occupied by Dr Neason Adams, his wife and his surgery. Number 2 was the infant school run by Mrs Bozman, wife of the Master Printer. (As one visitor put it 'the dispensary is his business; the infant school his recreation'.)

Adams was a physician and the most loveable of men. He became known as the 'St Luke' of Achill. Before him there was neither physician, surgeon, apothecary, chemist or midwife either on the island or within thirty miles of its inhabitants. His reputation has *never* been tarnished; he was, probably, the Mission's most indispensable prop. (It seems fitting, entirely, that Adams should have lived at Number 1.)

Neason Adams and Edward Nangle had been friends for years. Adams gave up a thriving practice in Dublin when he joined the Mission. In Achill he gave his services free. Amongst many local activities he remained a keen gardener who managed, somehow, to grow and ripen a little fruit on Achill. He used to give lettuces to his friends!

Number 3 when Charles probably first saw it, served as a Church (pending the completion of St Thomas).

Number 4 was the schoolhouse. Reading, writing, spelling, arithmetic, and scripture were taught.

In 1841, 72% of Ireland's population were illiterate and the figure on Achill was, probably, higher. Education was needed desperately. Edward Nangle's blazing determination to bring it to the people of Achill was second only to his blazing determination to bring them the Protestant religion.

The school at Number 4 was opened in December 1834. It was followed, quickly, by others at Cashel, Keel and Slievemore but hardly before the Roman Catholics had built three schools of their own in close proximity to Nangle's Protestant schools. These seven joined a single surviving 'hedge school'.[23] Both religions continued to build schools and so try to win the larger number of young, impressionable minds; even before Charles got to Achill the island had become 'over-schooled'. In addition there was an obvious need for tradesmen on Achill. Although Nangle may have tackled this problem earlier the annual reports of 1843 and 1844 show that twelve Achill youths (later increased to twenty) had been learning tailoring, carpentry, cobbling and printing; an 1844 Report shows that blacksmith, slater and plasterer tradesmen instructors had been recruited by the Mission. The training of young women had not been neglected. Later reports show that a 'skilful mistress' had been employed to teach the embroidery of muslin and that 'an extensive manufacturer in Belfast had engaged to supply the muslin with patterns stamped upon it and to pay for work when returned.' Evidently the mistress was up to her work; what she sent forward was 'deemed worthy . . . of a place in the Industrial Exhibition.'

Number 5, The Square, was the hotel. It was opened, probably, in 1838. It had five bedrooms and was built at the private expense of a single mission benefactor. Samuel Maynard and his wife took over its management in 1854. Most users of its accommodation came either to inspect the Mission or for the pleasure of seeing Achill Island for the first time. The hotel's charges were 5/8d per head per day for full board and lodging or – an attractive discount – £1.5s.0d. per week.

The hotel's visitors' books survived for many years but now seem to have disappeared; had they not done so they would have revealed some, at least, of the detailed substance behind the extraordinary interest which the Protestant Mission in Achill created. Without them it is possible to mention the names of only some of those people whose visit to Dugort was recorded elsewhere.

The Reverend Edward Stanley – not yet Charles's father's Bishop – went to Dugort in the Mission's earliest days. Stanley denied that Catholic and Protestant could not live together amicably; he sought peace, not war, between the religions. In 1835 he published a pamphlet on religion and education in Ireland in which he displayed, for an Englishman, an unusual knowledge of Irish history. 'Humanity shudders' he wrote, 'at the atrocities committed by English invaders yet we make no allowances for the feelings of hostility which have been transmitted . . . six centuries of misrule are not to be forgotten in a day.' And, concerning the widely held belief that the Protestant Church of Ireland was its *national* church, he wrote '. . .in the technical language of the law it may be so, but in the plainer . . . language of equity and common sense it never was . . . and never can be.' Stanley did not discover much religious harmony in Achill; he and Edward Nangle crossed swords. A pamphlet, which Stanley wrote in 1835, said something about Ireland worth remembering. 'Irishmen' he wrote, 'will not be driven but they may be led.'

Early visitors were Captain Sir John Franklin R.N. and Lady Franklin. Franklin had fought at Copenhagen and Trafalgar; he attempted the North Pole in 1818; and, by the time he went to Achill, he had become the greatest Arctic explorer of his day. In 1847 he was to lose his life as the Commander of what, it was believed confidently, would be the last and successful attempt to find the 'North-West Passage'.[24] Lady Franklin, on her own account, was a remarkable world traveller and the couple were not often united in England. Franklin, himself, was a religious man but it remains significant that, somehow, the couple found the time, and the wish, to visit the Mission together. (They did not stay in the hotel but in the Rectory as the private guests of the Nangles; this fact was duly reported in the *Missionary Herald*!)

Asenath Nicholson, a strangely dressed American lady, went to Dugort in the early 1840s and later published a book.[25] She lodged, uninvited, with 'the peasantry', wandered around the Colony buildings also uninvited, had a row with Elisa, the first Mrs Nangle (whose daughters giggled) and, as a generality, induced more heat than light. She walked, probably, to Keel ('no roads or footpaths') and on, through Dooagh, to Keem where she 'gathered a few amethysts' as if they had been peas from her garden. But, on the whole, she was not dissatisfied with what she found at Dugort. (She had, earlier, been in Dublin for some years. She once compared Dublin's many beggars to 'Pharaoh's frogs'; an allusion as opaque as some of her other activities.)

In 1842 a Mr and Mrs S.C. Hall – well-known travel writers who had heard much about the Mission – visited Dugort. They later published their *Ireland: Its Scenery, Characters etc.*, parts of which caused uproar in the Colony. The Mission, the Halls, wrote, had been 'a complete failure'. English subscribers to it were assured that 'they bestow their money for a worse than useless purpose'; and that 'the clergyman under whose control the settlement is placed' had not 'been an example of that gentle, peace-loving, persuasive zeal, that meek and unaffected grace which should distinguish an humble follower of the Lord and Master.' Edward Nangle was outraged. As part of a lengthy rebuttal – and Edward Nangle never used one word if three, four or even five could be pressed into use – he stated that the Halls had arrived at Achill Sound on a Tuesday (in June); that they crossed next day and spent most of it 'viewing the romantic scenery of Keem'; and that they did not reach Dugort until 'half past five' and left again 'two hours later'. (Remembering the distances involved this may not have been far from the truth.) The local Church of England clergy sprang to Edward Nangle's defence; this took the form of an address which was published in the Tenth Report of the Mission:

> Reverend and Dear Sir,
>
> Finding that a most unprovoked attack had been made on yourself personally, and the Achill Mission under your management by Mr S.C. Hall we, the undersigned clergy . . . feel bound to record our respect and esteem for your person and principles.
>
> We cordially extend to you the right hand of fellowship in your arduous and self denying exertions . . . We, unhesitatingly, contradict the misrepresentations lately put forth . . .
>
> We remain, Reverend and dear Sir, your faithful brethren in the Lord Jesus Christ . . .

There then followed the signatures of two Deans, two Archdeacons and no less than fifty-four Diocesan clergy. The incident illustrates the passionate opinions then held about religious affairs and the relentless vigour with which Edward Nangle defended both his Mission and himself.

Not long after the hotel opened three Frenchmen stayed in it. All wore 'the garb of gentlemen'. After using 'indecent language' and 'insulting conduct toward the female attendant' all were asked to leave. Before doing so Jean de Merveille committed his opinion of the colony to verse. This Edward Nangle chose to publish, in its original French, in the October 1849 issue of his *Missionary Herald*. In translation it reads:

Such a wild place I have never seen in my life
As the large colony, the sojourn of Saints.
There, is a village only recently built
By a man, the enemy of good wine and good cheer.
If you care for common sense and courtesy,
From the colony well away you will stay,
Better to go and sleep on the marshes,
Better still go and stay with 'Mr Le Sauvage' (The Wild One)
The colony is wild, 'Le Sauvage' is courteous,
Believe me, asylum is the foremost sadness.

A Mrs Savage (a lady remembered for her kindness) may have been the wife of 'Mr Le Sauvage' in line eight; 'the enemy of good wine and good cheer', in line four, can only have been Edward Nangle. Why did he choose to give such publicity to such an incident?

The Mission was, in many ways, an adventure in public relations. It depended, crucially, on moral and financial support given by a public in England and in Ireland. Early Victorian straight-laced morality amongst the upper and educated classes (the Mission's principal supporters) was largely illusory but its members tried hard – for the most part successfully because the press forbore to print all but a few of their indiscretions – to present a public image of unbending moral rectitude. The Colony, under Nangle's leadership, mirrored the society which supported it. As the *Missionary Herald* reported the affair it contained a clear suggestion of salacity. For Edward Nangle to cloak such an incident in a silence of his own making was to take a risk with his public which he could not afford; to report it made a virtue out of necessity. Publishing the rhyming verse in its original French obscured its meaning to some people, flattered others, and helped transfer the blame for what had happened on to the shoulders of France; the old enemy of England who could never be trusted with anything and certainly not with the reputation of a woman. To be dubbed, publicly, as 'the enemy of good wine and good cheer' was a small price to pay for the burial of an incident which was better buried. Edward Nangle was no one's fool.

In June 1855 Frances Blacker wrote that 'two gentlemen . . . just returned from the Crimea' had stayed in the Colony. One of them had been 'wounded severely by a sword cut all down his face.' A remarkable repair seems to have been effected. The wounded man – presumably an officer – had 'a silver plate across his forehead under the skin and a silver bridge to his nose!' This, as Frances commented, was 'hardly noticeable and one would only remark a trifling scar not looking at all warlike.'

Number 6 consisted of a house, office and yard in the nominal occupation of the Mission's Trustees. It is not known who lived there but it may have been John Carr, the Mission's bailiff for Achill; and, if so, it would have been also the Rent Office. (Carr was no friend of Charles. He re-appears later.)

Numbers 7 and 8 contained the printing office and the home of George Bozman, the master printer. (Mrs Bozman ran the infants school.)

The original printing machine, and founts in English, Gaelic, Greek and Hebrew had been a very early – and an *inspired* – gift to the Mission. In 1844, the Mission had bought a larger press, a stock of type, and other printing materials. Edward Nangle was a competent type-setter and printer. He took a close personal interest in his 'Achill Press' and, in consequence, it thrived. By 1836 it had produced two hymn books, a catechism and several pamphlets in Gaelic. Later it produced a number of larger books including the (now very rare) first printed bible in Gaelic. In July 1837 the first number of a monthly newspaper (dealing with the Mission's affairs) named *The Achill Missionary Herald and Western Witness* appeared.[26] Nangle was its outspoken, and often intemperate, editor. At that time newspapers were entitled to free distribution by post but, after the ninth issue, this concession was withdrawn. Withdrawal caused a towering rumpus – up to the House of Lords – the concession was restored and Edward Nangle discovered that the *Herald*'s circulation had increased from about 600 to almost 3,000 copies per month! Nangle took his own newspaper space to promote his own printing wares; his work was 'as neatly executed as in any Dublin office.' Because it did so much work free the press never appears to have made a financial profit (except, perhaps, in 1844, when it might have done so but for the misconduct of a carrier.) Nonetheless, intangible profits must have been great. The *Missionary Herald* kept the Mission's existence, progress, difficulties and needs continually in the eye of its public; and, without any great personal effort by Edward Nangle, it must have inspired numerous donations and other encouragements. It is worth sparing a thought for the administrative difficulties then involved in printing in Achill. Newsprint is heavy awkward stuff to handle. Neither it, nor finished printed work, mix satisfactorily with rain or salt water. What could be straightforward and accident-free in London and Dublin could be subjected to many frustrating difficulties in Achill.

Number 9 was the Post Office and the home of Henry M'Loughlin, the Achill Post Master. For its first nine years the Mission had been obliged to carry its own mails to and from Newport. The Tenth Annual Report of the Mission (for 1843) and a later news item suggest that the Mission had made, by the time Charles reached Achill, two separate contracts governing mail and passenger traffic to and from the island. In the first (probably) it contracted with Charles Bianconi, the Irish Coachmaster, at a charge of £80 p.a., to run a 'well appointed' return car service from the O'Donnell Arms Hotel in Newport to Achill Sound every Tuesday, Thursday and Saturday.[27] A similar service – provided, presumably, from within Achill – carried people and mail from Dugort to the Sound where, during the three-quarters of an hour allowed for the crossing, arrivals and departures swapped cars. Under what was a second contract (probably) the Post Office paid the Mission £20 p.a. for the carriage of their mails. Income from paying passengers and from the Post Office nearly equalled expenditure; Edward Nangle was confident that the growing number of tourists and Achill residents would 'ultimately' make the mail car a source of profit. (In 1852 an increase in the number of tourists made a daily car service necessary during the summer.)

In 1851, an application was made for a mail car service *within* Achill, but this was refused by the Post Office on grounds of insufficient volume. (This, in itself, in a community of 5,000 or more people, is a sharp comment on the level of literacy.)

Number 10 was used (after his posting to Skreen) by Edward Nangle; presumably he stayed there every summer with Sarah, his second wife (and, by 1859, a second family of four small children).

Number 11 was the 'Female Orphan House'. It had two gardens. When Charles first saw it it was still probably full of girls whose parents had perished in the famine. (It is believed that Edward Nangle, for this reason, took a special interest in it.)

Number 12 was occupied by the Mission offices. It may be thought of as the place where Edward Nangle did his thinking, editing and writing; and from which emanated those many ideas and 'instructions' which created the Colony Charles was to know.

Number 13 was occupied by a physician named Samuel Laird, about whom little is known except that he married Catherine Young, in St Thomas's, in May 1855.

Number 14 was occupied by Barnabas E. Quodling R.N., the inspector of Coastguards. He used Number 15 as his office. He lived, probably, with a wife (of whom nothing is known) but, certainly, with two daughters. (Both were married, in Achill, in the summer of 1855.)

It is easy, now, to forget the *crucial* part played by the coastguards in the nineteenth century in the prevention of smuggling and the saving of life. Three coastguard stations existed on Achill; one at Bullsmouth, one at Keel and one at Keem. (Charles lived, cheek by jowl, with the men who manned the Keem station.)

When Charles removed from East Anglia to Achill he exchanged one dangerous coast for another. Off Norfolk, danger came from currents and shifting sand banks; off Achill, from Atlantic gales. No one, yet, had sufficient experience of the technical difficulties involved in changing the method of ship propulsion from sail to steam. Countless unregistered, ill-manned, ill-equipped and ill-loaded ships of all sizes and descriptions put to sea thinking only of their profits. Fires at sea were common. Few 'sailors' could swim. On-board life-saving equipment did not exist. Charts were scarce but less scarce than men who could read them. Nobody had yet heard of Plimsoll's 'line'. Lighthouses were few and far between. The weather, as always round the British Isles, was *dangerously* unpredictable. Ships, usually, were insured above their value. The coasts of the United Kingdom were littered with the bones of wrecked, and then drowned, men, women and children and of what remained of their ships. It was only those few long-serving professional sailors and fishermen who knew how relentless, and how cruel, the ocean could be; that some enormous Atlantic 'sea' might exert a pressure of 6,000 tons per square foot; that, in an accident off Anglesey in 1854, the force of the sea had been such as to embed a gold ingot into ironwork 'as if the iron had been in a molten state when the gold was thrown against it.'

A reorganised coastguard service – operated by the Board of Customs in London – was created in 1822. Most of its staff – known as 'boatmen' – were recruited from the Navy after the war; all were required to be good seamen and of good character. The service was subjected to long hours of work (much of it at night) and to severe discipline intended to make smuggling and collusion between boatmen and public difficult. Round England the coastguard were required to deal principally with wrecks and smuggling; round Ireland with fewer wrecks and less smuggling but with the illegal (and so revenue reducing) production of poteen. Coastguard standing orders included these words: 'When a wreck takes place on any part of the coast under the charge of the coastguard every individual on the spot, or within reasonable distance, is to use his utmost exertion to save the lives of the persons on board and also to take charge of any vessel and to protect such property as may be saved from embezzlement of any kind.' The twin objectives – that is to save life and to preserve property – were explicit; and peremptory in the sense that, when necessity arose, they took priority over all other duties.

Wrecks, almost always, are unexpected. The arrival of the coastguards and of the local 'Receiver of Wreck' along some desolate Irish coastline could be, and often was, much delayed. Almost since the dawn of time a wreck, and its cargo, has been regarded as a gift from god by poor coastal dwellers capable of getting to it. Survivors, struggling to get ashore and save their lives, received scant attention. Somerville & Ross described an Irish wreck:

> As we stumbled down . . . someone . . . shouted, 'She's gone' . . . in that greedy pack of waves . . . she seemed the most lonely and tormented of creatures. About half an hour afterwards the cargo began to come ashore . . . Barrels were plunging and diving like a school of porpoises . . . some were big and dangerous, some were small and nimble . . . Ten men of the Royal Irish Constabulary can do a great deal . . . but they could hardly cope with a scattered and extremely active mob of four or five hundred. The people, shouting with laughter, stove in the casks, and drank rum at thirty-four degrees proof, out of their hands, out of their hats, out of their boots . . . With the drunkenness came anarchy . . . I began to know that there were men there who were not drunk and were not idle . . . and [I heard] an occasional rumble of cartwheels on the road . . . the casks which were broached were the least part of the booty . . .[28]

In the twenty years following 1854 twenty-three wrecks occurred in the Clew Bay area. The ships that perished – whether from the sea or by human fallibility – did so along a dangerous coast which lacked sufficient coastguard support. In December 1838, Francis Reynolds, an Achill coastguard officer, was murdered whilst in charge of a wrecked brig. Whether the Achill coastguards were any more effective in suppressing the illegal distillation of poteen is doubtful. The sixth Report of the Mission (dated 31st December 1839) discloses that Edward Nangle was President of the 'Achill Temperance Society.' Two meetings were held each month; one for 132 adults and the other for 166 juveniles. The latter were aged between five and fifteen. At the first juvenile meeting no fewer than sixty-three children acknowledged themselves to be familiar with the taste of 'spirituous liquor'. ('Spirituous liquor', with little doubt, was 'poteen'.)

After Waterloo, the British Government had good reason to reorganise the coastguards. Throughout the United Kingdom smuggling was not thought of as being 'a crime'; it was 'free trading.' Bribery and corruption were found everywhere; few people bothered their heads because smuggling deprived the Exchequer of legitimate revenue. Peace had thrown many 'daring professional men' on to a labour market in which wood cutting, farm labouring or unemployment offered few attractions compared to that of being an armed and prosperous smuggler. The south coast of England contained innumerable deserted inlets which offered an unlimited variety of short sea crossings to the Continent; and along which 'duty free' wines, spirits, tobacco and silk came one way whilst the best English wool went the other. It was estimated that 50%, or more, of all the spirits drunk in England had been smuggled. Of the four million gallons of gin made in a Dutch distillery the greater part was drunk, illegally, in England. France, never a tea drinking country, nonetheless imported six million pounds of tea every year most of which was 'on-smuggled' to England.

All this was reason enough for reorganising the coastguards but, in addition, the British Government continued to smart under a public humiliation imposed on it by Napoleon who used *English* smugglers for his own intelligence work during the war. In exile Napoleon disclosed that:

> They did great mischief . . . During the war all the information I received from England came through the smugglers. They are

> people who have courage and ability to do anything for money . . . I ordered Gravelines to be prepared for their reception . . . At one time there were upwards of 500 of them in Dunkirk. I had every information I wanted from them. They brought over newspapers and despatches from the spies that we had in London. They took over spies from France, landed and kept them in their houses for some days, dispersed them over the country and brought them back when wanted. They assisted the French prisoners to escape from England.

On our tour of Dugort this leaves:

The Rectory House, in which, by 1854, lived the Reverend Baker who had succeeded Edward Nangle.

The Eight Houses of Rock Lane. All were occupied in the names of six men and two women. Thomas M'Nulty in Number 1 gave evidence, in 1839, to a committee of the House of Lords on Education in Ireland; he was presumably a teacher. Nothing is known of the others; they may have been teachers (five of whom are believed to have lived rent free in mission houses), scripture readers or other senior employees, or associates, of the Mission.

Number 16. This lies at the lowest, and most easterly, end of 'The Square'. It was the house which Charles knew best during his first year on Achill. It was occupied by Murray Blacker, Frances his wife (and cousin) and their eldest, but still small, daughter Theodosia Violet (known as Violet).

By 1852, Edward Nangle had been in control of the Mission for nearly twenty years; these, instead of flowing in a quiet and continuous stream, had been interrupted – torn savagely apart – by the famine. This divided his administration into three phases. The first lasted from 1834 to 1845; eleven years of vigorous Protestant evangelism, the construction of numerous buildings and the attraction into Achill of a group of educated, intelligent, hardworking Protestant people. The second lasted from 1845 to 1849; four years during which survival, only, had significance. The third, post-famine, phase started in 1849; as far as Edward Nangle is concerned it may be said to have ended either in 1852, when he was posted to Skreen, or in 1883, when he died, so intimate was his continuing involvement with the Mission. The third phase – most of it witnessed by Charles – was an anxious one for the Mission and its founder. It saw the birth of *four* significant initiatives.

The first initiative concerned finance.

However Edward Nangle had defined his Mission's intentions towards the people of Achill it cannot have escaped his mind that, inevitably, he would be engaging himself in the more mundane matter of 'running a business'; or, to put this another way, that he intended to incur heavy, and continuous, expenditure for which a regular and dependable income of approximately the same size was necessary. As shown in note 19 on p. 308, not all of the Mission's Annual Reports can now be found but each available report contains a cash 'Income and Expenditure' account. These suggest – until the famine changed everything – that about 75% of its total cash income came from voluntary 'Subscriptions and Donations'; and that other cash income was sufficient to balance each account. ('Other income' included the *intentional* making of small, if irregular, profits on various Mission enterprises.)

Between the end of the famine and 1852 two things happened. First, 'Subscriptions and Donations' income started, *seriously*, to decline. The reasons for this were many. Before the famine, gifts from England and Ireland had been inspired by simple enthusiasm for missionary work and, from England, by loyalty to the Protestant religion. During the famine giving, from everywhere, had been inspired by simple charity. As the third, post-famine, phase of the Mission's existence struggled to its feet English enthusiasm for its work waned. Twenty years had passed since Emancipation; naked warfare between the two religions had come to seem like civil war without purpose. A new generation of English givers were emerging; charitable ideals were changing; and, *particularly* in England, countless other causes – many connected with the industrial revolution – called for sympathy and help. Ireland's political flirtation with revolutionary France in 1848 made some Englishmen angry and disinclined to help further anything in Ireland if they could avoid it. Secondly, the Encumbered Estate Court came into existence; this carried a shaft of hope, capable, perhaps, of providing escape from the threat of insolvency. The much delayed seventeenth Report of the Mission was unusual in that it was divided into two distinct parts; namely a normal annual report *and* 'A List of all Subscriptions Received for the Achill Purchase Fund.'[29] Edward Nangle had hoped that this special appeal would bring in £17,500, this being the price settled upon by the Encumbered Estate Court for the purchase of most of Achill (and some land on the mainland). In the event the appeal produced about £10,500; or enough to buy about three-fifths of the island. (In other words the Mission had failed to catch a significant part of the bus it had intended to catch. Why did the Mission even want to board such an apparently inappropriate vehicle?)

The seventeenth Report advanced, openly, two reasons. First, that the existing tenancy agreement was unsatisfactory and, secondly, that if the Protestant Mission did not buy Achill, then the – richer – Catholics would and 'the whole of our work here would be crushed.' Both reasons clearly were genuine; but, elsewhere in the same report, Edward Nangle expressed his wish 'to see the Achill Mission a self-supporting institution.' *This*, it seems, was the most important additional reason for taking the action he did; that is to say the replacement of the mission's rapidly diminishing 'Subscriptions and Donations' income by a more reliable land rental income arising from the Mission's new status as a substantial landowner. Although the Mission became the owner of much of Achill on 31st July 1852, their deeper expectations were not realised; largely because most of Achill's land was incapable of producing the rentals needed. The 1858 financial statement shows that 'Subscriptions and Donations' income had – as expected – fallen to 32% of total income and that other income had not yet been such as to render the Mission independent of further outside help. By 1864 – when Charles had been living in Achill for about ten years – matters had become *critical*; 'Subscriptions and Donations' had declined to 10% of total income. (From about this date Mission affairs went, steadily, from bad to worse.) The Society for Irish Church Missions helped but a 'serious falling away' of their own funds limited what they could do. The Land Act of 1881 led to a reduction of land rentals of between 30–40%; the Arrears Act cancelled a number of arrears of rent then due. The Land League's 'No Rent Manifesto' further damaged the Mission's financial position. In 1882 The Irish Society undertook the management of the *whole* of the Mission's missionary work but the later demoralisation of Irish society made it impossible for the Mission itself to keep its part of the bargain. Eventually, in 1915, the Achill Mission Estate was sold to the Congested Districts Board.

The second initiative concerned agriculture.

From its earliest days the Mission had put much effort into improving farming methods. Improvements, after the famine, were much needed. Originally Edward Nangle had intended to demonstrate what knowledge and hard work could achieve; and, quite quickly, the Mission's original grant of bog land round Dugort was running cattle and producing 'potatoes, oats and turnips'. The seventeenth (post-famine) Report announced the creation of a new Agricultural Training School. This was to be run by a 'qualified agriculturist' – Murray Blacker? – and worked by 100 boy pupils who 'will thus acquire such skills and habits of industry as are unknown among the peasantry of this island . . .'. Had this initiative succeeded it might have brought more long-term benefit to Achill than any other single thing which Edward Nangle attempted. Sadly, 1851 was too late; the cash required to support the school properly never became available. No more than forty-five boys ever worked the Training School farm. And, in about 1857, the project was abandoned 'for want of funds'.

The third initiative was more successful. (It formed no part of the mission itself.)

Religion and education apart, the only way of raising the standard of living in Achill was to attract in work which would bring interest and variety into people's lives and wages into their pockets. Achill possessed three marketable assets; splendid scenery, ozone laden air, and vast quantities of salt water fish. Within the limitation imposed by the difficulties of travel in the mid-nineteenth century the mission's hotel and mail car passenger service exploited the first two; the third was exploited by a Scot from Montrose named Alexander Hector who, in the mid 1850s, established an extension to his Montrose fishery business in Achill.

Hector was expert, particularly, in the matter of *ocean* salmon fisheries. He would have known of their existence round Ireland – and perhaps of the five round Achill – but how he and Edward Nangle came to hear of each other is unknown; certainly, Montrose and Achill are not close. Hector could not have reached the decision he did without more than one visit to Achill to see for himself what the island and its fisheries offered. As his new venture was to be *founded* on the canning of salmon he was bound to make sure of his supplies of salmon. The best known, and most prolific, of the five Achill ocean salmon fisheries lay in Keem Bay (below the house

The Reverend Samuel Boycott

The Reverend William ('Billie') Boycott

Burgh-St-Peter Church

Rear-Admiral Sir Charles Cunningham RN

James Blomfield Rush (murderer)

Ward Hunt

A blind ballad singer

Missionary settlement – Dugort

Village of Dooagh

Ruin of Boycott's Keem Bay house

The Reverend William Boycott (William II)

The Reverend William Boycott (William III)

Family portrait (taken in 1862). Charles front row, extreme left, Annie middle row, centre

Norwich Market in 1807

An immigrant ship – Dublin Bay

'Military manoevres'

The arrival of the Relief Column – 12 November 1880

Charles and Annie: members of the Relief Column (seen to right of door)

Boycott Expedition Medal (on reverse 'In Honour of the Loyal and Brave Ulstermen')

Lough Mask House: Annie, Madeleine, Assheton Weekes: three 'representative' soldiers

Rats! Manning asleep in Charles's Boathouse

'Cookhouse'

Charles and Somerset Maxwell

Departure from Lough Mask House – 28 November 1880

Earl of Erne

Haw Branch, USA

The Reverend William Douglass Boycott

Charles Cunningham Boycott (aged 56)

Murray Blacker

Great Yarmouth Row, No 35 (now Globe Row)

which Charles was to build); and some evidence as to how Hector came into possession of the right to take its salmon has survived.

In 1853 (as shown in the 'Valuation Book' for the area)[30] Murray Blacker became ('with others') the 'immediate lessor' of the Keem Bay salmon fishery. In due course Hector's name was entered as being its 'occupier' (or, in effect, its sub-tenant). A memorandum (in red ink) in the back of the Valuation Book suggests that Hector was not a Scot for nothing. This reads: 'I have heard this fishing is very valuable. I wrote to Mr Hector and rec'd in reply the note pinned' (alas no longer pinned) 'to this book. From the evasive manner in which he has written I could form no idea of its value but I have casually heard the rent was about £79.' Eventually £80 was entered: and this is the sum Hector paid annually to Murray Blacker as rent for the 'rights of fishing.'[31]

Salmon, turbot, lobsters, oysters, cockles and other sea fish, and game off Mission land, were all canned. Hector let it be known that he was willing to buy in carrots 'to any amount'. An unsuccessful attempt was made to produce cod liver oil, then in heavy demand for the relief of rickets[32] in industrial England. Four tinsmiths – who all, presumably, came from outside Achill – made canisters from 'tinned iron'; as many as 900 could be required in a single day. The fish was prepared and the canisters sealed by a boiling process at Keel. Subsequently they were shipped to London and other more distant overseas markets. Each canister was warranted for twenty years and bore a label printed by the Achill Press. In August 1858 – and perhaps in other years also – Hector entertained 150 Mission children to 'a delicious dinner of salmon, bread and potatoes'. At the same time Edward Nangle wrote: 'Mr Hector, since first he came to our island, has used his utmost energy and made every attempt to elevate and benefit, temporally and morally, all who have come within range of his influence.'

In August 1856 Edward Nangle had been able to hope, publicly in his *Missionary Herald*, that Hector's fishery business would be a permanent source of industry and employment. Upon one point of business Hector had always been adamant; he would employ only Scots foremen and he refused, absolutely, to place any Achill Irishman in any position of responsibility. Nevertheless, Nangle later paid tribute to the 'obliging and conciliatory manner' shown by the Scotsman towards Achill men and women, a number of whom were 'now cheerfully engaged' instead of 'pining in poverty'. Upon remote windswept Achill Hector's initial success had fallen like a gleam of sunlight seen through heavy cloud; but sadly Hector's prosperity lasted for no more than about twelve years. His Achill, and, more importantly, his Scottish fisheries depended, crucially, on the use of 'bagnets' which took far more salmon than did conventional nets. It was not long before bagnet success seriously alarmed Scottish riparian salmon fishery owners and legislation to forbid their use was passed. This, unhappily for Achill, blunted Hector's profitability; his business declined, and, eventually, it was wound up. Nonetheless Hector himself is still remembered on Achill with affection; Frances Blacker had been right when she said that he was 'a fine honest Scotchman'.

Charles and Hector first met when the fish canning business was in its first flush of success. Charles knew Hector for what he was; an independent businessman without formal connection with the Mission. Charles, himself, was in a similar position. The two, no doubt, became at least acquaintances; Hector needed, during the season, to keep an eye on his single, most prolific, source of salmon; Charles was fascinated by the regular daily summer routine which, on his doorstep, caught them. No doubt the pair of them often exchanged a salmon for a dram; their meetings enlivened by speculation as to why, through the ages, salmon swam, singly or in small shoals, so close to Keem's exquisite little beach.

The fourth initiative concerned the attraction in to Achill of a few resident gentlemen whose self-interest would keep them there; and whose initiatives, honesty, good conduct and public spirit would make Achill a better place in which to live.

Since its earliest days the Mission had depended, heavily, not only on the medical knowledge of Dr Neason Adams but also upon him as a man. Adams had been more than the St Luke of Achill; he had been its 'Good Samaritan'; loved by Catholic and Protestant; a physician who attended upon anyone and everyone; and who made no charge for the medicines he prescribed. Edward Nangle said of Adams that he had behaved himself, always, as a gentleman ought to behave and that his life had been a shining example of 'gentlemanly conduct.' In 1856 Nangle referred openly, in his *Missionary Herald*, to 'The importance of a resident gentry as a means of advancing the temporal improvements of a district'; and to this he added a postscript; 'The want of such residents is sadly felt in Achill.'

It is not difficult to see how, after the famine, this idea filtered its way into Edward Nangle's mind. He had the example of Neason Adams standing continuously before him; in 1850 he, himself, reached the age of fifty; in 1852 he had been posted away from Achill. He had, perhaps, become aware that Achill men and women needed more than education and a new religion; that what they needed were more men like Neason Adams; men who, in their own educated and cultured ways, would live amongst the people of Achill.

When in 1852 the Mission bought three-fifths of Achill it did so only because, as the Seventeenth Report makes clear, it lacked the cash to buy all of it. The Report goes on: 'in this difficulty three English gentlemen (Messrs Brassey, Holme and Pike) came forward with the sum of £7,000 for which they are to have a due proportion of the land . . . our friends were influenced by a desire to aid our Missionary work . . . and intend to give much employment to the people in reclaiming and improving their lands . . .' The lands lay along Achill Sound and were some way from Dugort. The inference seems clear; Brassey, Holme and Pike were to become 'landowning gentlemen'; and – Edward Nangle no doubt hoped – continually resident and active in Achill. In the event, and for reasons unknown, Brassey and Holme withdrew; and in 1861, William Pike bought their lands, so becoming Achill's largest resident landowner. Pike was a member of a well known Cork family of merchants and bankers; he built a good house and made a fine garden; he was hospitable; he farmed well; he brought up a family in Achill; he became a J.P. and Vice-Chairman of the Newport Board of Guardians; he had wide interests which included bird-watching. William Pike, certainly, showed himself to have many of the qualities required of a resident landowning gentleman. One satisfactory 'landowning gentleman' may not have been able to create, precisely, the leaven and leadership for which Edward Nangle had hoped; but, no doubt, one swallow was better than none.[33]

No cap quite fits Edward Nangle; the many contradictions in his character were extraordinary. Somerset Maxwell, a Mission Trustee (and of whom more later) wrote, in 1860, that he was convinced 'of the uncompromising truthfulness of his character'; but he decribed him, also, as being a 'Boanerges' of a man (by which he meant that he was a 'son of thunder' and 'a son of tumult')!

Edward Nangle's father had been a *Catholic*; his father's lax approach to the faith he held contrasted sharply with that of his two half-brothers (Edward's uncles) both of whom became Catholic priests. Edward's mother was Protestant; she – alone it is presumed – caused Edward to be baptised as a Protestant, but she died when Edward was aged nine. His father married three times; by his first wife he had five children, by his second (Edward's mother) nine, by his third, one. Edward grew up in a large, but religiously divided, family in which the majority of its surviving children, including Edward, had no living mother. He is believed to have attended four different schools. He went up to Trinity College with the intention of reading medicine but was persuaded into Holy Orders because, someone is believed to have told him, the Church offered a more socially acceptable career. As a young ordained clergyman (of the established and Protestant Church of Ireland) he held three curacies and the secretaryships of two religious bodies. While in Dublin Edward fell under the influence of several prominent Protestant evangelicals; and, when he became seriously unwell, into the care of Neason Adams and his wife who, for a time, nursed him in their own home in Dublin. Few people, knowing the mixture of soils into which Edward Nangle's fate had planted him, would have thought it likely that an untwisted sapling would emerge. That the sapling – never properly untwisted – grew on in the way it did is a tribute to the courage and determination which Edward Nangle, himself, succeeded in developing. (It is revealing that he *never* believed in Darwin's *Origin of the Species by Natural Selection*; throughout his life Edward Nangle believed that the Creator had 'created everything'.)

Edward Nangle and the Mission he founded and led cannot be separated. The famine – that 'most awful public calamity' – interrupted, perhaps fatally, what might have developed into a remarkable social achievement. He created, in the island he loved and out of nothing, a small civilisation. He tried, in his own way, to help the people of Achill. He tried, genuinely – in so far as any one individual could do so – to correct at least some of Ireland's disharmonies; these, in Achill, were exposed as in few other places.

Today Edward Nangle is remembered, only, as 'the founder of Achill's tourist trade'. It is an insufficient judgement.

CHAPTER THIRTEEN

DURING CHARLES'S YEARS IN IRELAND the Blackers were a well-known Irish Protestant family. They claimed descent from 'Blacaire', a King of Denmark who invaded Ireland about AD 900; their family crest is a Danish battle-axe. Their manor house of Carrickblacker, which stood above the River Bann in Co. Armagh, was built in 1692. Although it no longer stands, it is remembered for its elegance and for the care which successive generations of the family gave to it. Good husbandry ran strongly in Blacker blood.

The gods smiled on Charles when, as a boy in the rectory at Burgh-St-Peter, he first met the Blacker family. Three Blackers came to exert a considerable influence upon his life. William Blacker (born in 1776) became the foremost pre-famine Irish agriculturist, author, and land agent of his day; Murray Blacker, William's nephew, became Charles's life-long friend; Isabella Blacker – Murray's cousin – married Charles's elder brother Arthur.[34]

In February 1865, Sir Robert Peel, the then Irish Secretary (son of the former Prime Minister) asked, in the House of Commons, 'Who is [William] Blacker?' The question so astonished Lord Lifford that he wrote a pamphlet to which he gave the title 'Who is Blacker'. In this Lifford wrote:

> I doubt whether any Irishman, whose age is past thirty-five, and who has taken any interest in Irish landed property, is ignorant of who Mr William Blacker was. . . . Mr Blacker was an Irish gentleman, of good family and good fortune, who, for some twenty years of the first half of this century, devoted himself to the improvement, moral and physical, of the people of Ireland. His principle was, that the system of small farms was that most

> suited to Ireland, and that under it, properly carried out, a greater amount of produce could be secured than in any other way; while more than that, no other system promoted, in an equal degree, the morality and happiness of so great a number . . .

William Blacker became well known as an economist and monetarist, as an agriculturist, as a land agent, as a practical farmer and as the author of many books on agriculture in Ireland. In 1833 he won the Royal Dublin Society Gold Medal for his essay on the 'Management of Landed Property in Ireland'. Throughout his life he was convinced that the small farmer held, in his tenacious self-centred hand, the key to successful agriculture in Ireland; and that farming was the inescapable occupation of most Irishmen. His books explained what should be done; drainage, manuring and the rotation of crops were his passports to, and deliverers of, those larger yields which could be achieved (at least to some extent) on the small farms of Ireland. By *intensive* agriculture these small farmers, particularly in the north, were able to obtain heavier yields than were common even in England; that is eight to ten tons of potatoes, sixteen to eighteen hundred weight of wheat and seventeen to nineteen hundred weight of oats to the acre. By Blacker's system tenants of two and a half to five acres were able to keep cows for the first time. By the 1840s Blacker had become a much respected figure. In 1844 he was asked to give evidence to the Devon Commission on landlord and tenant relations and on currency and taxation.

As Agent to Lord Gosford's large estate in counties Armagh and Cavan – in the north of Ireland – Blacker gave farming dinners to which the tenants, and many others, were asked. These annual events resembled the Holkham 'Sheep Shearings' described in Chapter Three; like Holkham they included the giving of prizes, of talks and discussions and of demonstrations of good farming practice. A tenant at Gosford named John Bradford said of Blacker:

> When I came under Lord Gosford . . . I had no property whatever, nor meat for my family. I have now, thank God . . . through Mr Blacker plenty of provisions . . . I have two cows and a pig . . . and my land also is now in heart and produces as much in one year as it then would in three . . .

A second, Michael Clarke, had been in

> A state of despondency . . . my family in misery . . . he told me . . . that [my] place would be worth having if it got justice . . . as he was so kind I promised I would take heart again . . . Mr Blacker lent me a cow when I had got clover to feed her on . . . Now . . . the whole farm is in good heart. My health is got better . . . I am in the way of doing well . . .

Lord Gosford also owned, through his marriage, an estate in Suffolk; this lay at Worlingham to the east of Beccles and immediately across the Waveney from the Rectory at Burgh-St-Peter. No doubt William Blacker's work took him, from time to time, to Norfolk and Suffolk; it is certainly possible that he came to know the Boycott family personally; and that he met the boy who then wanted, so passionately, to go into the Army.

William Blacker died, still a bachelor, in 1850 at the age of seventy-four. His most influential years had preceded the famine. He tried, all his life, to teach the poor Irishman how to grow more food. The *Armagh Gazette*, in their obituary notice, wrote:

> Mr Blacker through a long life, maintained a character for strict integrity, philanthropy, and general usefulness seldom possessed by one individual. His many publications have for their object the improvement of the country . . . are well known; and his exertions for the advancement of modern farming both in the country at large and among the tenancy of the estate with which he was more particularly connected will be gratefully remembered by all, and there were many, who have benefited by his instruction and example.

William Blacker was not so much the Irish 'farmer's friend' as the Irish 'small farmer's friend'. Charles farmed larger acreages; but he could have found few men better than William Blacker from whom to learn his new profession.

Murray Blacker, like his uncle, was a highly intelligent man of character. He was eight years older than Charles. His father had died in India in 1823 where he had distinguished himself both as a professional soldier and as the Historian of the Maharatta Wars. His mother Emma then brought her three sons and one daughter home. Told, no doubt by his uncle, that Norfolk was the place in which to learn farming, Murray, at the age of twenty-three, bought a good house and farm of 354 acres at Toft Monks lying four miles to the west of Burgh-St-Peter. In 1851 Murray married a cousin named Frances Blacker; and, in 1855 Charles's elder brother Arthur married Frances Blacker's younger sister Isabella. The Blackers and the Boycotts became good friends.

Like his two elder brothers Murray was a strikingly handsome man whose courage leapt at two o'clock in the morning as furiously as it leapt at midday. He became a man about whom 'stories' gathered like iron filings round a magnet. By the mid 1850s he did *not* present a picture of excessive poverty! He still owned his Norfolk farm and house; he had leased 4,021 acres on Achill; he had taken for himself a fine house and a farm of 333 acres outside Claremorris on the mainland of Co. Mayo; and, in addition, he probably owned other properties. William Blacker's will cannot, now, be consulted because it was destroyed, by fire, in 1922[35]; but the probability is that both Murray and Frances (both being one of William Blacker's several nephews and nieces) each received a good inheritance from their uncle. (Later in life Murray was to become a very wealthy man; even his wife remarked that she had a high opinion of his financial abilities!)

On 31st July 1852 (under the powerful influence of the Encumbered Estates Court) a large part of Achill Island was sold by Sir Richard O'Donnell of Newport to the Protestant Mission.[36] In March 1853 the Mission leased 4,021 acres, lying at Achill's western end, to Murray Blacker; and, from about the same date, Murray started to live in No 16 'The Square'. In March 1854 Charles and Annie moved from Clonmel to Achill. A year later Murray sub-let 2,000 of his best acres to Charles for £42.10.0 p.a. The isolated lonely stage upon which Charles was to live, and farm, for nineteen years had been marked out.

It is possible, now, only to guess at why Murray rented the Mission land he did, why he was allowed to live in No 16 The Square, and why Charles should have decided to farm on Achill. At the time Murray was still a young and most enthusiastic farmer who had learnt his farming business in Norfolk; for this reason it is possible that he had been asked to oversee the Mission's Agricultural School at the same time as he, himself, farmed the Achill acres he had taken; and, if so, he became a legitimate occupant of a Mission house. Charles's reasons for deciding to live and farm on Achill may have been simple. Even today Achill is still a marvellous place. In the 1850s its remoteness, its gaunt beauty, its vast Atlantic storms were all, to a Norfolk man, something new. Charles was compelled to think of his health; the island's rich ozone-laden air may well have been, almost exactly, what his doctor had told him to find. And, some of the Keem Bay land which Murray had offered, was, by no means, bad; on the contrary some of it brought on animals, and particularly sheep, extremely well.

The first maps of Achill, to a scale of 6″ = 1 mile, were not published until 1839. These show that, before the famine, a loosely gathered group of thirty-nine Irish 'cabins' clustered about 150 yards above the beach at Keem (Charles did not see these before 1854 when, because of the famine, most had become even more derelict than they had been before it.) What the map does *not* show is that this group included one, very small, house of a character quite different from that of its thirty-eight neighbours; it had been very well constructed.[37] What Charles proceeded to do was to incorporate this small, but well built, house into his own, larger construction; and to take over an equally well constructed barn standing nearby.

The house Charles built is still dominated by a long west-facing (and incoming weather-facing) wall which contains only one small door and one small window; this, after 140 years, is still as sound as the day it was built. It is believed that the rooms facing south and the sea had 'great' – picture? – windows in them. The house had a slated roof. The outline of a carefully graded driveway which, almost from the beach, led up to the house is still – just – discernible. A small, unnaturally level, 'lawn' still stands in front of the house; this was built up, probably by Charles, using stones from the nearby and abandoned cabins. (Many stones are still visible in the lawns' lower supporting wall.) Today the three-sided yard is usually waterlogged because an old drain, which passed under the house, has become blocked. Knowing Charles it is unlikely that he would have wanted his horses far away; the doorway of one space within the building is large enough for a trap and the adjoining space could have stabled two horses. A small room at the north-east corner had a horseshoe forming a ring *deeply* embedded in a wall; its original purpose is obscure but anyone looking for it today will not find it; it was 'removed' in 1991. A barn stood nearby. This contains a well constructed arch and dressed stone. A little less than three-quarters of its ground floor was reserved for animals; a little more than one quarter contained a fireplace and could have provided accommodation for a man. An upper floor, reached by an external stair, provided storage. It was evident, to the professional architect who inspected both the house and the barn, that the quality of their construction was far superior to that of ordinary Irish 'cabins' (and superior to most of the buildings erected by the Protestant Mission; the church, only, excepted).

Whilst their house was being built Charles and Annie lived in a small 'iron' house of which Charles possessed two. Such houses were the 'mobile homes' of the age. When they moved into their new house one of their iron houses became a lock-up timber store. (Timber, on Achill, was *valuable*.)

One – intriguing – question remains. Who built the so well constructed small house and the barn?

Three, not unpersuasive, reasons suggest that it may have been William Blacker. First, while it may have been pure chance that took Murray Blacker and Charles to Achill, common sense suggests that some better reason did so; namely that, in 1850 when his uncle died, Murray either inherited, or otherwise took over, land and property in which his uncle had at least some interest.[38] Secondly, Edward Nangle tried hard to improve the islanders' essentially small-scale agriculture; whilst nothing has survived to show that William Blacker – the pre-eminent advocate of Irish small-scale farming – was ever consulted, it is likely that he was because he was the *obvious* man to consult. Thirdly the Valuation book (Book 29 – The Electoral Division of Slievemore held by the Valuation Office of Ireland) states that William Blacker was the 'Immediate Lessor' (or landlord) of 3,961 acres (later increased to 4,021 acres) lying at the western end of the island; and similarly, that he was the 'Immediate Lessor' of the Keem salmon fishery.

Persuasive as these arguments may appear thay are not conclusive. William Blacker, if he did lease the western end of Achill, can only have done so from Sir Richard O'Donnell but no formal or informal agreement can be found. Secondly, none of the (presently available) Protestant Mission's Annual Reports mention William Blacker's name. Thirdly, Valuation Books, as such, did not start in Ireland until about 1850; these present an ongoing picture of land ownership but not dates of change. As William Blacker died in 1850, a mistake about two men, both named Blacker – one a long established public figure and the other young and unknown – is certainly possible.

In June 1855 Frances Blacker went to Keem; she told her mother-in-law that the young Boycotts 'seem very happy together and extremely fond of each other . . . they live pretty comfortably.' Nonetheless comfort is relative. Charles was to admit, later and publicly, that his early years in Achill had been hard. The island, in 1855, was without roads; nothing remotely resembling a corner shop at which they could buy anything existed closer than the rough and ready Mission shop ten miles away at Dugort. They had to find their own food, cook it, and keep warm. There was no one nearby of their own sort from whom they might borrow anything or with whom they might become friendly. Nonetheless no more than a few tears may be shed for them! It was Spring. They were both aged twenty-three. They were in love. Waking each morning they 'cleaned their eyes' on the view which lay before them. On a spring morning Keem is exquisite. A place so lovely that angels – God's Messengers – 'fold their wings and rest' was written, first about Killarney, but their author, perhaps, had never seen Keem; that sparkling lovely little spot 'where the amethysts are gathered.' Sea, sky, mountains and islands stood before them composed as by the hand of a master of theatre whose only overseer was the weather. Within minutes what had been as sharp as any diamond could soften into mist and, as quickly, disappear under tearing storm-tossed cloud and furious driving rain. Their thoughts, as they gazed seaward, were Byron's:

> . . .
> There is a rapture on the lonely shore,
> There is society where none intrudes;
> By the deep sea and music in its roar
> . . .

Anyone with a knowledge of Achill is agreed, always, upon one thing; they never felt better in themselves than when living there. Achill's pungent ozone-laden air is, indeed, the 'elixir of life'. Charles – almost certainly – went there for his health; someone had given him excellent advice.

In Charles's early days at Keem his work as a farmer, the walking and learning of his new, mountainous – and boggy – acres, the suppression of vermin and the growing and otherwise procuring of food to support at least two people were inter-twined aspects of the same necessity; that is to establish himself, not only in a new profession, but in a new environment. Much of Charles's Keem Bay land was *steep*; the seaward parts of it so precipitous as to be extremely dangerous. Charles was often accompanied by Annie; one false step by either of them in darkness, dense cloud or in fog might bring destruction. In addition, Clew Bay (of which Achill forms the northern flank) contains deep water and lies partly open to the Atlantic; regular local tragedies had brought a most healthy respect for the sea among the people of Achill.

The farming operation at Keem was tailored by Charles to suit himself. It was neither heavily capitalised nor labour intensive. Achill's high rainfall and mild winters combine with the land of Keem Bay to produce *excellent* grass. An Achill rating officer, in 1853, judged Charles's land to be 'one of the best mountains in the parish of Achill for sheep and black cattle.' Charles reared both. In bringing on black cattle he was being no more than a typical Norfolk farmer; for many years the Scots had driven their 'large, thick, short-legged animals, usually hornless and of a black or brindled colour' to Norfolk where they were fattened before being driven on to the London meat market.

Charles's first ten years on Achill proved to be a fine time for farming throughout the United Kingdom. Repeal of the Corn Laws brought commercial prosperity; for a few years the Crimean War pushed up food prices. The population of the United Kingdom – except in Ireland – continued to grow. As always Ireland sent much food to England; the price of butter and wool, in Dublin, rose by 50% between 1850 and 1865; beef from 42/-d to 60/6d per cwt; mutton from 4 1/2d to 8d per pound.

Some of Charles's and Annie's own food came off the farm. As early as June 1855 Frances Blacker wrote that 'They have a servant and always mutton[39] and beer'. Charles, no doubt, kept a cow which required milking; Annie, no doubt, learnt to bake bread. Charles combined business with pleasure when he walked his rocky, boggy and heathery high mountain acres with a gun which might destroy an eagle – which 'abounded' on Achill – or a fox, before, moments later, getting him a hare, a woodcock, or a grouse.[40] Every so often he stalked a tender young goat from among the three or four semi-wild herds of goats which roamed his land. The trout in Lough Corrymore seldom grew bigger than ten inches but were good eating. The sea, close inshore, was *full* of fish. Lobsters were abundant. Clew Bay had oyster beds. The islanders had a saying 'when horse is weak, crab is fat'; crabs were good in the spring. Limpets, mussels, cockles, winkles and cranagh[41] (an edible seaweed) were to be found along the shoreline. Porpoises could be driven ashore and killed; in the Gaelic they were known as 'muckmurroughs', or sea pigs, because of their fattiness. Charles grew in Irish 'lazy beds'[42] above his house (the outlines of which are still, just, visible) his own potatoes and other vegetables. The potato blight came and went; some years – including Charles's first year at Keem – produced splendid crops of potatoes but others did not. Charles must have kept chickens because Frances Blacker wrote that 'pancakes is Mrs Boycott's only accomplishment in the sweet line!' Charles had an account (certainly from 1861 to 1874) with a merchant named Mulloy in Westport. From there he bought in farming necessities such as nails, pickaxe handles, chisels, scythes, putty and rope; and 'luxuries' such as candied lemon, a meerschaum pipe, sugar, mustard, coffee and Worcester Sauce for Annie and himself. Last – but certainly not least – were the amethysts! These could not be eaten but they could be collected from a little mine below Charles's house and then pored over and matched; and the one with the deepest colour put on the mantelpiece.[43]

It was a Robinson Crusoe life; food on Monday, short commons on Tuesday, a lovely – or a wretched – surprise on Saturday. Annie had been about thirteen when the famine started and seventeen when it ended; she had seen enough empty aching Irish stomachs to last her a lifetime. Throughout their lives together Annie was always at hand to remind Charles of what hunger – desperate, *hopeless* hunger – really meant.

During 1855 Frances Blacker (living in No 16 'The Square') wrote a number of still surviving letters to Emma, her mother-in-law, then staying in Brussels with her second son Julius. Emma was a vivacious, talented woman; Frances, evidently, on excellent terms with her. Violet – Frances's daughter, then aged two – comes under continuous notice but the letters are otherwise interesting for three reasons. First because Emma herself had already stayed in No 16; she knew the Colony. Secondly because both women knew the Boycott family in Burgh-St-Peter. Thirdly because both knew of the impending marriage between Charles's elder brother and Frances's younger sister Isabella.

Emma, herself, had been an exhibitor in a Colony exhibition of painting; Violet remarked that her grandmother 'draw beautiful'; Violet sent Emma 'twenty kisses and a hundred'. Violet had her second birthday and the Colony school was given a half holiday; there must have been a baker somewhere because Violet got a 'grand cake' from him. Although backward in one respect Violet's tongue 'is very forward'. Emma and the old Doctor living in No 1, it seems, had taken a liking to each other; he 'looked venerable in his white beard' and, later, made 'many enquiries about her'. Frances had a living in housemaid-cum-nursemaid named Kitty who 'does nothing but work' and who, apparently, wore shoes only on Sundays. (Frances wrote, also, of another household where the 'mistress was very disrespectful in manner' toward a servant who 'often told her so'.) Frances did some entertaining even though she found herself – in her small colony house – 'very short of plates and dishes.' She gave lunch to a visiting Bishop and 'the Boycotts sleep here that night.' William Pike (of whom more later) and his wife went to lunch and were given 'a beautiful salmon' taken out of the Keem Bay water at seven the evening before and new Keem Bay potatoes. In mid-July – probably on a night of full moon – Murray and Charles gave a picnic party at Keem. Murray took cake, pies and pastry from Dugort and Keem produced the usual salmon and new potatoes. 'The Pike party, who were the earliest departures, were not home till one o'clock in the morning so I [Frances] was very glad I had not gone . . . it is such a long shaky drive.' In the same letter Frances told Emma 'I cannot stand exercise.' Nevertheless, a few weeks earlier, Frances had – somehow – got herself to Keem where 'she made a mutton pie and a rice pudding one evening and a jam roll another.' Frances gave Annie some pudding recipes which she thought would please 'Charley.'

(This, probably, explains why Murray took 'pies and pastry' for the picnic!) On one occasion Frances ran into trouble with the time: 'My chronometer is broken, Murray has . . . my watch, the clock does not go, except when he is here, we are without time whatever . . . I may be . . . sometimes dining at eleven o'clock.'

Frances herself was much taken up by the prospect of her younger sister's marriage to a man she had not yet met. Arthur William – Willie – was aged twenty-five and still a curate. He managed a few days in Achill with Charles before his wedding and Frances's anxieties were laid to rest; she told Emma that she 'liked what she saw of him', that 'his manner and appearance were pleasing' and, perhaps with an eye to her sister's main chance, that his 'pecuniary prospects were better than expected.' The marriage took place in Kilcullen Church twenty-five miles south-west of Dublin on 2nd August 1855. Probably because of the difficulty of travelling only sixteen people attended; these included no one from either Achill or Burgh-St-Peter. Charles's father undertook to furnish a house for the couple and Charles's mother to provide all its linen; as Frances remarked, 'two nice wedding presents.' Isabella went away dressed in 'lavender silk, white crepe shawl and fancy straw bonnet trimmed with green feathers and silk lace.' They went, for one week only, to Killarney which was the place once described as being '. . . so lovely that angels fold their wings and rest.' Their return to England had two small tailpieces. They had to move house in a hurry and 'Mrs Boycott sent an old servant for a few days before them to prepare, and supplied them with ham, a piece of beef, a pair of fowl and some potted veal.' The second may have made Charles frown when he heard of it: Isabella met, stayed with, and liked a still young, newly remarried but one-armed Mrs Beevor (that is the Sophia who had been the pregnant and wounded widow of the murdered Isaac Jermy Jermy and his son).

Isabella, the bride to be, went visiting in Co. Cork where she saw a garden belonging to a poor curate: '. . . such a garden! 500 kinds of roses and a great number of each sort . . . a glorious sight'. The Curate's rose garden in Co. Cork was a far cry from Achill where, according to Frances, 'we are in danger of forgetting the existence of fruit and flowers.' Neither Frances nor the old Doctor's wife much cared for a doctor named Sayard. Sayard had married, and removed with his Dublin-born bride to Donegal, compared to which, the bride reported – and Frances re-reported – 'Achill was a Paradise. Nothing is to be got but by sending a special messenger thirty miles, two posts in the week, meat scarcely ever to be had at all and rarely eatable. Vegetables and fruit unheard of – not a house between them and the Rectory five miles off – so everything must be judged by comparison and one need not grumble after that.' Frances ended by remarking that Donegal must have been, for the bride, a great change from Dublin and she hoped 'Sayard atones for it all'; but Mrs Adams said, plainly, that 'the compensation is very inadequate'.

No one on Achill is ever far away from the weather. At the end of August 1855 Frances wrote

> of the escape we had yest'y of being washed away. About 9 o'clock in the morning there was a shower of rain, the heaviest I ever saw, the mountain was a mass of torrents . . . there was a river coming in from the road and roaring about the yard. A passage out was soon opened . . . but bye & bye there came such a flood opposite the front door that M [Murray] went out to look about a little. The whole Colony was collected opposite the orphan home which was quite under water even the upper rooms flooded the poor girls beds floating about & the large yard between it & the Dr's house was 8 to 9 ft deep. The water rushed in through the Doctor's gable filled his house into Mr Quodling's yard, right through their house and came out in waves at the hall door . . . In a minute our yard and stable were a couple of feet under water . . . you could hear the water under [our] floor . . . The poor Miss Quodlings were up to their knees in their sitting room trying [to] save the furniture.
>
> The old Capt[44] thought of nothing but his pet cat wh was carried out [by] the current down the road quite to the sands. He waded down after it & succeeded after 3 hours search in finding it half drowned. Baby [Violet] was nearly as wise; her difficulty was whether it would be better to cover the garden with Kitty's shawl or save the shawl & let the potatoes get wet! . . . it was a great excitement!

On 7th September 1855 Frances wrote her last letter from No 16. Violet had been naughty whilst her parents were busy packing for Claremorris and the mainland. She hid their 'nails hammer and other necessaries' and though she always protests 'won't do it again' it generally ends in her being sent off under a cloud. But – relief was at hand! In her first letter from the mainland Frances told her mother-in-law, 'I am very glad [Murray] need not go to Achill now Mr Boycott is finishing our packing.'

A traveller in 1839 described an Achill village as being a 'congeries of hovels thrown indiscriminately together as if they fell in a shower from the sky'; another asked himself, if he had been dropped in from the sky, whether he could have found his way out; a third likened the higgledy-piggledy collection of cabins to Kaffir Kraals. All three were apt descriptions of Keel, over which hung – in Alexander Hector's years and despite the 'ozone laden air' – a revolting stench of bad fish and seaweed. Dooagh was much the same except that it was divided into three parts; two of these lay on the high water mark but the third – named Tonregee – stood a little way inland along a stream. Keel was said to have a 'spa well'; and so, presumably, obtained its water from a central source. The huddling together was a reaction to poverty and the Irishman's liking for conversation and neighbourliness. The positioning of houses so close to the beach was another reaction to poverty and reflected the chance of finding food along the shore, driftwood as the sea might bring it in, and – occasionally – to the near miracle of an easily accessible wreck.

To construct anything in Achill – without the command of wider outside resources which money, only, could procure – was next-door to impossible. Stones, undressed and shaped anyhow, were the only material in easy supply. Rye straw for thatching could be saved but a baulk of sound timber to support a thatch had much the same value as a bar of gold; Achill *was* treeless. Whatever roof was constructed was held down by long plaited straw ropes from which stones were suspended. Walls were thick and filled with sea sand which, if it could be retained, kept out draughts. (The roofs were so contrived that rainwater fell into the sand, so consolidating it.) Even so people could, all too easily, find themselves in 'as much of a sop' inside a house as they would have been outside it; and, as an Irishman put it, 'a wild duck would take the rheumatism.' The cabin door was shut at night. The gaps round it, combined with other ways through the walls, usually coped with the smoke from a low night fire; but, even if it did not, it was warm and infinitely preferable to any quantity of cold night air. Warmth – from the turf fire which *never* went out – was vital to existence; the intake of food was too low for it to be otherwise.[45] Visitors to Ireland in the 1840s recalled how each new inmate to a workhouse was compelled to take a bath before putting on new clothes. The bath was looked upon as being an intolerable evil; the experience of washing the body likened to parting with a suit of clothes. The workhouse master insisted upon open windows and fresh air at night but an unhappy inmate declared that 'his open windows perished him wid the could': and 'no wonder we'd have a dread of it.'

It may be surprising to learn that an old Achill village still stands; not, in this case, as 'a congeries' like Keel, but in an unusual linear formation. According to the 1839 six inches to one mile Ordnance Survey map, and confirmed by what can be seen today, the village of Slievemore (or 'Big Mountain') then contained about 120 cabins. It is not known when it was built but it was abandoned during the famine. The inhabitants obtained their water, probably, from five tiny Slievemore rivulets which cross the contour line at intervals; 'water', probably, explains Slievemore's linear construction. Two graveyards – one old and over-full – stand side by side about its centre; Achill names – Lavelle, Burke, Kilcoyne, Patten, McHugh, O'Malley, Gallacher, McNamara – recur constantly.

Today the stones of the ancient cabins, picked clean by a century and a half of wind and rain, stand as silent sentries to a condition of life which is no more. The cabins are small. Their paths today are trodden only by sheep. Dung heaps no longer obstruct the narrow doorways. The lazy beds on which the people grew their potatoes are still – just – visible. The difficulty of making any sort of corner to a house using randomly shaped stones is evident. As an old Achill proverb puts it; 'Water is a thin man; it can come in by the smallest crack.' What a job it must have been to build a roof capable of keeping out Achill's torrential rains and ferocious storms! Slievemore, today, is a place in which to sit down and be quiet. Ghosts steal up and take your hands. Its southern prospect – Keel Lough, a curving strand of the whitest sand with the sea beyond it, the black forbidding heights of Minaun – is magnificent. It is not difficult to share so lovely a view with those long dead men and women and their pleading children who were driven out of their homes for that most elemental of all reasons: hunger.

In an undated (but written in 1855) letter Frances Blacker

remarked that Charles looked 'ill'; and, perhaps because he had grown a beard,[46] that she 'did not recognise him.' In October of that year she wrote, also, that Charles had come close to losing his life in a fishing accident. 'He and two men had been out herring fishing and just as they reached the shore . . . a breaker upset the curragh.[47] The two men jumped out but he was not on the look out and the boat turned over him . . . he was nearly suffocated his mouth and nostrils were full of sand and by the time the men could get the boat up he was quite insensible . . . A . . . few minutes revived him however but he says he has been very much upset ever since, so nervous he cannot sleep, but constantly starts up with a sensation of choking . . . it was . . . enough to shake a stronger man than he is.'

Frances's phrase 'a stronger man than he is' suggests that she had a clear understanding that Charles's health was not as good as it might have been. The after-effects of the accident – extreme nervousness and an inability to sleep – are not those of a normal young man in robust good health. It is difficult to resist the conclusion that, during the autumn of 1855, Charles suffered a relapse of his rheumatic fever; brought on by the accident, the strains of house building and by the necessity of living, in extreme discomfort, in a very small iron house. Breathlessness, arising from damaged heart muscle, is a symptom of rheumatic fever; it is not surprising, if his 'mouth and nostrils became full of sand', that he became 'quite insensible.'

Paul Henry lived and painted on Achill for several years after the First World War. His book (*An Irish Portrait,* published in 1951) refers twice to Charles. His first reference was short, '. . . I often thought I would have liked the man himself for having chosen such a wild place and so beautiful for his home.' His second 'story' about Charles was longer; it can only have been 'hearsay' but it has a ring of truth about it:

> Brian [O'Malley] was a sort of under-bailiff to Captain Boycott. Now Boycott could not bear to see people spitting, and he ordered every man on the estate who was seen to spit to pay a fine and rigorously enforced this. One day the Captain was shooting with Brian as his ghillie and Brian was caught in the act. The shooting

> had not been good and Boycott was in a bad temper and he gave Brian a good dressing-down. He then handed him a couple of brace of birds and told him to take them to Westport House, twenty-five miles away, and to 'Go at once.' Boycott could be a hard and exacting master and orders were orders so Brian saddled his horse and rode away, . . . his heart was sore . . . because the Captain had been so brusque and what was even worse had, contrary to custom, omitted to offer him any refreshment for the journey. And so into Westport where he delivered the birds at Lord Sligo's, and giving a feed of oats to his horse, strode into the hotel, took a room, ordered a meal, the best he could get, with plenty of drink, and told the ostler, whom he knew well, that the account was 'on the Captain.' To the credit of the Captain the bill was paid without a word. They were quits. Brian often repeated this story to me with a chuckle; he bore the Captain no grudge and the Captain bore no grudge to him.

In the early autumn of 1867 (probably) Charles and Annie suffered the miserable experience of having the house they had worked so hard to build at Keem destroyed by fire.

Staying with Charles and Annie at the time were William and Frances Day from Sussex, and their daughter Agnes who had been born in 1858. Agnes, all her life, remembered two things about the fire; first, that she had been carried out of the house and, secondly, that the fire had probably started in a grate on to which too many turves had been thrown. Memories of that kind suggest that she was then aged between six and nine; and, therefore, that the fire occurred between 1864 and 1867 (and, probably, during the warmer months of the year as it is unlikely that the Days would have taken a child to Achill in the winter). In 1987 the present author was told, with an apparent certainty of knowledge by a retired Achill cobbler, that Charles lived in his second Achill house for seven years. The cobbler's evidence, taken in conjunction with a later legal agreement (which caused Charles to leave Achill in 1874) combine to place the fire to a date in 1867 in which year Agnes would have been rising nine. Meteorological records show that the weather during the last days of August and the first half of September 1867 was wet and windy. If, as is quite possible, the Days' visit coincided with this, not untypical, late summer Irish weather, it is possible that someone – to keep the Day family warm? – overstoked a grate; and this being so, that the fire occurred between the end of August and the middle of September 1867.[48]

Fighting a fire which had taken hold was, in Achill in 1867, an almost hopeless endeavour; to draw, with difficulty and perhaps in darkness, a few buckets of water from the tiny stream was equally hopeless. After making sure that his guests and his wife were safe Charles would have rushed to release those of his animals unable to save themselves. That done, and having carried out what furniture and possessions – including an Irish linen bag full of amethysts? – Charles could do nothing except put his arm round Annie's shoulders and, with her, watch the fire burn itself out. So far as is known no attempt to repair the house was made. Neither Charles nor Annie had parents or brothers or sisters at hand to whom they could turn. But a way out of their predicament seems to have been standing ready; Charles and Annie may have had no relatives to whom they could turn but they did have one good and trusted friend.

When Murray Blacker sublet 2,000 of his Achill acres to Charles he kept the remaining 2,021 acres. Most of this was hard going; rocky, boggy, heather-covered barren land inhabited by eagles and by wild goats, by hares and by grouse, and by wild fowl on, and fresh water fish in, two distant loughs; but land which gave Murray the chance of enjoying the rights to the 'fishing, shooting, hunting and sporting', which he had acquired. The consequence seems clear; Murray could not enjoy what he had retained without a house of his own nearby. 'Corrymore' was built by Murray – it is believed – in 1856.

Over the years 'Corrymore' has been much added to, and much altered by, a succession of owners. The original house into which Charles and Annie moved is now the back of a much larger building having an inner courtyard. A feeling of 'romance' – extravagant fiction – still possesses people as they look up to it from far below and as they gaze out from it over Clare Island and the serenity of Clew Bay. 'Corrymore', for many years, has been a hotel. For a period after the First World War it became a celebrated one; celebrated, it is said, because of the excellence of its cook and because of its autocratic owner – a Major Dermot Freyer – who charged his guests as little, or as much, as he liked, or disliked, them.

In the mid-1870s a large notice board on the road below

Corrymore pointed upward to the hotel which was described as being once 'The Residence of the infamous Captain Boycott'. To the present author's question 'Why infamous?' the answer given was 'Well, he was, wasn't he?'

The author of an 1895 article in *Blackwoods Magazine* remembered he had met, in Achill, an old man who – chuckling as he spoke – recalled that Charles had 'got the better of the lawyers when giving evidence.' Charles's mathematical mind was first cousin to a legal mind; he admired precision and clear thinking. Charles, later, became a J.P. but not before he had himself undergone two, somewhat painful, brushes with the law as it was then conducted in Ireland. Both occurred on Achill Island when he was still a young man.

As, in 1855, Charles settled himself into Keem the earlier Protestant influence in Achill was waning; that of the Catholics was *waxing*. It was a good moment for the Catholics to try out, on a Protestant newcomer, what a little harassment might achieve. To this end a man named Clarke walked, on two occasions, from Bunnacurry – a Catholic stronghold in the east – to Keem for no reason better, it seems, than to pick a quarrel with Charles. On the second occasion Charles had Clarke removed from his house, whereupon Clarke sued for assault. A *Catholic* barrister then dismissed the case because no more violence had been used than was necessary. Clarke – financed, almost certainly, by the Catholic Church – appealed. The appeal was heard by a Mr Justice Keogh who, in the words of the Achill *Missionary Herald* (still, needless to say, staunchly Protestant), 'failed not to gratify the hitherto defeated wishes of the Popish party; and who, with a very hurried hearing of the defendant's case, reversed the [earlier] decision imposing on Mr Boycott a fine of £10 with costs.'

The second case was more substantial; it was entered as Boycott v. Carr and was heard during the Mayo Spring Assizes of 1860.

In early January 1860 a vessel named the *Neptune* was wrecked in Clew Bay. On 11th January John Carr, Bailiff to the Mission, claimed, in writing, that Charles had misappropriated to his own use some of the *Neptune*'s timber; Charles, as plaintiff, asserted that this amounted to 'a gross and malicious libel' and claimed £500 in damages. The trial took place, before a Judge and Jury, over a Thursday, Friday and Monday. It was reported, at some length, in two local newspapers but both reports appear to be 'selective' and garbled. An apparently unusual feature of the case was that Henry Lynch, the Jury Foreman, published his own comments on the trial. These included remarks to the effect that:

(a) The defendant (Carr's) own witnesses prejudiced his case. (Lynch referred to the 'very strong charge of the judge in favour of the plaintiff'.)

(b) The allegation that nine of the jury were for finding for Carr was incorrect; and that it was equally incorrect to say 'that those who were in favour of the plaintiff assigned no reasons for the view they took.'

(c) 'That . . . the insinuation that some of the jury were improperly influenced on behalf of the plaintiff between Saturday and Monday is grossly untrue.'

Lynch also wrote: 'The jury were unanimously of the opinion that the statements contained in Mr Carr's letter (in so far as they affected Mr Boycott) were false; but they did not agree in thinking it written with a malicious intention to injure Mr Boycott.'

(Doubt, now, surrounds John Carr's position within a rapidly declining Protestant Mission. The likelihood is that, officially and intellectually, he was still its bailiff but that, increasingly, he found himself doing an Agent's work. A letter from Somerset Maxwell [of whom more later] dated 14th June 1866 to another mission Trustee throws light on John Carr as a man: '. . . we do not stand clear to our conscience in being *only* known . . . to our tenants through the medium of a man in the position of life of Mr Carr'; long connection with property had taught him 'never to depend upon a bailiff or under-agent with a tenantry however trustworthy [he] . . . might be.')

Regrettably, 'the law', as it was administered in nineteenth-century Ireland, was not 'the law' as it was administered in England. W.E.H. Lecky – the distinguished nineteenth-century commentator and a man having a considerable knowledge of Ireland – discussed the differences between Irish and English law in Vol. II of his 'Leaders of Public Opinion in Ireland':

> In England, with the rarest exceptions, public opinion in all classes is on the side of the law, . . . In Ireland things are different . . .. The frequent impossibility of obtaining convictions . . . the extreme

> difficulty of obtaining evidence even when crimes are committed in open daylight and to the knowledge of numbers; the numerous cases of the murder of witnesses, . . . the great sums which Governments have been compelled to pay in order to transport honest witnesses or their families beyond the range of popular vengeance; are all signs of a diseased community in which the normal methods of administering justice often fail to work. It had, in consequence, been found necessary to combat crime by far more stringent measures than would be required in England. Suspensions of the Habeas Corpus Act, Insurrection Acts of great severity, frequent changes of venue, and the careful selection of Jurymen have all been necessary. Not only counsel but even judges, have constantly adopted a tone, in enforcing the guilt of criminals upon juries, which would hardly have been tolerated in England . . . Even in ordinary cases the Irish witness, with his cunning, his dexterity of fence, his dislike of simple and straightforward answers, his picturesque, diffuse, evasive phraseology, often gives an Irish trial an appearance which is very different to an English eye . . .

Distinguished as was Lecky the above extract from his writings does not go to the heart of the historical differences which separated English from Irish 'justice'. The essential difference was one of *acceptance*; no system of law can be effective if is not accepted by the people it controls. For many years England has accepted – and greatly prospered under – the precision of Roman law; for almost as long the Irish have never done so completely. Not all, but most, nineteenth-century Irishmen were Celts; as such they knew – dimly and *most* imperfectly – that, many years earlier, their forebears had lived under an ancient Brehon law. This was less precise than Roman Law. Vague memories of an ancient Brehon law is *not* to say that the nineteenth-century Irish either fully understood, or were always guided by, Brehon Law; murder, or the pursuit of witnesses for improper reasons, are crimes or offences under any system of law. But it does, perhaps, explain why English – or Roman – perceptions of a 'just verdict' were not always found acceptable in Ireland. The Irish were not so much a 'diseased' community as a different community; whose Celtic – and sometimes ill disciplined – blood was not Anglo-Saxon blood.

Two brushes with the law, as it was conducted in Ireland, were more than enough for Charles. As far as is known he never again 'sought justice' in an Irish Court.

* * *

Early in his years on Achill – and following a family tradition – Charles had been appointed a Poor Law Guardian. He became a Justice of the Peace for Co. Mayo in 1867. As a Justice he considered extending the railway to Achill; he approved the repair of three miles of road between Newport and Achill Sound; he pondered the difficulties which still afflicted so many of his poorer neighbours.

Keem Bay lies almost at the western extremity of the long, and mostly mountainous, south-facing flank of Achill. Those who lived further east, in its two coastal villages of Dooagh and Keel, looked out upon Clew Bay having, it is said, one small island for every day of the year; upon Clare Island; and over the bay to Westport and the lovely cone of Croagh Patrick, which is Ireland's 'sacred mountain'. Beyond Keel stretch two miles of hard white sand upon which Charles regularly exercised his horses. As he rode home again, along the rough, mountainous and overhanging-the-sea path which then connected Dooagh with Keem he usually stopped and enjoyed the view from a curious stone 'chair' which is still to be seen and is still known as 'Boycott's Seat'. Circumstances, occasionally, compelled him to make this dangerous journey after dark; but this does no more than emphasise that Charles was *always* the master of both himself and his horses. A.H. Knapp, about 1890, described the view from 'Boycott's Seat':

> Mighty Croaghan heavenward towering,
> From the bay of Keem below;
> Rears its crest with heather flowering
> Neath the western sunbeam's glow.
> Here its riverside exposing
> Beds of amethystine ore;
> There its mountain path disclosing
> Boycott seat and Corrymore.

So far as is known Charles never described himself as being a 'Captain'.[49]

The 'rank' came to him, probably, as an epithet and by degrees. In the first place it cannot have taken his new neighbours on

Achill long to learn that he had held a commission in the British Army. Many nineteenth-century Irishman, at heart, were would-be soldiers; many knew and admired the British Army; many loved military ranks and titles. For an Irishman to have referred to Charles as being an 'Ensign' would have been thought stupid and discourteous but to call a man who had served The Queen – however briefly! – a 'Captain'[50] was to give him a ringing title; it was polite; it was also to recognise qualities of background and education which, in a poor society, needed recognition. The *New York Times* (in April 1881) remarked that Charles won his 'familiar title of "Captain" by reason of his joviality and daring in sporting'. Feeling unwell – with his heart misbehaving – Charles could be silent and scarcely 'jovial'; but feeling fit with a gun, a rod or a horse in hand he could be – as the Spy portrait of him suggests – most good humoured and 'jovial'. The individuality and richness of a personality now dead are beyond precise reach but stories about him are not; the things which were his, the things he handled, link us all into the web of time. Charles loved children and they him but driving a trap down a steep hill in Achill he found he had beside him a frightened boy who wanted to get off; Charles drew the gun he almost always carried and said, in mock anger, 'I'll shoot you if you do!' His Irish cudgel – his shillelagh – has survived; it bears two, carefully incised, notches![51] He is believed – in his younger days – to have driven in the small hours furiously round Beccles with some cousins, everyone being dressed in white sheets and sounding off, loudly, on their hunting horns. What, probably, were the last pair of racing boots he ever owned are now in Taunton Museum; he gave them to a young man about to ride his first point to point.

The last reason out of which Charles's 'captaincy' may have grown came, probably, from the needs of his poor Achill neighbours. Edward Nangle had woken Achill from a *profound* sleep; with his Mission had come schools, religious warring, well-dressed tourists who poked about but who seldom spoke Gaelic, new ideas by the score, and even the chance of a paid job; to these heady innovations had been added the twin evils of famine and a surge in emigration. Comfort and help, advice and reassurance, a talk with 'a captain' who knew the outside world and the Protestant religion as it was conducted in calmer surroundings, were all, suddenly, required.

Charles brought into continuous residence a superior grasp of affairs; he stood, as a man of honour, where – or so it is believed – few gentlemen, in any continuous way, had stood before. He had been well educated. He came from a cultured family. He had common sense. It is recalled that, on Achill, he was as tolerant to Catholics as he was to Protestants. He knew the world outside Achill. A boy's 'boldness of character' had become a man's self confidence and courage. He was owner of the best social lubricant known to Irishmen: he loved horses and he rode them well. His Gaelic improved steadily; as the Reverend Daniel Dewer had written forty years earlier, '. . . he who will talk to them in the tongue of their fathers, which they regard as sacred . . . will be considered as their countryman and friend'. Charles brought with him, also, a family familiarity with the sort of 'captaining' which his poor neighbours needed; if the 'cure of souls' had been the first concern of his great-grandfather and grandfather and was the first concern of his father, then helping parishioners through their worldly anxieties had been, and was, the second. (In England the clergy of the established Protestant church accepted this commitment as being part of their ministry. Most did what was required of them quietly and without fuss; helped by the fact that almost all were gentlemen who, as such, had an easy access to those others best able to help.)

But, as Charles soon discovered, being a parish clergyman and a 'captain' in England, and being 'A Captain' in Ireland was not, always, the same thing. Sir Robert Peel said in 1828, 'There is no appetite for truth in Ireland.' In 1844 he said, 'There are many parties in Ireland who desire to have a grievance and prefer the grievance to the remedy.' A tendency to exaggerate, to flatter, to 'talk the blarney' – to mean one thing whilst saying another – to be evasive, characterised at least some nineteenth-century Irishmen. Charles, by his character, was almost exactly the opposite. He possessed a sharp perception of the difference between right and wrong, and, conveyed to him by the Irish themselves, a passion for what he called 'fair play'. He was bound, also, to listen to what his Irish wife had to say. She, no doubt, would have had a quick sympathy with genuine difficulty or with real distress; but, out of loyalty to her husband, a sharp tongue for any of her fellow countrymen's 'economies' with the truth. When Charles became angry with the grievances for which there was no real wish to find a remedy and the suggestions which originated, only, from an ulterior motive, she calmed him. But, as she calmed him, she taught him to tolerate – and more importantly to understand – the quirks and flourishes, the flatteries and the evasions, of Irish conversation and of Irish character. Annie, in a matriarchally-inclined society, found herself able to oil wheels which Charles may have had difficulty in oiling.

CHAPTER FOURTEEN

IN OCTOBER 1855 FRANCES BLACKER had written to her mother-in-law that Charles, with two companions, had been out herring fishing. This was eight years, almost to the day, since James Hack Tuke – the well-known Yorkshire Quaker – had seen, off Achill and during the famine, 'the bays . . . literally filled with shoals of mackerel and herring . . . the surface of the sea . . . alive with them'. If, wisely, Charles had gone out to reap from an abundance it is a matter of astonishment that, almost certainly, his companions did not share his enthusiasm. Why was it that James Hack Tuke had been forced to add, 'Around me stood groups of hungry creatures who looked down upon this inexhaustible supply of food wholly unable to procure it to allay their cravings'?

Mrs Woodham-Smith, in her well-known study of starvation (for lack of potatoes) in mid-nineteenth-century Ireland, posed her doubts concerning Irishmen and their fish in these few words: 'It is difficult at first to understand why the Irish people, thousands of whom live near the coast, did not eat fish. They were starving . . . yet fish abounded . . ..' To answer the – astonishing – question 'why did the Irish not catch and eat more fish?' it is necessary to divide Ireland's fish into their 'catchable' groups.

Several good reasons prevented the development of a deep water Irish fishing industry. First, the catching of large quantities of deep-water fish required the construction of specialised ships, ports and equipment for which the capital required was neither available from within Ireland nor willing to come forward from England. Secondly, most Irishmen lived in scattered 'agricultural' communities to which no means of fast bulk 'fish' transport existed. Thirdly about three million (or more) Irishmen earned no money with which to buy in food regularly; as Sir Robert Peel had remarked, they 'grew it'. (The position in nineteenth-century England was quite different. There capital moved easily to wherever it could earn a profit. Fishing fleets, ports and distribution systems – which, quite soon, included refrigeration – were all developed without difficulty.)

No obvious answer to the question 'Why did the Irish not bother themselves to catch the fish in their freshwater rivers and loughs?' seems to exist. The quantities available were vast. Rivers and loughs were not to be found everywhere – Achill, for instance, has no rivers and few loughs – but in general, Ireland's inland waters were as close to being 'everywhere' as anywhere in Europe. Had a steady demand for means of catching fresh water fish existed there can be no doubt that cheap hooks, lines and nets would either have been made at home or, otherwise, have become available. Few inland fisheries were protected. Dr Johnson, the London physician, had no doubt about the quantity of salmon: 'The salmon alone that penetrate into every lake in the interior . . . would seem sufficient to feed half the people.' Had it been a brown trout – so common in Ireland as to be thought of as vermin – a roach, a tench, a carp, an Irish 'white trout', a fat eel or an out-of-condition spawning or spawned salmon yanked, in November, from a tiny header stream and then smoked (as had been the custom, for centuries, in Wales), that a hungry Irishman *wanted* there was little to have stopped him from helping himself.

Ireland has a long indented coastline. As the population expanded many poor Irishmen found themselves living along it because food could be found there. Mussels and edible seaweed could be gathered; and, if the will to do so had existed, abundant and excellent fish could be hooked or netted close inshore. A writer, in 1906, listed the fish actually caught in nets[52] in Charles's tiny bay at Keem; these included red and grey mullet, ling, mackerel, gurnet (which fed on crabs and tasted like them), plaice, sole, sea bream, pollock, devil fish, skate, scad, conger, cod, dogfish and turbot plus what the author called 'sweet williams'. (The list might have included salmon since Keem's ocean salmon fishery was, perhaps, the most prolific in Ireland; also crabs and lobsters since both were common.) There is no lack of evidence to show that those poor people who lived along a shoreline were assiduous *gatherers*; less often met with is hard evidence to the effect that men kept boats and fishing gear as a matter of course and used them *regularly* to catch inshore fish. (Some evidence, indeed, is to the contrary; that, 'when the potato failed, Irishmen all over Ireland pawned or sold their [fishing] gear to buy meal.')

An 1856 issue of the Achill *Missionary Herald* recalled memories of the landward side of the Sound crossing place in 1831 where there had then stood 'the remnants of a building which had once been used as a salt factory and the roofless gables of which told a tale of failure and desolation . . .' Vague as this remembrance is it has a ring of truth about it; salt was essential for preserving fish. In bygone times much salt was procured by the evaporation of sea water; the 'factory', probably, had been the building in which the salt had been kept dry. Until, in 1834, Edward Nangle brought new life to Achill it had slumbered in lonely isolation. Cut off from the world – as it had been – it is possible that, in some earlier period, Achill men and women had built themselves their own salt factory; and that they had managed to preserve their own gluts of fish. But, and if so, why had they allowed their 'factory' to fall into 'failure and desolation'?

Frances Blacker well understood the business of preserving fish and its urgency. On 1st and 29th August 1855 she 'reported to Brussels' that she had been busy either 'curing' or 'kippering' salmon; and, on a 'Monday' night – it was probably in September – that she and Murray had spent the whole of Sunday 'salting and pickling' 245 mackerel which had been sent from Keem. It is certain that Charles and Annie knew how to preserve fish.

Sound commercial reasons prevented the development of an Irish deep water fishing industry but the same can *not* be said either of Ireland's inland, or of its inshore, fisheries. Why did the Irish prefer – as it were – to die from not eating potatoes when so many might have lived by catching fish taken from one of the finest freshwater and saltwater stocks of fish in the world? To broaden the question; how did the nineteenth-century eating habits of the Irish develop?

Seven or eight hundred years earlier a small Irish population ate well enough. They kept bees and so had honey; guests in the great banqueting hall at Tara received portions of meat appropriate to their rank; and, earlier still, a hostess (by some miracle!) had been able to milk her cows no less than three times in one day. Friar Michael (of Kildare), early in the fourteenth century, referred in a poem to 'flour-cakes' 'puddings rich' 'meat that princes can bewitch' and 'to flesh, fish and meat all the best that men may eat'. This – admittedly vague and incomplete – picture is one of a vigorous and lively people eating from a range of varied and balanced foods. This situation seems to have lasted until the period 1100–1300 when a significant change in Irish domesticity occurred. During these 200 years most of Ireland's querns – hand-held stone mills for the domestic grinding of grain – were destroyed, deliberately, by the owners of water mills in order to increase their own sales of ground flour.[53] Whilst, for many years, this can have had little effect on Irish eating habits it attacked family independence: people were *forced* to buy in their flour.

In the year 1600 Ireland's total population was about 1.25 million people. Sufficient good land was available to allow that number to base their foods upon 'milk and meat'. They ate 'griddle cakes' – made presumably from flour which had been bought in – 'mutton, curds and buttermilk'; and plenty of uncooked watercress which grew wild in many of Ireland's streams. This constituted a well balanced diet; it is not surprising that Irishmen, then, were 'well shaped, agile, rarely overweight'. At about the same time the English were surprised that 'the rich and varied resources of fish . . . were not tapped by the natives'. The fact, of course, was that so small a population could still pick and choose where it lived. It was easier to live where animals – and so meat – did best; and this, in Ireland, is on good grass land to be found, more frequently, inland than by the sea. Having no real need either to catch fresh-water fish or to face the difficulties and dangers of deep water fishing the probability is that Irishmen, gradually, fell out of the taste and flavour of fish.

About the year 1600, the first potato is believed to have been planted in Ireland. The new plant from the New World took exceptionally strong root! It was not long before Irishmen discovered that the potato was easy to grow, easy to dig, easy to cook, easy to eat, that its taste never cloyed, that its foliage smothered weeds, that it was prolific and that it could be kept for about nine months; and, because potatoes are bulky and heavy, that it was better to grow and eat them locally. Shakespeare died in 1616. He used the word 'potatoes' only once when he caused Falstaff to exclaim, 'Let the sky rain potatoes.' The poet was to the point; it was as if a new, cheap and abundant foodstuff *had* rained down on damp rainy Ireland; and upon a country in which the potato usually flourished as in few other places.

From about 1675 the impression is that the potato had taken firm hold in Ireland. Thomas Dingley then wrote of Irishmen eating only potatoes and milk (and of 'sitting upon their hams like greyhounds in the sun'); in 1690 John Stevens agreed about the potatoes and milk but added that some bread, also, was eaten; John Duntan – evidently an enigmatist – wrote that the Irishman's food 'is not in the least degree better than they allow their pigs'; Robert Leigh, in 1684, wrote, less enigmatically, 'ye great support of the poor sorts of people is their potatoes which are much used all over the country'. By about 1715 'a potato diet' had come to be 'regarded as the diet of the poor' who were then described as being '. . . sorry slaves who subsist on a rig [a ridge] of potatoes'. In November 1739 a severe frost 'entirely destroyed the potatoes the chief support of the people'. Arthur Young, the celebrated agriculturalist, toured Ireland in 1789. In Co. Wexford – comparatively fertile and with a long coastline – he found that the poor ate herrings, bread and pork; of Co. Kerry – less fertile and with a long and mountainous coast – he wrote: 'Their food in summer potatoes and milk; but in spring they have only potatoes and water and sometimes they have herrings and sprats'; in Co. Antrim he wrote only of distressed weavers who ate 'milk, potatoes and oat bread' (and only a little butter because they sold most of what they made). Arthur Young wrote, also, of four inland counties in which he found food restricted, virtually, to potatoes and milk, a little butter and oaten bread; they had 'no fresh meat at all except Easter Sunday and Christmas Day'. Young, it seems, did not mention fresh-water fish; of anadromous fish he remarked only, and in reference to Co. Kerry, 'They never eat salmon'. Volume IV of the *New History of Ireland* (1691 to 1800) states that 'a potato diet was invariably regarded as the diet of the poor.'

Arthur Young's tour of Ireland in 1780 coincided, roughly, with the date when Ireland's population began to grow *very* fast; by 1800 it had reached about five million; by 1821 it had grown to over six and a half million; by 1831 to over seven and a half million; and by 1841 – the last census before the famine – to over eight million people. The Devon Commission reported in 1845 that the potato 'enabled a large family to live . . . at trifling cost and, as the result, the increase of the people has been gigantic.' Dr James Johnson, the London physician, went in to a cabin in the early 1840s and found the family 'squatting round the fire eating potatoes . . .' At the same time he remarked that 'the fisheries were not worked one tenth as much as they might be; the Irish are by no means fond of fish.' As Dr Johnson returned to London the scenery of disaster had fallen into place on Ireland's potato-studded, but virtually fish-free, stage. The stage had been long in building. The destruction of querns had played its part in limiting the perceived range of foods which the poorer Irish might cook and eat; until about 1780 a small population, having no compelling reason to catch fish, had lost the wish to eat it; from about 1800 the abundance and availability of the potato had begun to induce a dependence upon it; and, by a date unknown, the poor Irish had reached a stage such that they possessed neither the means, nor the knowledge, to cook anything except potatoes. Bread, and ovens in which to bake it, had become virtually unknown. Meat was eaten only *very* occasionally. For lack of cash, for lack of shops, for lack of roads, for lack of any system of marketing, 'the poor Irishman' was unable, virtually, to buy in anything.[54]

In sharp contrast to what had become normal amongst Ireland's poor, two small Irish communities (at least) did catch and eat fish regularly. The lives of the Blasket Islanders has been described, vividly, by Thomas O'Crohan in *The Island Men*. The men, women and children of the Claddagh quarter of Galway City, whose life and business was fishing in Galway Bay, were portrayed in the *Illustrated London News* of 23rd February 1873.

Thomas O'Crohan was born in 1856. He became a skilful and resourceful fisherman, but he did not live on fish alone. He had milk and potatoes. He mentions bread and porridge and the occasional rabbit and hunk of seal meat, but fish was his staple. Fish oil gave his house the boon of some sort of light at night. Like Hack Tuke Thomas once saw an immense shoal of fish close inshore. By an almost superhuman effort he and his friends netted eight thousand 'May mackerel; every one of them as long as your arm'; and they 'washed and salted' all of them before, exhausted, they went to bed. Thomas also went line fishing; life then became a 'cruel and toilsome job'; and, sometimes, a dangerous one by reason of sudden storms and the occasional arrival inshore of 'monsters' – that is sharks and whales. But – and Thomas was careful to add – 'those who were taken up with this business never knew privation or hunger'. Thomas *never* 'sat upon his hams'. He was capable of prolonged physical effort. He described his parents, 'My father was a middle-sized man, stout and strong. My mother was a flourishing woman as tall as a peeler; strong vigorous and lively, with bright shining hair.' He described, also, his four elder sisters; 'stout young women they were in those days, up to their bellies unloading boats, as sturdy and strong as any girls that ever were in Ireland.'

The *Illustrated London News* article on the people of the 'Claddagh' – who lived in Galway – consisted of two, carefully drawn, sketches and a short article. The latter remarked that the '. . . *fishermen* and their families live pretty much by themselves, keeping up many peculiar habits of domestic and social usage[55] as if they were a distinct tribe'; and adds 'they differ much from the ordinary type among the western peasantry'. One sketch is of six adults; their carefully drawn 'portraits' suggest physical strength, resolution and robust good health; their unsmiling faces suggest a fierce independence. The second sketch is of three boys and two girls; all are good looking; all their faces are young and, with one exception, still soft; all leave little doubt that, in due time, they will resemble only their elders.

After the famine the poor Irishman's mind was held fast by two emotions; pleasure at being alive strove with fear of another – *terrifying* – potato famine. Of necessity neither did much to change the poor Irishman's eating habits. Thomas Carlyle saw the famine's immediate aftermath; 'all creatures . . . cling to the potato as the one hope or possibility they have or dream of . . .'. Carlyle returned to England via Donegal, where he noted that 'the people won't fish or can't'. On Achill – and despite the example set by Alexander Hector – people continued to eat, mostly, potatoes. In August 1864 the Achill *Missionary Herald* wrote that, whilst Ireland's seas abounded with fish, the people's (fishing) 'boats and implements were of the most primitive construction' and that little had been done to turn 'this source of wealth' to advantage. In 1870 W.S. Trench published his *Realities of Irish Life*, in which he wrote, 'The sea . . . abounded with fish but there were no nets, no boats, and no one to organise the simplest fishing operation.' An Irish commercial directory of 1879 suggests that little fish was sold outside

Dublin and a few fashionable coastal towns such as Waterford and Youghall.

> The top o' the mornin' to you, Mick,
> Isn't it fine an'dhry an' still?
> Just an elegant day, avic,
> To stick the toleys on Tullagh Hill.
> The field is turned, an' every clod
> In ridge an' furrow is fresh an brown;
> So let's away, with the help o' God,
> By the heel o' the evenin' we'll have them down.
>
> As long as there's plenty o' milk to churn,
> An' plenty o'pyaties in ridge an' furrow,
> By the winter fire we'll laugh to scorn
> The frown o' famine an' scowl o' sorrow.
>
> There's a time to work, an' a time to talk;
> So Patsy, my boy, your pratin' shtop!
> By Midsummer Day, blossom an'stalk,
> We'll feast our eyes on a right good crop.
> Oh, the purple blossoms, so full o' joy,
> Burstin' up from our Irish loam.
> They're better than gold to the peasant, boy;
> They crown him king in his Irish home![56]

Patrick Coleman's lines capture the anticipation and the excitement, under a warm spring sun, of planting potatoes in Ireland but not the trials and tribulations which, so often, followed. Of the importance to the poor in Ireland of the annual potato crop there is no doubt. Gerald O'Tuthaigh in his *Ireland before the Famine* states that, by the mid-1840s and the start of the Famine, the potato had become the sole food of about one third of the Irish people and a major component in the diet of almost all other Irishmen. Sir Robert Peel came to much the same conclusion when, at the time of the famine, he wrote, 'Four million of the Irish people might be considered exclusively to rely' upon the potato. The Devon Commission said of the poorest Irish that 'in many districts their only food is the potato, their only beverage water . . .'.[57]

Most educated Englishmen, in the early years of the nineteenth century, never knew whether to take William Cobbett seriously or not; he exaggerated wildly but he was also a most intelligent and perceptive man. At a date before the Great Famine brought the potato into such public notoriety he wrote this strange piece:

> A potato is the worst of all things for man. There needs nothing more to inflict scrofula – a swelling of the glands – on a whole nation. It distends the stomach, it swells the heels and enfeebles the mind. I have no doubt, that a whole people would become idiots in time by feeding *solely* upon potatoes. Like other vegetables, this root in moderate quantity, is well enough in the way of sauce, but as the main article of the meal, as the joint to dine on, it is monstrous . . .

For a large number of poor Irishmen, both before and after the famine, potatoes *were* the joint they dined on; they ate little, or nothing, else.

It seems impossible, now, to calculate how many pounds of potatoes the poor Irishman was able to grow on whatever quantity of land happened to be 'his plot of land'. Plot sizes are seldom mentioned and then without the all important distinction between English statute and Irish 'acres'. 'The Poor (Ireland) Relief Act' of 1847 acknowledged the existence of men who possessed *less* than one quarter of one statute acre but not their number. The size of any man's actual holding of land bore little or no relation to the number of mouths that had to be fed from it; the number might be any figure between one and ten or even more. All that can be said with certainly is that land holdings, amongst the poorest Irishmen, were very small; and that the quantity of potatoes which could be grown on them was correspondingly small.

The annual yield of potatoes can vary considerably.[58] Yields depend upon soils and rainfall, upon variety, upon manuring, upon seed quality (and the regularity with which seed is changed), upon the suppression of weeds and upon disease; yields depend, *also* upon the skill and knowledge of the cultivator. Whilst Irish soils and rainfall tend to produce heavy crops, and a popular but coarse and watery nineteenth-century variety named the 'Lumper' cropped heavily, the typical Irish peasant was better known for his ignorance and 'laziness' than he was for his skill and hard work.[59] Particular doubt surrounds two aspects of peasant cultivations; the ability to manure properly and regularly; and the determination, under all circumstances, to reserve about 1/8th part of one year's crop as seed for the next.[60]

For lack of reliable evidence to the contrary it is thought probable that the poor Irishman did not dig his potatoes until he was ready to eat them; this had the advantages of safe storage and of preventing them from being 'greened' by exposure to light. (In general pigs do not much care for raw potatoes.) In the spring, as the weather became warmer, the Irishmen became obliged either to dig his remaining crop (to prevent sprouting) or, by early April, to dig them so that his land could be prepared for the next crop. Either course of action was likely to lead to a storage difficulty and consequential risk of damage.

After the Act of Union – and after the defeat of Napoleon! – Irishmen fell under increasing criticism from England. Why were the poor in Ireland *so* very different from the poor in England? 'Mr Punch' declared the Irish to be, by their very nature, 'the laziest and dirtiest people in all of Europe, if not the world.' *The Times* asserted that the root cause of Ireland's woes was the 'proverbial lassitude' of her people and that their great fault was 'volatility'. Professor M.W. Senior (of Oxford University, a member of the 1833 England and 1844 Irish Poor Law commissions and a man remembered for his 'comprehensive, mature and luminous thinking') wrote, 'I saw in the west [of Ireland] an immense population, apparently almost entirely unemployed, even in the early part of the harvest . . . tens of thousands of people who appeared to be entirely idle, their fields overgrown with weeds, their houses in a state of ruin; their persons foul and wretched, and altogether in a state of destitution which I did not believe existed in any portion of the world.'[61] Mrs Woodham-Smith, in her *Great Hunger*, wrote, 'The discreditable state of Ireland, the subject of adverse comment throughout the civilised world, her perpetual misfortunes, the determined hostility of most of her population, even their character, provoked intense irritation in England.' James Finton Lalor (an *Irish* patriot) bemoaned the 'disunion, dishonesty, defect of courage and faults of conduct' which characterised Irish resistance to England; Irishmen, he said, 'are cowed and conquered at the very point when an Englishman only begins to be thoroughly roused . . . better worth for us than a pike in every hand would be three drops of English blood in every heart – the bulldog breed that will not sink but boils the higher for every blow.' Bernard Becker, an American journalist, joined the chorus of criticism when he wrote that the Irishman 'will work nobly for a spurt'; and that, in the west, the men were 'neither good fishermen nor good farmers – at least I know that they neither catch fish nor pay their rent.'

All these criticisms, and many *many* more, were directed at the Irish living *in* Ireland. Less common was reflection about the poor Irish when they were *not* living in Ireland. Professor Senior also wrote, 'The Irishman does not belong to the races that are by nature averse to toil. In England or Scotland or America he can work hard . . . no danger deters, no disagreeableness disgusts, no bodily fatigue discourages him.' James Johnson, author and frequent visitor to Ireland, wrote, 'I may here remark that when the Irish labourers come over to this country, and are employed in hard work, as navigators etc., they are found unequal to the task till they are fed for some days on bacon, bread and potatoes. They are like horses taken from grass and incapable of hard work till fed for a time on hay and corn.' Bernard Becker (the American journalist) wrote also '. . . Irishmen do a vast quantity of the roughest kind of work (in England) and in the United States. In the latter country it is a matter of notoriety, supported in my case by the evidence of my own eyesight, that almost all the hard labour is performed by Irishmen and Negroes.' Finlay Dun, in his 'Landlords and Tenants in Ireland' described Michael Royen as 'a tall active man of fifty; who, in 1800, worked on a farm near Leeds where he has been regularly employed for eighteen years . . . has hoeing by the piece, when he works from four am to nine pm.' The Reverend John O'Rourke, in his history of the famine, wrote:

> The English press berated the landlords and equally bitter and insolent was their tone towards the Irish people. Accusing them of many inherent devices, denouncing their ignorance, their laziness, their want of self reliance. But a liberal English journalist, taking another viewpoint, said '. . . those vices . . . were not an essential part of Celtic nature. Has not the Irish Celt . . . achieved distinguished success in every country of Europe but his own?'

In Ireland the poor Irishman was lazy and dirty; he displayed 'lassitude and volatility'; his person was foul; his condition discreditable; when he worked he did so only 'in spurts'; he lacked moral courage and did not, always, tell the truth. The Reverend John O'Rourke also expressed his doubts about the misfortune which gripped Ireland when he wrote: 'The state in which he (the Irishman) is to be found in Ireland today must be, therefore, accounted for on some other theory than the inherent good-for-nothingness of his nature.' In 1865 a Cambridge professor declared that, 'It is idle . . . to explain Ireland's misfortunes by saying that the Celtic is naturally inferior to the Saxon race.'

An eminent London physician recently described a satisfactory diet in these uncomplicated words:

> . . .for vitality, energy and enjoyable, illness-free living we need a generous intake of the 'protective foods' in which the thirteen vitamins, ten trace elements and two essential fatty acids together with other important nutrients are concentrated. . . . Day by day we need a basic core of fibre-rich whole foods; whole-grain cereals, green leafy vegetables, with yellow/red ones, salads and pulses being specially protective, fruits, nuts, oils from a choice of many vegetable seeds, some dairy products and preferably some fish and meat products. (*The Times*, 3rd June 1992)

To eat *well*, to eat *wisely*, is to eat *widely*. An adequate intake of all the essential nutrients is essential for health and activity and is necessary, particularly, during pregnancy and lactation and for children as they grow. Potatoes contain a, perhaps surprising, number of essential nutrients but if the range of foods just listed is necessary for 'vitality, energy and enjoyable illness-free living' it is self-evident that potatoes, eaten alone with water, must be incapable of producing the same result.

In 1862 a German, Ludwig Feuerbach, declared, '*Der Mensch ist, was er isst*'; 'Man is what he eats.' Today the science of human nutrition is still not understood completely but the truth of Feuerbach's aphorism is obvious; mother's milk, with the addition of air and water, will not build a fifteen-stone Irish muscle-man; only a sufficient, and nutritionally well balanced, diet will perform *that* miracle. (The consequences of malnutrition upon children are very serious; lack of iron and other essential nutrients prevents the full development of the brain; lack of protein is likely to stunt physical growth; and lack of vitamins is likely to make children less able to resist disease.)

The 'shortcomings' of potatoes as a food for human consumption becomes apparent under two, *exceptional* circumstances; that is when they are eaten alone (or, virtually alone) and when they are 'damaged' before being eaten. (This second possibility is discussed below.)

The consequences involved in eating potatoes *alone* consists of three nutritional shortages and one nutritional absence. The shortages are: of fats (which supply energy and which are digested slowly)[62]; of riboflavins (or vitamin B2) required for the utilisation of energy from food (and which is present in potatoes only in very small quantities); and of protein (probably). Protein is required, primarily, for the growth and repair of the body (any surplus of protein is converted into energy).[63] In addition potatoes are *devoid of Vitamin B12.* B12 combines, normally, with folic acid in the creation of blood. Raw potatoes contain folic acid but *much* is lost in cooking. Poor blood causes anaemia. Anaemia is a form of physical weakness.

The above nutritional deficiencies will not kill a human being but they combine to create feelings of malaise of which 'lack of energy' is the dominating characteristic; to say that a human being suffers from 'tiredness and weakness' is to say that he 'lacks energy'; to say that he 'lacks energy' is to say that he finds it almost impossible to do a hard day's work. These expressions and words match, closely, the words used by Englishmen when describing – and criticising – the Irish; that is to say 'laziness', 'volatility', 'idleness', 'dirtiness', 'defects of courage' and an inability to work except 'in spurts'. Conversely the Irishman, living outside Ireland and so not being confined to a potato diet, became a healthier human being; he became neither 'averse to toil' nor did danger 'deter, disagreeableness disgust, nor bodily fatigue discourage him.' (*No one* should be surprised by this; today everyone understands that if a man is required to work hard and continuously he *must* be fed properly.)

The human body is complex. Ultimately it is controlled by the mind. Mind and body cannot be separated. The mind reacts, initially with hesitancy but ultimately with certainty, to the condition of the body. If, in the long term and in one way or another, the body is denied both the social privileges usually accorded to it and the energy-giving mixture of foods it needs, the order from the mind to 'slow up' becomes imperative. The mind obeys its own instructions; it, too, 'slows up'. Mind and body are capable of adopting modes of conduct in which mental and physical activities are well below their respective optimums. Sloth, laziness, lassitude, lack of fixity of purpose, the poor potato-eating Irishman's inability to keep himself clean, an unwillingness to undertake mental or physical work were attitudes imposed by the brains of individuals; but those which became publicly apparent did so, for the most part, through bodily inactions; the avoidance of effort is the body's natural defence against under- or mal-nutrition. Because so many generations of the Irish people had existed only on the potato some of their disabilities had become – almost but not quite – hereditary; nineteenth-century domestic squalor, for example, had become almost 'normal'. The chain of misfortune could not be broken until the impoverished Irishman had begun to eat far more widely; as he did when he lived outside Ireland.

In addition to the nutritional deficiencies already described the 'poor Irish' were obliged to endure one 'self inflicted' source of ill health (by the drinking of too much poteen), four other deficiency conditions arising from shortages of Vitamin A, of calcium, of Vitamin C and of milk and one other disease – pellagra – normally little known in Europe.

Poteen

The private distillation of poteen (or Irish whiskey) was illegal but its local manufacture was widespread. Poteen was drunk both by adults and children. (The danger from drinking poteen is damage to the liver. The liver is one of the three *vital* organs of the body.)

Vitamin 'A'

Many poor Irish lived solely on potatoes but these neither contain retinol (Vitamin A) nor carotene which can be converted to retinol in the body. Retinol is essential for good vision in dim light; its absence in the food of children can often be the cause of actual blindness in children.

For most of the nineteenth century 'poor eyesight' went unnoticed by the medical profession. Two 'straws in the wind' suggest that 'blindness' – however defined – was, by no means, unknown in nineteenth-century Ireland. First, Ireland is believed to have contained a large number of itinerant ballad singers and entertainers who, whether blind or partially sighted, gave their entertainment in exchange for food and lodging. (The Dublin ballad singer illustrated in the plate section was blind.) Secondly, many poor families went to bed 'with the sun' as a matter of course.

Calcium
Potatoes do not contain much calcium. Calcium builds and strengthens bones. Lack of calcium, particularly in children, leads to stunted growth and to the disease of rickets in which leg bones often become deformed.[64]

Vitamin 'C'
A lack of vitamin C causes scurvy. Whilst new potatoes (and particularly their skins) contains *ample* Vitamin C the content reduces steadily as the potato ages. Scurvy broke out, periodically, in nineteenth-century Ireland and usually in the late summer when the poor Irish had eaten no potatoes for several months.

Milk
Milk is the most complete of all human foods. It supplies a range of nutrients essential to human well being. Its virtual absence from the diet of almost all the poor Irish was a most serious misfortune. Two reasons make it virtually certain that no more than a handful of the poorest Irish were able to keep a cow; that is to say lack of cash with which to buy her in and lack of pasture on which to feed her. A clergyman told the Devon Commission, 'it was a fortunate man who has milk for his family.' A shortage of milk had become general, probably, by about 1800 when domestic cheese-making appears to have ceased. Patrick Coleman published his 'pyaties' lines (quoted on p. 178) in 1900 when he was still in his early twenties. His line 'As long as there's plenty of milk to churn' may owe something to youth, to a dawning understanding of nutrition and, perhaps something, to Irish optimism.

Butter milk is referred to occasionally. It is the acidulous milk from which the butter fat has been removed. (It should not be forgotten that nineteenth-century milk yields bear no resemblance, whatever, to late-twentieth-century milk yields.)

Pellagra
Maize was supplied by England to Ireland, as a famine relief food, in 1845 and 1846 and again from about 1878.[65] Maize, ground and cooked in water, became a popular dish; it was known as 'stirabout'. Fairly large quantities of stirabout were eaten in 1845 and 1846. Larger quantities, over a longer period, were eaten locally and regionally during the potato failure which started about 1878,

and with which Co. Mayo was much involved. (It is not known when the consumption of maize, 'in stirabout form', ceased.)

Niacin (a 'B' Vitamin) facilitates the utilisation of energy from foods. Maize contains niacin but in a form such that little is absorbed into the body. If no other foods are eaten with the maize (as is believed to have been the case in both famines) the progressive disease of pellagra is a likely consequence. In its first stage the skin of a sufferer darkens, thickens, and becomes scaly and irritable; at the same time the patient suffers diarrhoea and is weak, lethargic and depressed. In its second stage the victim suffers severe mental disturbance leading, often, to insanity. During the Great Famine a Quaker relief worker wrote the following lines about children he had seen:

> . . .shrivelled are their lips;
> Naked and coloured like the soil, the feet
> On which they stand, as if thereby they drew
> Some nourishment as trees do by their roots;
> From earth the common mother of us all.
> Figure and mien, complexion and attire,
> Are leagued to strike dismay; . . .

It seems likely that the author of these lines had, unknowingly, seen children who were suffering from the first stage of pellagra. If so the *second* stage – severe mental disturbance or worse – was more or less inevitable but it must be remembered that, for most of the nineteenth century, insanity was never well defined nor clearly understood. It was associated, often, with blindness, paralysis and extreme debility; and thought of as being a terrible and mysterious visitation of providence for which there was neither cure nor relief. The inclusion of the blind and those suffering from extreme debility (both of which can be seen, now, to have likely nutritional origins) and the paralysed amongst those thought of as being insane increased the perceived total of the insane, but it is unlikely to have falsified other evidence which suggests, forcibly, that insanity was common in Ireland during the second half of the nineteenth century, and during the early years of the twentieth century.[66]

'Mr Punch', in 1848, said it had made a new discovery; the Irish were all mad and the obvious cure for their distress was wholesale incarceration in the new lunatic asylums. (Mr Punch, perhaps, was exaggerating; but if he was *lying* he had chosen a curious subject to lie about.) R.N. Salaman, in his book on the potato, remarks that two troubles, 'opthalmia leading to blindness and insanity had increased notably'. Sir William Wilde, a distinguished Dublin doctor (and father of Oscar Wilde) said that those left behind after 1845–49 were disproportionately poor, weak, old, lame, sick, blind, dumb, imbecile and insane. ('Imbecile' means of 'weak intellect'.) Margaret Crawford, in her *Famine: the Irish Experience*, implies that pellagra (and so insanity) was present in 1845–49 but that it *was* obscured by other conditions. She suggests that it was present during the second 1878–80 regional famine.

Despite the difficulties of diagnosis the number of lunatic beds in Ireland seems to have increased very sharply between 1850 and 1914. Before 1850 there are believed to have been 2,802 insane beds in Ireland; by 1851 there were said to be 4,623; by 1861, 7,831; and, by 1914, no less than 21,000 in a population which, since the Great Famine, had declined by a third. The provision of more and more lunatic beds, it was said, had failed to keep up with the demand for them; and that insanity in Ireland had 'gone beyond the control of Central Government'. Two other aspects of insanity in Ireland seem to have made their impression; the *youth* of sufferers and the fact that so many were *male*. Some United Kingdom statistics (of 1914) confirm the impression that the lunacy rate in Ireland was high: in England and Wales, the rate per 100,000 of the population was 298; in Scotland 283; but in Ireland it was 490.

The potato

What *is* the potato? Does it – like the hornéd moon – have its darker Side? or Sides? Before answering this question it must be said, *immediately*, that, correctly harvested, correctly stored, cooked and eaten in reasonable moderation the potato is an excellent and nutritious vegetable. Vast quantities are grown almost all over the world and eaten, almost all over the world, without the smallest ill effect.

But the fact of the matter is that the potato is a member of the botanical family solanacaea and that it does have darker sides to it. The family contains some 150 members, of which 142 are of no present significance to man. The family includes the tomato and sweet pepper, both of which are wholesome; the tobacco which has narcotic, sedative and other unwholesome properties; the henbane and the mandrake both of which have narcotic and poisonous properties; the 'deadly nightshade' which has poisonous berries; *and* the potato.

The potato plant (solanum tuberosum) is an unusual one in that it possesses – so to speak – a 'dual personality'. On the one hand its below-ground tuber is the excellent vegetable that everyone knows; on the other hand its above ground green stalks, green leaves and green and hard seedballs are toxic. In addition, modern – that is post-Second World War – research shows that all parts of the potato plant contain glyco-alkaloids and that these, under certain conditions, are capable of causing neurological disturbances and gastro-intestinal disorders.

No one – in his right mind – eats the green and bitter tasting stalks, leaves or seedballs of the potato. But what is to be made of the glyco-alkaloids?

The glyco-alkaloid content of sound potatoes is low and most of what they do contain is found in their skins. The glyco-alkaloid content of damaged potatoes – that is those which have become rotten, which have been greened or blighted or which have sprouted – can be considerable. Because potatoes keep, at best, for only nine months the poor Irishman of the nineteenth century found himself, eventually, eating his 'last potatoes'; these, almost certainly, had been 'damaged' and so contained varying quantities of glyco-alkaloids. Disturbances to the nervous system may include drowsiness, laboured breathing, weakness, paralysis and a lack of consciousness (and, very occasionally, to death); disturbance to the gastro-intestinal tract may cause inflammation, haemorrhage, ulceration, abdominal pains and diarrhoea.[67] No one, now, can be certain that the Irishman of the nineteenth century was subjected, periodically, to ill-health caused by eating potatoes which contained glyco-alkaloids because medical knowledge was, then, insufficiently advanced; but the presumption must be that glyco-alkaloid toxicity did, from time to time, add to the discomforts (if nothing worse) of poor Irish families.

Prolonged malnutrition caused by eating only (or virtually only) potatoes induces, in human beings, mental insensitivity, lassitude, poor eyesight, the collapse of personal standards and general 'malaise'. To be deprived of milk, nutritionally, is most serious. Prolonged indulgence in poteen is likely to damage the liver. Periodical glyco-alkaloid disturbance to the nervous system (and to the intestinal tract) may well have added their portions of discomfort to what, already, had become a weakened physical frame. As has been said, mind and body cannot be separated; ultimately the mind falls into step, and into sympathy with, the body that carries it.

When (about 1849) James Finton Lalor bemoaned the 'disunion, dishonesty, defect of courage and faults of conduct which characterised Irish resistance to England' he said, also, that 'Irishmen . . . are cowed and conquered at the very point when an Englishman only begins to be roused, and to fight savagely; and, more wanted, I fear, and better worth for us than a pike in every hand would be three drops of English blood in every heart – the bulldog blood that will not sink'. In saying this Lalor was in *error*; he had been born long before anyone had any real knowledge of nutrition.

What the poor Irishman, living in Ireland, needed was good square *meals*;[68] washed down by *milk*.

CHAPTER FIFTEEN

WILLIAM BOYCOTT – THE THIRD RECTOR – was born in Norfolk on 12th January 1799 when England was at war with Napoleon and when the weather had been, quite exceptionally, severe (the snow had been fifteen feet high and turnips had to be split with a beetle and wedge). William was an almost exact contemporary of John Henry Newman and of Edward Nangle; aged seven at Trafalgar in 1805, seventeen at Waterloo in 1815 and thirty-one when he succeeded to the Rectorship in 1829. He had been educated at Winchester and at Cambridge. The harvest – upon which so much still depended in England – had been exceptionally bad in 1812; well off as he was William had found himself obliged – from time to time – to scrape his plate like everyone else.

William served his curacy at Honingham, a Norfolk parish about nine miles west of Norwich. There he fell in love with Elizabeth Georgiana Beevor – known always as Georgiana – a niece of Sir Thomas Beevor. William and Georgiana were married in Honingham Church on 25 September 1829. About a year later their first son Arthur William – Willie – was born. Georgiana, then, was tall and slim; and, by no means, unhandsome.

Both William and Georgiana had been born and bred in Norfolk. William was to prove himself a good father and a liberally minded Rector; nothing suggests that he was not in sympathy with the liberal outlook which characterised so many Norfolk families. Georgiana herself can only have been much influenced by the strong liberal views held by Sir Thomas Beevor (the head of her own family) and his remarkable friendship with William Cobbett. Looking after, and caring for, the poor became an important duty of the new Rector and his wife. The French revolution had, indeed, 'redefined the rights of all men everywhere'; even in quiet peaceful

England it was William and Georgiana's generation which was required to take notice of this fact. The new Rector had a duty to be fair to all points of view; good quiet sympathetic local government was much needed in rural England.

During William's years the family farm still consisted of ninety-three acres of typical Burgh-St-Peter 'upland'. William – the 'Black Squire' – employed in his Rectory a coachman, a cook, a nurse, a housemaid and a kitchen-maid. He had succeeded, on the death of his father, to the handsome Manor House[69] – and another lot of servants – in the fashionable Norfolk village of Great Ormesby. This fine house stood across the road from the Church and had been bought by Billie when he sold his 'Yarmouth Rows' house. It was lived in by Charles's Aunt Emily (a well to do spinster who left Charles several pieces of good silver) until she died in 1863. (The house had about five acres of paddock and a fine garden.)

When William II started his ministry in 1829 his surname, according to the usual spelling in the church registers, was 'Boycatt'. In 1841 he started signing the books in the name of 'Boycott'. To modern ears this seems to be a somewhat surprising thing to do, but, in 1841, it was probably not so; no great importance attached to the precise spelling of surnames and 1841 was a census year. The change may have been caused by nothing more significant than a demand for accuracy in the completion of the 1841 census return. (The 1841 census is believed to have been the first correct one.)

In June 1842 John Morse died as a very wealthy man and a large landowner. He had appointed William as one of his three executors. His will contained the provision that '. . .every person who becomes entitled to the rents of the estates shall take the surname of "Morse-Boycott".' (This, presumably, was by way of acknowledgement that the two John Boycotts had been the original begetters of the Morse wealth.)

The history of the clergy of England is part of the history of England. Gladstone said that what the Church needed was 'Saints, Theologians, Pastors, Preachers, Philosophers, Gentlemen and

Men of Business'; and, for much of the nineteenth century, this is, broadly, what England got. Thirty or more years earlier – in Billie's day – far too many clergy had been also either farmers, politicians, courtiers, sportsmen, *bon vivants* or – like Billie himself – academics. Examples of oddity were, by no means, uncommon. A parishioner tried to explain why a clergyman had been absent from something by saying, 'If it rained and he stayed away from the scene of his ministrations then the explanation was that it rained and he stayed away.' A clergyman – bothered by a recalcitrant wife – put his woes into verse:

For me, I neither know nor care
Whether a person ought to wear
A black dress or a white dress.
Plagued with a trouble of my own
A wife who preaches in her gown
And lectures in her night-dress.

In Jane Austen's *Mansfield Park* a fashionable young lady met, and liked, a young clergyman; later she reflected – with gratitude – that the uniformity of modern dress had not betrayed the young man's profession. An Archdeacon of Salisbury asked the Clerk of a remote country church, in 1874, how often Holy Communion was celebrated; eventually the clerk blurted out 'Aw, we do never have he. We've got no tackling.' A parish in Dorset had been held by a Rector who celebrated Holy Communion four times a year on the first Sunday of every Quarter; if Easter Sunday did not fall correctly then the parish had no *Easter* Communion. Strangers went, on a Sunday, to a country church but found it deserted. Eventually they were told 'Parson he had the service yesterday. He do sometimes. He lose himself and forget the day.' But, on the other hand, the Reverend R.A.J. Suckling (a friend of the family, one of the Patrons of Burgh-St-Peter, and a *devoted* clergyman) was the Rector of a London parish for fifty-five years.

At much the same time the Church found itself obliged to accept its share of coping with the social consequences of the industrial revolution and the population explosion which it caused. New factories surrounded by sprawling shanty-built, roadless, drainless and filthy 'new towns' appeared overnight along the empty and unknown valleys of Yorkshire and Lancashire. These, in effect, contained neither churches nor clergy nor any source of church income by which the construction of churches, or the employment of clergy, might be funded. Nonetheless churches and parsonage houses *were* built and 'the church' became enlarged and strengthened by its new commitment to industrial England. (The fourth Boycott Rector served part of his curacy in Leeds.)

The Church of England touched – or attempted to touch – almost every aspect of life in nineteenth-century England. It refused – absolutely – to be categorised into this, or that, compartment. Many clergymen thought that they were, indeed, 'God's messengers.'

During William's years as Rector three important events occurred. First, the Corn Laws were repealed in 1846; this led to an *immense* increase in Britain's world-wide trade. Secondly, The Great Exhibition took place during the summer of 1851; this demonstrated, to the world, that not only were England's manufacturing skills supreme but that London, in effect, had become the capital of the world.[70] Thirdly, in 1869, the Suez Canal (which had been built by the French) was opened. Six years later the British government acquired a major financial interest in it; and, in so doing, it placed a vital world artery into British hands.

On Sunday 30th March 1851 a curious 'one off' event occurred; everyone who went to a recognised church on that day was counted. Two churches then existed in Burgh-St-Peter. The 30th March attendance figures in William Boycott's Protestant (and 'official') church and John Powley's Methodist Church were as follows:

				Average attendance over previous 12 months	
	Morning	Afternoon	Evening	Morning	Evening
Parish church	31	42	–	25	50
Methodist church	55	120	40		about 150

Four points need to be made. First, that whilst the Methodist Chapel stood in the centre of Burgh-St-Peter village, the Church was two miles distant; walking from the village to the church and back involved a round journey of four miles which meant that a labourer was 'on his feet', in effect, for seven days out of the seven.[71] Secondly, the Methodists conducted no weddings or funerals. Thirdly, the Methodists had *always* been very strong in Norfolk. (The first Norfolk and Norwich 'circuit', consisting of twenty-one 'meeting places', had been formed by Wesley in 1783.) Fourthly, Wesley himself had been a 'mighty little man'; once seen he could *never* be forgotten. (It is fair to say that in Burgh-St-Peter honours as between the two churches were about even.)

Burgh-St-Peter was part of the Poor Law Union of Loddon and Clavering which catered for forty-one parishes. Although the surviving records are, by no means, complete, the average number of inmates was about 190 but the poor of Burgh-St-Peter – between August 1845 and October 1851 – seem to have been more noticeable by their absence than by their attendance at the workhouse. William Reynolds, at the age of eighty, was admitted in 1848 for no better reason than that he was aged eighty; Samuel Browne was admitted because he was 'cursed by the itch'; one Burgh-St-Peter man contrived – somehow – to leave before he had been admitted; John Abel became infirm; Frances Freeman 'died in the house' (but at the age of seventy-six); Samuel and Sarah Browne – and their three, no longer young – children went in and out repeatedly, usually because 'they had no work'. There is no evidence that anyone from Burgh-St-Peter misbehaved himself whilst in the workhouse. A local offer to sell something (in Burgh) was accompanied by a sentence saying that 'The neighbourhood [was] respectable and that the Poor Rates [were] very moderate.' (There is little doubt that much of this was due to the Rector's conscientious work.)

In August 1857 an interesting 'non-event' occurred. Commissioners (of whom the Rector was one) were actually appointed to construct 'The Lowestoft and Burgh-St-Peter Ferry' over the River Waveney at, or close to, the Church and Staithe.[72] The proposed work included a new road from the far bank of the

Waveney to Lowestoft and the improvement of the old road leading from the church and past the Rectory.

The 1841 and 1851 census returns suggest that even Burgh-St-Peter might be subjected to 'The ever Whirling Wheel of Change'. At the 1841 census Burgh had work for only one carpenter, one tailor, one blacksmith, two shoemakers and two bricklayers; but in 1851, not only did the village have an additional carpenter and shoemaker but it also had one butcher, one dressmaker, one wheelwright, two shopkeepers, one schoolmistress, one fish merchant *and* one Policeman! Why? It seems reasonably clear that, by the middle 1850s, Burgh-St-Peter had some chance of becoming a 'dormitory addition' to the growing town and port of Lowestoft. That nothing, in fact, ever happened to disturb Burgh-St-Peter's isolation may suggest only that Lowestoft had an over-inflated perception of its own ability to grow: Great Yarmouth was, by far, the larger, and more important, town.

(The site of the proposed 'over the Waveney' link to Lowestoft is now a boat and yacht marina on the Burgh-St-Peter side; nothing, except water, connects the two banks of the river. The area round the far bank is now a nature reserve.)

Thomas Edward Branthwayt Boycott – Tom, the third son – was born two years after Charles. Whilst his pulpit plate in the Church describes him as having been a 'Captain R.N.', this is unlikely to be true as his name appears in no Royal Naval List; he *is* mentioned, however, as having been a Second Mate in the Merchant Navy in 1857 when he was aged twenty-three. What Charles thought of Tom is unknown. What his father thought of him is reasonably clear; although Tom did receive his inheritance his freedom to spend it was, *most seriously*, curtailed. Tom died in 1879 having contributed little – except, perhaps, an ability to drink too much – to the family fortunes.

In the summer of 1862 Charles and Annie went back to Burgh-St-Peter when the whole Boycott family had their photographs taken on the rectory lawn. Georgiana stands – thinly – between her husband and her eldest son; Isabella sits beside Willie; Edmund stands to his father's right; Annie – wearing a smart hat – sits centre stage; Charles, and his strong unyielding face, sits on the ground to the right; Tom sits centre stage (as, perhaps, was too often the case); William – who became the fourth Boycott rector – half lies on the ground beside Tom; Emily Boycott and Owen Dinning sit to the left of the group.[73]

Between Waterloo and Charles's fifteenth birthday in 1847 the coaches of England and the organisations behind them reached a standard of efficiency equalled nowhere else. A coach and four tearing through a sleepy village, or seen across open country, had been a splendid sight; its posthorn a 'clarion o'er the dreaming earth'. Crowds went to watch the coaches leave, or return to, their London Headquarters. ('The Swan with Two Necks' in Lad Lane – which many Norwich and Ipswich coaches used – 'The White Horse' in Fetter Lane and 'The Angel' in the Strand were three of them.[74]) Some people went to admire the horses; others to appraise the way they were driven; others to criticise the turnout; and not a few to hero-worship a noted coachman. But, mostly, they came to enjoy 'the splendid spectacle . . . whether setting out with horses with backs up and very much on their toes, with sparkling harness and coachwork and not a spot of mud or dust anywhere, or arriving with a tired sweating team and the whole turnout robbed of all its glitter by a thick coating of mud or dust . . . it appealed to the Englishman's love of . . . horses which in those days played a greater part in the ordinary man's life than ever before or since.' When light allowed there was another London horse spectacular to be seen; the night 'mails' *all* left the central post office, at high speed, at eight pm *precisely*. The coachmen were a breed apart. Their usual daily stint was fifty miles but a man named Thoroughgood drove the London to Norwich coach over 112 miles every day, for two years, without a break; Jo Walton 'faultlessly dressed' drove 'The Star' to Cambridge and back every day. Not everything, always, went right; in February 1830 the London coach took three days to reach Fakenham in north Norfolk because of snow; in May 1833 the horses of a Norfolk coach panicked[75] and, attempting to leap a toll gate, 'smashed it to atoms and fell'. Coachmen were, usually, 'engagingly indulgent to school boys'; Charles's lifelong passion for horses may owe something to a kindly coachman. Coaches went '*up*' to London and '*down*' to the country. Travelling on them was *not* cheap; the 'free' baggage allowances was only fourteen pounds. It was important to load coaches properly. 'Coaches' said Tony Weller – Sammy's father and a man who knew because he was, himself, a coachman – 'is like guns – they requires to be loaded with wery great care afore they go off'. Journeys were divided into stages, marked, almost always, by inns at which horses were changed and passengers comforted. Count Pecchio, an Italian living in England in 1827, wrote: 'At every inn on the road, breakfast, dinner, or supper is always ready, a fire is burning in every room, and water always boiling for tea or coffee. Soft featherbeds, with a fire blazing up the chimney, invite to repose; and the tables are covered with newspapers for the amusement of the passengers. The English Inns would be real enchanted palaces, did not, at last, the bill of mine host appear to dispel the illusion.' 'The Scole Inn', twenty-five miles from Burgh-St-Peter on the London to Norwich coaching road, was one of the most celebrated of the old coaching Inns.

By 1862 the coaches, as a form of public transport, had been gone for ten years. The old coachmasters had died hard. 'If you get upset in a coach,' they had proclaimed, 'there you are; but if you get upset in a train where are you?' Their question remained unanswerable; except by doing what everyone did which was to get on the next train and to hell with the – quite serious – risk of being in an accident. R.L. Stevenson caught the magic of the new partnership between steel and steam in his *From a Railway Carriage*:

> Faster than fairies, faster than witches,
> Bridges and houses, hedges and ditches,
> Go charging along like troops in a battle.
> All through the meadows the houses and cattle;
> And all of the sights of the hill and the plain,
> Fly as thick as driving rain.
> And ever again, in the wink of an eye,
> Painted stations whistle by!

For a nation – and, before long, much of the world – which had revered the horse and its speed and strength above all things to travel by rail was to travel on a magic carpet. The rhythmic noise made by the trains, their speed and capacity, and their promise of more and better to come caught everyone's imagination as it had never been caught before. Suddenly people could travel to see, and stay with, their friends and relations; to keep business appointments hitherto impracticable; to visit places of which, before, they had only heard; and to take cheap 'day excursions' to the sea or some interesting event (which, in the spring of 1850, had included taking an excursion to Norwich to see the execution of James Rush). The railways introduced, also, another concept; the idea of, and need for, punctuality. Trains waited for no one.

When the time came to return to Ireland, Charles and Annie went 'up' to London – the old coaching expression was still not dead – by train to catch the 'Irish Mail'. This splendid conveyance became the first 'named' train and, probably, one of the fastest running anywhere. Two 'Mails' left London and Dublin every day; these departed Euston at 7.25am, and 8.25pm (GMT) and Dublin at 6.15am and 6.45pm (Irish Time – 25 minutes behind GMT). (These trains, and their timings, continued substantially unchanged until 1884.) They played an inanimate, but crucial, role in the conduct of Irish affairs. The British Government, in London, carried the ultimate responsibility for the government of Ireland; but it could not do so effectively without a constant stream of information and advice from Dublin. The thoughts, opinions and decisions of the cabinet and government in London, and of the Lord Lieutenant and 'Castle' in Dublin – whether kept fluid in the mind of a man who became a 'Mail' passenger or committed to writing and sent by the post – could move between the two capitals only as fast as a day or night 'Mail' and a paddle steamer could convey them. (The telegraph had been invented but had not yet become a commonplace 'tool' of management.)

At 8.25pm, precisely, the Dublin night 'Mail' pulled out of Euston Square station. It was a sight of which every Englishman had every right to be proud. The train belonged to the London and North Western Railway company; or, as it was known, the 'LNWR'. The LNWR claimed to be 'the premier line' world-wide; and, appropriately, each carriage bore a representation of 'Britannia ruling the Waves' (which she *did*). The train consisted of 1st and 2nd class carriages only; the Mail declined 3rd class passengers. The carriages were painted 'plum and spilt milk';

that is, off-white above and a purple chocolate below. As already stated the scheduled elapsed time between London and Dublin was eleven hours and thirty-five minutes; during this period passengers travelled 330 miles which included sixty miles by sea. The external splendour of the coaches was not reflected, in the 1860s, in their internal comfort. Whilst the first class compartments were well upholstered – the sitting down was comfortable – the short wheelbase of the carriages made them rock and shake in motion. The coaches had no corridors, lavatories, heating, communication cords nor, distressingly often, any light at night.[76] (It was not until 1873 that lunch baskets could be bought at Chester by *day* 'Mail' passengers. The 'Aristocrat' at 5/-d contained a pint of claret or sherry, chicken, ham or tongue, bread, cheese and butter. For those who could neither afford 5/-, nor drink a pint of claret or sherry, a 'Democrat' was available for 2/6d; this contained a pint of ale or stout, cold ham or pie and bread and cheese but no butter.) The opportunities given to passengers to stretch their legs and find a station lavatory were neither as frequent, nor as assured, as many must have wanted and some must have wanted desperately. The 'Mail' stopped, 'briefly', at Rugby and at Stafford. It did not stop at Crewe. It stopped for ten minutes at Chester but not again until it reached Holyhead. (It was possible to run, non-stop, from Chester to Holyhead only because the world's first water 'take-up' troughs had been installed near Colwyn.)

Charles and Annie's train reached Holyhead at the unsociable hour of 3.05am. They then transferred, probably, to one of the City of Dublin Steam Packet Company's large paddle steamers which sailed to Kingstown (now Dun Laoghaire). From Kingstown only six miles remained; these they did on Ireland's oldest line, the 'Dublin and Kingstown.' (Laid, originally to the English gauge of 4′ 8″ but re-laid, in the 1840s, to the standard Irish gauge of 5′3″.) They reached Dublin's Westland Row Station (now Pearse) at 7.35am Irish time. Charles – Annie probably reminded him – adjusted his watch; they had no time to spare if, as seems probable, they had decided to go straight home. A private 'car' was a necessity if they were to catch their next, westbound, connection at Broadstone.

Broadstone Station was the Dublin terminus of the Midland Great Western Railway. The M.G.W.R. was, uniquely, 'Irish'; it is impossible to imagine either it, or its Dublin terminal, being built in England. Stephenson's new union of steel with steam took the most vigorous root in a flowing tide of invention, of capital provision and – for the most part – of economic prosperity but this was not so in Ireland. Nonetheless it seemed unthinkable – to *both* Englishmen and Irishmen – that so large a physical part of the United Kingdom should languish without railways. Broadstone Station, as it greeted its passengers, was a most curious oddity; an elephant of more hues than white. It stood in magnificent isolation; for lack of custom six, or fewer, trains used it during each 24 hours; the station building was constructed, massively, of granite in the *Egyptian* style; its forecourt was bisected by the branch of a canal. (This was crossed by pedestrians by a swing bridge which had to be swung; and, by 'cars', by a pontoon which had to be moved out of a water lay-by before it could be used.)

The M.G.W.R.'s morning 'mail' drew out of Broadstone – flagged by a splendidly dressed guard – at 8.30a.m. Like the 'Mail' from London to Holyhead it provided first and second class accommodation only; like it, also, the first class carriages were comfortable enough to sit down in but the coaches shook and pitched over a permanent way in the construction of which insufficient capital had been sunk. For the first part of the journey the line of brown carriages, hauled by an emerald green engine, followed the course of the Royal Canal. Thereafter it proceeded west at no more than moderate speed on its own magic, if poorly-laid, carpet; to Galway, to Mayo and to Sligo; toward Lough Carra, Lough Mask and Lough Corrib; toward Croagh Patrick and Belmullet's 'ever changing skies'; and to the mountains and sunsets of the west.

At Mullingar the Sligo carriages were detached. At Athlone the Mayo carriages were detached and re-attached to a new – also green liveried – engine. With an Irish nicety the class of engine from which this particular one would have come were named after racehorses: 'Eclipse', 'Voltigeur', 'Harkaway', 'Birdcatcher', were four of them. However, the hard fact was that the 'fast half' of the journey had been completed; only the dawdling half remained. From Athlone onwards, whilst the operating responsibility for the service remained with the M.G.W.R., the stock ran on a permanent way owned by the Great Northern and Western Railway (the G.N.W.R.), of which Lord Lucan – a large Mayo landowner –

was Chairman. As Chairman he engaged himself in what became known as the 'Lucan Line'. In 1879 the *Illustrated London News* considered that the G.N.W.R. was the 'worst managed railway in the world'; in the same year the *Irish Times* described as 'incomprehensible' the time it took, usually, to travel from Dublin to the West.

Slowly 'Eclipse' – or was it 'Birdcatcher'? – hauled its load toward the setting sun. The train ambled to its stops at Roscommon and Castlerea. Any passenger still awake at Ballyhaunis may have been enlivened by a passing glimpse of Croagh Patrick. The land became poorer; it was self evident that, hereabouts, neither land values nor land rentals could, ever, be high. No one, in 1862, was dying of starvation; but the countryside through which the train took its passengers had been devastated by the famine. As the journey lengthened so evidence of a shortage of capital for the proper development of a railway system multiplied; the quality of station buildings deteriorated; some booking halls were left open, partially, to the weather. As was to be written later the 'cause of weakness' in the railways of Ireland '. . . was the total want of domestic capital . . . and the unwillingness of English capitalists to embark their funds in a country whose social and political position they viewed with distrust'.

After leaving Ballyhaunis the train next stopped at Claremorris; there, in all probability, Charles and Annie's outward rail journey to Dublin and England had started; and there, in all probability, Murray Blacker – full, as always, of strongly held opinions on any and every subject – was waiting to meet them. They had been on the jolting merry-go-round of the new railway age for some time; as Count Pecchio had observed a bed – in Murray's comfortable house outside Claremorris – would 'invite to repose'. Next morning – or perhaps the day after – Charles and Annie repacked their bags, saddled their horses, loaded their pack-horse, said their goodbyes and rode away to Achill. After nineteen miles they passed through Castlebar where they might have seen the railway being extended to Westport (which it reached in January 1866). A further twelve miles brought them to Newport where they, and their tired horses, spent the night. Next morning they needed to leave early. Annie, their baggage – and their saddlery – had to be ready for the first available space on the ferry boat at Achill Sound. Charles and the horses – with himself, bareback, on one of them and with his boots, probably, round his neck – had to be ready to scramble and swim across, within a few minutes either way, of slack water.[77]

In 1862 – thanks to the Mission – a small hotel stood on the island side of Achill Sound but Charles and Annie would have had no time to waste; they were still, at least, fourteen miles from home. Charles needed time to go down to the bay and catch something for supper; Annie needed time to make, and bake, bread. They were home again.

The two English counties of Norfolk and Suffolk were famous for the quality, and the variety, of their game.

Before the Game Reform Act of 1831, game, as Elizabeth I had ruled, belonged only 'to the men of the best sort and condition'. Until 1831 no one had been allowed to sell game; in consequence only a tiny proportion of the population of England ever sat down, *legally*, to a partridge or a young pheasant – or indeed any other game – for its dinner. The 1831 Act legalised both the shooting and the selling of game by the simple purchase of licences to do so. Nevertheless the 1831 Act failed to convince many people that *anyone* possessed any right to own game because pheasants and partridges – and all other game – were *wild* and free to move to wherever they wished; indeed game flew 'all round . . . with golden glittering eyes'. Such arguments found little, or no, favour with the owners of sporting estates. These claimed – with at least some justice – that they had themselves raised much of their game, that they employed gamekeepers to feed it and care for it, and that they enjoyed entertaining their friends to shoot it; the birds and animals, they maintained, were *theirs*.[78]

Despite the many arguments the preservation of the English way of life was too important to be put at serious risk. England, after Waterloo, was a curious place; proud of itself, proud of Nelson, and proud of Wellington, but there was more to its pride than pride in two, great, commanders. Englishmen – whether poacher or politician – had a quite extraordinary pride in, and love for, England; 'This other Eden, demi-paradise' as Shakespeare had described it. A simple 'love of England' possessed the nation; to poach, or not to poach, was no more than a passing detail of little real importance compared to the overwhelmingly important fact of being an *Englishman*.[79]

From Waterloo in 1815 until the end of Charles's life in 1897, poaching[80] – throughout England but especially in East Anglia – had become an important business. There was a never failing market for game. This was so because game in Norfolk and Suffolk was so plentiful, because it was such good eating, and because game in the cities and towns of England commanded such high prices. A large poaching gang of more than twenty men, led by a well disciplined and retired non-commissioned officer from the Napoleonic Wars could be, and was, a formidable opponent; of whom even the bravest gamekeeper was wise to be wary.

'Revolution' in France did not end with Wellington's victory at Waterloo; on the contrary revolutions in France and Europe continued for much of the nineteenth century. From Waterloo in 1815 to about 1848 it was not difficult to argue that whilst the French had been defeated it would still be possible for England to lose the peace she thought she had won. High unemployment, high food prices, bad housing and the unfair operation of the Corn Laws brought deprivation and misery to many poor families living in the English countryside. To become a successful poacher became an easy way of getting a good meal; and, if the game could be sold, of earning money. Fanny Burney, the diarist, had already remarked that a revolutionary instinct might cross the channel from France and that its cause might well be 'The Game Laws'. At much the same time a Lord Melton had voiced the establishment's viewpoint. 'It therefore seems to me that they [the game laws] should at all times be most respectfully guarded.' Horace Walpole – a Norfolk man – remarked: 'I never admired Game Acts but I do not wish to see guns in the hands of all the world, for there are other "ferae naturae" besides hares and partridges; and when all Europe is admiring and citing our institutions I am all for preserving it where it is.' The law stood – no doubt correctly – firmly on the side of the preserver of game.

Whilst 'a poacher' had always been someone who unlawfully took game the word carried, until the Game Reform Act of 1831, a wider meaning than is now, sometimes, remembered. Until 1831 the right to take game had been given to very few people. In consequence many gentlemen and landowners found themselves excluded from an inner circle but, like most Englishmen, they loved their 'sporting'. Whilst most managed to shoot – either as guests or by permission of the qualified or by helping themselves to what they could get on common land – there were many angry complaints about the number of 'patrician poachers' who shot or hunted without permission from anyone. 'Give me leave to tell you, Sir,' wrote one irate sportsman to a Derbyshire game preserver, '. . . that if you will take Care to preserve your game from Poachers, and behave with a little more civility to the Gentlemen Sportsmen, you will not have so much reason to complain.' (What, in those days, distinguished the patrician from the working-class poacher was the fact that the latter poached only for the food, or income, it might bring.)

Poaching was an uncertain business. The aims of individual poachers were not, always, either the same or entirely clear. The first-time man – creeping, darkly, out of his village – well knew that he might be caught in his first ten minutes or that he might never be caught. Some young man – with a girl in the back, or the front, of his mind – wanted to put his courage to the test more than he actually wanted a partridge to eat. Some men poached simply to feed their hungry families. A – by no means insignificant – number 'went out at night' for the sheer excitement of doing so. Other men went out to kill as much game as they could and to make a profit. In June 1843 (when Charles was aged eleven) a man was caught taking a pike – value 6d – unlawfully from a Norfolk river; in his defence he pleaded that 'he had no work and no other way of getting a livelihood'.

After Waterloo many landowners in England, and particularly in East Anglia, owned coverts in which game was, almost always, to be found. After the 1831 Game Act trespass became a criminal offence; so overcoming the common law principle that there could be no private ownership of birds or animals in *ferae naturae* – that is to say – in a state of nature. In addition the legal freedom to sell game altered both the quantity of game available and the methods of killing it. An ever more wealthy society's need for recreation, a sharp increase in the number of sporting guns and a demand, at almost any price, for game to eat, led, all too often, to open warfare between armed poachers and gamekeepers. The gamekeeper, himself, filled an essential position in this 'warfare'. The Lord of the Manor had the power to appoint gamekeepers, so conferring upon them a semi-official position. A gamekeeper had the power to seize a poacher's gun and his dog; and, if necessary, the poacher himself. Gamekeepers were chosen for their courage, intelligence, resolution and physical strength. A number were wounded; and, on average, about two were killed every year in England. The gamekeepers[81] occupied the first – and by far the most effective – defence against the poacher.

The mid 1830s saw the first breech-loading gun and its counter part, the machine-made cartridge. These two innovations brought a much increased safety to shooting and, in the case of the cartridge, the boon of safe easy and *precision* loading. Nonetheless the old slow-to-fire muzzle loading gun with its counterparts – the ramrod, the powder flask, the pouch for shot, the box for caps and flints, the wads, the cleaning gear needed after twenty shots or so – took a long time to die; many men clung to their old guns and their old ways for years.[82]

Breech-loading much increased safety, and the ability to fire so many more shots in a day coincided with an ever enlarging English society's need for physical relaxation. Money and the new skills given to the artificial rearing of game – particularly pheasants and partridges – much increased the total quantity of game. At the same time England adapted itself – slowly – to the continental idea of the 'battue'; that is the driving of game over standing, and waiting, guns. Whilst this allowed more people to shoot so dramatic a change was, by no means, welcome everywhere; East Anglia – by now becoming far removed from the new industrial areas of the north – remained deeply rural. Change, in the name of such familiar creatures as pheasants and partridges – and hares and duck and woodcock and snipe[83] – seemed unnatural. Crops began to suffer as game – particularly hares – increased. To the old school, who loved the hard exercise of a day's shooting and who took hills and dales, icy water, and snowdrifts in its stride, the new ways of shooting driven game seemed unnatural; they denounced it as being cruel and, certainly, not worth the trouble and the expense of organising it. The art of rearing strong well feathered fast flying birds and then presenting them over a line of standing guns was not learnt overnight; and, when it was, it was not everyone who could hit a high strong pheasant with the wind in his tail. (A certain Royal Duke, shooting in Norfolk, hit nothing but a keeper shooting beside him downed everything with the cry 'your Highness's bird'. Eventually, the owner of the shoot ran up shouting, 'You are a lying humbug. He has not killed one and you know it.') Not surprisingly, immature, or badly shot, birds were disliked by the poulterers and this aroused the sarcasm of the Duke of Wellington: 'The poulterers of London refuse to buy pheasants killed by the gun. They must have them snared . . . very soon they will require that all be hen pheasants . . .'

Most poachers who were caught were caught by gamekeepers but, occasionally, one of two mechanical devices did the catching. The mantrap, when sprung, caught and held a man's leg in a vice-like – and very painful – grip. The spring gun was mounted on a pivot; its firing mechanism was controlled by radiating wires fixed to surrounding trees and, when a man walked into a wire, the gun pivoted and fired. Neither device was particularly effective against experienced poachers who took care to avoid them; indeed some poachers moved the weapons and, occasionally, caught an unwary keeper. But, for the most part, the mantrap and the spring gun caught only loving – and wandering – couples; passers-by whose hats had blown off into the wood; autumn gatherers of blackberries and nuts; people unsteadied by liquor and the occasional clergyman-cum-botanist who, usually, had no idea that the wood he was in was defended by these appliances. (Mantraps and spring guns were proscribed – in effect outlawed – by an Act of Parliament in 1827; the Act was introduced by Lord Suffield, a well-known, and large, Norfolk landowner.)

Few normal poachers, at heart, were dishonest but some dishonest professional poachers certainly existed. Thetford, a small Norfolk town lying south of Norwich, was cursed by a group of eighteen professional poachers in about 1849. Included amongst these men's many misdeeds was the fact that they had shot and killed a mild-mannered and popular gamekeeper. Some time later an odd-looking man named Ben Knight joined the Thetford gang. Knight dressed himself in animal skins and professed a deep hatred of all gamekeepers but – curiously – he was extremely generous with his cash. It was soon discovered that Ben Knight was, in reality, a Robert Boughen who had been hired to put an end to the Thetford gang's activities; and, in this, he seems to have been largely successful. (The survivors of the Thetford Gang reformed themselves into the 'Ixworth' gang.)

A London game dealer remarked that there may have been as many as 19,000 suppliers of game to the many 'city' markets; killed, if not in one way, then in another. Regardless of the law the poulterers hung up their game for all to see and to covet.

Poached game was an article free from direct production costs but it was not free of other costs, all of which had to be met by the final buyer. These included something to the cold – and often hungry – poacher (and, very occasionally, to his half brother, the dishonest gamekeeper); something – before the advent of the trains – to the innkeepers who drew beer for the local keepers *and* the local poachers but who, also, collected in and then held game for the next coach; something to the coachmen and guard who hid, and then dropped off, the deader of their passengers by some special arrangement which only they knew; something to the barrow boys who carried the game to the poulterer's shops; and something larger than 'something' to the poulterers who displayed the game in their shops and who took the risk that, for some reason, they might not sell it. (One poulterer had been obliged to throw 2000 partridges into the Thames because the weather had, suddenly, become warm.)

In 1863 Charles started to receive anxious letter from home. It was not long before doubt became certainty; Willie – Charles's elder brother – had cancer of the bladder. He was in continuous pain. In 1864 he was only able to conduct one baptism and one burial in Aldeby church. In January 1865 he baptised his second son and last child with the names of William Douglass. On 23rd June 1865 the third Rector wrote a sad letter to the Dean of Norwich: 'It has pleased God to overrule our plans. My son is inflicted with an incurable . . . disorder which . . . causes him at times so much suffering, and always so much of bodily weakness . . . as to force on him the conviction that he cannot do that justice to the parish which he desires – and which I venture to think he has hitherto done. Indeed his voice is the only power remaining to him. He thinks it right, therefore, to resign into your hands the trust which you committed to him.'

Willie died on 13th August 1865. He was buried in his own Aldeby churchyard. He left behind his wife Isabella and their five, still young, children; Frances, aged nine, who was never to marry; Emily, who was to marry Herbert Goodwin, a mathematical don at Cambridge; Madeleine, who was to marry Assheton Weekes (who became a clergyman); St John, who was to marry Nina Marryat and emigrate to the U.S.A.; and William Douglass, who was to marry Alice Godfrey and become the last Boycott Rector of Burgh-St-Peter.

The loss of Willie threw the family into some turmoil; he had become a well-prepared, and well-educated, heir-apparent to the family Rectorship. The people of Burgh-St-Peter had every right to expect that when the mantle fell upon his shoulders Willie would carry it, not only with distinction, but with an historical understanding of, and sympathy for, the way of life of the people of Burgh-St-Peter.

Who ought to succeed? Charles and Tom had set out already upon their own careers. Edmund had been ordained at the age of thirty-five but was far from strong. His father's choice fell, almost inevitably, upon his youngest son William Boycott. (William had been born in 1843 and had, already, been ordained.)

When Willie died Edmund, the fourth son, became the brother with whom Charles seems to have had most in common. At his birth in 1835 Edmund had been a tiny little fellow of whom his Father remarked, 'They put him on the drug scales, weighed him against a dose of rhubarb and gave him the rhubarb afterwards.' As a baby Edmund was extremely small; his mother made tiny, and most beautiful, vests for him, one of which is still in the ownership of Donald Scott of Wisborough Green in West Sussex. Nevertheless – and eventually – Edmund did grow sufficiently to be sent to the Fauconburg School in Beccles, where he stayed until he was nineteen.

Edmund married a by no means poor lady named Mary Dundas Scott in 1864. Edmund and Mary had three sons (which included twins) and two daughters. All their children – with the exception of one daughter – had been born in the south-west of Ireland because, for a period, Edmund had worked there; he was in the employment of the Children's Hospital in Great Yarmouth which owned land in Ireland.[84]

Towards the end of his life the third Boycott Rector undertook some internal repairs to the fabric of Burgh Church, during which he discovered a mural of 'Knights on Galloping Horses and a Sanctuary and an Altar'; he was of the opinion that these might have been illustrations of the murder of Thomas à Beckett. Although the Rector found himself obliged to obliterate what he had found he reported the matter to the Norfolk Archaeological Society, who, in 1872 and in its Volume VII, carried a short article about his discovery. (William also said that he had made a careful sketch of what he had found but this, like its original, has disappeared.)

Georgiana – it is believed – was a good mother to her large brood. She kept house well; she disciplined her children; when necessary she became their nursemaid of last recourse; she argued – no doubt successfully – with the army of tinkers and tailors who called, constantly, upon the Rectory House. When her last daughter was born she was aged forty-six. As the years passed she became – for a reason now unknown – very thin and an increasingly difficult woman with whom to deal. Willie's death in 1865 and Charles's – more or less permanent – absence in Ireland may have caused her more unhappiness than the world ever understood. It is possible that, by 1865, she had reached a stage in her own life such that she could no longer endure the thought of another, lonely, winter in Burgh-St-Peter. As was her habit she did nothing by halves. When her eldest son died, she decided – in quick time – to leave Burgh and install herself in the, now empty and waiting, Manor House in Great Ormesby.[85] Although this was an unwifely thing to do affairs turned out better than might have been expected. Isabella and her five – fatherless – children moved into the Burgh Rectory so giving them a home and making it possible for Isabella to keep house for her father-in-law. The Boycott daughters seem to have followed their mother into the comforts of the Manor House; they may well have thought that they had a better chance of finding themselves husbands in Ormesby.

When the third Rector died in 1871 Isabella moved, temporarily, to Rugby. She moved back to Beccles – and into a fine old house named Roos Hall – which she then shared with Edmund Boycott and his wife. Isabella died in 1874 and was buried, next to her husband, in Aldeby. At her death her five children all became *Charles's legal wards.*

William Boycott died on 30th October 1871 at the age of 73. Charles was his executor. He was buried in his own churchyard four days later. He had been a kindly, hardworking, liberally minded, scrupulously honest and loyal servant to his parish for forty-two years; when he died he left it in excellent order. He had excelled in doing his duty to his family, to his parishioners and to anyone else able to establish a claim upon him. It is, unfortunately, by no means certain that he ever established any real mastery over his wife; when she became argumentative and domineering he is believed to have retreated to his library where he read until the storm had either passed on or had subsided.

Nothing, now, suggests that William Boycott had been a totally committed 'Man of God'. His inner convictions never *compelled* him to worship God with all the strength at his command.

A FAREWELL TO ACHILL

Isle of the Eagle, farewell to thy mountains
With all their bright blossoms of purple and gold;
No more shall I sit by their murmuring fountains,
Or from their bold length the Atlantic behold.

Dear Glen of the oaks, with thy garden of roses,
Where the birds ever sing and the breezes are mild;
Unbosomed in mountains thy beauty reposes
Like fairy land opening in midst of the wild.

The flocks wander free on Kildownet's green Highlands,
Where the blue winding Sound joins the ocean again;
And the clouds rest in crowns on the rock-girdled islands,
Like nature proclaiming them Kings of the main.

Thy peaks fade from view, but where-er it betides me
In memory oft by that wild shore I'll dwell;
Now the hills close thee in other scenes are beside me,
Beautiful Isle of the Eagle – Farewell.

CHAPTER SIXTEEN

ABOUT 1871 OR 1872 CHARLES and Annie reviewed their lives. They were both aged thirty-nine. They were happily married. They had no children, and, probably for this reason, were more than usually sympathetic to each other's points of view. Since the fire they had no house to call their own. The getting off, and returning to, Achill was still, physically, almost as time consuming, and as tiring, as it had always been. Such social life as the Mission had brought to Achill was not what it had been. Charles had acquired at least three small mainland land agencies in addition to the two small Achill agencies from Lord Sligo and Murray Blacker; all required regular visiting but doing so could be dangerous. (John Moran, the Achill cobbler, remembered that Charles always put on an old coat and hat when passing a certain wood on the Corraun peninsula.) There were other reasons which suggested the wisdom of a move to the mainland. First, Charles had become a good farmer; he wanted a larger and better farm. Secondly, and since his father's death in 1871 and the earlier death of his elder brother, he had become head of his East Anglian family; he had a duty to make himself less inaccessible. And – no doubt – a third reason was not backward in coming forward: Charles wanted to start – what had been impossible from Achill – racing horses.

In 1872 an attractive opportunity on the mainland of Co. Mayo came Charles's way; he was offered a farm and a house on Lord Erne's Lough Mask land and the Agency for both it and Lord Erne's other Co. Mayo property. Both the land, and the house, stood on the eastern, or Ballinrobe, side of Lough Mask[86] and about three and a half miles from Ballinrobe. The property consisted of a good general farm, a good house, good yards, good buildings and stables, two islands on Lough Mask ('Black' and 'Carrigeenagur') and, for good measure, an ancient, but ruined, castle[87] which stood by the farm buildings. Sporting rights went with the offer. A large – almost palatial – boathouse stood by the lough; Charles could cast a fly against the notorious Lough Mask brown trout. A long driveway, passing through trees and parkland, led from a quiet side road to the house. The view from the house itself – towards the setting sun and the Mountains of Maamturk – was no less splendid than had been the views to which Charles had become so accustomed on Achill. Charles was never the man to rush, headlong, into anything; but it cannot have taken him long to accept Lord Erne's offer.

It is never easy either to 'move a farm' or to sell a property in so remote a place as Achill; for this reason the agreement between Charles and Lord Erne did not become effective until 1st May 1874. Charles then took, for thirty-one years, Lough Mask house and '388 acres 2 roods and 39 perches plantation measure' (or 629 acres statute) and the other property which has been described. The lease stated that no compensation for improvements would be paid unless 'in respect of permanent buildings and the reclamation of waste land . . .' The agreed rental was £402 p.a. for nine years and £500 p.a. for the remaining twenty-two years. It is clear that, when Charles signed this agreement, he intended to make Lough Mask House and farm his home for the rest of his life.[88]

The third Earl of Erne lived in Crom Castle on the shore of Upper Lough Erne in Co. Fermanagh. The Earl's physical individuality was marked; his whiskers were white and bushy and his face large, square and pockmarked. He owned (in 1883) 40,386 statute acres in Ireland (and properties in Dublin). Of this total 31,389 acres lay around Crom Castle, 4,826 in Co. Donegal, 1,996 in Co. Sligo and the remaining 2,184 acres – or about 5% of his total holdings – lay in Co. Mayo. The Mayo acreage was divided; part lay some distance away at Kilkenny near Castlebar whilst the remainder lay round Lough Mask House. Like other large landowners in Ireland Lord Erne preferred to employ either Englishmen or Scotsmen in positions of authority; this may be one of the reasons why Charles, it seems, had little difficulty in renting Lough Mask House and the *good* farm round it.

The population of Co. Mayo was about 95% Catholic. The fact that Charles had come from so unusual a *Protestant* background – so far as is known – was never remarked upon.

Charles's early years on Achill had seen an easy acceptance of an Irish post-famine agricultural prosperity. Economists and agriculturists in England and Ireland had begun to see farming in Ireland in a new – post-famine – way. These – matching their thoughts to a sharply declining Irish population – believed in the creation of larger, more heavily capitalised, farms upon which small farmers (in effect labourers) could find paid work. This policy was put into some effect in Counties Galway and Mayo where several Scottish and English farmers had settled. Many such individual arrangements had been made possible by the Encumbered Estates Court, which, when it freed an estate of its accumulated debt, converted it into a property which could become profitable; in other words a previously bankrupt owner had been replaced by a new, profit-producing, owner. This, more or less, is what Charles became. The land he farmed on Achill (as a tenant of Murray Blacker's) had been relieved, previously, of its (O'Donnell) debt encumbrances by the Encumbered Estate Court. Much the same thing happened when he took the Lough Mask farm; the rent he then paid allowed him to make a reasonable profit. Padraig G. Lane, in his *General Impact of the Encumbered Estates Act of 1849 on Counties Galway & Mayo* remarks that 'Captain Boyquett (sic) of later fame, became prosperous through farming land in West Mayo.' There is no doubt that Charles *did* become – at any rate for a time – prosperous. He did so because he was a sensible man, because he had Norfolk farming in his blood, because he had studied William Blacker's books and because he was honest; *and* because he refused to pay more than a sensible rent for the land he farmed.

About two years after Charles and Annie had settled themselves into Lough Mask House and farm, agriculture, throughout Europe, began to suffer its longest, and worst, depression. The causes were two; bad seasons and the invasion by America's so called 'prairie farmers', of English and European grain and beef markets. America was still a young country; still full of young men surging westwards who, suddenly, found themselves possessed of three powerful commercial advantages. American railways – for a period and to encourage the new settlers even further westward – carried grains at below cost; improved marine engines made possible the building of cheap ocean freighters (the cost of sending a ton of grain from Chicago to Liverpool dropped from 67/-d in

1873 to 24/-d in 1884); and, because the new American wheat farmers were forced to invent harvesting and other machines capable of doing the work for which there was no labour. In consequence cheap American wheat flooded into Europe; English wheat prices fell from 45/2d per quarter in 1875 to 43/10d in 1879, to 35/8d in 1884, to 31/11d in 1890 and, in 1897 – the year in which Charles died – to 26/2d per quarter.

Only the United Kingdom – *wedded* to free trade since the repeal of the Corn Laws – and Belgium refused to impose import duties on foreign grain. For a year or so Ireland's stock farmers continued to be cushioned but, in general, the United Kingdom – which, of course, included Ireland – was forced into a long period of most serious agricultural depression. By 1883 England's annual wheat crop had been reduced by one million tons; her dependence upon American cereals had grown by leaps and bounds; and the old 'safety mechanism' – that is the *inverse* relationship between wheat yields and wheat prices – had been destroyed. English farmers were forced to reduce their labour force by 92,000 men; English farming technology – which had led the world – withered; speculators bought good wheatland for a song and either converted it to keep sheep or further exhausted it by cropping without manuring. Rural rents fell sharply; East Anglian 'high farming' – as Charles had known it as a boy – more or less ceased to exist; English farmers, who had been the proudest and most hard-working of men, sank into a strange embarrassment; bankruptcies and auctions followed as the night follows day.

The urbanisation of England had begun.

Charles's years in Ireland came to a head – and more or less to an end – with the slow gathering together of *two* major questions. Who ought to be the principal owners of the land of Ireland? And when – if ever – should political independence be granted to Ireland?

Because Ireland has never been conquered completely her land laws had become *immensely* complicated. Large landowners often owned too much; and, all too often, seemed oblivious of the fact that the ownership of property had its duties as well as its rights.[89] 'Tenant Right' – that is the custom that if a man paid his rent he could not be evicted – operated in parts of Ireland only. In addition the quite exceptional poverty of so many Irishmen could not be corrected because no wealth-producing industrial base – apart from Belfast – existed. Slowly, discontent in Ireland found its reflection in English politics; slowly, the growth of an increasingly strong Irish party at Westminster began to tilt England's political balance; slowly, the question of who ought to govern Ireland demanded an answer. Easy solutions were *not* to be found. Few Englishmen knew Ireland personally; Gladstone, for example, went to Ireland only once. Many Irishmen, who had fled Ireland during and after the famine, settled themselves in England; their opinions could not be entirely ignored. Ireland herself remained overwhelmingly Catholic. England, in command of the world's oceans and of much else beside, was deeply reluctant to see the homogeneity of the British Isles destroyed.

Not everything, always, went right for Ireland. The Fenians consisted mostly of small Irish farmers, labourers, clerks and shop assistants; they drew support not only from Ireland itself but also from those 'new Irelands' which post-famine emigration had created in America, in England, in Australia and in New Zealand. In 1867 the Fenians thought that their moment had arrived but, in this, they were incorrect; the British Government's intelligence was too good and an inadequately organised uprising failed disastrously. At about the same time the Pope issued an astonishing encyclical. In this he listed some ninety 'errors and perverse doctrines' which included 'rationalism, science, democracy, the writings of the press, secular education and the enveloping power of the state' and said that 'The Pontiff can neither be, nor ought to be, reconciled with progress, liberation or modern civilisation.' This, in effect, amounted to a papal declaration of war upon the spirit of the age; not surprisingly, even in Ireland, it came to nothing.

Gladstone, when told in 1868 that he was to become the Prime Minister of a – so called – 'United Kingdom' is reputed to have paused, and then to have said 'My mission is to pacify Ireland.'

Gladstone's intellectual brilliance, his mastery of detail and his determination to get to the bottom of every problem put before him, produced in 1879 an Act to disestablish the Anglican Church of Ireland and his first Land Act. The latter began to address Ireland's underlying, and complicated, land difficulties; it also established Gladstone as a man who cared personally about Ireland. Nonetheless his 1879 Act was, to the ordinary citizen – whether Irish or English – almost unintelligible; few perceived that it was a significant step in the right direction. The Act conceded four important principles. First, that the peculiarities of Irish Land Tenure should receive statutory recognition; second, it curbed the absolute power of the landlords; third, it legalised the, so called, 'Ulster Custom' of tenant right and compensation for disturbance and for improvements made; and, fourthly, it tried to create a peasant proprietorship. All these were solid achievements; they emphasised that the ownership of property had its *duties* as well as its rights.

But neither Rome – nor a new Ireland – could be built in a day; time for reflection was needed. The complexities of the ancient Irish land system could scarcely be modernised in one Land Act. It is, indeed, pertinent to ask 'What *is* a peasant?' The answer is that a peasant is someone who is tied to a particular place by reason of the land he tills; that is, the '*pays*' from which the French word '*paysan*' is derived. The tenacity with which the peasant clings to the soil, and the soil to him, gives a 'peasantry' its endurance and character. The peasant is not, usually, a 'political animal'; but that is not to say that he cannot be roused when his rights to his land are threatened. (The peasant is a formidable *resister*; the land he farms is all he has.)

It was equally impossible for England to throw off her international responsibilities. A multitude of tasks constantly awaited the Imperial Government in London. The Crimean War had to be fought and the Indian Mutiny suppressed; the unification of Italy, the American Civil War and the Franco-German war all required the closest attention; the South African war and, only a few years later, the First World War, had to be fought and won; the Royal Navy, upon which, ultimately, everything depended, needed constant thought and the constant spending of vast sums of money; the economy, and domestic affairs at home, demanded never-ceasing attention. It is the fact that, throughout the nineteenth century, the House of Commons found itself continually faced by 'too much business'. This was nobody's fault; it was the price of Empire and world-wide Admiralty.

In 1875 and 1877 two new stars began to light the Irish stage. Charles Parnell – an aristocratic leader of men and a man with strong American connections – was elected to the House of Commons. Michael Davitt, no aristocrat but an intensely patriotic Irishman of transparent integrity (who had been born in Co. Mayo and who, throughout his life, '. . . nothing common did, or mean

. . .') was released from an English goal. Parnell and Davitt joined hands; both saw, clearly, that only 'the land of Ireland' could unite the people of Ireland (both, long since, have passed into the web of Irish history).[90] Both men, of course, were Irishmen before they were anything else; but both, in their own ways, never seem to have lost, at least some, regard for England; perceiving, perhaps, the immense burden of Empire which she carried.

In December 1879 Davitt went to the U.S.A. where, with John Devoy, the American Fenian, he created an alliance of revolutionary and constitutional nationalists dedicated to the support of the two great issues which faced Ireland; land ownership and political independence.

During 1879 several large public demonstrations of hostility to the existing order took place. The poor malnourished Irishman (particularly in the west and despite the fact that, by 1880, he may have had about fifteen acres of land) became convinced that the landlords, great and small, were responsible for his hunger and misery. The cry everywhere (and not only in Co. Mayo) contained much the same revolutionary message; 'Down with the intruder! Down with tyrants! Every man must own his own land, every man must have his own home!' Co. Mayo became the centre of hostility to England; every week saw some violent extension of this hostility. In their unity of purpose the Irish crowds were not dissimilar to those crowds of Frenchmen who, ninety years earlier, had imposed their will upon France. Earl Grey, already, had warned Parliament that 'Ireland . . . is the one deep blot upon the brightness of British honour'; John Stuart Mill, the economist, had already warned England that the condition of Ireland 'is now more dangerous . . . than at any former period'. A great upheaval, a great moment of Irish self-assertion, seemed imminent.

The National Land League of Ireland was formed in the autumn of 1879; Parnell and Davitt became its national leaders; the parish priests its most influential local leaders. The Land League was a lawful organisation; it was *not* begotten by oratory. Its sympathies lay, openly, with a wronged, impoverished and near starving people who sought the support of all Irishmen everywhere and, most particularly, from the 'new' breed of Irish-Americans. The League's essential task was to organise resistance to the landlords; for the immediate purpose of preventing evictions and for the ultimate purpose of transforming the Irish tenant farmer into the owner of his land. Professor Moody has described the crisis into which Ireland then fell:

> The so-called 'land war' of 1879–82 was the greatest mass-movement of modern Ireland. An elaborate system of 'moral-force warfare' was developed; process-serving and evictions were made the occasion of great demonstrations; families evicted for non-payment of rent were sheltered and supported; an embargo was placed on evicted farms; persons involved in prosecutions because of their league activities were defended and the families of those sent to prison were cared for; and the terrible weapon of social ostracism, the boycott, was perfected as the ultimate sanction of the league against all persons who violated its code. For the first time the tenant farmers, as a class, stood up to the land-lords. The passions roused by the agitation inevitably erupted into violence and outrage, but it was just because the Land League was technically a lawful organisation that the government had so much difficulty in coming to grips with it.

Charles, at Lough Mask House, was still, primarily, a general farmer; his land agencies were minor. He did *not* grow large quantities of potatoes. 1872, 1873, 1877, 1879 (and 1883) were all bad, or *very* bad, potato years. (In 1877 the Co. Mayo potato yield was reduced to 1.4 tons per acre.[91]) In January 1880 Charles, as a local Justice of the Peace, became obliged to consider the fact that, round Claremorris, there were no less than 300 families 'on the edge of starvation'. In the following month Charles seconded a proposal that no new roads should be built in Co. Mayo (as had been done in the Great Famine) unless the owners *gave* the land.

Rain fell, almost continuously, on Ireland in 1879. Peat, the only source of warmth and comfort, could not be dried. The poor of Co. Mayo – and other counties like it – found themselves without enough food, without money with which to buy in 'stirabout', without dry peat with which to keep warm, without credit at the shops – many shops had, already, extended far too much – and without work either in Ireland or in England. The poor Irishman became 'pale, thin, bloodless and silent'; he seldom smiled; he was, indeed, malnourished. By the end of 1879 no less than 142,000 Mayo people were in need of relief; nearly 48,000 had become workhouse inmates. Many Irish poor law unions were bankrupt.

The eyes of the world – including many eyes in America – began, yet again, to converge upon Ireland.

The poor Irishman who, otherwise, might have starved in 1879 and during the first seven months of 1880, was saved by private charity. Late in 1879 two relief committees were formed in Dublin. One – chaired by the Duchess of Marlborough (the wife of the Lord Lieutenant) – distributed gifts from England. The second – chaired by the Lord Mayor of Dublin – distributed gifts from elsewhere.[92] Both committees transmitted food clothing and supplies rather than money. Few people who worked for either committee received any salary. By the end of May 1880 the funds of both committees were seriously reduced; nevertheless food, somehow, was found. The Land League, whose object was active political agitation, helped with relief; amongst other things it distributed 500 tons of food and clothing received from the U.S.A. The Royal Navy carried relief to many offshore Irish islands. The Duchess of Marlborough was greatly admired; she found herself solving 'problems which had perplexed statesmen'. By what, at the time, seemed to be a dispensation of providence the summer of 1880 was warm and dry; the new potato crop could be dug in good time.

In February 1880, when hunger in and around Ballinrobe had become most serious and the relief organisations in Dublin were in full swing, sixty-five people around Ballinrobe signed 'a memorial' to the Lord Lieutenant. This requested that an already planned canal, one mile in length, should be dug from Ballinrobe to Lough Mask (so connecting Ballinrobe by water to the sea at Galway) and bringing 'unskilled work to hundreds in need of it.' 'C.C. Boycott J.P.' was the fifth person to sign the memorial; his signature appeared below the signatures of a Parish Priest, the Clerk (to the Ballinrobe Council?) and two large local landowners about whom nothing detrimental is known. His signature, so high up the list, suggests that either he had, himself, taken some part in the initiative or that he welcomed it. (In the event the canal was never dug: £6,000, perhaps, was too much money to spend?)

A general election in April 1880 returned Gladstone to power as Prime Minister, William Forster as the Irish Secretary[93] and Earl Cowper as the Lord Lieutenant. The Land League put forward its own Parliamentary candidates and won a resounding victory; to return a landlord to Parliament, it said, would be like 'choosing a wolf to guard sheep.' Parnell was elected to Counties Meath, Mayo and Cork, but chose Cork; the Reverend Isaac Nelson (an Ulsterman and a Protestant) became the member for Co. Mayo. Parnell proceeded to the leadership of a militant Irish party at Westminster. But – and despite the famine relief efforts already made – Ireland was still, by no means, out of its wood. In April 1880 the 'starvation months' still lay ahead; no one could foretell either the oncoming weather or the size of the next potato crop. At the end of May 1880 James Redpath (an American) said, 'Everybody knows there is a famine in Ireland'; nevertheless few people knew how severe, and how widespread, hunger still was.

Forster's (and Gladstone's) immediate proposal was intended to conciliate Ireland; their 'Compensation for Disturbance Bill' proposed that a landlord should pay compensation to an evicted[94] tenant for improvements already made to a land holding. The Bill passed the Commons by 225–199 votes but was rejected by the House of Lords by 281–51 votes. Rejection by the Lords had very large consequences for Charles, for England[95] and for Ireland. The Land War proceeded, immediately, to new levels of violence; the landlords, as a whole, redoubled their efforts to evict defaulting tenants; the Queen's Writ – more or less and for a period – ceased to run in Ireland. England – the British Government – was left with no alternative but to enforce the old law. Of necessity, exceptional powers of coercion were authorised by Parliament in London.

Charles's past 'good conduct', an earlier popularity, a sympathy for the lot of so many poor Irishmen amongst whom he had lived for so long, a love of horses and an ability to ride them well counted for nothing. Old loyalties were swept away; suddenly, pertinent, sensible questions were not asked. Past friendships between a farmer and the men who worked his farm, between a man and his groom, an angler and his ghillie, a gun and his beaters, became of little account. No guillotine was erected in Merrion Square – or outside the Courthouse in Ballinrobe! – but, for a time, the passionate appeal of the 'land for the people' united all Irishmen; Protestant and Catholic, Celt and Saxon, Farmer and Labourer, Priest and People, The Orange and The Green, all joined hands. America watched. Almost to a man the Catholic clergy supported the League; Father O'Malley of The Neale – not far from Lough Mask House – played an important part in the first 'boycotting'.

(Father O'Leary led the campaign of hostility against William Bence-Jones.)

To the simple uneducated Irishman living in Ireland the Land League presented an irresistible appeal. To those Irishmen who had already emigrated to the United States, to England, to Australia and to New Zealand the appeal was more remote; they had already found somewhere else in which to work and where good food could be bought. But, to Charles, the Land League represented something different; he could see no prospect that the Irish, left to themselves, could govern themselves. Many people in England, and not a few in Ireland, agreed with him.

CHAPTER SEVENTEEN

LORD ERNE'S COUNTY MAYO LAND was divided into two parts; *good* land, farmed by Charles, lying midway along the Ballinrobe side of Lough Mask, and poor land lying some distance away near Claremorris (upon which no trouble ever arose). It was never easy for Charles and Lord Erne to meet; or for either of them to appreciate, fully, the difficulties which then, and increasingly, separated the politically stable County of Fermanagh in the north from the poor, infertile and increasingly turbulent County of Mayo in the west.

In the autumn of 1880 Charles was rising forty-nine years of age; a time of life – fixed by Aristotle – when human faculties are at, or near, their peak.

Charles and Annie had no children but, in the Autumn of 1880, they had living with them in Lough Mask House four 'young' people. These were: Assheton Weekes, aged thirty; a niece named Madeleine Boycott, aged nineteen, and two nephews and brothers named St John Boycott, aged seventeen, and William Douglass Boycott,[96] aged sixteen. Madeleine, St John and Douglass had been Charles's wards[97] since the death of their mother (one of Murray Blacker's sisters) in 1874.

Charles, in 1880, was what he appeared to be; an efficient, determined, hardworking and clever tenant farmer and minor land agent; a man who was determined to go on making a success of his life. (A Mrs Brabezon-Combe remembered him as a handsome man of fastidious habits.) He was meticulously honest; when, eventually, he left Ireland he is believed to have owed no one a penny. His handwriting divides into two groups. The first was small, neat and level, and suggests that he was much concerned with the ordinary things of life, that he was able to concentrate his mind, that he wasted nothing, that he understood the importance of detail and that he was a practical man with much respect for the law. The second group suggests that he was capable of becoming a formidable opponent to anyone who challenged his beliefs; and that, had he been less cautious, he might 'have achieved great things.' By 1880 he had laid out about £6,000 on Lough Mask House and farm. He had always been able to create a good working team of people. He was, probably, the largest local employer of labour. He played, 'at almost every noon hour', the old Irish game of handball with his men. After he had moved into Lough Mask House he started to keep a small string of racehorses which he often rode himself. He shot and fished well. He hunted when he could. He is believed to have owned land in Co. Galway; he certainly owned about a hundred acres at Kildarra not far from Lough Mask House. All these were qualities in a man which the ordinary Irishman found it impossible not to admire. A Madame De Bovet was later to write that, on Achill, Charles 'had left an excellent impression on the people who had worked for him'; or, as someone else said, he had 'pulled along admirably with his tenants for years'. In February 1880 a local committee report said, 'There is not even a registered Agent, save one, Captain Boycott, who manifests every disposition to do his best for his own people.' In his 'Tapestry of Toil' the Reverend Desmond Morse-Boycott has this account of how Charles and a young girl first met on the shores of Lough Mask:

> I was enjoying myself, as a child will, among the tall reeds . . . when suddenly the head and shoulders of a man appeared . . . wild, yellow-red hair, wind-blown, sticking straight up from the forehead, and a ragged, bushy beard framed the face, while the widest-opened fiercest blue eyes under a contracted brow fixed themselves on me.
>
> The remembrance of those eyes is as sharp today as when they first met mine. To my childish mind the face seemed to belong so rightly to the reeds and the lake that I was greatly interested . . . we stared at each other for a full minute; then, coming forward, but keeping low among the reeds, the man spoke to me. I answered, and thereafter for a long hour we sat together . . . finally my father . . . appeared, and his surprised 'Hullo! Boycott' told me to whom I had been talking so gaily and happily.
>
> And just here is my cause for gratitude for, in greeting my father and indicating my small self my new-found friend gave utterance

> to the astonishing pronouncement: 'A very remarkable little girl, most clever and intelligent.' . . . Small wonder I treasured the remembrance and, suffering from what today would be called a deep inferiority complex, such praise helped me more than can well be expressed and the chance words did good beyond my telling throughout my childhood.
>
> . . . Captain Boycott told my father . . . that the reason for his sudden appearance in the reeds was that he hid awhile before taking, as was his custom, a different path back . . . I quite understood that it was to avoid being murdered en route.

Charles's handwriting analyst added a postscript to his report in which he said that, if Charles had been prepared to take risks, he might have achieved much. But, when crisis struck in 1880, his many responsibilities in and around Lough Mask House – as husband, as guardian to three children, as friend, as employer, as Agent, as farmer with many animals on his hands, as householder – prevented him from taking foolish risks; he was, also, faced with the ever present chance of recurring, and serious, ill-health. He became 'a prisoner'; a resilient, strong-featured, courageous man from whom complete freedom (for the time being) had been withdrawn by the Land League.

Annie had become a lady of character. Like her husband she was aged forty-eight. When Charles was away – as J.P., as Agent, or when racing his horses – she attended to the farm. When, as almost certainly happened from time to time, Charles suffered a relapse of rheumatic fever, she packed him off to bed. She never, it seems, complained; she just got on with whatever job next required to be done.[98]

Assheton Weekes had lived with Charles and Annie for several years; he became almost a son to Charles. He had been, earlier, an officer in a cavalry regiment. He loved horses, and, no doubt, took over much of the responsibility for looking after Charles's farm and race horses. In the early winter of 1880 Lough Mask House was enlivened when Assheton Weekes and Madeleine Boycott announced their engagement. (They were married, in Dublin, in January 1881.)

Three members of Charles's household refused to leave his employ. These were Johnny Meany, an experienced groom and a retired jockey; Judy, a physically diminutive cook; and Harriet, a parlourmaid.

The summer of 1880 was a good one; potatoes grew well. Nevertheless the Irishman remained discontented. He still felt – dimly and dumbly – that he possessed an ancient Brehon *right* to the land of his fathers. He became 'thankless, independent and defiant' towards his landlords, so many of whom were absentee, feeble in their conduct of affairs or, simply, disinterested in the future of Ireland.

About 20,000 people attended a Land League meeting at Cong – about six miles from Lough Mask House – on a Sunday in July 1880. A band played patriotic tunes; broad-sheets reviling landlords and landgrabbers alike were read eagerly; one group announced 'On, on, in your masses, dense, resolute, strong to war against treason, oppression and wrong'; another proclaimed 'The Land for the People'. Many men were armed.[99] One speaker declared that 'he looked upon the Land Question as being the very marrow of all Irish grievances' and that 'The Land League was determined to carry on the war until they had banished landlordism root and branch.' Another said 'The man who takes the land from which another is evicted is worse than he who uses the pistol.' Most of those who listened so attentively were simple Irishmen of Celtic origin. What they cared about was the *land* of Ireland; its history, its earlier occupiers, and its ancient villages so many of which had been abandoned because of famine and emigration. 'Those who toil must own the soil' became their catchphrase and the following lines their talisman:

> To rise like lions after slumber,
> in unconquerable number;
> shake thy chains to earth like dew,
> Which in sleep has fallen on you;
> you are many, they are few

Father John O'Malley, the Catholic Parish Priest of The Neale – a hamlet lying between Lough Mask House and Cong – led his people along the road from The Neale to Cong. (O'Malley was well known to Charles.) He was loved by his parishioners because of his character, his humour, his conviviality, his ability to speak in public, and because – like too many Irishmen – he 'loved the bottle'. O'Malley lost no time in coming to his points. 'My heart' he said, 'swells with pride because of my hope that the days of our bondage will soon be over and we will soon be what we ought to be – freemen.' He then told his audience four things; that he himself had been appointed 'President of The Neale branch of the Land League'; that the temporal salvation of his listeners depended on 'the success of the Land League'; that 'the designs of the Irish landlords have ever been to annihilate the Irish people'; and 'that the proper place for the priest . . . is . . . at the people's head.' This was strong persuasive talk; nicely calculated to fire those simple people who did not, really, understand the political revolt then taking place and to heighten the anxieties of those who did.

In May 1880 the London *Times* said, 'The Land Question in Ireland has now been worked up to a point far transcending all former extravagances . . .'. Gladstone himself did not, fully, appreciate what was happening. 'I did not know,' he later confessed. 'No one knew the severity of the [impending] crisis.'

Monseigneur D'Alton, the author of a book published in 1928, had evidently known Father O'Malley personally. O'Malley, D'Alton wrote, was of the militant order and had considerable sympathy with all those who held extreme views on Irish political questions. He was known, indeed, to have very friendly feelings 'even toward the physical force section, and . . . was in entire sympathy with the Land League movement. His brother-in-law was an old Fenian and . . . to the home of Father O'Malley . . . Davitt and the Chief Land League leaders were frequent visitors . . . One of the first bitter struggles between landlord and tenant was fought . . . on the estate of the Earl of Erne. His Agent was Captain Boycott, well known on the turf and not unpopular until the division between landlord and tenant became so sharply defined.'

Lord Kilmaine (a neighbour of Charles's) wrote personally to the Lord Lieutenant on 25th October 1880. '. . . the parish priest, Mr John O'Malley, a most prominent member of the Land League, has advised [the tenants] not to pay their rents unless they receive a substantial reduction. Mr O'Malley is a positive curse to the neighbourhood. He makes the most violent speeches . . . and has openly . . . justified . . . murders . . . It is the openly expressed opinion of the peasants that no amount of police protection will prevent Captain Boycott, of Lough Mask, being shot this winter.' (That Charles escaped may owe something to poor marksmanship but, more probably, to his vigilance and to the fact that – strange as it may sound – no one really *wanted* to kill him.)

George Moore, a Catholic and the owner of a large house and over 12,000 acres not far from Ballinrobe, was, no doubt, an acquaintance of Charles's because they both loved racing and horses. On 11th September 1880 Moore published a letter in the *Mayo Examiner* in which he pleaded that 'the calamities which threaten the country' should be averted and 'that there are many landlords who are anxious to march with the times . . .' 'Landlords', he said also, 'do exist, will exist and must exist' but what Ireland needed was *more* landlords so that their land holdings – and so their rentals – would be, not larger, but smaller. He hoped for 'a peasant proprietorship which would develop and spread over the whole island until the balance of wealth was more evenly adjusted'; and ended by hoping that 'The policy of the [Land] League should, now, be one more of conciliation than hostility.' But – and alas – Moore pleaded in vain. The Compensation for Disturbance Bill had been rejected, already, by the House of Lords; 'coming events' had, indeed, 'cast their shadows before'.

On Sunday 19th September 1880, in a town named Ennis in Co. Clare, Parnell delivered his famous 'shun him' speech. To his own rhetorical question: 'What is to be done to a tenant who bids for a farm from which another has been evicted?' he said, 'you must shun him on the roadside . . . in the streets of the town, . . . in the shop . . . in the market place, and even in the place of worship, by putting him into a moral Coventry, by isolating him . . . as if he were the leper of old . . . there will be no man . . . to dare the public opinions of all right thinking men . . .' Two things seem clear. First: that this speech was the origin of the idea of 'boycotting'. Second: that Parnell had no idea that Charles even existed.

On 22nd September 1880 a 'process server', accompanied by seventeen members of the R.I.C.,[100] started serving ejectment notices on a group of Lord Erne's tenants. Although Charles had, apparently, threatened to start issuing these hated documents the poor people did not think he was serious and only three were served. The fourth house was occupied by a Mrs Fitzmorris who, with her girl friends and waving a red warning flag, shouted, 'You'll not serve my house as long as I have life in my body.' A shower of mud, stones and 'manure' followed and, eventually, the 'process' party was forced back into Lough Mask House. On the following day the women – barefoot as usual – 'indulged freely in shouts and yells and in threats at what they would do to the process server if only they could get at him'. Only one, additional, process was served for the good reason that all the householders, by then, had left their houses.

On the following day (probably) Charles's farm was invaded. The *Connaught Telegraph* of Saturday 25th September wrote that:

> The tenants around the quiet district of Lough Mask had quite a trying and exciting time . . . [when] . . . thousands [probably about 100] of human beings might be seen swarming on the hillsides that surround . . . Lough Mask . . . Whilst awaiting the expected arrival of the police a curious scene was enacted. By one sudden impulse every man . . . rushed down towards the . . . residence of the very unpopular agent . . . and at once hunted away every labourer, follower and servant in and around the place . . . Ultimately it was resolved to *starve* the agent out of the place and to induce their respected and kind landlord, Lord Erne, to rescue them from such a neighbour.

Later, a Martin Branigan (who worked for Charles), described the same event:

> I was afraid to stop . . . about fifty or sixty . . . came into the field; cannot say who they were whether the neighbours or not; did not know any of the fifty or sixty persons; the horses got frightened; none of the people came nearer than 100 yards from me; none of the party spoke to me and yet I was afraid of them and went away with the horses; one of the men that was working with me told me the business of the fifty or sixty people; . . . told Mr Weekes . . .: Mr Boycott was not at home.

'Crowds' can be strange phenomena! The 'crowds' (of perhaps 100 people) who descended upon Charles's farm did so, probably, either because they were actually hungry or because they felt themselves, genuinely, to be oppressed. No one knows how this particular crowd was divided between men and women but, if hunger was the principal reason why they assembled, then women, almost certainly, were in the majority. Angry crowds often try to impose 'natural justice' by destroying, or pulling down, walls, fences and gates. A crowd, usually, has chosen its own leader. Crowds are often violent and impulsive but they can be easily alarmed by rumour; and, if rumour turns to certainty, they may panic. Crowds are seldom either fickle or wholly irrational. They seldom attack individuals; their 'enemies' are often small groups of people who, in themselves, seem to personify the apparent injustice against which the crowd is demonstrating.

Next day Father O'Malley arrived and was 'most warmly received'. After giving some 'private instructions' he went to Ballinrobe. On hearing the news the leaders of the Ballinrobe Branch of the Land League (which included Father O'Malley) set out for Lough Mask House; and, a procession having been formed, the crowd proceeded towards – or back to? – The Neale where Father O'Malley congratulated them on 'the great victory they had achieved and the noble example they had set.'

Charles, immediately, found himself in real difficulties; the first 'boycott' had, indeed, begun. It was as hard, then, to run a farm without labour as it would be difficult today to run one without tractors. Annie found herself in similar difficulties. Both Charles and Annie – and Assheton Weekes – must have been astonished by the violence of the events which, suddenly, had erupted against them. Nonetheless the demands of the farm waited for no one. Charles had started harvesting. He had animals and a number of chickens and geese which demanded immediate attention. Assheton Weekes and Johnny Meany had their hands full in caring for the working, and race, horses. St John became the herdsman and attended to about 300 sheep and perhaps fifty steers (attending to sheep in those days was no sinecure; foot-rot was common). St John himself later wrote, 'I was always followed by two of the police who were not allowed to help me' but he often heard a voice saying, 'Tell the police to turn their backs and I will help you'. (St John never did so for fear of getting the R.I.C. into trouble.) Douglass, probably, became the 'odd job' boy. Madeleine, no doubt, helped her Aunt, did what she could on the farm and kept a sharp eye on Assheton Weekes. No one in Ballinrobe would 'wash Charles a cravat or make him a loaf'. The poor – and undernourished? – crowds who had invaded Charles's farm on 23rd September could not live on it but they seem to have returned regularly to break fences and gates, to fell trees, to damage hedges, and to trample and steal Charles's crops. What had been a well ordered private house and farm had been turned into a muddy, and disordered, public establishment. Everyone still living in Lough Mask House was required, suddenly, to adopt a new, and most unexpected, lifestyle. Charles, it is believed, used to draw back the curtain of a room and say, 'If they want to shoot me they damned well can!'; someone remarked 'he'll not hear the birds sing in Spring.' All that Charles is *known* to have said is: 'I can hardly desert Lord Erne; and, moreover, my own property is sunk in the place.'

On 25th September two things happened. First, Lord Mountmorres was murdered not far from Lough Mask House.[101] The Dublin *Evening Mail* described his murder as being 'the coping stone of a huge edifice of lawless outrage which had ruled the west of Ireland under a reign of terror as powerful . . . as that of the French Revolution.' Murder, of course, is *totally reprehensible*. Nonetheless Bernard Becker – an American journalist – has this, most curious, account of 'Irish murder' in his book *Disturbed Ireland*:[102]

> I have heard it talked over by every class of persons, from a landholding peer to a not very sober car driver . . . no horror is expressed . . . the humour of the situation overrules every other consideration. That poor people . . . should shoot one of their own class instead of the hated agent is a fact so irresistibly comic as to provoke . . . hilarious comment . . . Nobody appears to care about the general, and social, aspect of the case.

The Irish today do NOT customarily murder each other. Is it possible that prolonged malnutrition, partial blindness, pellagra – and too much poteen – could, so seriously, damage an Irishman's perception of what was right and what was wrong?

Secondly, Lord Erne's Lough Mask tenants despatched their

first letter of complaint about Charles to Lord Erne; this was signed by thirty-seven tenants. Charles, it appeared, had been a tyrant; he laid down petty laws; he never had a civil word for anyone; he stopped tenants from using certain paths; he claimed, improperly, from the Erne estate; he sent a process server, and police, to serve ejectment notices; and so on to the number of fifteen, miscellaneous, 'misconducts'. The tenants asked Lord Erne to 'choose between your old and faithful tenants and this unknown upstart'; they informed him that other local landlords had given 'larger reductions in rent'; that Charles had become 'an object of scorn and contempt'; and, as they hoped, 'you will at length look after us.' To this Lord Erne replied, politely, on 1st October. He said that if the charges against Charles had been made 'as occasion arose' he would have examined them; secondly, that he had not raised his Lough Mask rents for thirty-two years; thirdly, that he had done more for his Co. Mayo tenants than he had done for any others; and fourthly, he rebuked them by saying that your present conduct is 'due to your having been mislead by bad advice.' He ended by adding, 'My agent . . . and his family must be guarded by police to save them from death and insult.'

The tenants replied on 7th October. They deprecated that 'all power' should be in the hands of men like Rutledge (who had been sacked for dishonesty in 1862) and Boycott; emphasised their own poverty; denied that Lord Erne let his land cheaply, saying, 'Your agent and Thomas Rutledge have between them the fat of the land leaving us all the rocks, old walls, heath and brushwood'; complained that Charles had overcharged them for seed potatoes and had supplied poor quality manure; *and* that Charles might thank himself for being 'in such a disreputable position.' (Like their first letter their second was signed by thirty-seven people.)

To this Lord Erne replied, sharply, on 13th October. He refused to admit the 'Justice of the complaints, which, from all I have previously heard of [Charles's] character I believe to be entirely without foundation.'

(At about this date Counties Mayo and Galway were proclaimed as being 'Disturbed Areas.')

On 14th October Charles signed his first letter to *The Times* in London:

THE STATE OF IRELAND

Sir, The following detail may be interesting to your readers as exemplifying the power of the Land League. On the 22nd September a process-server, escorted by a police force of seventeen men, retreated to my house for protection, followed by a howling mob of people, who yelled and hooted at the members of my family. On the ensuing day, September 23rd, the people collected in crowds upon my farm, and some hundred or so came up to my house and ordered off, under threats of ulterior consequences, all my farm labourers, workmen, and stablemen, commanding them never to work for me again. My herd has been frightened by them into giving up his employment, though he has refused to give up the house he held from me as part of his emolument. Another herd on an off farm has also been compelled to resign his situation. My blacksmith has received a letter threatening him with murder if he does any more work for me, and my laundress has also been ordered to give up my washing. A little boy, twelve years of age, who carried my post-bag to and from the neighbouring town of Ballinrobe, was struck and threatened on 27th September, and ordered to desist from his work; since which time I have sent my little nephew for my letters and even he, on 2nd October, was stopped on the road and threatened if he continued to act as my messenger. The shopkeepers have been warned to stop all supplies to my house, and I have just received a message from the post mistress to say that the telegraph messenger was stopped and threatened on the road when bringing out a message to me and that she does not think it safe to send any telegrams which may come for me in future for fear they should be abstracted and the messenger injured. My farm is public property; the people wander over it with impunity. My crops are trampled upon, carried away in quantities, and destroyed wholesale. The locks on my gates are smashed, the gates thrown open, the walls thrown down, and the stock driven out on the roads. I can get no workmen to do anything, and my ruin is openly avowed as the object of the Land League unless I throw up everything and leave the country. I say nothing about the danger to my own life, which is apparent to anybody who knows the country.

CHARLES C. BOYCOTT

Lough Mask House, County Mayo, October 14th

The Irish Land Act Commission of 1880[103] (known as the Bessborough commission) resulted, in 1881, in Gladstone's Irish Land Act. The Bessborough Commission interviewed Charles in

Galway City on 22nd October 1880; that is about a fortnight before his name became widely known. The Commission were anxious to discover what Charles thought about his existing situation and to satisfy themselves that he was a truthful witness; he was asked no less than 167 questions. Although it is believed that the Commission's report was delivered, privately, to Gladstone shortly after Christmas 1880, the report itself did not become public until several months later; by which time Charles had been compelled to leave Ireland temporarily and his surname had become a household word.

Charles's answers to the Commission's questions make clear that he had an excellent grasp of the then situation in Ireland.

Q18467. Lord Erne, it appears, had offered his Lough Mask tenants a reduction in rent of 20% but the tenants demanded 25%. Charles stated that he had referred the matter back to Lord Erne who refused to grant more. Charles then took out nominal 'ejectment processes'.

Q18473. Did Charles foresee any difficulties in having the ejectment processes enforced? He replied that any tenant evicted for non payment of rent would be reinstated 'as is done everywhere in Ireland now.'

Q18474. Asked to account for this Charles said: *First*, that the Parish Priest (of The Neale) had said how easy it was to reduce the parishioners only to those who had the 'Land League at heart'; *Secondly*, that it was well known that Charles did not support the Land League; *Thirdly*, and for that reason, 'the edict had gone forth that he was to be banished from the parish.'

Q18478. Why did the people suppose you went against them? 'By bringing ejectment processes.'

Q18488–18493. Charles explained that 1878 had not been a bad year but that the price of cattle had dropped sharply and that local tradesmen had, without warning, stopped giving credit.[104] But, and despite this, Lord Erne's tenants were 'snug holders' and 'middling well off.'

Q18494. It was not inability to pay their rents that prevented the tenants from paying? 'I am certain of that in my own mind.'

Q18495. Is Lord Erne liberal in his dealings? 'Yes.'

Q18496. Did Lord Erne continue in this way? 'No, he does not. Within the last two months I had instructions from his Lordship to withdraw from it.'

Q18499. Had Charles ever experienced local ill feeling? 'Never.'

Q18523. Are you worse off than the surrounding landlords or agents? 'I am. I have been picked out as a victim to show the power of the Land League. I am, unfortunately for myself, a farmer as well as an agent.'

Q18541. What would happen if Charles gave up proceeding with the ejectment notices? 'The work people would come back and everything would go on smooth.'

(N.B. This may, or may not, be true. Father O'Malley was a determined man having the then formidable power of the Land League behind him.)

Q18543 Were your farm servants turned out by an order from the Land League? 'Yes, a mob came up to the place.'

Q18547. Were the people who invaded your property malicious or afraid? 'There is not a single individual in the country who is not afraid. Even a juror is afraid to go to Court. Every man in the country is in fear, and they say that even the protection of the police is of no use because they say the moment the police are taken away they will be shot the same as Lord Mountmorres.'

Q18548. The Commission asked 'if every man in the county is afraid, of whom are they afraid? 'Charles replied, 'It is more than I can tell. That is my only answer.'

(N.B. Almost certainly the many poor Co. Mayo Irishmen who Charles knew were, in 1880, badly nourished, poorly sighted, and, as a consequence of pellagra, often dim-witted. Many lacked moral courage and were incapable of doing that which they knew to be right. Charles had no better understanding of the true cause of this than the poor Irish themselves.)

Q18551. Were the poor people connected with the Land League? 'Every man is a subscriber to the Land League. Every man pays his shilling . . .'

Q18574. Is the district intimidated by the Land League? 'I am certain of it.'

Q18592 and 18593. Charles confirmed that Lord Erne had spent money on buildings, fences and roads, but from the answer to Q18593 it appeared that this expenditure had been, in total, little more than £80 to £100 over about eight years.

Q18599. Was the agency worth much? 'No, it is not.'

Q18600. Would it be better for Charles to resign? 'When acting for Lord Erne, and things got into trouble and all that, I would not leave; but, if I got things quiet, I would ask him to take up the agency from me.'

Q18603 and 18604. Charles considered there was no objection to him personally or to him as an Englishman.

Q18607. Would your servants help you if they were not terrified? 'I believe so.'

Q18612. Charles said that he had a letter from the bailiff on Lord Erne's Castlebar property 'stating that I might come on any day, for the tenants would pay.'

Q18614. Are you on good terms with Father O'Malley? 'Yes.'

Q18623. Charles stated that, quite recently, he had raised his men's wages.

Q18629. Having regard to the condition of the country, ought Charles to give up Lord Erne's agency? 'No.'

On 23rd October it became known that the Government in London intended to proceed, in law, against fourteen prominent members of the Land League; these included C.S. Parnell and J.W. Nally. The news was received with astonishment. Many sensible people thought that no jury could be found to convict the fourteen accused and that Gladstone's insistence that public order in Ireland be maintained was an impossibility. Parliament was prorogued for several weeks. Many people judged that the Cabinet, in London, was on the point of breaking up. Extra troops were sent to Ireland. The Irish Secretary issued a memorandum reminding the Irish magistracy of the power they already possessed for the maintenance of public order in Ireland.

On 24th October Bernard Becker went to Lough Mask House. There he discovered Charles and Annie – helped by a bull-terrier – herding sheep and guarded by 'two members of the R.I.C.[105] in full uniform and with carbines loaded.' Becker later described what he had found, already, in the west; the almost absolute wretchedness of so many poor Irish;[106] the acceptance of murder as a – more or less – unsurprising event; and Charles's extraordinary situation in which normal farming was no longer possible. Becker's excellent article appeared in several newspapers and attracted widespread and – in loyalist circles – *horrified* attention.

On 29th October the Dublin *Daily Express* (a paper which, in

Dublin, represented Ulster opinion) published a – somewhat startling – letter from 'Combination'; this proposed the creation of a fund of about £5,000 'to save Boycott's crops'. 'Combination' soon turned out to be a Protestant Land Agent named Manning. Manning's idea was adopted in Protestant Ulster with enthusiasm. Subscriptions poured in. All those Protestants who, earlier, had been alarmed by the activities of the essentially Catholic Land League had found their cause; a cause which Charles himself was almost bound to support.

One of the more surprising things which, subsequently, did not happen is that religious ill will – as between Catholics in the south and Protestants in the north – never seems to have manifested itself. The fact is that Charles was not just a Protestant by birth and upbringing; he was, most markedly, a Protestant. That nothing unseemly occurred suggests either that Charles was much better liked than is usually admitted or that nineteenth-century religious differences in Ireland were of less importance than is supposed.

On 1st November Charles was obliged to attend the Petty Sessions Court in Ballinrobe in connection with the Branigan case. Charles, in his second letter to *The Times*, dated 3rd November, described what next happened:

> I was suddenly surrounded by a yelling, hooting mob of 500 persons. Had it not been for the prompt manner in which the constabulary . . . closed around me, I should infallibly have been torn in pieces by the infuriated mob. Shortly after my arrival at the barracks, which we reached with much difficulty, the resident magistrate and sub-inspector of constabulary joined me and requested I would not go into the town until the crowd had dispersed. My servant, in attempting to bring my horse and dog-cart to me, was assaulted and forced to seek refuge in the yard of the constabulary barracks. A requisition was sent from the resident magistrate to the officer in command of the 76th for thirty men; and it was not until they arrived at the constabulary barracks, where they were forced to fix bayonets to assist the twenty-eight police, that my man was able to bring my dog-cart to the infantry barracks, where I had been detained for three hours . . . On my return through Ballinrobe on the following day I was hooted and groaned at; and my cart, which I had sent to the town for necessaries for my house, was ordered off the public streets, and the shopkeepers refused to execute my

orders. The spirit of terrorism towards me is decidedly on the increase and the determination to hunt me out of the country more openly expressed.

After this affair Charles must have found himself, for about a week, 'living in limbo'; that is to say in 'an unfavourable place' on the 'borders of hell!' Nevertheless – and despite the fact that Annie had been 'confined to her room' for several days – Charles did his best to go on presenting a normal, and fearless, front to the Land League. It was, not infrequently, remarked that 'he bore a charmed life'. But, as far as is known, he was never shot at by a marksman who took careful deliberate aim. He was, quite often, shot at; but – unaccountably! – he was never hit.

In early November – despite the 'boycotting' – Charles is believed to have gone to Galway (to see his land there?), to Dublin (on business?) and to the centre of racing at The Curragh where, no doubt, he hoped to make – at least provisional – arrangements for the future well-being of his horses.

By the end of the first week in November a 'Boycott Relief Expedition' from Ulster had been, more or less, decided upon. (Charles, it is believed, did his best to stop this from happening; he needed no more than about twelve men to finish his harvest.) Tension began, slowly, to mount; plans to transfer additional soldiers to Ballinrobe were made; troops began to patrol the roads leading to Charles's house; the – inefficient – telegraph between Ballinrobe and Dublin was kept, permanently, open; additional magistrates – including Thomas Hamilton the Senior Irish Magistrate[107] – were drafted into the Ballinrobe area. On 8th November Forster, the Irish Secretary, called a press conference in Dublin and ruled that, whilst the Government intended to help Charles, they could not allow more than fifty men to go to Lough Mask House to actually get in his harvest. This cooled some – but by no means all – of the mounting excitement.

On 9th November further military reinforcements from Dublin and The Curragh proceeded west to Ballinrobe; and, by the following day, about 900 soldiers (from different arms of the services)[108] and a small 'army' of war and newspaper correspondents had arrived. Ballinrobe was seething with excitement! Could it, conceivably, be true that an armed body of Ulstermen was on its way to help Charles 'get in his turnips'?

On 10th November the 'Boycott Expedition' was reported as being ready to leave Ulster. Whilst Charles had succeeded in 'saving' a large part of his grain crop he still needed to complete his harvest. The rumour that he was about to play host to a number of Ulstermen filled him with – justified – trepidation; even the R.I.C., billeted on his land, were prevented from buying food in Ballinrobe. But, and despite his mounting difficulties, Charles remained defiant; Bernard Becker described his 'bowed grey head and slight spare figure' which was, by no means, in submission to his most unusual circumstances.

On the same day, in Ulster, the fifty volunteers from counties Monaghan and Cavan showed themselves to be 'stout and respectable' – and cheerful – young men (whatever anyone else might call them!). They had been told that they were going to County Mayo to save the crops of a brave and courageous English gentleman. On 11th November the two separate county parties merged under the command of Mr Manning, Mr Goddard (a solicitor) and Captain Somerset Maxwell, who was then aged seventy-seven. Whilst waiting on Athlone station the volunteers were issued with revolvers but told to conceal them.[109]

The Dublin *Daily Express* donated food and supplies.[110] The party travelled on to Claremorris by a scheduled – and *not* a special – train.

At Claremorris station the volunteers found themselves facing a substantial reception party. This consisted of one Field Officer and twenty other ranks from the 1st Dragoons, 150 officers and men of the 76th Regiment, two troops of the 19th Hussars, Colonel Bruce and a number of Royal Irish Constables, several Resident Magistrates, an ambulance wagon under the command of Surgeon-Major Reynolds (who had won a V.C. at Rorke's Drift in South Africa), and a large group of war and newspaper reporters. James Daly – Editor of the *Connought Telegraph* – enlivened the large, and patiently waiting, party with a vigorous denunciation of landlordism.[111] Not surprisingly the *Freemen's Journal* remarked that they had never seen 'a sorrier or more wretched crew than the volunteers' whilst the 'loyalist press' described a group of 'fine young men' making 'a brave show of indifference.' (The loyalist description was correct; the volunteers *were* an excellent lot.)

At about 4.30pm – it was November and darkness was fast coming on – the marching party set off on their fourteen-mile march to Ballinrobe. Heavy rain is said to have fallen 'continuously.' For a reason now obscure the escort of 150 men of the 76th Regiment were relieved, at Hollymount, by a similar number from the 84th Regiment. Several delays occurred; it was not until nearly five hours had elapsed that the by now wet and weary volunteers reached Ballinrobe.[112]

On the following day (12th November) the weather had improved. The military column – smaller than on the previous day – reformed itself and marched on, for a further three miles, to Lough Mask House where it was received by Charles and Assheton Weekes, both of whom were armed. Not many people watched; most of those who did were women.

That evening Charles gave a dinner party for those army officers, volunteer officers and magistrates who intended to spend the night at, or near, Lough Mask House.[113] The volunteers made themselves as comfortable as circumstances allowed; everyone found a tent. Manning, Goddard and Somerset Maxwell retreated to Charles's large, carpeted and almost palatial boat house; accompanied, for a reason now unknown, by the correspondent of the *Daily Express*.

The expedition's first night in Lough Mask House is believed to have been very wet. The process of turning Charles's tidy paths and well-kept lawns into an – appalling – quagmire had begun.

On 12th November there were about 900 soldiers in and around Lough Mask House and Ballinrobe and about 7,000 in the west of Ireland. Charles continued, resolutely, to defy the Land League. The eyes of the world were, by now, focused upon events in Lough Mask House.

On Saturday 13th November the task of 'saving Charles's crops' began; this meant the lifting of eight acres of turnips, seven acres of mangolds, two acres of potatoes and the threshing of twenty acres of already cut corn. The Royal Engineers 'scooped out' a cooking trench upon which the volunteer cooks placed gigantic pots of potatoes. Three or four members of the party started on the threshing, using Charles's 'modern' – but still very small – hand-thresher; the remainder, accompanied by their officers and escorted by police and a patrol of the 19th Hussars, marched out to Charles's fields.[114] That night the Monaghan men returned soaking wet and refused to sleep in their tents, but seemed happier when moved into a hayloft. A rumour reached the camp that it was to be attacked that evening; sentries were doubled, a password given out and extra soldiers from the 84th moved up but nothing untoward happened.

14th November was a Sunday. It was thought wrong for men to work on that day. In the afternoon a divine service was held in the hayloft.

At about this point it is necessary to remember that, in 1888, a large number of 'Irish Documents' were sent to London for use during the – long drawn out – trial of Charles Parnell. A quantity of 'Boycott' documents were, almost certainly, then sent to London but virtually *all* of these have since disappeared. Nevertheless Thomas Hamilton's – the Senior Resident Magistrate at Lough Mask House – concluding report (dated 28th November 1880) has survived. In this Hamilton said that the 'general good conduct' (of all those soldiers and police involved) 'had been admirable' but that 'the organised and systematic obstruction offered by the Land League . . . had been much enhanced by the difficulties of the undertaking; and that, but for the ready and cheerful assistance rendered by the Military and the Police, . . . the expedition must have proved a failure.'

The *Connaught Telegraph* of 20th November reported a meeting in Dublin of the National Land League; from this it is clear that the Ulster expedition had been a considerable success. Indeed 'it had become a question whether Captain Boycott, or the people, shall win', and, the report went on, 'Abandonment of the project, now that we are pledged to it, would involve imputations which there could be no answering.' The National Land League also asked that '"they" shall not discourage our effort to repair the harm already done in Co. Mayo.' It is, of course, easy to make too much of this. The Ulstermen had only a limited objective. When they had secured Charles's crops, and threshed his corn, the only thing remaining to them was to return home. In the meanwhile the eyes and ears of the western world – including American eyes and ears – remained *glued* upon Charles and his exciting affairs. Rumour – and threatening letters – abounded. Some bored gentlemen of the press thought that, if no one else would attack Lough Mask House, they ought to do so themselves. The steady 'disappearance' of Charles's geese and sheep caused astonished comment. The poor telegraph service (The 'story on the top of a stick') between Ballinrobe and Dublin came under continuous criticism. The small hotel in Ballinrobe became crammed with 'a closely laid strata of guests' but a number of soldiers were still quartered – and half drowned – on Ballinrobe's green. The scarlet of the soldiers' uniforms became muddy and dishevelled. Nonetheless, it remained true that no one dared predict what, next, might happen. The Land League could *not* lawfully be suppressed; the Ulstermen may have won a battle but they had not yet won a war.

On much the same day it was reported that Charles was not looking well.

On the next day Father O'Malley began to react to the apparent success of the Ulstermen. He proposed that a delegation of Lough Mask House and farm employees, led by himself, should go north to meet Lord Erne. O'Malley – astonishingly – then believed that Lord Erne might agree to sack Charles as a counterweight to the success of the Ulstermen. O'Malley's idea was debated by the National Land League in Dublin on 19th November but was sharply rejected; it had become obvious, to at least some Land League members, that they were, in reality, *winning*.

On 16th November there was a short-lived excitement when Charles, and a troop of Hussars, searched successfully for some missing cattle which ought to have been on Charles's farm at Kilmaine. The *Freemen's Journal* remarked that this incident reminded them of Don Quixote when 'the warriors bold searched for its wandering beeves.'

On 17th November three small excitements occurred. First, a well known man named J.W. Nally[115] – who is said to have been out shooting but who, also, may have been out drinking – penetrated into the camp. Nally was accompanied by a man named Joyce who pretended to be a clergyman whose – astonishingly – simple message was 'the land for the people.' This caused the camp guard to be called and 'after a lively exchange of compliments' both visitors were ejected. Secondly, when the 'Gentlemen of the Press' arrived for their daily visit, Colonel Twentyman – in command at Lough Mask House and believed to have been a kind-hearted but choleric officer – refused the press entry on the ground that no less than forty-seven of Charles's sheep had been slaughtered by the military. The matter was referred to the overall Commander (Brevet Brigadier – General Bedingfield R.A.) who countermanded the earlier order. Thirdly, it was announced that

Charles and Annie had decided to return, temporarily, to England because it was impossible for Charles to farm 'when I can neither buy nor sell'; and because he, himself, had become unable, both mentally and physically, to undertake any active duties.

On 18th November it is known that Lord Erne went to Dublin. The Reverend Desmond Morse-Boycott, in *A Tapestry of Toil*, has this curious account of a train journey which Charles may have undertaken in order to meet Lord Erne. 'He' – Charles – 'was in danger of his life. One day the angry peasants saw a funeral cortège making its way to the station where the bier was placed on the platform . . . As the train steamed in the lid of the coffin flew open and the corpse of Captain Boycott darted into a first class carriage.'[116]

On 20th November Michael Davitt returned to Ireland from the U.S.A.; too late to take any part in the 'Boycott affair' but not too late to emphasise to his many friends in Ireland the depth of American support for Ireland.

By about the same date it seemed unlikely that any surprising incident would upset the steady flow of events round Lough Mask House. The Ulstermen were working well. Such of Charles's crops as could be sold were fetching good prices. Somerset Maxwell had abandoned the boat house and was staying with Lord and Lady Ardilaun near Cong. A professional photographer named Wynne had taken some excellent photographs of the 'camp' and its occupants. Fifteen of Ballinrobe's inhabitants had been charged with obstructing Charles – on his lawful business – on 1st November. What, about a fortnight earlier, might have become a dangerously explosive situation had fallen – far – short of expectation.

The 21st November was another Sunday. A clergyman named Brodie took a service which was attended by the Ulster Volunteers and a number of soldiers. (Charles himself went to Hollymount Protestant Church which stood a few miles away. Whilst there he was guarded by a young officer of the R.I.C. who never forgot the experience.)

By Friday 26th November the Ulster Volunteers had finished their work.[117] That night everyone was kept awake by another *tremendous* storm which, finally, completed the ruin of Charles's well-trampled park and his lawns and paths. On the following day (27th November) conditions were better and everyone set about striking camp with a will. At about 2pm the volunteers – accompanied by their officers, some soldiers, the press and several newspaper artists – assembled outside Charles's front door. Somerset Maxwell read out a courteous letter from Charles in which he thanked everyone for their help and expressed the sadness he felt at being obliged 'to quit, with my wife, a happy home where we had hoped to have spent the remainder of our days.' A great cheer went up when Charles walked down his front door steps and shook hands with everyone. A Regimental cook borrowed a scabbard and beat the time whilst the assembled company sang 'Auld Lang Syne' and 'For They are Jolly Good Fellows'.

Not many local people watched the departure to Ballinrobe of 'the queerest menagerie that ever came to Connaught', but Father O'Malley was one. He found himself entangled with an old lady. 'Did I not warn you' he said, 'to let the British Army alone? How dare you come to intimidate those two thousand heroes after their glorious campaign? I'll make an example of you. Be off!' Later O'Malley was interviewed by the press. To them he emphasised that it was the 'three Fs' that Ireland needed; that is Fixity of Tenure (of land), Fair Rents and the Free Sale of Land. He hoped that, before long, Gladstone would, indeed, grant just that. But O'Malley also said that some 'extraordinary event like the Boycott expedition' had been a necessity; without it the eyes and ears of the western world would not have been fixed, for so long, upon Ireland and its difficulties.

Assheton Weekes – who lived with Charles throughout the first 'boycott' – put pen to paper in a letter to the *Freeman's Journal*. In this he made three points:

First: That Charles had been tried, and condemned, 'on false issues.'

Second: That Charles and his workmen had been on amicable and friendly terms and that his employees had no wish to leave his employment.

Third: That 'the cause of all the ill will' had been because Charles could not, honestly, recommend a greater reduction in rent than Lord Erne had already granted.

Reveille sounded early on 28th November. It was still dark when the volunteers and soldiers marched away from Ballinrobe to catch their trains. Charles and Annie – accompanied by a dog, a parrot and a few suitcases – left Lough Mask House early on the same day in an ambulance wagon (drawn, it is believed, by four grey mules) and escorted by a troop of the 19th Hussars. As Charles caught up, and passed through, the Ulster Volunteers he took off his hat to them; they had done their duty. On Claremorris platform Charles walked, quietly and unconcernedly, amongst those of his friends who had managed to get to the station to see him off (these included J.W. Nally!). On arrival in Dublin Charles and Annie were escorted to the Hamman Hotel in Upper Sackville Street by detectives. A police constable was posted outside the hotel's front door. Charles may have intended to spend a few days in Dublin – there was talk of a banquet – but two threatening letters, and the unwillingness of the hotel's proprietor to continue giving him a room, forced him to leave. He left Dublin on the mail boat to Holyhead on 1st December 1880.[118]

So ended an odd, and unique, affair. Davitt later remarked that 'the boycott incident' had cost the British Government £3,500 but that the value of the crops saved had been £350. The Masonic Grand Lodge in Belfast expressed 'their sympathy with Captain Boycott and his family during the cruel persecution to which they have been opposed by the Land League.' The truth, of course, was that much of Ireland was in ferment; for the time being the Land League was, virtually, all powerful; it was not easy to decide, at any given moment, who actually *governed* Ireland.

As Charles left Ireland about ten other landowners were being persecuted, similarly, in Co. Mayo alone.

PART THREE

AN 'UNSOUGHT INTERVAL'

(December 1880 – August 1881)

CHAPTER EIGHTEEN

AFTER CHARLES LEFT LOUGH MASK House at the end of November 1880 'boycotting' became both widespread, and notorious, in Ireland. The Cork Defence Union published a leaflet on the subject on 1886.[1] In its 'introduction' it said, '. . . a peaceable subject of the Queen is denied food and drink and . . . is ruined in his business; . . . his cattle are unsaleable; . . . the smith will not shoe his horse, nor the carpenter mend his cart; old friends pass him by . . . making the sign of the cross; . . . his children are hooted at . . .; he sits apart . . . in the place of public worship; all for doing nothing but what the law says he has a perfect right to do . . .'

The same leaflet listed 101 'boycotting cases in the County of Cork.' A much abbreviated account of ten of these follows:

Daniel Rourke (Blacksmith) No one permitted to employ him because he disobeyed the orders of the League in working for 'boycotted' farmers.

Mrs Hosking (A schoolmaster's wife) Did not belong to the League. Refused provisions.

Dennis McCarthy (Farmer) Completely 'boycotted'. Wife stoned and her clothes torn 'by the mob' when attending Chapel in December 1885.

T. M. Beamish (Landowner and farmer) Partially 'boycotted' since 1880. Servants and labourers compelled to leave his employ. Three of his animals stolen, killed and eaten. A tenant shot. Now dead.

Edward Gardiner (Cattle buyer) Purchased cattle from 'boycotted' persons. Attacked on public road and left for dead.

R. Williams (Farmer) A body of armed, and disguised, men went to his house at Christmas 1885. When he appeared he was fired at and wounded in the back and legs.

Johanna Donaghue (wife) Children attacked. When Joanna defended them she was pelted with stones and violently attacked by a dog.

Timothy Collins (Farmer) Closely 'boycotted'. At midnight his cattle shed set on fire. Rescued his cows and saved his house. Badly burnt. Overcome with terror.

Patrick Donneley (Artisan) Closely 'boycotted'. Wife and daughter joined League but he refused. Left alone for two years. Found dead by roadside.

A curious example of 'boycotting' occurred in 1882, when a publisher was punished for committing two 'offences'; these were that he came from the 'North of Ireland' and that he was hospitable to 'obnoxious people'.

Some individuals were not 'boycotted' but were left in no doubt as to what the 'Land League' thought of them:

Horace Townsend 'The lying, oily, slippery, paid Agent of the syndicate.'

Beardy Pateshall 'The Plotting Pliable worker from the slums of an unknown English town.'

Smith-Barry 'The Bastard Head of the Exterminating Crew.'

The verb 'to boycott' started to appear in the dictionaries of the world about the year 1900. The verb was 'coined' in the priest's house in The Neale, in late September 1880, in a conversation between James Redpath, the well known American journalist, and Father O'Malley. Redpath was searching his mind for a word – round which uneducated people might get their tongues – to signify hostility towards a landlord or land agent. O'Malley thought for a moment and then said, 'How would "to boycott" do?'

To 'boycott' was legal in as much as it could not be proceeded against under the law because no offence, known to the law, had been committed. This was its strength. It soon became a most unpleasant, much feared and widely used social weapon in Ireland; and, before long, in the world. It was, almost always, used against individuals or against small family groups.

Parnell and the Land League won 'their war' against Charles without much real difficulty and in a, more or less, gentlemanly way. But, after Christmas 1880, gentility came to an abrupt end; 'boycotting' became a terrifying, and often long lasting, punishment for an offence which no judge or jury had even considered let alone ruled upon.

Before Charles 'invented' boycotting[2] the verb 'to ostracise' (first used in 1588) meant one of two things; it could mean 'a temporary banishment by which a too popular, or too powerful, citizen was sent into exile' or it might mean, 'banishment by general consent; exclusion from society favour or common privileges'. 'To send to Coventry' meant 'to exclude a person from the society of which he is a member on account of objectionable conduct; to refuse to associate, or have intercourse, with him'. Neither of these well tried sanctions fitted the new requirement; neither 'ostracism' nor 'sending to Coventry' exacted sufficient penalty. In May 1882 Gladstone defined 'boycotting'. 'What is meant by boycotting? In the first place, it is *combined intimidation*. In the second place it is combined intimidation made use of for the purpose of destroying the private liberties of choice by *fear of ruin and starvation*. In the third place, that being what "boycotting" is in itself, we must look to this; that the creed of "boycotting", like every other creed, requires a sanction and that *the sanction of boycotting* – that which stands in the rear of "boycotting", and by which alone "boycotting" can in the long run be made thoroughly effective – *is the murder which is not to be denounced*.' As the years passed, and acts of 'boycotting' multiplied all over the world, it was realized that even Gladstone had not succeeded in hitting the 'boycott' nail, precisely, on the head. The *Oxford English Dictionary* now defines the word as follows: 'To continue in refusing to hold relations of any kind with (a neighbour) on account of political or other differences, so as either to punish him or coerce him into abandoning his position. The word was first used to describe the action instituted by the Irish Land League towards those who incurred its hostility.'

A silver commemorative medal was presented in early 1881 by the Orange Order to the men who took part in the Lough Mask House Relief Expedition.[3] The medal bears the following inscription:

Obverse	The Imperial Crown and the words 'IN HONOUR OF THE LOYAL AND BRAVE ULSTERMEN'
Reverse	'THE BOYCOTT EXPEDITION. LOUGH MASK 1880'

(Space was left, on the Reverse, for the name of each recipient to be inscribed.)

The ribbon is orange with two green stripes which indicates that the medal is connected with agriculture. It was designed by a professional medalist named John Woodhouse (Junior) and struck by West & Co (then of Belfast). Seventy-one medals were struck and awarded to:

The Officers of the Expedition	3 (Manning,[4] Goddard and Somerset Maxwell)
The County Monaghan Party	32 (Presented to the recipients by Lord Rossmore on 17th February 1881)
The County Cavan Party	25
Individuals from Dublin	7
Special Awards	3 (The Earl of Enniskilling, the Royal Irish Academy and the *Belfast Newsletter*)
Required by law	1 (The British Museum)

The only known (but incomplete) list of recipients is contained in the *Belfast Newsletter* of 15th November 1880. (Charles himself was the *recipient* of help; rightly, he was not awarded a medal.)

'Boycott' medals seldom come on to the open market. (The medal awarded to Robert McBride of the Monahan contingent was bought by the author in 1984.)

A Member of Parliament named Major-General Burnaby, and William Day (who, with his wife and small daughter, probably stayed with Charles and Annie at Keem at the time of the fire), acted as 'Joint Secretaries' to the appeal for cash to reduce Charles's financial loss at Lough Mask House.

At the time Mr Gladstone was both Prime Minister *and* Chancellor of the Exchequer.

On 8th December 1880 Charles wrote, personally, to Mr Gladstone. He said that he had laid out about £6,000 on improving and stocking his farm; that some tenants could, but would not, pay their rents; that large numbers of police and soldiers had been sent to Lough Mask House; that fifty volunteers from the north had completed his harvest but that he had only asked for twelve; that when the soldiers, the police, and the volunteers from the north were ordered to leave Lough Mask House he had been compelled to leave also; that his house and farm had been, at least temporarily, made valueless; that hardly a night passed without some further injury to his property; and that, in effect, there was an absence of law in the west of Ireland. Charles emphasised that these misfortunes were not of his own making. He hoped that H.M. Government would first investigate his complaint and then compensate him.

To this Mr Gladstone replied enigmatically; he said that 'he is not sure in which way he is to understand your request for assistance' which 'had been very largely afforded to you in the use of the public force.'

To this Charles replied immediately. He regretted that his meaning should be doubtful. He said (again) that he had lost £6,000: that it was a mistake to think that he had been assisted – largely – by 'the public force'; and that he had asked for only 'twelve labourers'. But, instead of such a small number, 'an army had been sent into Mayo, not to assist me but to preserve the public peace.' He ended by emphasising his regret that 'Her Majesty's Government, having failed to protect, would do nothing to compensate him.'

On 28th December (after Christmas) Mr Gladstone wrote again telling Charles that he had referred the whole matter to the Irish Government in Dublin. His concluding paragraph was, by no means, hostile to Charles's point of view: 'Mr Gladstone is glad to observe the natural sympathy which your case has aroused in the public mind.'

During the first week in January 1881 Charles was away from Burgh-St-Peter canvassing public support and he was not able to reply to the 28th December letter until 7th January. He then asked two questions. Did Mr Gladstone admit the truthfulness of his claim? *Or*, was he challenging Charles's right to compensation? (To this, second, question there was a barb; several supporters of the Government had declined to join 'the Boycott Committee' because to do so might be thought of as an act of hostility to Mr Gladstone.)

No reply to Charles's 7th January letter was received until 20th January. Mr Gladstone then, and in effect, reiterated that the whole matter had been referred to Dublin to whom any further enquiries should be made.

To this Charles replied sharply (he was, it seems, beginning to smell a rat). He started by saying that 'the terms in which your several communications have been expressed has been somewhat ambiguous' and continued by saying that the Cabinet letter of 14th December had led Charles – *and* his friends – to conclude that the Government had rejected official compensation; and, this being so, Charles's Committee had appealed to the public whose response had been most generous. 'Subscriptions had reached them from every quarter.' Nevertheless this, particular, public outlook had been short-lived; the – apparently erroneous – idea that Charles would be compensated officially had caused private subscriptions to 'dwindle away'. But then – having lost the financial sympathy of these friends – Mr Gladstone's most recent letter had told him that no such meaning was to be attributed to it; and, in consequence, I have 'lost my hold on the generosity of my fellow countrymen.' And, (in effect) I have 'gained nothing from the Prime Minister save a barren expression of sympathy accompanied by a delusive hope of substantial assistance'.

The altercation with the Prime Minister ceased at this point. The argument with him reveals two, important, aspects of Charles's character and abilities. First: he was frightened of no one. Secondly: his letters to Mr Gladstone were written in excellent English; like all Charles's letters they were clear, concise and to the point.

Their names are now unimportant, but a large number of Englishmen – many of them distinguished – either actually contributed to the Boycott Relief Fund or would have liked to do so had not Gladstone's attitude stopped them. The Stock Exchange, in London, opened a list to which £180 was contributed. Lord and Lady Erne gave generously. On the 12th December 1880, in a letter addressed to William Day, Lord Erne wrote,

> Mr Boycott has been my agent for five or six years and I always found him doing his duty by me and my tenants. They never complained of him in any way until lately when they brought most frivolous charges against him. I shall have great pleasure in . . . . [illegible] as one of his Committee, and doing anything in my power to assist him.

Lord Erne's good opinion of Charles never wavered.

In all about £2,000 was collected from the public. Charles always claimed that the 'first boycotting' had cost him some £6,000; or, in other words, that he had lost about £4,000.

The fact, of course, was that Gladstone was both Prime Minster *and* Chancellor of the Exchequer. He had a duty not to spend public money unnecessarily. (Charles was the *first* 'boycotted' man to lose money; but he was, by no means, the last.)

In January 1881 Charles had his portrait painted by 'Spy'; it appeared in *Vanity Fair* on 29 January 1881. (A copy appears on the back of the cover.)

The portrait depicts a strong forceful man of about fifty. His hair is thin but he wears a luxurious beard. His nose is large and prominent; Napoleon is said to have remarked, more than once, 'Give me a man with a nose'. Charles's eyes were portrayed as being blue. His hands are not visible. His clothes fit him excellently; he wears a darkish, well cut, Norfolk jacket. All in all he is depicted as being a strong, resolute man, well accustomed to standing – squarely and cheerfully – on his own two feet. If being kicked out of Ireland about six weeks earlier had distressed him this fact is concealed. (To appear, in 1881, in a Spy cartoon, was a sort of 'Oscar'; a mixture lying somewhere between an O.B.E. and an appearance on *Desert Island Discs*.)

Late in 1881 Charles gave Annie a small, but beautifully made, gold brooch in the form of a sheaf of corn. The back is inscribed – in tiny lettering – 'Annie Boycott, from her husband, Harvest Lough Mask, 1880.'[5]

In November 1880 the 'intensely loyal' Grand Orange Lodge in Belfast passed a resolution in which they openly recognised the effect the Land League was having upon 'the lives, liberties, property and trade of all . . . well disposed persons'. The Grand Lodge also expressed sympathy with 'Captain Boycott . . . and his family during [their] cruel persecution'; and expressed their admiration of 'the devoted and brave conduct' which had characterised the Boycott Relief Expedition. They also petitioned the Queen, telling her that '. . . in Ireland true liberty has ceased to exist and intolerable tyranny prevails; life is not secure, right is disregarded, the processes of law cannot be enforced and dishonesty and lawlessness disgrace the land'.

Grand Lodge soon saw that something had to be done *quickly*;

too many houses and farm properties were being abandoned. The Property Defence Association (P.D.A.) was formed by the Orange Order in early December 1880; its members became deeply concerned by the calamities into which Ireland seemed to be falling. The P.D.A.'s intentions were to uphold the rights of property, to maintain a freedom of contract and to insist that individuals had liberty of action. (The P.D.A. operated in fifteen Irish Counties. Lord Erne became a member.)

On 10th December 1880 the P.D.A. began to accept at least some responsibility for abandoned properties by putting in Ulstermen as caretakers until such time as the rightful owner either repossessed himself of his property or put it up for sale. Nothing, now, has survived to show that Lough Mask House was looked after by an Ulster caretaker but it is almost certain that this was the case. (Nothing, it seems, was either lost or stolen whilst Charles and Annie were away from Ireland.)

Having been thrown off his farm and out of his house Charles, in the Spring of 1881, found himself the possessor of leisure. He used it to do what he had wanted to do for some time; that is to go to the United States of America. He and Annie – travelling as Mr and Mrs Charles Cunningham – left the Rectory at Burgh-St-Peter and went – mostly on pleasure but to some extent, also, on business – to Virginia. After landing in New York Charles, Annie, and Charles's nephew St John,[6] travelled on, by train, through Washington and Richmond (the capital of Virginia) to the small Virginian County of Amelia. There they stayed with their old friends Murray and Frances Blacker. Twelve days at sea, plenty of sleep, good food, agreeable company, and the twin prospects of meeting the Blackers again and of seeing America had worked wonders; Charles was in *excellent* health and spirits. As he went ashore his travelling companions said their goodbyes with *vivas*; he had been well liked.

The American press were on the quayside, in strength, to meet him. The *Richmond Despatch* (of 7th April 1881) started a long article about Charles and the condition of Ireland, with these words:

> There was nothing remarkable in the appearance of the little party as they stepped down the gang-plank . . ., and yet, but a few months since, these new arrivals were more talked about,

> more written about, more villified, more sympathised with, and generally subjected to more unsought notoriety than any single family at that time residing in the wide range of Her Britannic Majesty's dominions.

Under the sub heading of 'A Man of Nerve' the *Despatch* described Charles:

> In appearance Captain Boycott by no means gives the idea of a hard taskmaster or a cruel, grasping man. He is of medium height . . . of muscular build, broad-chested, upright as a dart, and carries his forty-nine years lightly indeed. His face is expressive of good humour; but the key to the character he has earned for the possession of an indomitable will, nerve and courage, is to be found in the somewhat small grey eyes, in which firmness and determination are plainly visible. The beard, moustache, and whiskers once dark brown are worn full, and are already plentifully besprinkled with grey. Partial baldness displays a well shaped head; the protuberant forehead indicating the possession of intellectual faculties of a high order. Captain Boycott is genial, not to say jovial, in manner and appeared to be on excellent terms with himself and the world in general. During no part of the conversation that took place between himself and a *Herald* reporter did he give vent to any bitter expression relative to the tenantry whose cordial hatred he so successfully acquired. He is a polished gentleman in diction and gesture who successfully affected – if, indeed, he did not sincerely feel – a profound commiseration for the condition of the people among whom he has spent over a quarter of a century.

Annie, as buoyant as her husband, did not escape her small share of the questioning. Asked 'whether she did not find it a very trying time during the last few months of her family's residence at Lough Mask', the lady responded with an eloquent shrug of her shoulders; 'Oh, dear me! Please don't talk about it; we want to forget that unpleasant episode altogether.'

Murray Blacker first saw Virginia in 1871; six years, only, after the end of the American Civil War. By 1881 the scars of that conflict were beginning to heal; but the State of Virginia, whose plantations and farms and fields had borne most of the fighting, had, by no means, fully recovered.

When, in 1861, the Civil War started, Virginia found itself pulled this way and that; it had always enjoyed strong links with its neighbours. It was overladen with a sense of history and of obligation, not to part of America, but to all of it; seven of the first twelve Presidents had been Virginians. It might have become the most southerly State within the 'union' North; indeed, at the very beginning, it voted so to become. A few days later Virginia changed its mind and joined the South; convinced (or if not convinced then persuaded by several pressing considerations) by the size and profitability of its Richmond slave market, by the fact that its own agricultural prosperity and its easy aristocratic way of life depended upon slaves, and by the inevitable conclusion that, whatever it did, Virginia's farms and fields were likely to become battle grounds. Neutrality was never an option in the weeks leading up to the war.

Richmond became, immediately, the Confederate capital; not least because of the Tredegar ironworks which supplied about half of all the Confederate ammunition and ordnance. Thousands of Confederate officials, the sick and the wounded, prisoners of war and soldiers in transit – and their prostitutes – trebled Richmond's population. As had been feared much heavy fighting took place on Virginian soil. 'Union' strategy was to blockade and isolate the South, cut it in two, and capture Richmond. All these objectives were ultimately achieved; Richmond fell on 3rd April 1865.[7] The 'South' surrendered (at Appomattox Court House in Virginia) on the 9th April. (Abraham Lincoln, the sixteenth President, was assassinated five days later.)

No Richmonder who lived through the city's final 'evacuation' fire ever forgot it. Bridges, factories, houses, mills, warehouses, and virtually all the city's windows, were destroyed. The reaction of Richmond's inhabitants to such a disastrous outcome to the war were varied. On the one hand its 'mob' (including many poor immigrant Irish) 'discovered that the gutters were awash with whisky, rum and brandy, . . . and, bold from drink, "Confederate" deserters and stragglers, escaped Union soldiers . . . blacks, poor whites and impoverished aristocrats . . . burned and looted . . .' On the other a Mrs Robert Stannard, a beautiful Richmond hostess, 'sat outside her magnificent home in her best clothes and quietly watched her mansion burn to the ground.' Panic-stricken dogs and cats 'ran the streets, ignoring the squeals of thousands of rats . . .' Immediately after the war Virginia lost her cherished identity; in the eyes of the 'North' she became nothing better than 'District No 1'. The city went uncleaned. An unprecedented crime wave followed the war. Negroes and Northern opportunists ran the government of Virginia and its legislature.

Whilst Richmond was quickly rebuilt Virginia's old plantations and fine houses could not be cured of their ills so quickly. Virginia had been fought over, dug over, pillaged and 'occupied' for four years. War casualties had been heavy. Many of its houses and farms and estates had mistresses but no masters. Before the war many of its inhabitants had been 'wealthy' in the sense that they had 'abundant means at their command'; 'means' had consisted, not of money, but of slaves. These, for the cost of their food and clothing, worked their master's land, stocked his 'larders' and provided servants for his house and plantation. Peace, and the overnight disappearance of all slaves brought to Virginia's landowners more than a sudden poverty; it destroyed their way of life.[8]

By 1870 Murray Blacker had been a Deputy Lieutenant of Co. Mayo for five years and one of its Justices of the Peace for fourteen years. He lived in a fine house outside Claremorris. What caused him to remove to Virginia? The underlying reason is to be found in his character. By no stretch of the imagination could he have been described as a placid, accepting man; on the contrary he was a fiery, impatient, courageous and uncompromising one who required the circumstances of life to fall towards, and not away from, himself. By 1870 – and despite the fact that he was, himself, an Irishman – he had become increasingly intolerant of Ireland's political uncertainties and its intermittent violence. Violence erupted, it is believed, into his own drawing-room (presumably in Claremorris which was never, in itself a placid and accepting place) when he was having tea. To his fury an Irish malcontent shot at him through a window. Although the Fenian bullet (if it was one) missed its target it pierced the target's silver teapot twice. In what might be described as a 'passion of ill-humour' Murray started to pay better attention to *The Field* correspondence about 'farming in Virginia' which had started in March 1870.

Most of *The Field*'s correspondents were Englishmen who can never have travelled far. Almost to a man they displayed a starry-eyed ignorance of the realities of farming in a foreign country whose staple crops were not those of England or Ireland and which, so recently, had endured so calamitous a civil war. These people wrote that 'hundreds of farms' were available, that taxes were light, that Englishmen would be well received, that there was no scarcity of water, that 'railways intersected Virginia in all directions', that Virginians made good neighbours – the 'ladies, especially, being well educated and considerate' – that game was abundant and that 'An Englishman hunts a pack of English hounds.' 'English Farmer', on the other hand, would have none of this rubbish. It was his opinion that Virginia was a 'wilderness'; that its land was 'worn out'; that 'few people unaquainted with farming can form any idea of the expense, trouble, time and labour that it takes to restore a worn out soil to a state of profitable cultivation'; and that labour was difficult to get and 'very bad'.

The whole truth, of course, lay neither with the pie in the sky optimists nor with 'English Farmer'. The State of Virginia occupies a large area. Whilst two of its post-war ills – the lack of slaves and the lack of capital – affected almost every aspect of daily life its third misfortune was not so all-embracing; not *all* of its thousands of farmers had been killed and not *all* its farms had been fought over, dug over, and pillaged. Bargains – good farms at reasonable prices – were to be found. The difficulty was to find them.

In May 1871 Murray went, himself, to Virginia. He was then aged forty-seven. He was an intelligent energetic man who had devoted the working part of his life to farming. He had served his farming apprenticeship in South Norfolk; he still owned the same working farm in that county of fine hard-working farmers. He owned, and worked, farms in Claremorris and Achill. He had probably inherited his uncle's library. As he sailed away to America he had few equals as a practical working farmer and as a judge of land, buildings and stock. He returned home in July 1871. He then lay under an obligation to tell his fellow readers of *The Field* of his Virginian experience but this took him six months. (His letter to *The Field* was published on 17th February 1872.)

Murray's letter was, *by far*, the longest published by *The Field* about farming in Virginia. Its encouraging 'come hither to Virginia' impression was heightened by the obvious diligence displayed by its author, by the fact that he had been accompanied by an apparently honest and knowledgeable local land agent, and because he had walked almost everywhere whilst carrying his few possessions on his back. Within his grand total of 3,000 words Murray devoted 800 to his journey out, to New York, and to hotel, food and prices. (Whilst in New York he visited several Irishmen 'whose parents are my tenants' and who were all 'delighted to see anyone from the old country!') He stated seven points about settling in Virginia concerning which he 'required to be satisfied.' His inspection of about eighteen farms lying south-west of Alexandria occupied 1,000 words. From that area of Virginia he moved (by train) to the small tobacco-growing county of Amelia. There, in about 400 words, he found that land could be purchased 'on very moderate terms say from £1.15.0 to £3.0.0 per acre; at the latter price with house and offices'. He was critical of crop yields because the land was 'in no case manured.' (In remarking upon this – to English eyes – farming phenomenon he wrote that 'the yards in which cattle are confined become choked with manure; this difficulty is often overcome by moving the yard and not the manure.') He then employed 600 words in descriptions of Virginia's timber and trees, its fruits, its birds ('. . . the wild turkey . . . is a splendid bird for the table') its snakes ('The rattlesnake is considered a very honest snake as he always lets you know if you approach too near him') and its insects. In his final paragraph he said he had been 'introduced to the neighbouring gentry' – who had treated him 'with marked kindness' – and that he had satisfied himself 'that the accounts [he] had read in *The Field* as to the advantages of Virginia as a field of emigration for a person with capital had not been overdrawn.' In effect, Murray's *Field* letter added a voice to the support of those Englishmen and Irishmen who had contemplated farming in Virginia. (Times, however, change; professionalism deepens. To modern eyes Murray's letter would be considered long on rhetoric but short on hard professional knowledge of farming.)

Murray moved to Virginia in the spring of 1872. About October of that year he printed a prospectus entitled 'From England to Virginia'. It contained four documents:

No 1 A copy of his original letter to *The Field*.

No 2 An 'Expression of Confidence' in Murray as 'an agent for the sale of lands in the county of Amelia' signed by eight gentlemen of that county.

No 3 Comments on his second visit to Amelia by Murray dated, in Amelia County, 2nd September 1872.
No 4 A list of twenty-eight (unidentifiable) farms for sale.

Taken together, Documents 2, 3 and 4 establish that, by the autumn of 1872, Murray had set himself up as an agent for the sale of farm properties in Amelia County. Taken individually, Document No 4 is now of little practical interest. Document No 3 is of interest because, in it, he announced that his brother, the Reverend Maxwell Blacker of Pimlico, London, and 'C.C. Boycott Esq, J.P. of Claremont, Claremorris, Ireland' would give information about Murray's Virginian enterprise to people living in England and Ireland respectively. Document No 2 (the 'Expression of Confidence' in Murray) is of interest for three of its declarations. The first declared that Murray will 'more certainly than anyone we have met guard immigrants against the ruinous evil of purchasing poor lands at high prices and the community against purchasers without capital'. The second said that 'The extensive acquaintance and connection of Mr Blacker and his companions with a very superior class of British and Irish farmers and gentlemen compel us to believe that they will be the means of introducing promptly a body of agriculturists whose business habits, social qualities and practical knowledge of farming will be of incalculable value to the state.' The third declaration made the, potentially significant, point that whilst the eight signatories to the document addressed themselves only to the people of Amelia County, they hoped to see 'the agency of Mr Blacker extended to the counties of Powhatan, Nottoway, Cumberland and Chesterfield'.

Up to about this point Murray's affairs seem to have been proceeding satisfactorily, but the fact is that the 'Blacker Immigration Scheme' never succeeded. Whilst Murray himself was able to buy in a splendid plantation property and to grow successfully for thirty years what to him then were strange crops in strange soils and under strange climatic conditions, his band of 'young gentlemen' never found their El Dorado; Amelia welcomed, but failed to hold, its farming immigrants. Why did Murray succeed where his young men failed?[9]

First, because Murray was a tough and experienced farming businessman who had committed himself to Virginia and who had enough capital to buy in, and go on buying in, whatever labour he needed to work his land in a *very* difficult labour market. Secondly because 85% of his Document No 1 was irrelevant to farming in Amelia whilst its remaining 15% failed to provide what his young men most needed; that is practical guidance concerning Amelia's soils and rainfall, recommendations about continuing soil fertility and advice on how to sow, grow, harvest and sell Amelia's particular crops. The third reason is less precise. Murray and the eight men who signed Document No 2 referred, frequently, to the desirability of attracting 'gentlemen' out to Virginia. Although the need for 'capital' and a 'practical knowledge of farming' were both mentioned as being desirable, too much emphasis was placed on the circumstances of an immigrant's birth and too little upon his capacity to turn a pig's ear into a silk purse. Murray's 'prospectus' still carries the – slightly sweet – smell of one surviving upper class Virginian Society standing, too eagerly, to greet another like it. Fourthly, the young men themselves seem not to have been without fault; most had a 'grand time riding, racing, gambling and courting the local girls.' (Three dozen sturdy, experienced – and married! – English yeomen farmers from East Anglia might have left behind a more enduring record.)

Murray purchased his own Virginian property, named 'Haw Branch',[10] from a Mrs Harriet Mason on 10th August 1872. The property then consisted of a splendid old frame mansion house and 1,229 acres of well-timbered, and well-watered, land in Amelia County. The land grew excellent tobacco; much of the woodwork in the house is carved in tobacco leaves. The land also grew good grass which produced good horses; the plantation kept up its own private racecourse. As a family the Blackers had grown accustomed to living comfortably in fine houses; Murray and Haw Branch fitted each other exceptionally well! In 1872 Murray, as an Irishman with money, held strong bargaining cards; Mrs Mason – 'no businesswoman' and a widow with five children – held poor, somewhat anxious, cards. Murray bought Haw Branch and its land for $17,513; or for $14.25 per acre. The strong cards, without doubt, were Murray's; what sort of bargain did he drive?

Document No 4 of Murray's 'prospectus' listed twenty-eight properties in Virginia which his young men might have bought. Four of these contained no house and seven were not priced. The twenty-one properties which had a house and which were priced included one at $28.00 and one at $17.00 per acre. If these two are ignored the suggested average selling price of the remainder was about $9.50 per acre. Whilst evidence of this nature can only be speculative it nevertheless suggests that when Murray bought Haw Branch for $14.25 per acre he had not driven a hard bargain; indeed it is believed that Mrs Mason thought she had received 'an excellent price . . .' Under all the circumstances the transaction reflects some credit upon Murray; he might have behaved very differently. Murray could be, and often was, an impatient, impetuous man; but, at heart, he was a kindly one who had been born into an upright and honourable family. (It is to be doubted if Charles would have been his lifelong friend had it been otherwise.)

In the early days of the Immigration Scheme Haw Branch became its social, and business, headquarters. Murray may have conducted an agricultural school there for his young men; if so, he was doing no more than follow in the footsteps of his distinguished uncle. It is certain that Murray had inherited money; it is equally certain that he made more of it by his skill and acumen as a farming businessman during the thirty-one years he worked the Haw Branch Plantation. An obituary notice later said that he was 'Supposed to be one of the richest men in Virginia' and this may well have been true; his wife had remarked already that 'Murray is very fortunate in his speculations, they always turn out well . . .' Murray and Frances entertained handsomely at Haw Branch and Murray became well known for the quality of the many horses he bred and kept. Horses and farming – farming and horses – were his life; 'It was wonderful . . . how well mannered, and how well schooled, his horses were.'

When Murray Blacker bought Haw Branch in 1872 'slavery' was still 'writ large' in Virginia. Before the Civil War slaves provided all the labour required to manage the house and its land. As almost always in those earlier days, in upper class houses, the mother – the wife – was then expected to, and usually did, *rule* her household; her responsibilities were too many, too varied, and too interlocking to make any other arrangement practicable. As always Haw Branch had been virtually self-sufficient; the plantation produced its own vegetables, fruit, grain, chickens, pigs, sheep, and cattle; its mill supplied flour and cornmeal; its forge 'yielded handwrought nails, hinges, chains, horseshoes and bits.' The kitchen – as a precaution against fire – stood twenty yards behind the house; slaves carried 'delicious food' – cooked by 'Aunt Prudence' or, later, by her daughter 'Pink' – to a semi-basement dining-room in which twenty-four people could, and often did, sit down. Various other outbuildings stood round the kitchen; a deeply dug, and therefore cool, dairy; a deeper dug and even cooler ice-house; a smoke house which cured suspended 'hams, shoulders, middlings and sausages' (its door possessed a round hole through which the plantation cat was able to tackle its rats and mice); an oyster house (in which, in season, oysters were kept alive in sea water in barrels and which were fed on cornmeal; as they ate so they 'made a peculiar hollow sound'); a weaving room which, for the most part, made slave clothing; and a school house in which the children of the family took their lessons. No description of a laundry house has survived but one, undoubtedly, existed. A mill for grinding grain used to stand on a nearby stream.

Little of the life which had been so familiar for so long at Haw Branch survived the Confederate surrender at nearby Appomattox Court House on 9th April 1865. Mrs McConnaughey records that 'the carriage horses' did so because they 'had been hidden successfully in the swamp'; and that a few cattle and hogs had evaded the Confederate and Union armies *and* the 'carpet-baggers'.[11] By far the most serious injury suffered by Haw Branch was the overnight loss of wealth which, previously, had resided in the ownership of enough slaves to run the place as a successful family home and plantation business ('successful', in this context, did not mean the earning of a large, freely spendable, cash surplus; it did mean the earning of a general sense of contentment in the way of life lived by everyone – including the slaves – at Haw Branch.[12]) On, or very shortly after, 10th April 1865 most of those who had been born slaves simply 'melted away'; those few 'freemen' who stayed on required to be paid. Being paid did not, often, mean that labour worked harder. To the post-emancipation question, 'How does Negro labour compare now with what it was?' the usual answer was, 'It takes three Negro men now to do the work of two then.'

Stories about Murray gathered like moss on a bank. 'He was very thin and would put on more and more coats as the weather got colder, sometimes wearing as many as six; into these coats he would tuck his long beard and then ride over a jump throwing one hand in the air and crying "Ovah". He broke his hip – over a jump – at the age of seventy-eight! He owned sixty – or more –

pairs of woollen stockings but would not allow them to be washed; instead he rotated, or 'aired', them on a line in the house. (George Washington, it is said, owned fifty-six pairs: both men, perhaps, disliked stockings which had shrunk in the wash.) He kept a tame snake against rats but his cook was terrified, and, eventually, killed it. Murray charged into her kitchen shouting, 'Where is my serpent?' He found the corpse, stuffed it and mounted it over his front door. He never let a business opportunity slip; when sugar became scarce he bought in a boatload and supplied 'the whole neighbourhood at lower prices than could be had elsewhere.'

Murray lived on at Haw Branch until 1903, when he sold it to a German émigré. He then moved into Richmond; 'Blacker Street' still recalls him. He had been instrumental in forming the Deep Run Hunt Club in Richmond; L.H. Handcock, the Hunt's first master, was one of his sons-in-law. Frances, Murray's wife, died in Richmond in about 1907. Three years later – and long after Charles's death – Murray went back to England. He died at Goldingham Hall – the house he had bought in Suffolk – in August 1913 at the age of eighty-nine.

Nothing has ever suggested that Murray accepted any personal responsibility for the individual success of any of his young immigrants. Few, it is believed, survived for long after 1877. It is now easier to ask questions about Murray's Virginian enterprise than it is to answer them. Why, if he hoped to expand his agency business into four other American counties, did he not take more trouble to ensure success, rather than failure, in Amelia? Why did he decide to reprint, verbatim, his almost irrelevant *Field* letter as part of his 'prospectus' instead of originating a new, 'purpose-designed', document? Did his natural impetuosity blind him to some Virginian facts of life? Did it come as a surprise to him that he could not start up his own, large, property at Haw Branch, whilst, at the same time, keeping a fatherly – and professional – eye on twenty or more young would-be farmers?

Charles's 'business' with Murray had been neither long nor tedious. In the first place Charles had an obligation to see any of Murray's young men from Ireland who were still there to be seen and who Charles might have encouraged, originally, to try their hand in Virginia. Secondly, Murray had given Charles a Power of Attorney over his remaining United Kingdom affairs; this may have needed attention.

* * *

Charles's enjoyment of Haw Branch must have been intense; it was spring after what had been, for him, a long winter. Having been unwell he was in good health; he was the guest of his best – and most trusted – friend; America, Virginia and Amelia County were all new to him. Haw Branch is a lovely house in which to be asked to stay. He was looking forward to seeing, on his return journey, 'the elevated roads, the Brooklyn Bridge, and other American "big things".' St John – then rising eighteen – must have rubbed his eyes when, for the first time, he saw Haw Branch; horses galore, miles of good land on which to ride them, a private racecourse on which to race them, and two uncles who, between them, knew all that was worth knowing about horses! It is scarcely surprising that, as far as it is known, St John never again wished to leave America.[13] In 1965 Haw Branch reverted to Mrs Mason's family. In that year her great granddaughter (Mrs Gibson McConnaughey and her husband Mr Cary McConnaughey) bought back the house and the 120 acres of land which still went with it.

Charles was not the first man to find a cool refreshing wind stirring round the 'Statue of Liberty'. If Charles ever felt free to speak 'the truth, the whole truth and nothing but the truth' about the 1880 'boycotting' he did so, in Haw Branch, in the spring of 1881; whether riding alone with Murray or sitting with him in the long dining room of that charming house.

Part Four

August 1881 – June 1897

Chapter Nineteen

The third William Boycott (and the fourth consecutive Boycott Rector of Burgh-St-Peter) was the Rector for seventeen years until his death – of epilepsy[14] – at the age of forty-six on 28th June 1889. He had been sent to Shrewsbury School and to Cambridge where he obtained a B.A. degree but where he, also, failed a (voluntary) Theological Examination. He then became a curate in several different places – but including St Mary's, Leeds – until his father died, when he became the Curate of Burgh-St-Peter. In May 1872 – on the presentation of Charles and the Reverend Smyth-Thorpe – he became the Rector.

William married Charlotte Oxley, the daughter of Charles Oxley (of The Hall, Ripon, in Yorkshire), on 7th January 1869 when he was aged twenty-six. Charlotte bore him a daughter named Georgina – but perhaps Georgiana! – who never married but who, later, became a patron of Burgh-St-Peter church, and a son named Edmund Alfred Cunningham. (Edmund was ordained late in life; he suffered from some 'physical imbalance' which prevented him from becoming the fifth Boycott Rector. By all accounts he became – like his father – a most enthusiastic yachtsman.)

When William III became the Rector the family fortunes were not, probably, what they had been but this William leaves little impression of clerical poverty. Charlotte may have brought in money. Certainly, in 1887 and 1888, William owned what must have been a fine boat; a yacht named *Selina* which had been built in Norwich by a boat builder named Mollett and which was registered in the Lloyds Yacht Register of 1887 and 1888.

Not much is now known about the 4th Rector. The impression is that he spent many of the spring, summer and early autumn months sailing the North Sea in a succession of boats which he kept in Lowestoft; and to which he usually walked. Sailing, it seems, was the love of his life. When he died the *East Anglian Daily Times* wrote, '. . . this most accomplished yachtsman who practically lived on the water in the summertime simply returning on the Sunday to his parish, which adjoins the river, to conduct divine service'.

Whilst serving his curacy at St Mary's Church in Leeds – a *vast* building – William came under Dr James Woodford, later the Bishop of Ely. Woodford was a bachelor. He treated his curates with much kindness and he was recognised, far and wide, as being an outstandingly good preacher. In one of his sermons in St Mary's he posed the rhetorical question: 'Why do respectable working men not worship?' He then proceeded to tell his congregation that they should 'Talk it out, sift it, and then come and tell me what we can do to take the stones out of the path and make the way easier . . .'

The Church attendance census of 1851 had administered a jolt to the security of 'the Church' in England. As decade followed decade an increasing number of people found themselves unable to believe in the actual existence of an all-seeing and all-merciful God who cared for them as individuals. Not a few churches in England still possessed, and read from, bibles which stated, *categorically*, that the world had been created in the year 4004 BC.[15] Thomas Huxley – a Fellow of the Royal Society – *ridiculed* this notion; he insisted that the world was of an immeasurable antiquity and that to suggest otherwise was foolishness. The Natural History Museum in London became known as 'Nature's Cathedral'; Huxley himself spoke of the 'priesthood' of science; and of 'the church scientific.' He asserted – vigorously – that the battle was not between 'scientific enlightenment' and 'religious darkness' but rather that there was no battle to be fought; quite simply the world was of an *immense* antiquity.

It seems probable that Willie – who should have become the fourth consecutive Boycott Rector but who died before his father in 1865 – *did* believe in the existence of a merciful, and all-seeing, God. It is by no means certain that William III did.

In Ireland 'boycotting' had become a powerful weapon; the threat of it 'intimidated the stoutest heart'. Thousands upon thousands of poor Irishmen joined the Land League. This seemed to promise the *ascendancy* of the common people and, more importantly, the descendancy of the landlords. The Land League was supported by a militant press 85% of which gave it active support. The situation in Ireland, in the early 1880s, was without parallel in the United Kingdom; the catalogue of outrages, of murders, of gun rule, of the persecution of both 'guilty' and innocent men, of the wounding and disfigurement of innocent animals, poisoned much of the Irish countryside. Considered rational judgements on affairs became almost impossible. Time for quiet considered reflection was, most urgently, needed.

The moral weakness, induced by hunger and exceptionally bad living conditions of so many of the poorest Irish in the late 1870s, was all too apparent. These men and women found it impossible to resist the – temporary – strengths of the Land League; many cowered under its close and vigilant sway. Most poor Irishmen disliked 'the outrages' but they lacked the moral courage to resist. This did not mean that they were unaware of what the Land League was trying to win; that is, at least some, measure of independence from England.

W.E. Forster, at the time, asked an Irish audience why Irishmen, so famous for their bravery in the field, were so destitute of moral courage? And why, sometimes, they paid their rents *in secret*?

At the time about 140 newspapers were published in Ireland; of these an overwhelming majority supported the Land League and its policy of 'peaceful passive resistance'. Two well-known local papers were published in Co. Mayo; both the *Connaught Telegraph* and the *Mayo Examiner* supported the League. James Daly – the Editor of the *Connaught Telegraph* – became a public, and much respected, figure because of the vigorous and effective support he gave to the League. The weekly *Irish World* was published in the U.S.A. but many copies found their way to Ireland; this particular paper maintained, *consistently*, that the land of Ireland belonged to *all* the people of Ireland.

When he returned to Lough Mask House in August 1881 Charles had become an international figure; much admired and respected by those who knew him in Ireland[16] but, naturally enough, held in some doubt by those who did not. By 1881 'boycotting' was in full swing throughout Ireland. Most people probably knew that a man named 'Boycott' had been a locally well-known farmer, sportsman and rider of horses in Co. Mayo and that he had given his name to this 'new'(but not original) form of punishment. The difficult truth was that 'boycotting' covered a multitude of errors and sins of commission and omission. A man could be 'boycotted' because he, actually, deserved it or because he did *not* deserve it; it is difficult, now, to decide which caused the greater disturbance to the social equilibrium. Countless people, all over the world, knew Charles Cunningham 'Boycott' by reputation; was *this* the man who had, apparently, behaved so badly? Time – of course – might have healed matters; but new acts of 'boycotting' went on, and on, and *on*. The opportunity of positive action – conferred by the word – to right old injustices, old immoralities and old 'unfairnesses' played, not only on weaknesses in the Irish character, but also upon Ireland's long subservience to England.

The question which gradually brought Charles face to face with reality was simple; were circumstances in Ireland such that he would be wise to go back to England? His third letter to *The Times*, published in June 1882, suggests that he was already sufficiently persuaded by events to begin to answer his own question. As always his letter was terse:

TO THE EDITOR OF THE TIMES
Sir, – There are two classes of tenants in Ireland. One consists of men who have struggled to keep their engagements and have pinched and impoverished themselves to do so. These men have paid their rents. The other class have threatened their landlords, subscribed to the Land League, attended seditious meetings and kept their money in their pockets.

How does the Arrears Bill deal with those two classes? The former have paid their rents, and so nothing is done for them; the latter, as an acknowledgement of the power of the Land League, are to have two years rent presented to them – one by the State, the other by their landlords. Is this policy anything but a premium on dishonesty and an encouragement of sedition; and is it not certain to foster illegal combination and agrarian outrage in the future?

In fairness the State should place the tenant who has paid in the same condition as the man who has refused to pay rent.

Your obedient servant
C. C. Boycott

June 1st (1882)

Disposing of a *good* farm, in a poor and *very* disturbed countryside and moving himself and a wife back to England was not something that could be done overnight. Charles seems to have had little doubt about whom he hoped would buy Lough Mask House and farm. In a letter addressed to James Daly (written in England and dated 20th March 1886), Charles said, 'I do not like the idea of your losing Lough Mask – take my advice – you will have a property for your children after you.' (In fact the Daly family did buy Lough Mask House and farm and have lived there, contentedly, ever since.)

If Charles did not, already, know the Adair family who lived in both Northern Ireland and in Suffolk he would have known of them. He was offered the job – which he had no doubt he could do – of Land Agent to some 14,000 Adair acres lying along the Norfolk and Suffolk County boundary.

The late Victorian period saw a significant shift towards a national and an international viewpoint and towards a London which had become both the magnet, and the capital market, of the world. English lawyers, English bankers, English brokers and English insurance agents became powerful. London became the focus of artistic life; new galleries, new theatres and new concert halls were built, not only in London, but in many provincial cities. German opera, Norwegian drama, French impressionism and Russian ballet all found their, almost inevitable, way to London. Many of London's ancient roads were rebuilt, so reflecting the fact that they passed through the capital city of the world's greatest Empire. London itself became neither the principal city of England nor the principal city of the British Empire; it became 'the Capital' of the human race.

England *accepted* social inequality but, in so doing, she succeeded in giving close attention to the law and to the necessity of, at least some, social discipline. There were still many poor in England; but these – it sometimes seemed – were playing a part in something greater than themselves. Personal incomes rose. The old laws of nature began to loose their grip. Clean water began to flow, medicine began – just – to cure,[17] excrement began to go down into its own sewers, gas and electricity replaced candles and oil lamps; a man-made order began to supersede the seasonal rhythms of the natural world. But – and despite this – England's bureaucracy was smaller, its institutions were more extensive, its churches were fuller and its homicide, suicide, divorce and illegitimacy rates were lower than those of most other countries. It was an extraordinary 'spring time'; and, like the magical beauty of an English spring, it could *not* last.[18]

CHAPTER TWENTY

IN 1885 GLADSTONE WAS AGED seventy-six. He had worked with an immense professionalism to understand the Irish problem but almost all his colleagues were the saddest of disappointments; they displayed only 'a huge and bottomless ignorance' of the – so wet but also so lovely – island lying across the Irish Sea. Ireland had been Gladstone's anxiety for years. 'Ireland, Ireland' he had written in 1850 'that cloud in the west, that coming storm . . .' And, during the first five years of the 1880s, 'feelings in Ireland were running so high, distress was so acute, opposition to government so concerted, violence so endemic' that sensible good government from London was almost impossible. Eventually a deal was struck; Parnell was released from prison in exchange for his promise to do his best to make Gladstone's second Land Act work. This led to Forster's resignation and to his replacement by Lord Frederick Cavendish. But – on the very day that Cavendish arrived in Dublin – he and his companion were murdered in Phoenix Park.

By the previous Christmas Gladstone is believed to have realised, in his heart, that Ireland must be given, at least some, measure of Home Rule. But, to not a few thoughtful Englishmen, this Gladstonian concept of what was right for Ireland seemed madness from almost every other point of view. Were the Irish – such *close* neighbours – fit to govern themselves? The British Empire – controlled from London – stood at its peak of world-wide authority and influence. What message would a largely independent Ireland convey to the world? What message would a continuously mutinous Ireland convey to the world?

Parnell had become the leader of a united Parliamentary group at Westminster of eighty-six Irishmen who had been elected to win self-government for Ireland (a quirkish fate had decreed that

Parnell's total of eighty-six Members *exactly* matched the Liberal majority over the Conservatives). What best to do about Ireland had come to eclipse all other national anxieties. It was common knowledge that Gladstone had come to the opinion that, at least some, measure of self-government for Ireland was essential; his formidable intellect, the intensity of his Christianity, and his immense capacity for reading had given him a greater knowledge of, and sympathy for, Ireland than was possessed by any of his political contemporaries. He believed that all people should govern themselves if they were capable of doing so. Gladstone came to see, in Parnell, Ireland's man of destiny. As an orator Parnell could move granite this way and that; shafts of the brightest sunlight shone from his helmet; and – *above all* – he was still only forty years of age.

By now committed to 'Home Rule for Ireland' Gladstone became Prime Minister again in January 1886. In June he introduced the second reading of his 'Irish Home Rule' Bill to a House of Commons overcharged with excitement and packed to bursting.

The future status and condition of Ireland presented itself to the nation – which, of course, *included* Ireland – in the sharpest contrasts of right and wrong. Political fervour ran high; many old political allegiances were forgotten. The many aspects of government which Gladstone's proposals would have withheld from Dublin seem, in retrospect, of greater importance than those he intended to confer. The Crown, peace and war, defence, foreign and colonial relations, customs and excise, trade and navigation, post office, coinage and legal tender, would all have remained in the hands of the Imperial Parliament at Westminster; one may exclaim 'Whatever was left to argue about?' (There was, of course, some confusion of language; people who thought the words 'Home Rule' were only another way of saying 'self-government' were to be forgiven for their mistake.) The fact was that whilst Gladstone's 'Home Rule' proposals involved the grant of a larger measure of authority to Dublin than had ever before been contemplated, they did *not* amount to actual self-government.

Opposition to Gladstone's 'Home Rule for Ireland' took three forms. First, it carried the implication that 'Ireland' was a political entity but this was not the case; the loyalists in the north had no desire to be controlled from Dublin. (As Lord Randolph Churchill put it, 'Ulster will fight and Ulster will be right.') Secondly, it was maintained that 'the loss of Ireland' posed a threat to the security of the Royal Navy upon which the Empire depended. And, thirdly, lay the nagging fear that the Irish were, simply, *not* fit to govern themselves.

Gladstone himself described the issue of 'self-government for Ireland' as being the gravest, but also the simplest, issue submitted to the nation for fifty years. Coercion in Ireland had achieved nothing and would achieve nothing. The alternatives were to continue to govern the Irish by coercion or to allow them to manage their own affairs in such a way as would maintain their honour and consolidate the unity of the Empire. His proposals, Gladstone said, would carry the following benefits. First, the consolidation, and not the weakening, of the Empire. Secondly, the cessation of a heavy, constant and demoralising waste of public treasure. Thirdly, the abatement (and eventual extinction) of ignoble feuds in Ireland and the proper development of Irish resources. Fourthly, the redemption, by England, of a stigma fastened upon her in respect to Ireland – almost from time immemorial – by 'the judgement of the whole civilised world'. Fifthly, the restoration to Parliament at Westminster of its dignity and efficiency and its ability to progress public business.

The Opposition challenged every facet of the Gladstonian vision of an Irish future. They maintained that the Empire *would* be weakened; they asserted, with vigour, that Gladstone's policy was a shameful surrender to violence and a public admission of failure to govern Ireland as she ought to be governed. Men stood – with the greatest conviction – on both sides of a precipitous national divide.

In the summer of 1886 Thomas Lees fought Northampton in a general election. He was aged forty. He had been born in Ireland and had been trained at Trinity as a barrister but he had served, for most of his life, as an officer in the Royal Irish Constabulary. He was an old friend of Charles's.[19]

The simplicity of the issue facing the electorate of Northampton – and the difficulty of being woolly headed about it – cut deeply into local political loyalties. The Liberal vote was reduced by defections to the Conservatives and further reduced by those Liberals who voted as 'Dissident Liberals'. A local newspaper editor wrote that 'The concession of a separate Irish Parliament . . . is one of such enormous difficulty and the method of conciliation is so novel that great allowances should be made for those who shrink from making the experiment.' No doubt this caused additional Liberal defections but it also did much to bring the – all important – issue of Ireland squarely before the electors. (Many Englishmen still thought that the Irish were a race of blood-thirsty savages unlikely, ever, to be capable of self-government; or of associating as equals in the family of civilised nations.)

Northampton was represented in the Commons by two well-known Liberals named Labouchère and Bradlaugh. At the 1886 election these two candidates were joined by a man named Turner (who stood as a Liberal Dissident) and by Thomas Lees (who stood as a Conservative). Lees was no politician; his family motto was 'An honest man's the noblest work of God' and it may have come as no political surprise to Lees that Bradlaugh described him as being 'green'. Nevertheless Lees spoke in a 'manly straight-forward style'; no one could doubt that he did *not* agree with Gladstone's proposals.

In June Lees arranged an open-air meeting close to the centre of Northampton, which Charles addressed. *His* was the authentic voice of Irish terrorism. In his person, and by what he said, he confronted the electorate with the most notorious single aspect of Irish affairs and the aspect which gave rise to the greatest doubts about the ability of the Irish to govern themselves. (In 1886 Charles was aged fifty-four. He was still as upright as a dart, grey haired, grey bearded and with a twinkle in his eye; *and* at peace with himself.)

Thomas Lees welcomed his old friend Captain Boycott. Speaking at the Far Cotton meeting Lees said that the arguments in favour of Home Rule for Ireland were 'vapoury, sentimental and illusory'; twenty-five percent of the electorate of Munster and Connaught were illiterate; they were required to *say* for whom they voted because they could not read.

Charles was received 'with applause'. He said the coercion which made the law respected (in Ireland) was not coercion to the law-abiding part of the population. Only those who had experienced 'boycotting' could understand its nature. It was unpleasant to go to market escorted by police with fixed bayonets and to see Land League sentries placed outside shopkeepers' premises. He had been forced to obtain his food by stealth. Without notice some

400 men (?) went upon his farm and compelled his labourers to leave his employ. He had seen children posted as sentries to beckon the men who were waiting to shoot him. Ireland was ruled by the unwritten law of the Land League. Cattle were mutilated. Men's noses were cut, their ears slit and women were pulled out of bed and their hair cut off because they refused to be ruled by the Land League. He (Charles) had been helped by Ulstermen who were as different as 'Russia from Northampton'. He felt sure that, at the critical moment, the electorate would 'declare for the maintenance of the Unity of the Empire.' Another newspaper concluded:

> Mr Lees may derive plenty of encouragement from the Far Cotton meeting; and I have no doubt the speech of Captain Boycott, whose name furnished the appellation of that inhuman system 'boycotting', will go a long way towards opening the eyes of the electorate of Northampton as to the real state of things in the sister isle.

In the event Gladstone's proposals were defeated by thirty votes. Thomas Lees did far better than anyone expected. A journalist described the subsequent scene in the House of Commons 'as being impossible to describe'. The Conservatives cheered themselves hoarse. The Irish party waited for a lull and then, rising en masse, sang out 'Three cheers for the Grand Old Man.' It had, indeed, been a fateful decision. Had Gladstone been right or wrong? Is it possible to imagine that the Protestant majority in the north of Ireland would ever have accepted a Catholic government in Dublin? It is possible, always, to take a horse to water; but impossible to make it drink.

Chapter Twenty-One

THE STORY OF CHARLES'S WORKING life in Flixton is the story of two, separate, things; that is his work as the Agent to the Flixton Estate and the rebirth of the old Bungay races.

As 'The Agent' Charles and Annie lived, rent free, in the Agent's House (known as 'The Priest's House') which stood close to Flixton Church. But they may, also, have lived, temporarily, in a fine old Beccles house in which Napoleonic prisoners of war had been lodged. These, using a diamond, had signed their names on the window panes, and, as soon as he saw them, Charles is believed to have added his own. (Unfortunately the ground floor of the house was later damaged by fire and all the glass broken.)

The Suffolk Record Office, in Lowestoft, now holds all the 'Flixton Papers.' These include two 'letter books' in which Charles – as Agent to the estate from 1886 until his death in 1897 – wrote about 970 'official' letters of which he wanted to keep a copy. Those which can still be read present a good picture of the 'agency' work which fell to Charles at the end of the nineteenth century; and of the prolonged agricultural depression which continued to haunt rural England.

The original Flixton Hall had been a beautiful building which had been destroyed by fire in December 1846 (the available water had turned to ice!). The house had then belonged to the Adair family for two hundred, or more, years. King Charles II is said to have admired it greatly and to have asked to whom it belonged; 'Oh, some Popish Dog'; to which the King is believed to have replied, 'The dog has a very beautiful kennel.' The Adairs were Catholic and were large landowners in East Anglia and in Northern Ireland. A member of the family named Lord Waveney had been the Lord Lieutenant of Co. Antrim since 1883, and it may well have been he who had suggested that Charles might become the Flixton Agent.

Sir Hugh Adair owned the Flixton Estate during Charles's years as its agent. Charles's appointment to Flixton could hardly have been bettered; it took him back, almost, to the village in which he had been born and gave him work which he understood. He had been a successful farmer for thirty years; he had, at least some, experience of being 'An Agent'; he understood good, bad and indifferent land; he knew something about houses and property; he understood animals; and he loved horses, which still did all the hard work on the farms of the world.

During Charles's eleven years as Agent most of the official letters he wrote (in 'letter books') have survived. Although poaching was still common in England his few letters on the subject suggest that the Estate was not much bothered by real poachers; and, only occasionally, by the better-off kind who, with a friend, 'happened to be walking on estate land with a gun and a dog.' In October 1887 Charles surprised two well-dressed men – and a boy who was carrying two pheasants – whom he thought had been poaching. Charles told Sir Hugh Adair that he preferred to make an example of such men rather than making an example of 'some half-starved' men who poached 'from necessity'. Six years later Sir Hugh and his son told Charles that they proposed to attend the local Court when two Flixton poachers were to be tried. Charles urged them to adopt a sympathetic line as 'poachers are but mortal and as keenly alive to revenge what they might construe as a . . . hard case; and, till the winter shoot is over, I should not like to have their attention drawn this way.' In January 1894 two local men were caught poaching, *by night,* on the Flixton estate but, on this occasion, Charles took a more severe line; he recommended that both be proceeded against. Charles's experience of poaching at Flixton did not amount to much; due, probably, to his forbearance and to his memories of so many poor, near starving, Irishmen.

Throughout Charles's years at Flixton agriculture continued in crisis; there was scarcely a tenant farmer on the Estate who did not, at one time or another, plead either poverty or extreme poverty. Charles well understood his own position; that he was a servant to the tenants and that his duty was to help and support them. But he also knew that he had a duty to Sir Hugh Adair; and that he was required to chide, and sometimes to discipline, the tenants. It was Charles's rule that, come what may, he was in his office from ten to twelve every Thursday and Friday morning.

There is a story that, in his very early days, a number of tenant farmers found themselves in a large hall in Bungay somewhat nervously awaiting the – famous or infamous! – new Agent's arrival. He – having driven himself to Bungay in a smart dog-cart with a Dalmatian bounding along under the axle – is said to have walked, in silence, to the head of the table. There, after the briefest of pauses, he drew from the pockets of his immaculate Norfolk jacket a pair of pistols which he laid on the table with their barrels crossed. 'Good morning,' he is supposed to have said. 'I am glad to be no longer in Ireland.'

Charles's first letter-book letter started on 19th March 1886. His handwriting was small and his style terse. He noted that a Mr Hammond had accepted an estate farm and that he, Charles, would 'take an early opportunity of coming over' to see it (as, indeed, he saw regularly all the farms on the estate). Charles was compelled to work hard; in four years he managed to give himself only twelve days' holiday. Sir Hugh Adair – despite the fact that he was building himself a new Flixton Hall – was frequently away from the Estate in Aldeburgh or in County Armagh.

Twice a year the Agent gave 'Audit Dinners'. These usually took place at 'The Magpie' in Harlestone or at 'The King's Head' in Bungay. Rents were paid. Endless conversations took place between men who had the same professional interests but who did not, often, meet; jokes, much conviviality and the drinking of innumerable glasses of sherry and port, and the eating of a fine dinner, followed; and, every now and then, someone had to be helped home! (The Agent paid the bill through one of the Estate accounts.)

Keeping an Estate going in such difficult times was no sinecure. The work Charles did demanded a practical knowledge of farming and numerous skills. He had little patience with those who bungled, or broke, their engagements. 'As it is three weeks and a day . . . and you have failed in your performance of contract . . . I write to say that I consider the agreement off and shall not accept delivery.' He was, invariably, a stickler for detail and for adherence to his word but he was, also, kindly; '. . . a throat is not to be trifled with . . . the sale can wait until you are fit.' He always apologised if an apology was necessary; 'Am sorry you had to hurry the good grey mare so much yesterday. As the down train was five minutes late I just caught it . . .' He wrote to a tenant farmer in February 1888, 'I was sorry not to see you at our Audit. I hope nothing serious prevented you?' He wrote to a tenant named Jax: '. . . you were credited with £31.19.0 – [but] . . . you forgot the £6.8.6½ cash in hand.' The Estate suffered a severe winter storm; 'of course you must have your bedroom window put in and get it done as soon as you can . . . the gale on Sunday will cost the Estate not less than £1,500 for repairs to Farm Houses, Buildings and Cottages and that is just double what I have allowed a year for repairs. The park is a sad sight to see . . . my allowance for repairs for a year went in an hour.' He wrote to the Leadenhall Market in London that 'venison at 6d per lb was a fair price for a good buck *before the House rises.*' The impression is that Charles struck up a particular friendship with the Head Gamekeeper who, usually, produced an income for the Estate between October and February by the sale of game. On one occasion Charles paid the Head Gamekeeper at the rate of 2d per head for 36 hedgehogs, 209 rats, 52 jays, 11 hawks – variety unstated – 41 stoats, 7 cats and 289 rabbits. (A large number of hares were also shot but these, invariably, were given away to those who worked on the Estate.)

During Charles's years a new gatekeeper was appointed. This man was not allowed to have children living with him for fear this might produce too many small dirty faces to stare at arriving guests. (Towards the end of the century this was well understood.) In April 1895 Charles became irritated by a failure to repair a public right of way. He asked by 'What Act of Parliament and which section of such Act, your Parish Council call on Sir H.E. Adair, as a private individual, to repair such a path.' He was driven, constantly, by the need to be economical; 'Please get the wooden floor repaired; times will not admit of new work.' Several estate houses, it seems, were not supplied with good drinking water and this seems to have puzzled Charles for a few days. Eventually he wrote saying that the water ought to be boiled and filtered and that a sample should be sent to an analyst.

During Charles's years at Flixton East Anglian farmers were enduring depression after depression. '. . . cattle cannot pay at present prices. Stores are dearer than beefs; I expect next month they will be cheaper. The lambs are very fine . . .' Charles wrote to a Mr Jiggins – a most faithful tenant – saying that Sir Hugh 'desires me to state his sympathy with you . . . in the present state of agriculture' (the sympathy extended to a reduction in rent of £30.0.0 per annum!) Charles wrote to another tenant saying how sorry 'he would be to break so long a connection' and thanked him for his 'cordial and hospitable greeting when I came to Redingfield.' In August 1887 Charles had been able to tell a tenant that Sir Hugh had 'reduced his rent to £40.0.0 per annum.' In December of that year Charles wrote to another tenant saying 'As soon as the half year's rent, due in April, is cleared up I will give you the order for the drain pipes.' Charles found himself forced into writing to a Mr Cracknall to say 'that he had had no reply to his request that a half years rent should be paid on 6th April'; and, to another, '. . . you are trying me too far and further I will not go. I have to request you will come and see me today, between 10 and 1 o'clock; or you will have a much more unpleasant visitor.'

The Flixton Estate, of course, contained a number of *good* farms: 'I send you particulars of the Middleton Hall Farm. It is a real nice farm, in good working order, with a good house, a good double cottage, and first class farm buildings. There is an unusual quantity of pasture and that of good quality . . . there is a capital dairy with a pump in it.' Later Charles wrote to a Mr Goldbach saying that he had a farm on which the rent 'is absurdly low.' From time to time an offer to take a farm simply could *not* be accepted. 'Sir Hugh Adair desires me to tell you that he declines your offer of £200.0.0 for the house, offices, cottages and 454 acres of land.' To one particular candidate for a farm Charles said that he would be pleased 'to show you over' and that he was 'anxious to get some new blood into the district.'

One of Charles's difficulties concerned a young man named Danby. 'If you cannot get a fair amount of work done in a day I must get someone else.' Danby, it seems, was both stupid and lazy because Charles next asked Sir Hugh to sack him; but, in the nick of time, the whole Danby family, including the young man, got flu. Charles found himself writing to a lady to enquire, 'Why you expect Sir Hugh to do the outside painting to your house and premises?' On another occasion Charles found himself sharply disillusioned – in a typically 'Irish' way – by a young man who 'wanted to have hold of both ends of the stick whilst his wife held on by the middle.'

Sir Hugh completed his new version of the old mansion in 1892. Despite the fact that it had, precisely, sixty rooms and 365 windows it does not seem to have attracted the same admiring opinions as had been given to the earlier house. Charles was a realist; he knew that if the new mansion was not, immediately, a great success he was bound 'to get some of the blame' (which he did!).[20]

Charles raced his horses, most enthusiastically, in Ireland and, later, in England. Racing is a rich man's occupation; Charles was never that and the truth is, almost certainly, that he spent more money on his horses and racing them than he ought to have done. His colours were green, rose sleeves, and black cap; these he carried, quite often, himself. It was written of him that he *always* showed 'indomitable pluck in the saddle' and that his 'boldness and resolution never forsook him.' He held, 'a high reputation upon the turf, his integrity in running his horses never once being doubted, whilst he was never behind in "settling" with the ringmen . . .' He won, at Sligo, on a horse 'much addicted to a display of self-will' after a tussle with another ridden by Johnny Meany who, subsequently, entered Charles's employ as a groom. 'Finella' ('a grey of beautiful shape'), 'Dame Durdin', 'Martinet', 'Guerilla', and 'Aphrodite' all raced, in Ireland, in Charles's colours. At the beginning of his 'unpopularity' Charles heard that 'the boys' intended to knock him over at the Ballinrobe races but he frustrated their intentions 'by giving their leader' – said to have been J.W. Nally – 'a mount on his second best horse and riding boot-to-boot with him from start to finish.' (Charles did his best to continue his racing career in England but the truth is that his pocket was *never* deep enough.)

In 1888 Charles became the Secretary of the Bungay Race Committee and played a leading part in re-starting the old Bungay Steeplechases. These took place on open ground within a large bend of the Waveney (now the Bungay Golf Course). In 1895 Charles, and the Steeplechase Committee, probably erected an extra stand, so popular had the 'Bungay Races' become. In earlier days 8 or 9000 people might drive, in their carriages, on to the racecourse 'at 1 o'clock and stop till 5. Very pleasant . . . dine at the ordinary at the King's Head at 5½ with forty others . . . to the theatre in the evening.'

* * *

In December 1888 Charles was examined (but not cross examined) on the events of 1880 as part of the Parnell Commission Enquiry (that is about events which, for the most part, had occurred eight years earlier).

Q29508 Did Charles live in perfect friendship and peace with his neighbours? Yes.

Q29510 Did he take part in field sports and receive friendly treatment from all classes? Yes.

Q29517 How many tenants were there? About 35.

Q29530 For what reduction in rent did they ask? 5/- in the £ (or 25%).

Q29531 Did you agree? They came to me several times; they handed in memorials to the Earl of Erne; I sent these to him; he sent me his replies which I read out.

Q29532 What was the result? That he would allow 10%; no more and no less.

Q29533 In your opinion was this a fair reduction? Yes.

Q29534 The tenants would not accept 10%? No.

Q29535 Why? They dare not. They said the 'law of the land' now was 5/- in the £1.

Q29536 Did they say from what source came the 'law of the land'? No.

Q29546 Why did your employees leave your employ? They were ordered to leave.

Q29551 What then happened? I had no one to work for me. I got up about 4am. I had to feed and water my horses and clean out the cowsheds for the girls who did the milking. Then I went into my fields to pull turnips and throw over the beet for the cattle to eat. Then I would come in and have a bath and breakfast. Then I would put the horse into the water cart and go all round the farm.

Q29558 What occurred in Ballinrobe on 1st November? I was mobbed and hooted and hustled by about 500 (?) people. The police protected me. I went inside the barracks. A Company of Infantry was called out with 30 loadings (I think it was) of ball cartridges. I was confined to barracks for three or four hours. Eventually a police escort was obtained to follow me to Castlebar where I had business.

Q29559 Did you receive the rents from Lord Erne's Castlebar tenants? Yes.
Q29560 What deduction was made? 10% or 2/- in the £.
Q29563 What happened to your farm? I had several off farms. The walls were thrown down and the cattle driven off. The legs of some sheep were broken by being driven over walls and a mare had its eye knocked out.
Q29571 Did you, in September 1881, return to Lough Mask House? Yes.
Q29572 Did you, at the end of September, go to Westport? Yes – to attend a stock auction.
Q29573 What occurred? I was hooted and mobbed and my effigy was first hanged and then burnt in the market square.
Q29576 Who were the principal Land Leaguers in your neighbourhood? The Rev John O'Malley.
Q29582/3 Did matters improve for you? I was allowed to go about in peace in 1882. I was allowed to hunt.
Q29585 Beyond the question of collecting rents do you know of any reason to account for your treatment? None whatsoever.

The last known portrait of Charles is a pencil sketch by Sidney Prior Hall done as Charles gave his evidence to the Parnell Commission. The portrait is of a heavily bearded, elderly but still handsome man. It appears in the plate section.

William Douglass Boycott – known always, as Douglass – was born in 1864. He was the last member of the family to assume the title, in 1889, of 'Rector of Burgh-St-Peter.'

Douglass was educated at Rugby and Selwyn College, Cambridge. He was an undistinguished student in both places but he seems to have been not unknown – as a young man – for his love of parties and even greater love for complicated practical jokes, one of which he is believed to have played on the Fellows of his own College. He is said to have written an almost unreadable letter to the College Bursar telling him that 'an Eastern Potentate' intended to lunch in the College on the following Wednesday with a view to sending his son there. On the following *Tuesday* the front door bell rang violently and a swarthy, middle aged, eastern 'gentleman' –

beautifully made up – was admitted. The visitor spoke only the most execrable English, complained that the food was not fit for a dog, picked his teeth with his fork, belched and left abruptly saying, loudly, that nothing could persuade him to send his son to such an appalling college. (A charming letter of apology, of course, followed; but whether the still angry Fellows found themselves able to accept it, is, of course, another matter!)

After leaving Cambridge Douglass served his curacy in Jarrow before taking up, as Rector, the family living of Burgh-St-Peter in 1889. He may, at this period of his life, have been extravagant. Certainly, in 1899, he resigned the living of Burgh-St-Peter and proceeded to the neighbouring – but much larger – parish of Wymondham as its *Curate*. (There he delivered the annual 'Papillon Lecture' from which he earned a little extra money.) Later he refused a living in Norwich because it involved attendance upon those about to be hanged for murder. At about the same time he started the writing of a book to be called *Life in God's Family*. Although this is believed to have sold quite well, it is now, virtually, unknown; even his children never knew of it, and, when he died, no copy was found amongst his possessions.

The opening chapters of Douglass's book are austere; its author seems to emphasise the role of the Church as being a separated community; almost a 'Holy Club'. This leads him to make what now seems to be an extraordinary demand; namely that the members of the family have a duty to maintain an enmity towards the enemies of the head of the family. In the meanwhile he had accepted the living of Upton, a small village lying close to Acle and The Broads; indeed it may have been the charm of Upton – and its most lovely church – which caused Douglass to 'think again'. In his early years at Upton he made two, remarkable, friends. A.K. Watson had been a Senior Wrangler at Cambridge, was a master at Harrow, an atheist and a Communist; Jim Scott – of the large Norwich engineering firm of Lawrence & Scott – was a confirmed atheist. This did not prevent them from becoming close friends of Douglass; and even from attending services in Upton Church.

It seems that what had really changed was not the underlying logic of Douglass's book but its applications. It became clear that what constantly exercised his mind was the extraordinary figure of Jesus himself as this is to be discovered in the four Gospels. It takes little imagination to see that all the many sayings and acts of Jesus could not be incorporated into any generally acceptable religious doctrine; the dichotomies are too numerous. Such difficulties may have strengthened his friendship with Scott and Watson who – quite apart from their avowed atheism – adopted the most radical opinions about most generally accepted standards of behaviour. This particular difficulty may account, also, for the persistent sense of inadequacy which, to the end of his life, Douglass felt about his own sermons; his diary, for the last year of his life, repeatedly notes this.

Although Upton Vicarage was by no means grand, Douglass felt increasingly uncomfortable at living within such comforts as it possessed. He became unsparing in his devotion to his parishioners. On one occasion a Doctor decided that ice was essential to save the life of a child; Douglass solved that problem instantly by riding on his bicycle to Yarmouth and returning with the ice (fortunately it was in the winter!). He did much the same thing to get a doll for a child. Even today there are some people who still remember him vividly; to have met him, even casually, was something to be remembered and treasured.

He wrote beautiful English. When he first went to Upton his Church was in a sad tumble-down state. He seems to have had friends far and near – arising from his book and his memorable practical joking? – to whom he appealed for help. He described his Church; 'Lofty proportions, the peculiar grace of its arcade, the regularity of its windows, perfect and interesting specimens of fully-developed perpendicular, its side altars and their lights . . . the brilliant colouring of the screen, font and pillars, the stained glass of its windows make a church which, tho' smaller than many Norfolk churches, is second to none in its beauty.'[21] Part of the money for which he appealed was intended to cover the cost of rebuilding the tower which had, largely, fallen down around itself. A professional stonemason actually re-laid the old stones but Douglass did his share of the work; he carried up all the stone himself.

Douglass became the climax, and ultimate truth, of the long Boycott ministry. In some ways he anticipated the most profound religious minds of the twentieth century. In his letters 'from prison' Dietrich Bonhoeffer – who formed the confessional church in opposition to Hitler – asked what Europe would need; and came to the conclusion that it would not be clever men, not moral men but *simple* men. Alan Ecclestone – who abandoned a brilliant academic career – spoke of the need for the Church to devise a way of life that was 'in keeping with its Title Deeds'; and, by 'Title Deeds', he meant the words and acts of Jesus as reported in the four Gospels.

Douglass Boycott came to hold the traditions of the Church in which he had been brought up in the greatest respect and affection. He sought by any and every means to create a path through which he, and others, might pass. It is scarcely possible to imagine a more fitting conclusion to the long Boycott ministry in which Samuel, William I, William II and William III had all played their parts. Douglass justified the sequence because, quite simply, it led up to him. He came to see that the basis of his ministry could only be, not the doctrinal complexities of any form of the Christian religion, but the simplicities of the reported words of Jesus himself.

Douglass died, aged sixty-eight, in 1932.[22] He was buried, under a simple oak cross, immediately outside the porch of the Norfolk church he had loved and which he had served. (Rotting oak no longer disfigures his burial place; it is now unmarked.)

When, in 1899, Douglass Boycott accepted the curacy of Wymondham, he severed the long family connection with Burgh-St-Peter. The Rectory House then contained, no doubt, a valuable clerical and family archive going back, probably, to Samuel's years as Rector. But – and despite this – Alice, Douglass's wife, is believed to have lit a succession of the most magnificent bonfires! A few things which had belonged to Charles – his riding boots and his Shillelegh – with two clear notches cut in its handle – were given away. None of his papers escaped.

Charles had 'an accident' in December 1894 which 'kept him in Dublin'; in April 1895 he was 'not well'; in December of that year he had difficulty in 'getting about'; in March 1897 his doctor 'ordered' him to Brighton. A month later Charles himself said, 'The change has done me good. Like an old horse it has kept me on the road a few months more but the Doctors are all agreed that I have not much longer to live.' All these were incidents leading to his death – in The Agent's house – on 19th June 1897, at the age of sixty-five. His burial service in Burgh-St-Peter Church was conducted by the Reverend Douglass Boycott, who had been with him during the 'siege' in Lough Mask House. His gravestone was erected by Sir Hugh Adair.

Charles could scarcely have chosen to die on a more significant day. The weather was calm and hot. Almost the whole of the Royal Navy – its presence in one place, its Admirals, its bands, its picket boats, its array of signalling flags, its visiting ships – were lined up in The Solent and beyond to mark Queen Victoria's Diamond Jubilee. Bells were rung deliriously; England, indeed, went on holiday! No one had time to remember the death of the excellent man who had not only given his name to the English language but also to the languages of the world.

There is little doubt that Charles, when crisis struck in the autumn of 1880, held much of himself in an undisclosed reserve. He was a man of high courage and of fine integrity. When forced to leave his house and farm in Ireland he did so calmly and without complaint. His answers to the lengthy examination imposed on him by the Bessborough Commission were models of clear thinking and of concise good English. He was not afraid to quarrel, to some extent publicly, with the leading English politician of the day whose views on Ireland did not accord with his own. Adversity did little more than wash over him; he had not earned, and he did not deserve, his notoriety. (Eponyms are rare and curious 'creations'; they may be born as quickly, and as easily, as 'boycott' was born in October 1880.)

Charles died as a 'technical bankrupt' due, almost certainly, to the losses he suffered when, eventually, he was able to sell his property round Lough Mask House; and – it must be said – to the additional losses he suffered because of his passion for racing horses.

It is impossible to maintain that Charles was 'a great man'. His character was tested – perhaps severely – in Achill for eighteen years, but little is known now of the lonely life that he and his wife led there; all that may be said is that a lesser man might have abandoned it. He was tested, severely, in the autumn and early winter of 1880, but this period was too short to make any proper judgement possible. He was tested again – by the complexity and the uncertainty of Anglo-Irish politics – between the autumn of 1881 and early 1886, but the tide of events was, by no means, then all hostile to him. He proved himself to be a kindly, and thoughtful, servant to the Flixton Estate. It would be foolish to place him in the ranks of 'the great and the good'; but that he had some claim to greatness may not be far from the truth.

Towards the end of his life Charles became stiff and rheumatic. A bitter March wind from the north-east had been blowing round 'The Priest's House' for days. He is believed to have pulled out his gun and fired two shots from his dressing-room window at the weathercock on Flixton Church. 'That'll teach that bloody bird,' he muttered.

EPILOGUE

PARNELL DIED IN 1891; DISGRACED, in some eyes, by his affair with Mrs O'Shea. Gradually the large landowners in Ireland sold their properties; Ireland became a country of largely peasant proprietors. Government support for the development of rural industries, for the formation of co-operative societies and for the encouragement of fisheries was given. The North of Ireland (around Belfast) continued to be prosperous and innovative. Ireland continued to be of strategic importance to England.

During the First World War Irish nationalism grew fast. In 1918 it was thought that Ireland might become a valuable industrial base in addition to being a significant producer of livestock and other agricultural products. A general election was held, in Ireland, in 1918; De Valera then became its President. In 1920 the British Government passed a 'Government of Ireland' Act which made provision for *two* Irish Parliaments; one, essentially Protestant, governed the six Northern Counties of Londonderry, Antrim, Tyrone, Fermanagh, Monaghan and Armagh; the other, essentially Catholic, governed the remainder of Eire. A treaty of separation, as between the six northern counties and the remainder of Eire, came into effect in 1922.

The 'union' between England and Ireland had lasted for 122 years.

★

'The first man to whom this system of ostracising was applied, as if he were a leper, was a Captain Boycott . . .. This Boycott was a coarse, vulgar tyrant, and treated the poor peasants as if they were so many dogs. He evicted unfortunate tenants with as little remorse as if he were exterminating wolves . . .'

Ireland Past and Present D.P.Conyngham. 1884.

⋆

'After some twenty five years military service, Boycott went to Ireland in 1875 to become the land agent of Lord Erne and to farm about five hundred acres in County Mayo . . . That he was a rigorous, and often ruthless, servant to his noble master there is very little doubt . . . [he] behaved in general towards the underling with a nineteenth century ruthlessness which was so characteristic of that age of progress.'

So the Land Leaguers 'sent the man to Coventry . . . they stopped his food supplies, interrupted his mail, tore down his fences and prevented him from getting in the crops. Boycott fought back.'

Review of the film *Captain Boycott.* John Pudney. 1947.

⋆

'You couldn't, with any punch of effectiveness, say about a bad landlord or agent or landgrabber, "We'll Featherstonehaugh or Cholmondeley or Twentymen or Marjoribanks him". . . . No, BOYCOTT just happened to be a good word, two clean clear forceful syllables; and, as such, it is something in the dictionary while the man is nothing.'

Review of the film *Captain Boycott.* Benedict Kiely. 1947.

⋆

'Lough Mask House, the home in 1880 of Captain Charles Cunningham Boycott . . . a military man of a notable density of skull and paucity of imagination.

Boycott woke one morning to find that his servants were absent, and that . . . no-one would speak to him . . . Boycott was steadily reduced to a state of desperation and before long he suddenly departed never to be seen about Lough Mask again.'

Connaught – The counties of Galway, Mayo, Sligo, Leitrim and Roscommon in Ireland. Jean Jennett.

★

'A great deal of excitement was caused all through Ireland, early in November (1880) by the war on "Captain" Boycott – an Englishman, agent of Lord Erne . . . An agent of the worst type . . . a paltry, mean-souled fellow . . .'

Life of Michael Davitt D.B. Cashman. 1979.

★

'Captain Boycott was my great great great uncle.'

'Emma, that is nothing to be proud of.'

An exchange between the author's niece Emma Viney and a mistress at her school in England. 1980.

★

'BOYCOTT, the largest council estate in Droitwich, is to change its name. A survey of the 2,000 homes showed that residents did not want to live on an estate named after Captain Charles Cunningham Boycott, notorious in the 1870s for his repression of Irish peasants.

Residents' Association chairman, Mr Larry Wright, had claimed it was "like living in somewhere called 'Hitlersville!'"'

Berrows Journal. 1984.

★

'Captain Boycott, a wealthy and implanted landowner in the West of Ireland, so cruelly abused his position and tenants (already aggrieved by having their lands taken away and given to this Englishman) that they, led by their priests and quasi-political leaders, refused to acknowledge his existence or that of his constabulary and troops. This meant that he collected no rent nor harvest, a situation that persisted for some five years which finally resulted in his expulsion from Ireland by his political overseers (perhaps the Earl of Connaught) . . . you should bear in mind that this tale is widely known . . .'

(from a private letter to the author dated November 1985)

★

'Captain & Mrs Boycott . . . were curiously free from any form of animosity against the Irish.'

N. China Sunday News. 1931.

★

Quoted in New York as being written in a letter by Charles Cunningham Boycott to a friend: 'I go for my annual holiday to dear old Ireland: it is my one treat of the year.'

New York Times. 1889.

★ ★ ★

'Words are like leaves; and where they most abound,
Much fruit of sense beneath is rarely found.'

Alexander Pope.

NOTES

Part One: England – Ireland

1 The words are taken from the service (not now often conducted) for the Churching of Women.
2 Burgh Castle (it remains standing just west of Great Yarmouth) is not to be confused with Burgh-St-Peter.
3 The Church of England does not concern itself with 'records' (as, for example, does Guinness). In December 1988 a correspondence started in *The Times* about long-serving clerical families. By this evidence six families in England and two in Scotland had experiences similar to the Boycotts'; no doubt there were others. (One family, the Leirs of Ditcheat in Somerset, held that living in unbroken succession from 1699–1917; the last Leir incumbent was succeeded by a son-in-law so that members of that family were in continuous occupation of the same rectory for 247 years.)

   The family surname was changed from Boycatt to Boycott, almost certainly, in 1841, when the decennial census return for that year required to be completed.
4 The Glebe is a piece of land for the use of the incumbent. It seldom exceeds a few acres. The incumbent is free to use it himself or to let it.
5 The Boycott family tree, on p. xiii, in its left-hand margin, lists those who have held the advowson of Burgh-St-Peter, and so the right to present to it, between 1713 and 1977. In 1977, by an Order in Council, a number of local benefices, including that of Burgh-St Peter (which had already been united with Aldeby and Wheatacre) were united into 'The Benefice of Raveningham'. The same Order established a team ministry of one rector and three other ministers and a patronage board whose duty it became to present the rector. Charles Arthur Boycott, the patron of Burgh in 1977, was appointed a member of this patronage board.
6 Paine was a Norfolk man and a champion of the common man. He was born in Thetford in 1738 and worked, for a short time, in Diss.
7 The expedition was commanded by General Hoche, an allegedly efficient officer then aged twenty-eight. Inevitably Hoche found himself much in the hands of the sailors. In 1796 the French Navy had not recovered from the upheavals of the revolution; training, morale and general efficiency were all low; Brest, the naval base at which the expedition assembled, was in a state of chaotic disorder.

   Forty-five ships were mustered; these included eighteen of the line and thirteen frigates but only seven transports. The soldiers numbered 14,750. The line ships and frigates were all, of necessity, burdened with troops and stores, and, in consequence, were under provisioned with ammunition and food. The stores included a large supply of arms for the insurgent Irish. An over large staff was embarked (including one lady dressed as a boy). Hoche and the naval commander sailed together in a frigate named 'Fraternité'; Wolfe Tone, in French uniform, in one of the ships of the line.

The fleet stole out of Brest on 16th December 1796 when the days were short and the nights long. Order, counter order and disorder within the intricate sea approaches to Brest resulted in three collisions and the loss of one seventy-four gun ship and 1255 men by shipwreck. The expedition's unseamanlike departure was observed by Sir Edward Pellew, in command of the Brest Inshore Squadron of British frigates; but it proved impossible for Admiral Colpoys, in command of the main blockading squadron, to bring the French to battle.

At sea the fleet set course for Ireland but without the 'Fraternité', which became separated and which, in the event, was never seen again until all was over. The subordinate commanders opened their sealed orders only to find that these contained no instructions as to the place of landing. In desperation the fleet made for Bantry Bay (in the extreme south-west of Ireland) in the belief that this was in accordance with the overall plans (but whether it was also General Hoche's remains obscure).

At this point – as might have been expected in late December – the weather intervened decisively. Fog was followed by a terrible storm which split and scattered the French fleet. Many ships never got into Bantry Bay and those that did failed to land their troops.

Eventually a disorganised expedition straggled back to Brest. By engagement in battle, capture, shipwreck and scuttling the French lost thirteen ships and some 4,000 men. Hoche had but one consolation; if Colpoys had caught the overloaded and disorganised French fleet as it first cleared Brest a disaster of dreadful proportions would, almost certainly, have occurred.

8 Humbert – a revolutionary general and said to have been a former dealer in goat and rabbit skins – landed in three ships (with *English* colours flying) in Killala Bay, Co Sligo, in August 1798. He marched south into Co Mayo picking up a number of wildly enthusiastic out-of-the-bog Irish insurgents as he went. Before he could be brought to account, and despite the help of his 'helpers', he succeeded in routing, with ignominy, a militia force outside Castlebar. The 'Castlebar Races' are still recalled with mixed merriment and bitterness. The French, eventually, were treated with honour; but from the Irish insurgents a terrible retribution was exacted.

9 Much rough, dirty water passed under the bridges of Dublin and London during the 'negotiations' about Union. No consensus between the opposing points of view was ever achieved. The Union Bill was passed, eventually, by a majority of forty-three votes, but the vote had been scarcely a free one. Everything at the Crown's disposal had been devoted to 'the single object of carrying the Union'; '. . . the virus of corruption extended and descended through every fibre and artery of the political system, including crowds of obscure men who had it in their power to assist or obstruct.'

10 In 1800 Charles Napier, the 'soldiers' friend', and upon the base of whose statue in Trafalgar Square is inscribed the words 'Erected by Public Subscription, the most numerous subscribers being Private Soldiers' was

aged eighteen: John Moore (Light Infantryman, trainer and the officer who conducted the retreat to Corunna) was thirty-nine: Arthur Wellesley (victor in the Peninsula and at Waterloo and, later, the Duke of Wellington) was thirty-one.

11 America declared war on England in 1812 in superficial anger at the blockade; behind the declaration lay a notion that she might acquire Canada whilst England's back was turned.

Anomalies in the economic struggle were many. In 1807 Napoleon, compelled to winter an army in Poland, required 50,000 greatcoats. He was only able to obtain them from England. He paid for the coats but received none as the Royal Navy intercepted the consignment before it reached Hamburg.

12 A globe will show one surprising fact about the British Isles; that is their sea centrality. The Island of England 'lies wholly in the sea and set at the precise centre of all the land of the earth. No other spot upon the globe either fulfils, or can ever be made to fulfil, these two conditions. Turn the globe as you will, contrive and consider as you please – in the end the hard geographical fact will remain that England, alone of all the communities of men, has the sea centrality of the world.'

13 It was quite possible for strangers to be 'compelled to employ guides, walking on stilts, to lead them across'. Even as late as April 1862 accidents could still happen. 'On account of the breaking of a sluice gate in the Fens near Lynn the sea has reasserted its sway over 50,000 acres, and steamers are plying over farms, roads and luxuriant crops.'

14 In 1778 Mrs Siddons played in Norwich for seven nights; 1200 people heard Handel's Judas Maccabaeus sung in St Peter's Church; over 900 people heard a symphony given by an orchestra of one hundred musicians.

15 A common four year rotation ran: wheat, turnips, barley, clover. A six year rotation went wheat, barley, turnips, barley with clover (or other grasses) clover, other grasses for two years. Another six year rotation retained one year fallow.

'Drunk or sober, sow wheat in October' is an old Norfolk maxim; perhaps owing its origin to the importance of maintaining a rotation.

16 (a) Most ploughmen worked in one daily 'journey' of eight hours. In Norfolk, when daylight allowed, two journeys each of five hours were worked (man and horse went home to dinner at noon). Whilst most English ploughmen moved at one or two m.p.h. Norfolk teams did three or four. By these means a Norfolk team might plough two acres a day, a performance undreamt of elsewhere.

(b) After 'rotations' become established a visitor to Norfolk noted that almost every farm labourer knew the crop which any field had just carried and what it would next carry.

17 George III – a progressive farmer – ran two farms at Windsor; he called one his 'Flemish' farm and the other his 'Norfolk' farm.

18 It is believed that the word 'coke' in connection with a hat, may be eponymous. The predecessor of the bowler was a similar hat, made originally to the order of William Coke of Holkham. (The bowler, in the hat trade, is known sometimes as a 'coke'.)

19 Worsted is a village to the north of Norwich.

20 John Morse was born in 1745. He had become a prominent figure in the life of Norwich before he and his sons inherited so much from John II.

He had been High Sheriff of Norfolk in 1779 and Mayor of Norwich in 1781 (he was to be Mayor again in 1803). From a second marriage in 1800 to Elizabeth Ann Hall he had a third son, also named John. This John, in 1844, changed his name to Morse-Boycott. At his death John Morse-Boycott left 'immense estates' in Dorset, Devon, Suffolk and Lincolnshire, some of which may have come down to him indirectly from John II. Certain beneficiaries under his will were obliged to take the surname of Morse-Boycott exclusively, or after, any other surnames.

21 A Reverend Thomas Page (no doubt the same man) married Horatio Nelson's parents (the Reverend Edward Nelson and Catherine Suckling) in Beccles Church on 11th May 1749.

22 Samuel's portrait is the property of Donald Scott of Wisborough Green, Sussex, a descendant of Samuel's. The portrait still hangs in its original, and fine, frame.

23 A terrier is a periodical inventory of church property.

24 Samuel built before dining rooms came into general use. (Meals were eaten in parlours on small tables brought in for the purpose.)

25 On 2nd January 1773 Samuel buried a manservant named William Osborne in the porch of Burgh-St-Peter church. Thousands of shoes walked over Osborne's memorial stone before it became covered by a large door mat. If, today, the mat is drawn aside only the following lettering remains:

William Osborne
Died Dec 30 1772
Aged 73 years
diligent servant
BOYCATT
(perhaps 'he received')
of an Earthly
. . ... Wages
Bag . . .. with holes
Having served . . .. In that calling
The Lord Christ

'Bag' is clear as a group of three letters; 'with holes' is clear. It must be presumed that Samuel chose both the place of burial and the wording of the inscription. (If he was alive today it would be interesting to ask him a few questions!)

26 In 1785 Lt Charles Cunningham RN, who came from Eye in Suffolk, was aged thirty. He had already seen seven years active service in the West Indies where he had distinguished himself. Whilst on that station he served as First Lieutenant in the 'Hitchenbroke' commanded by Nelson. At his marriage England was at peace and Cunningham, probably, unemployed. In 1788 he went to the East Indies and was promoted Commander.

27 Three references (one, conceivably, flawed) attest the existence of a second 'Mrs Boycott'. First, a Peter Routh letter of May 1774 refers to Samuel 'and Mrs Boycott' in the context of man and wife. Second, the 'imperfect' piece of evidence suggests her, quite natural, presence as a witness to Mary's marriage in 1785. 'A. Boycott' signed the register. (John II had a daughter named 'Anne', but she almost certainly died in infancy.) If 'A. Boycott' was not Samuel's second wife nothing suggests who else she might have been. Third, Venn's Biographical History of Gonville

and Caius College (Vol. II) states that Samuel married Mrs Gordon of Northwold.

Northwold is a village in north-west Norfolk. Gordons (one a lawyer) appear frequently in the parish registers of the period. Three male Gordons, any of whom might have been the wanted widow's earlier husband, died in 1752, 1753 and 1756. Confusingly, the marriage register discloses that, in December 1750 'Wm Green of Eccles Esq. and Anne Gordon' were married. If she is the lady in question then (a) she and Samuel may well have been contemporaries and (b) whilst her initial was 'A' – in agreement with the signature of a witness to Mary's wedding – confusion has entered, somewhere, between her two surnames of Gordon and Green.

(To add, even further, to the 'Gordon' confusion a marriage took place, in 1772, in Burgh Church, between 'Edward Mapes Esq.' and 'Anne Gordon' 'of this parish'. Samuel did not officiate but he was a witness; perhaps at the wedding of a new sister-in-law temporarily resident in Burgh?)

28 As early as 1794 Norwich found itself garrisoned in some strength on account of internal unrest. 'At this period the revolutionary feeling had found its way from France to England, and in no place was the admiration of what had been effected in France, . . . greater than in Norwich . . . the officers (of the garrison) could hardly appear in the streets without insult from the populace. At night, if they went out, they were knocked down; and attempts were made to sow disaffection among the soldiers. Desertion became frequent, . . . there was a society in Norwich for the encouragement of desertion. It was amply supplied with funds; and the members secreted the soldiers, provided them with coloured clothes and money, and then despatched them to their respective homes.' (Sir James McGregor, surgeon to the 88th or Connaught Rangers who served in Norwich at the time. Quoted in *Perlustrations of Great Yarmouth*, Vol. III).

29 Threshing machines were found particularly objectionable. They took away work in general and work in the winter. (The latter was usually done indoors and so allowed a wage to be earned in bad weather.)

30 This Sir Thomas was an interesting innovator in his own right. He believed that every man, no matter what his station in life might be, should be able to earn a pension. Many notebooks still remain in the Beevor archive which testify to the week by week working of a successful Provident Society which this Sir Thomas established in Attleborough in 1847 and which secured old age annuities to retired labourers.

31 Young Samuel's death happened in the year the family moved to Burgh-St-Peter. He was the first member of the family to be buried there.

32 The President of Magdalen College, Oxford was elected by the Fellows for life. He was required to be a man 'of good and reputable conversation, approved in knowledge, good morals and conditions; of discernment in spiritual and temporal concerns; of forecasts and circumspection also'. As President Martin Routh became the 'Head over all the Scholars, Fellows, Clerks, Ministers and others' living in the college. Unlike the Fellows the President was permitted to marry.

33 Most of the Boycott/Routh archive in Magdalen College derives from letters which Martin Routh had not, as it were, methodically thrown away. They were discovered after his death, behind, in, and under furniture in his Magdalen rooms. They include four of William's letters to Martin, only one of which concerns the Sacrae research work. For the most part this

is lighthearted and presages, only, the despatch of documents; it is not one which Martin would have wished to keep. Martin's apparent lack of method, it seemed, was confined to non-essential material.

34 Billie came seventh in the Mathematical Tripos, so becoming the 'Seventh Wrangler' of his year. In his time the universities were far from being well attended centres of great learning. Of Cambridge G.M.Trevelyan wrote 'But if Cambridge shone at all, it was only in comparison with Oxford. Owing to the permanent influence of Newton the Mathematical Tripos was a real test of knowledge . . . It had an enduring effect on the intellectual life and traditions of the University . . .'

35 Billie and Charles Harvey had been exact contemporaries in Cauis. Harvey was a Norwich man and a lawyer who later became the Recorder of Norwich and its member of Parliament. Upon coming into a large inheritance Harvey changed his name to Savile-Onley.

36 Holkham Hall is a fine Palladian mansion in north Norfolk built by Thomas Coke to house the tapestries, statues and paintings he brought back from his own Grand Tour of Italy in the mid-eighteenth century.

The house and its owner were well known as being the centre of Whig opinion in East Anglia. It is possible that Billie, as a young and promising Whig, had been entertained there; perhaps with Mary, as evidently, she knew it also.

37 The word 'Guillotine' is an eponym; so called after a Frenchman named Ignace Guillotin.

38 Early in 1793 on the outbreak of war, Charles Cunningham R.N., in command of a brig, had carried Admiralty despatches to Lord Hood, Commander-in-Chief Mediterranean. He later took command of a frigate which he had helped capture from the French. In August of the following year, and immediately after the subjugation of Corsica, Hood sent Cunningham home, overland, carrying his own despatches to the Admiralty. '[He] . . . has cruised with infinite diligence, zeal and perseverance, under many difficulties [and] . . . is charged with my despatches, and is competent to give any information their lordships may wish to have. I beg to recommend him as an officer of great merit, and highly deserving any favour that can be shown him.'

Cunningham left Corsica on 11th August and arrived in London 1st September despite the compelling necessity of avoiding capture, en route, by the French army and by gales in the Channel which held him at Helvoetsluys for several days. Was it only a sense of duty that drove him so hard and so fast? Was he greeted, when he got home, by a happy wife and two excited little girls? If not, did he know what to expect? Had Lord Hood chosen him, from amongst a number of his Captains, as his London Courier out of compassion? There is no way of knowing.

39 Of Anne, as a person nothing is known. She was one of several daughters of Thomas Smythe, of Dereham, who may have been a Dereham solicitor. Her grandmother was one of Nelson's sisters. The Smythe family came originally from Kent but had been established in Norfolk for many generations.

40 At Magdalene College Cambridge the position of 'President' was dissimilar to that at Magdalen Oxford; at Magdalene Cambridge the President was elected by the Fellows as their representative and, if necessary, as a countervailing force to the Master of the College who was appointed by an hereditary 'Visitor'. In Kerrish's day the appointment of President was for life or until resignation.

41 The surviving Kerrich archive in the British Museum consists of forty-six volumes of manuscripts. The five local churches which Kerrich certainly knew were Aldeby, Fritton, Redgrave, Toft Monks and Wheatacre; nothing, in any of them, suggests a stepped tower.

42 No physical internal feature separates nave from chancel. The roof line is continuous. (The screen which, today, divides nave and chancel, is recent.)

43 The wherries were locally designed to meet local needs. They were made of oak and were clinker built. They varied in size between the Wanderer of eighty tons burden and the little Cabbage able to carry four tons (and much of it 'on the cross' or smuggled). The majority carried 25–35 tons and had a length of fifty feet, a beam of twelve feet, and a draught of three feet. Apart from a tiny cabin aft, the boat consisted only of stowage and the narrowest of decking along which the wherryman walked when obliged to 'quant', or pole. The mast foot was weighted so allowing the mast and the single black tarred sail to be quickly lowered and raised again by one man as the wherry 'shot' the many bridges. Owners gave them countrified names like Pillbox, Rifle, Hit or Miss, Beer Tub, Ginger and Rat Cage. In their heyday there may have been two to three hundred working the waterways. One observer said that he had seen 'nine dozen wherries and timber carrying keels' being loaded and unloaded together along the Yarmouth Quays; and making 'a gallant show'. (One wherry has been preserved and is still afloat.)

44 Norfolk is not well endowed with stone. Bricks were required everywhere.

45 Large scale smuggling across the North Sea had been indulged in for centuries. This account of an incident is taken from Norfolk Annals for 14th February 1822. 'A smuggling boat landed eighty tubs of gin and brandy on Snettisham beach. The crew of the preventive boat seized the cargo, a portion of which, with their boat, was rescued by the smugglers, who had the assistance of about 100 persons, some of whom were armed with bludgeons and fowling pieces. Twenty or thirty horses and carts were in waiting to remove the contraband goods. Two of the smugglers were wounded in the affray.'

46 A wetland copse.

47 'It is a very pretty sight to watch a party of these little gulls, looking snow-white in the distance against the rich brown of the newly turned up soil, paddling amongst the clumsy clods with dainty, red-webbed feet, and continually lifting their white wings to balance themselves on the rough ground . . .'

48 A decoy consists of a number of ditches – or 'pipes' – which radiated outwards from the shore line of the decoy lake or water at carefully chosen places; in the 1860s Fritton had sixteen. Each pipe was about sixty yards in length and full of water to about 18″ depth. Each was netted overhead and opaquely fenced on both sides by reed screens in which small apertures had been left at intervals. The pipes were wide and inviting at their mouth, but curved and tapered down to the purse net at the far end. Tame 'decoy' ducks – quacking with delight at the food thrown into the mouth of the chosen pipe by the decoy man (hidden by the screens) – were followed by wild birds eager to know the cause of the sudden excitement. When the pipe had filled to his satisfaction the decoy man's little dog started to jump in and out of the pipe through the

apertures; his sudden appearances and disappearances were fatally alluring to the wild birds, particularly mallard and teal, who scrambled and flapped along behind him and ever closer to the purse. At the point of no return the decoy man showed himself. The suddenly panic stricken wild birds tumbled themselves into the purse, whilst the decoy ducks, as they had been taught, swam quietly back to the mouth for fear they might show the wild how to escape. Things, of course, could, and did, go wrong. The decoy ducks could misbehave; a heron could have chosen to fish in the mouth of the same pipe as the decoy man had chosen; hawks could only be shot, but, if so, the cure was worse than the disease; a pike could roll at the wrong moment; an otter could be about. But, mishaps apart, a decoy was a cunning resource.

49 There was a sharp increase in the number of cheap guns on the market after Waterloo in 1815. Surplus government stocks and captured – mostly French – rifles were sold off to 'gunsmiths' who sprang up everywhere. These shortened and furbished the guns to fire pellets instead of ball.

50 Archbishop James Ussher worked out the chronology of the Old Testament to arrive at this date. Ussher died in 1656. A number of such bibles still survive.

51 The diocese of Norwich then included Suffolk; this meant, interalia, that Burgh-St-Peter lay around its centre and not, as it is today, at a diocesan extremity.

52 Edward Stanley had three, unusually interesting, children. Arthur became the well-known Dean of Westminster and author. Owen commanded H.M.S. *Rattlesnake* on a voyage of discovery and survey of the Great Barrier Reef, and, on the way, gave his name to the central range of mountains in New Guinea. Mary had the charge of fifty nurses in the Crimea.

53 The Act was implemented nationally by three Commissioners and locally by professional land agents and valuers acting as Assistant Commissioners. The Assistants 'scurried from one parish to another offering advice, settling disputes, confirming agreements and effecting compulsory commutations'. Every field, house, garden, road, path, pond and plot was numbered, mapped and assessed. About one sixth of all the parish tithing maps were, ultimately, sealed and signed by the National Commissioners; these then became known as 'first class' maps. The Burgh map, drawn to a scale of 1″ = 3 chains (or 66 yards) by Richard Barnes, a surveyor of Lowestoft, is one of the 'first class' maps. It is an informative and beautiful piece of work and is now preserved in the Public Record Office. (It includes drawings of the Church, Staithe and Rectory.)

54 The Boileau letters are preserved in the Norfolk Record Office. They were written to Lady Elliot in Brighton who forwarded them to 'John' in India, who, later, brought them home again. The author retained her sense of humour: 'If I become a heroine nobody need despair I think.' She also retained her curiosity: 'By the bye' she interposed in one letter, 'you have never told me who your liberal lover was . . . and whether you love him this time?'

55 The actual outcome of the demand (to which he acceded) that Charles's father would 'refund' part of his tithe receipts is not clear.

56 A memorial (not now easily found) in the Abbey Church in Wymondham records the death of Isaac Jermy and his son Isaac Jermy Jermy on 28th November 1848 (that both were murdered is not stated).

57 Gossips, at the time, believed that Isaac Preston Jermy and Rush were half brothers.
58 Sophia was, always, an attractive and spirited woman. Years later, as Lady Beevor, a maid wailed 'Ma'am there's a burglar in the house' to which Sophia replied 'Show him up. I haven't seen a man in months!'
59 The Nore mutiny was revolutionary. Its leader was in open sympathy with the French. An unknown number of United Irishmen joined the mutineers.
60 Charles Cunningham wrote A Narrative of Occurrence that took place during the Mutiny at the Nore in the months of May and June 1797. This was not published until 1832. It does not bear his name nor does it indicate the date on which he wrote it. Whilst he may have drafted it using a diary kept during the mutiny, doubt, inevitably, exists as to its accuracy. Subject to this qualification the narrative suggests, first, that the Admiralty knew that the *Clyde* remained loyal; second that Cunningham, because of this, had inside information about the mutiny; and, third, that the Admiralty had instructed Cunningham (and another Captain) to extricate their ships at the first opportunity. At a meeting on shore (during the Mutiny) between Captain (later Vice-Admiral Sir) Henry Blackwood, Charles Cunningham and Parker, Cunningham had to be restrained, forcibly, by Blackwood, 'from sealing Parker's fate'.
61 A portrait of Charles Cunningham by Henry Wyatt and two 'portraits' of H.M.S. *Clyde* by William Joy (the first at midnight as she started her escape from the Nore and the second at Sheerness at dawn the following morning) are in the Royal Naval Museum, Greenwich.
62 The marriage took place at Honingham, Norfolk on 25th September 1829. (William had been the curate at Honingham.)
63 The Bungay Spa was said to be a lucrative business. Despite this belief a Norfolk tailor who 'from a weakness fixed upon his Ancles and Knees became incapable of walking, but after a Fortnight's Cold Bathing, he so well recovered the use of his legs, as to run away without paying for his immersions'.
64 The Military Secretary was then Lord Fitzroy Somerset who, in 1852, became Lord Raglan and, in 1854, Commander-in-Chief British Forces, Crimea. At Waterloo Fitzroy Somerset was still a vigorous, high-spirited young man. A sniper's ball smashed his right elbow, but a surgeon amputated his arm and 'tossed it away'. 'Hey,' shouted the patient, 'bring my arm back. There is a ring my wife gave me on one of its fingers.'
65 The 'Blackheath' source is contained in Boase's Modern English Biography and the Roughton anecdote in 'Maria Pasqua' by Magdalen Goffin.
66 Hanworth Church tower as it is today does not lend itself to the type of escapade described; but the incident is in keeping with Charles's character.
67 Major-General John Boteler Parker was the Lieutenant Governor of the Academy and the second son of Admiral Sir Hyde Parker, Commander-in-Chief of the British Fleet at Copenhagen in 1801. (It was Admiral Parker's signal to discontinue the action which caused Nelson to raise his glass to his blind eye and remark 'I really do not see the signal.')

When a young man J.B.Parker fell in love with Fanny Wilson (the elder sister of Harriette Wilson, the last of the great London courtesans) and she, genuinely, with him. They had a daughter. After service in the Peninsula Parker and Fanny lived together in open amity as Colonel and Mrs Parker, but, in 1814, he suddenly married so deserting Fanny and the child. At Waterloo he lost a leg; this caused him great pain for the rest of his life. He was Lieutenant-Governor of Woolwich from 1846 until his death in 1851.

Parker had been in good company when he philandered with Fanny Wilson. His Commander-in-chief in the Peninsula and at Waterloo – the Duke himself – had paid Harriette Wilson's price. Upon being threatened by public disclosure, Wellington – true to himself as always – gave the celebrated reply 'publish and be damned'.

68 The cost of buying a Commission about equalled the cost of establishing a boy in any other profession. The purchase of Commissions was abolished in 1871.

Part Two: Ireland – England

1 The 39th Foot became The Dorset Regiment. It is now part of The Devon and Dorset Regiment.

2 Charles's file in the Public Record office contains three letters to the Military Secretary written on third and twenty-first April and on fifteenth June 1848 by a surgeon named Thomas Mant. Mant's handwriting is vile but the impression is that he had come to know Charles well and that he was trying his best to help him obtain his Commission. This, in turn, suggests that Charles's parents may have consulted Mant about Charles's health in late 1848 or early in 1849. It is possible, also, that William Vaughan Donovan (who witnessed Charles's marriage) did so because he had come to know Charles as a patient.

3 The coaching organisation created by Charles Bianconi (an Italian from Milan) stood comparison with the best in England. Bianconi operated principally in the south and west of Ireland. His 'cars' carried up to sixteen people. These were open but were provided with heavy waterproof leather aprons. Bianconi's cars were clean, smart, carefully driven and punctual. Bianconi's headquarters and principle stables were outside Clonmel; he kept about 1300 horses there.

4 During the sixth and seventh centuries Ireland is believed to have contained 184 Tuath. So large a number illustrates the extent of political fragmentation which then existed. Ireland, in its totality, was not easy to conquer.

5 Robert Peel was Irish Secretary from 1812 to 1818.

6 The exact ratios are:
1 Statute acre = .617347 Irish acre, or
1 Irish acre = 1.619835 Statute acre.

7 Much that was good in the area round Belfast stemmed from sensible land customs. In general, landlord and tenant shared a common outlook; tenants enjoyed security of tenure; agrarian outrage was absent; money could be invested safely both in farms and in domestic cottage industries particularly in the linen industry. A sound foundation for private and public investment and enterprise not only existed but stood ready to welcome, and share in, the industrial revolution as it developed in England.

8 The word 'corn' can be confusing. It denotes the leading crop of a 'district';

in England it is wheat, in Scotland oats and in the U.S.A. it means maize (or Indian corn).

9 *Mayo Examiner* – 6th March 1880.

10 (a) The famine experiences of the third Marquis of Sligo – for whom Charles is believed to have held a small Achill agency – is not uninteresting. In 1845, in the year the famine started and at the age of twenty-five, the Marquis assumed his title and inherited 115,000, mostly useless, acres round Westport. In August 1846 the starving people of that town 'dropped to their knees before him' and with two others, he ordered 1000 tons of flour from America. This reached Westport ten months later and were sold to the starving people at half price; Lord Sligo himself bearing 5/8ths of the resulting loss. He 'spoke out' in the house of Lords. At Christmas 1848 he told the British Government – in a letter to *The Times* – that it was responsible for the situation in Ireland and that 26,000 people in Westport were destitute of food, fuel and clothing. He closed Westport House. Few rents came in. He was forced to borrow. After the famine he found himself obliged to eject many of his tenants from their, more or less, useless land; or, as he himself put it, be ejected himself. The third Marquis of Sligo's portrait suggests that he was an honourable man; what is known of him during the famine years does not belie this impression.

(b) The voluntary work done by the Quakers during the famine was outstanding. '. . . a few courageous men left homes in Middlesex and Surrey, and penetrated to the remotest glen and bogs . . . never since the fourteenth century did pestilence, . . . glean so rich a harvest . . . The population sank so fast that the living could not bury the dead . . . often the wife died in the midst of her starving children . . . Into the midst of these horrors did our heroes penetrate . . . pouring nourishment into parched lips, from which shot fever-flames more deadly than a volley of musketry. Here was courage . . . And who were these brave men? They were Quakers from Clapham and Kingston!'

11 It is thought that in 1848/49 20–30,000 people, already much weakened, died of cholera. Ideas of the time as to cholera's cause and treatment are illustrated by the way the British Army in India tackled the condition. '. . .because of the erratic pattern of empty beds when it struck, some soldiers believed that the disease had been introduced by the Wandering Jew who walked in a figure of eight pattern. The treatment was often no more enlightened. For example, there was the rack, which . . . was a bed of open webs to which the stricken was secured and roasted over a spirit lamp. If the disease did not kill the patient the various treatments would.'

12 Russell was small, almost a dwarf. (Later in life he married a largish lady from which time he became known as the 'widow's mite'.)

13 When his Conservative government fell (immediately after the repeal of the Corn Laws and on a parliamentary 'technicality') Peel, in effect, retired although he remained a member of the House of Commons. On 29th June 1850 he was thrown by a new horse near Hyde Park Corner. He died, three days later, aged sixty-two.

14 A colony of Ulster Irish moved into the Ballycroy area (close to Achill on the mainland) in the sixteenth century. Before it died out the Gaelic spoken on Achill was thought to have an 'Ulster-Gaelic' intonation.

15 It is possible that the word 'Achill' derives from 'Aguila', the Latin for eagle; certainly, in Charles's day, the Golden Eagle and the white Tailed

Sea Eagle – or Erne – were common. If so the connotation may include 'look out point' (which Achill is).

16 Ozone is oxygen in a state of condensation; it then possesses 'a peculiarly pungent and refreshing odour.'

17 Theresa McDonald, in her *Achill: 5000 BC to 1900 AD* states that three old church sites exist on Achill; one at Slievemore, one at Kildarnet and a third at Dookinella.

18 Stoney became, later, the Rector of Castlebar and a member of the Achill Mission's Management Committee.

19 In writing about the Achill Protestant Mission reliance has been placed on four sources:

a) The Achill *Missionary Herald* (of which several complete copies exist)

b) Such annual Reports of the Mission as, now, can be found. These are:

2nd Published Dublin 1836 British Library, London
6th 31st December 1839 R. Irish Academy Library, Dublin.
8th 31st December 1841 R. Irish Academy Library, Dublin.
9th 31st December 1842 R. Irish Academy Library, Dublin.
10th 31st December 1843 R. Irish Academy Library, Dublin.
11th 31st December 1844 R. Irish Academy Library, Dublin.
15th July 1848–May 1849 National Library, Dublin.
16th 31st December 1849 R. Irish Academy Library, Dublin.
17th 31st December 1850 R.C.B. Library, Dublin.

(The 17th Report had, attached to it, a separate list of all subscribers to the Achill Purchase Fund.)

c) A 'statement of affairs' dated 30th January 1858, issued by 'The Mission' and now to be found in the R.C.B. Library.

d) A copy of the Income and Expenditure account for the year ending 31st December 1864 (bound in a copy of the Achill *Missionary Herald* for that period and held by the National Library in Dublin.)

20 The eating of maize almost certainly led to the disease of pellagra – see Chapter 14.

21 The charge of 'souperism' – the taunt – was not new to Nangle. In 1839 he had given evidence to a House of Lords Committee. During the hearing he referred to the Mission as trying to raise the people in every way. '. . . it is hard to avoid reproach' he said. 'Sometimes we are accused of being ready enough with our preaching because it costs us nothing, but that we will not give anything to the poor people; then, when we strive to better their temporal condition, it is insinuated that we attempted to induce them to change their religious profession by bribery.'

22 The water-colour is in the ownership of Colonel F.E. Nangle of Ardglass.

23 The 'hedge school', as its name implies, was an itinerant school. It was taught by a man who, usually, believed in what he was doing and attended by children whose parents, at least, wanted them to learn.

24 Franklin was a determined man. Because, as he thought, he knew the Arctic so well he applied to lead the 1847 N.W. passage expedition. To this the First Lord of the Admiralty demurred, saying 'you are sixty'. 'No! No! My Lord' replied Franklin 'only fifty-nine.'

25 *Bible in Hand – Ireland's Welcome to the Strangers*. Asenath Nicholson. Hodder and Stoughton. London 1926.

26 'The Achill Missionary Herald and Western Witness' was the paper's *short*

title. Its full title (composed, presumably, by Edward Nangle) reads: 'The Achill Missionary Herald and Western Witness; Being a monthly Journal Exhibiting the Principles and Progress of Christ's Kingdom and Exposing the Errors and Abominations of that Section of the Rival Kingdom of Anti-Christ Commonly called the Papacy, together with a practical exposure of the Civil, Social and Political delinquencies of the Pope's emissions in attempting to establish his wicked usurpation throughout this world generally and especially in this Kingdom.'

27 Bianconi's cars to and from Achill were probably Irish 'Jaunting Cars' able to carry a driver and four passengers who faced each other behind the driver.

28 *Some Experiences of an Irish R.M.* Somerville & Ross.

29 The list was printed in Achill and appeared as a booklet; it runs to over 100 small pages of small print. It contains about 9,500 names; of these over 2000 contributed directly whilst the remainder did so through local collections. One, anonymous, individual subscribed £300; eight, including the Primate himself, subscribed £100; several people gave 6d; 'a friend' sent 2 1/2d; forty-six members of the 'Norwich Protestant Society', between them, subscribed exactly £5.0.0.

30 Valuation Books started, in Ireland, about 1850 the year in which William Blacker died. The books present an ongoing, and progressive, picture of land ownership but no dates of change. Whilst William Blacker's name appears as the owner of 3961 acres and as the owner of the Keem Bay salmon fishery, this evidence, because of its date, cannot be regarded as conclusive. (Prior to 1850 such information was contained in Grand Jury Books but these were destroyed by explosion in 1922.)

31 These ocean salmon fisheries have existed since time immemorial. It is not known who owned them or how they were conducted. They may have been handed down in families. Several men and a boat were needed to work each fishery and it was necessary to fish every day throughout the summer season. Organising the gangs, disciplining them, paying them and then disposing, rapidly, of the catch was, probably, beyond the continuous capacity of any one family and, for this reason, a number of families may have shared the rights and the profits. This may explain why, in William Blacker's case, the valuation book entry reads 'Wm Blacker and Others'.

32 The word is believed to be eponymous; after Dr Ricketts of Newbury who became adept at curing children with 'swollen hands and small legges'.

33 William Pike leaves behind him one, other, impression; he refused to be brow-beaten by Edward Nangle!

34 Arthur and Isabella had five children all of whom were destined to become Charles's wards.

35 This, irreversible, act happened in Dublin on 28th June 1922 during the Irish civil war. 'Half an hour' after midday the conflagration reached two lorry loads of gelignite sticks stacked in the Public Record Office. The city was rocked by a huge explosion; the greatest Dublin had ever known. It was described by an eye witness, in a letter published in the *Irish Times*, the following day:

'Black as ink, shot up 400 feet into the sky, a great column of writhing smoke and dust, not more than fifty feet in diameter at the base. It spread into an enormous mushroom some 200 feet up and flared in the sun with lurid reds and browns, through which could be seen thousands of white snowflakes, dipping, sidling, curtseying, circling, floating as snowflakes do. But the shower was not falling, it was rising. Higher it rose and higher . . . Tons of bricks and mortar fell into the river . . . and for the next hour documents going back to the twelfth century drifted over the city . . .'

36 By all accounts Sir Richard and Lady O'Donnell, in themselves, were good upright people. The O'Donnells owned an estate of 80,000 acres (most being very poor) round Newport and on Achill which had become unmanageable by reason of debt.

The Encumbered Estates Court was set up in 1849 to deal with numerous Irish estates of which the O'Donnell estate was typical; and to rid Ireland of its impoverished, and usually insolvent, landowners. Its three commissioners were given power to free estates of inherited 'encumbrances', to order sales, and to give any purchaser a 'clean' freehold title to what he had bought. It had been hoped that its activities would encourage careful English farmers and businessmen to invest capital in Irish farming. In the event, and during the first eight years of its work, some 3200 properties were sold to 7200 purchasers of whom only 300 were Englishmen. Several of these Englishmen farmed well, and profitably, in Counties Mayo and Galway. Irish purchasers, however, are remembered, for the most part, as being an unprincipled lot; speculators as careless of their land as they were of its poor tenants.

37 Both house and barn have been, recently and carefully, inspected by a professional architect. He is certain of their superior construction.

38 As already explained William Blacker's will was destroyed in 1922.

39 W.M. Maxwell (author of 'Wild Sports of the West') took a shooting party to Achill; he bought a Keem sheep which, he explained to his guests, was a mountain district 'celebrated for the flavour and fatness of its sheep'.

40 Irish hares are not the same as the brown English hare; they are stockier, have shorter ears, and a white tail. Irish grouse were larger and heavier than the red grouse of Scotland.

41 Cranagh (or Carageen) makes a jelly like pudding and is still gathered in Achill.

42 The, so called, potato 'lazy beds' were usually small and rectangular. Seed was laid on the beds and covered by spoil thrown up from a surrounding trench. Lazy beds could be used on steep land and gave good drainage in what, usually, was a wet country.

43 There is a story in the family that a mysterious 'linen bag' once existed containing 150 precious stones; said, vaguely, to be emeralds or rubies. The stones were thought to have been collected by a 'much travelled' member of the family but in the context of rubies or emeralds the cap fits no one. Were these stones Achill amethysts (a clear bluish violet stone)? The amethyst used to be known as an 'amatist' and judged to follow 'the ruby in dignity'. Amethysts are of quartz or rock crystal. Rock crystal is called, sometimes a 'diamond'; especially when attached to the name of a place – e.g. 'An Irish diamond' (the old amethyst mine is no longer accessible).

44 Almost certainly Captain Dyer R.N. (If so he served on the Mission's Court of Local Management' which consisted (in 1839) of Dyer himself, Dr Adams, two Missionaries and the Steward. They met twice weekly.)

45 Visitors usually expostulated at the choking blinding smoke they were obliged to breathe inside the cabins. James Johnson, a London Physician

and writer on Ireland, went into a cabin without a chimney in 1844 and found the family squatting round the fire eating their potatoes in a clear atmosphere. He noticed that the smoke accumulated downwards under the roof until it reached the doorway by which it then escaped, so establishing an equilibrium between a suffocating upper region and a lower level of clearer air for anyone either squatting or lying down. It is not difficult to imagine the consternation, followed by the disturbance to the delicate balance between the clean air and the smoke, caused by the sudden arrival of a well-dressed, rather grand, English speaking visitor to the family circle (which, as often as not, included a frightened pig). The visitor, refusing any invitation he might receive to sit down because there was nothing on which to sit except the dirty floor, remained standing; and choking, in the upper and by now swirling, smoke cloud.

46 Prior to the mid-1850s men, often, wore side-whiskers but during the Crimean War beards became fashionable.

47 Curraghs were constructed with a light wooden frame over which tarred animal skins were stretched. Having no keel they were fast and could turn on a sixpence but were dangerous except in a calm sea. They carried, usually, three men but could be carried to the water by two.

48 As his account with Mulloy's of Westport shows, Charles, for a year or so around 1867, seems to have been under financial pressure. This may have been because he had taken over responsibility for farming all of Murray Blacker's land, or because the loss of his Keem Bay house had forced him into spending more money than he had expected.

49 Charles could not have become even an honorary 'Captain' in consequence of his brief career in the British Army as an Ensign. His name appears nowhere in any local Mayo Militia etc. records.

50 References in Irish literature to 'Captains' are not common. In an article on Dr McHale (The Roman Catholic Archbishop of Tuam) he, on one occasion, went to inspect – without invitation – a Protestant school near Delphi (south of Westport) to which about thirty Catholic children had been admitted. The Bishop discovered that no Catholic 'emblems' (crucifixes and pictures of the Blessed Virgin) were displayed on the walls; in consequence he stated that until these were displayed, he 'could not permit it' – 'it' being the school – 'to exist'. To this diktat the school mistress (a woman whose 'free English blood . . . boiled and stirred!') told the Bishop that she would 'consult the Captain' (John Lyons; Journal of the Westport Historical Society Vol. 4 No 1 p44.)

51 This hangs over a fireplace in the house of Mr J Benest of Nicholas Hayne, near Wellington, Somerset.

52 Nets were then suspended from floats made of tarred sheepskins. The neck aperture was tied, closely, round a bung. The bung had two holes; one through which the net was secured and the other through which the float was inflated.

53 The word 'quern' originated from the Danish word 'vroe' or handmill; it means 'stones for crushing'.

54 By the early years of the nineteenth century the idea, amongst the poorest Irish, of using money to buy in something they needed (except, that is, their rent money) seems, virtually to have 'flown away'; money no longer had much day-to-day purchasing reality. In March 1817 – under the exceptional pressures exerted by the famines of 1816 and 1817 (see p. 117) Sir Robert Peel, the then Irish Secretary, wrote that the poorest Irish 'are

not buyers of food but growers of it and have no money to purchase if what they usually grow fails them'. E.C. Large, in his *Advance of the Fungi*, records that if a 'banknote came into the possession of a poor Irishman he would not infrequently pawn it to raise cash.'

55 One peculiarity of the Claddagh was their heavy gold hereditary wedding rings.

56 Coleman wrote these lines in 1900 when he was still in his early twenties. In the year 1900 there was more milk (the population of Ireland had been reduced).

57 It is not easy to define 'the potato eating poor' in nineteenth century Ireland. Almost all Irishmen, then, loved potatoes (Frances Blacker told her mother-in-law that 'she was Irish enough to prefer potatoes and buttermilk to almost anything else'). Throughout the nineteenth century most Irishmen were 'farmers' in the limited sense that they depended on their land to provide their food; but the word 'farmer' could mean a prosperous grazier who lived well above subsistence level, a small 'subsistence' farmer, and a 'labourer' who depended on a tiny patch of land to keep his family and himself alive. Most of Sir Robert Peel's 'four million' came, primarily and without doubt, from the labouring class but the famine and emigration did not mean that this class disappeared; on the contrary it persisted, particularly in the west (and in Co Mayo), throughout Charles's years in Ireland.

58 Professor Lyons, in his *Ireland since the Famine*, estimated the yield in Ireland, between 1850 and 1859, at 4.6 tons per statute acre. In England, during the nineteenth century, the average yield was about 6 tons per acre. In *The Great Famine*, it is stated that, in Co Armagh (and under the influence of William Blacker), yields of eight to ten tons per acre were obtained. (Modern yields of twenty, or more, tons per acre bear no relation to nineteenth century yields.)

59 In 1880, in Co Mayo and in Charles's time, good disease-free seed was imported. This ought to have yielded well but failed to do so because the seed was planted too close together.

60 In a book published in 1896 an unknown reader pencilled in, opposite to a relevant paragraph, these words: 'it was simply due to the usual practice of growing potatoes from bits of tuber, and not from seed of the flower – and using for this purpose the worst tubers.'

61 When Professor Senior saw so many people unemployed during 'the harvest' he may have been under a misapprehension as to how the potato 'harvest' in Ireland was usually conducted.

62 Lack of fats in a meal usually means that no one then enjoys that contented feeling of having 'eaten well'. Dr Johnson, the London physician and a frequent visitor to Ireland, referred to this lack of satisfaction from eating only potatoes when he wrote 'Rarely indeed have the labouring classes more than two meals (of potatoes) in the twenty-four hours; and if these were well boiled the pangs of hunger would be insufferable . . .' The remedy, he continued 'was the all-but universal custom of half boiling potatoes so "leaving the bones in".'

63 The potato consists of 80% water and 20% solids. The solids consist of 85% starch and 15% of 'other nutrients'. 'Other nutrients' include about 1.8gr of protein per 100gr of solids.

This, comparatively large, quantity of protein suggests that those people who ate only potatoes ingested ample protein but this may not have been so for four reasons. First, the prior call upon the available protein is for the growth, and repair, of the body; but, in the special circumstances which governed the life of the 'poor Irishman' this may have needed more than, normally, was the case. Secondly, man is part of the animal kingdom and so better adapted to the absorption of animal protein than vegetable protein. Thirdly, the poor Irishman was deprived of potato protein during every May, June, July and August. Lastly, it is impossible, now, to say how many pounds of potatoes the 'average poor Irishman' ate in every 24 hours.

64 The word 'Rickets' is believed to be eponymous; after Dr Ricketts of Newbury who became adept at curing children with 'swollen hands and small legges'.

65 Maize was supplied, also as a famine relief food, in the year 1800 but nothing is now known of its then consequences.

66 Two Doctors (of Medicine) travelled widely round Ireland in 1879 and 1880. They referred, frequently, to 'mental depression' which may have been their words for a form of insanity. If so this may have been either a normal, but secondary, symptom of pellagra contracted between 1845–1849; or the secondary symptom of pellagra contracted in 1879 (or earlier).

67 In Lewisham, in 1979, a group of seventy-eight schoolboys were taken ill after eating potatoes which, later, were found to contain an excess of glyco-alkaloids. Of these boys seventeen were admitted to hospital; of these, three were described as being 'seriously ill'.

68 If his meals had included fish – so much the better!

69 The Manor House, itself, no longer exists.

70 A few trees (and many sparrows) were left standing (and chirping) in the main Exhibition Hall. When all was almost ready an official suddenly asked himself what might happen if a sparrow should happen to shit upon the Queen's head whilst she carried out her inspections. As no one could answer this delicate question the matter was referred to the Duke of Wellington. He, by then, was becoming tired of the stupid questions he was required, constantly, to answer. He is alleged to have said 'get a blasted sparrow hawk.'

71 It may well be asked 'Why was the Church so isolated?' There are two reasons. First, because in earlier days the village had been moved westward to prevent the spread of plague from Lowestoft; secondly, because the Church itself had often served as a navigational beacon before the Waveney had been better confined to its, now recognised, channel.

72 A staithe was a recognised loading and unloading place for river traffic. Staithes existed at St Olave's, Somerleyton, Burgh-St-Peter, Alderby and Beccles.

73 Emily Georgiana (Charles's eldest sister) became engaged to marry Owen Dinning in the summer of 1862, but he is believed to have died on the day before the wedding. Emily – not surprisingly – became distraught. (It is likely that Owen had no living parents and, in consequence, he was buried amongst the Boycott graves in Burgh-St-Peter churchyard.) Emily – eventually – married a hard-riding and hard-swearing man named Charles Harrison; by him she had three sons and two daughters.

74 William Chaplin ran a large coaching business out of London. He owned five yards, employed 2000 people, and kept sixty coaches and 1300 horses.

A coaching centre existed at Hounslow at the junction of the roads to Bath, Gloucester and Exeter; this had stabling for 2500 horses.

75 The word 'panic' is eponymous. Pan was born covered in hair and with the feet, legs, ears and horns of a goat. He loved music; hence the 'Pipes of Pan'. Pan is supposed to have caused the panic amongst the Persians at Marathon. Strictly speaking we should talk of being seized by panic fever.

76 Carriages were lit by rape oil lamps. These, before departure, were tossed up, already lit, by a man on the platform to his mate who walked along the top of the carriages; this individual caught each lamp and inserted it, through a special hole, into the compartment below. The lamps were designed to stay lit for the six and a half hours between London and Holyhead but, not infrequently, the jolting of the train caused the wick to drop when, after emitting one final belch, the lamp went out.

77 At about the time when Charles first went to Achill the effective width of Achill Sound had been reduced to about one hundred yards by the construction of stone piers on both sides; but it is doubtful if these would have been of much help to horses either swimming or scrambling across.

78 It was not only the man in the street who found himself – from time to time – in a muddle. Blackstone – the great English lawyer – had written '. . . by the law of nature every man from the prince to the peasant has an equal right to take game.' Nevertheless Blackstone, more or less, contradicted himself when he wrote 'for the good of society rights to take game could be restricted.'

79 Ellenborough's wartime law of 1803 (which stayed on the Statute Book for years) did not, specifically, mention poaching but made it a capital offence to 'resist lawful apprehension' by shooting at, or attempting to shoot at, some official trying to do his duty. Since apprehension by a gamekeeper was lawful and 'shooting, stabbing and cutting' were part of the nocturnal business of poaching the laws against poaching were, in effect, considerably strengthened. Early victims of this new law were four young Norfolk poachers who were executed in 1804. At about the same time a new law much increased the severity of the punishment when several men cooperated together in some poaching foray. Because the punishments were so severe many men attempted to resist arrest; this, often, compounded the punishment.

80 An analysis of the occupations of 299 convicted Norfolk poachers between 1821 and 1861 produced some surprising 'wrong-doers'. Whilst 230 – or 73% – of the 299 were labourers who, almost certainly, poached because their wives and children were hungry the others probably 'went out at night' for different reasons. The occupations of this group included a farmer, a weaver, a carpenter, a shoemaker, a baker, a gamekeeper (!), a bricklayer, a pumpmaker, a beerhouse keeper, a stationer, a basket maker, a botanist, a fish dealer, a leather cutter and – astonishingly – a Commissioner of Assessed Taxes.

81 For obvious reasons gamekeepers, almost always, wore some kind of 'Estate' uniform. The gamekeepers on one well known Norfolk estate wore red waistcoats with eight brass buttons beneath a velveteen jacket and a hard 'Billycock' hat.

82 Immediately after the Napoleonic Wars the market for sporting guns was flooded by Government surplus and captured, muzzle loading, guns. These

were shortened and refurbished – usually by incompetent local gunsmiths – to fire pellets.

83 The snipe shooting over the Whitecast Manor land, not far from Burgh-St-Peter, was celebrated.

84 Edmund was ordained by the Bishop of Norwich in 1870 when he was aged thirty-five. He served his curacy in Caistor lying midway between Great Ormesby and Great Yarmouth. He then became the Rector of North Cove with Willingham which lay close to Beccles and over the Waveney from the Burgh-St-Peter rectory. North Cove had no rectory house but Edmund and his family lived, first, in a good Beccles house and, later, in Roos Hall with Isabella. Edmund travelled out to the U.S.A. with Charles and Annie in 1881. Ill health forced him to resign his North Cove living in 1891. He died in 1900.

85 Georgiana died in January 1876. She is commemorated in one of the south facing windows of Ormesby Church.

86 The word 'Mask' may, at one time, have been 'Measg' or 'Measca'; so called, it is said, because the waters of Lough Mask mingle with the equally chalky waters of Lough Carra to the north and Lough Corrib to the south.

87 The Castle is said to have been built by an 'English Baron' in 1238. In 1338 it belonged, probably, to Sir William Burke (of the Co Mayo branch of that powerful family). At one time it was owned by Thomas Bourke. In 1618 it may have been owned by the Butler family (Burke, Bourke and Butler are all well known names in Irish history).

88 On 2nd July 1877 Charles and Murray Blacker (Charles signing for Murray under a Power of Attorney) sold their Achill lands and property to the Reverend Warburton Welford for £2925. (Murray Blacker and his family had removed to Virginia in the U.S.A. in 1872.)

89 In 1870 about 45% of Irish landowners were resident on, or near, their property; about 22% were resident elsewhere in Ireland; and about 23% (or nearly one quarter) were either never, or seldom, resident in Ireland.

90 In 1886 (probably) Charles Boycott and Davitt are believed to have met, by chance, in London. There was no ill will between them; indeed they are said to have had an excellent lunch together.

91 Exhausted Irish seed may have been used in 1879. In 1880 'Champion' seed, supplied from England, was planted. This seed yielded excellently but only when planted at the correct intervals (which was not, always, accomplished by the Irish peasant.)

92 Gifts came in from many sources most being connected with England. These came in from Dublin itself, from England, Scotland and Wales, from France, from 'British Troops in Kandahar, from Madras, Bombay and the Nizam of Hyderabad, from South Africa and Canada, from Buenos Aires, from Tasmania and New Zealand; and, of course from America. (Nearly half of all the money received consisted of gold received from Australia.)

93 W.E. Forster was a brave upright man who had, at least some, knowledge of Ireland.

94 The number of evictions and 'outrages' increased alarmingly:–

Year	Evictions	'Outrages'
1877	2177	236
1878	4679	301
1879	6239	863
1880	10,457	2590

95 By no means everyone, in England, was astonished by the rejection. Many Englishmen still thought of the House of Lords as being 'a House of Gentlemen'; and an authority to which the highest interests of the country might, safely, be committed.
96 William Douglass Boycott became the fifth and last Boycott rector of Burgh-St-Peter (and the present author's grandfather).
97 Guardians appointed under a will have no enforceable duty to act but, almost always, do so. In Common Law a guardian stands in loco parentis; and must take the day to day decisions that a parent would take.
98 Madeline, as a grandmother, told her grandchildren that Annie made her 'peel potatoes' and 'refused to let her sit in front of the fire'. There may well be an element of truth in this! Someone had to peel the potatoes and there may well have been a shortage of peat in the house.
99 Many arms, it is believed, came into Ireland from the U.S.A.
100 This was a large number. They had, probably, received wind of trouble.
101 At about the same time a Co Mayo agent named Ferris died of his (gunshot) wounds and an employee of Lord Ardilaun, living near Cong, was shot and killed.
102 Becker did not know Ireland and had no Irish friends. On arrival in Ireland on 24th October 1880 he went, immediately, to Lough Mask House. He returned there on 10th November. In the meanwhile he travelled in the poorer Irish counties.
103 The four members of the Commission who interviewed Charles were: Lord Bessborough, a 'model' Irish landlord; Baron Dowse, who had been Attorney General for Ireland since 1872; the O'Connor Don, a distinguished Irishman; and Arthur Kavanagh, who was an extraordinary man having been born with only the rudiments of arms and legs. (Despite this handicap Kavanagh travelled far and wide, hunted, fished and shot. He dissented from the Commission's findings and submitted a minority report.)
104 '. . . money had been very cheap. Any man who borrowed a hat or coat went into the bank and got £5,.0.0. . . . The banks paid the rents by their unbounded liberality in giving money. The people are in debt now in all directions . . .'
105 The Royal Irish Constabulary – known as the R.I.C. – were a quite exceptionally fine and well disciplined body of men. All were splendid physical specimens. Many young R.I.C. officers were the sons of gentleman and had graduated at a University. Colonel Bruce, who commanded the R.I.C. at Lough Mask House, wrote that he 'very frequently partook of Captain Boycott's hospitality.'
106 Becker described the poverty in Co. Galway: '. . . pale cheeks, high cheek bones and hollow eyes tell a sorry tale not of sudden want, but of a long course of insufficient food . . . there is something strangely appalling in the pallid looks of people . . . (who live in the finest air in the world) . . . there can be no falsehood in their gaunt famished faces, no fabrication in their own rags, and the nakedness of their children.'
107 Hamilton was said to be a man of 'iron' nerve. He was chosen, constantly, for the most arduous and critical work.
108 In 1880 the British Army was not at its best. Many units reached Ballinrobe wet and tired and having left behind several items of equipment. The troops involved included:
1st Dragoons (now the Blues and Royals):

19th Hussars (now the Light Dragoons):
76th Regiment (now the Duke of Wellington's Regiment):
84th Regiment (now the York and Lancaster Regiment [disbanded in 1968]):
Royal Engineers:
Army Service Corps (now the Royal Logistic Corps)
Army Hospital Corps (now the Royal Army Medical Corps).

109 As far as is known no practice ammunition was issued. To become an even passable shot with a revolver (which has a very short barrel) is difficult.

110 The food was said to be good. The *Daily Express* supplies included:

2 sacks of oatmeal	6 stoves
3 barrels and 1 sack of biscuits	2 cooking stoves
3 cwt tinned meat (in cans)	1 gross Lucifer matches
2.5 cwt bacon	4 foghorns (for signalling)
2 large hams	100 empty sacks
1 large cheese	Towels and blankets
25lbs butter	Soap
25lbs tea	Candles
1 cwt sugar	Tins (for drinking)
25 tins Swiss condensed milk	Plates
25 tins concentrated coffee and milk	Knives and forks (including carvers)
6 drums salt	Flare lanterns
30 lbs tobacco	Dark lanterns
14 gallons whisky	6 carts and 6 horses

111 Daly had become President of the Co Mayo Land League. He advised the people to 'feed your families, pay your suppliers and, if you have any money left, pay the landlords'. After 1881 Daly came to the view that the Land League had deserted the social group to help which it had been formed. It is said of Daly that he was 'the most undeservedly forgotten man in Irish history'.

112 The *Freemen's Journal* remarked that the scenes in Ballinrobe were 'the nearest approach to any army beheld since Humbert and his Frenchmen were at Castlebar in '93'

113 For such an occasion Charles used, probably, his Crown Derby Dinner Service which is now in the ownership of Dr W. O'Sullivan of Killarney. (Each piece bore a red hand-painted 'mark' to indicate that it was manufactured between 1782–1820).

114 Harvesting in 1880 was hard work. The present author has a newspaper illustration of Charles driving a two horse reaping machine and of his wife and his niece bundling up the corn. Assheton Weekes – in a smart bowler – and two armed constables of the R.I.C. stand guard. Two of the female servants who refused to leave Charles's employ peep out from afar. Charles – not surprisingly! – looks anxious. (The picture actually shows three pretty girls doing the bundling up but this is a mistake.)

115 Nally was an outstandingly good athlete and an attractive well known local man. It is believed that he and Charles were friendly. His intrusion into the camp was, probably, no more than a – slightly drink taken? – joke.

116 Coffins were used, sometimes, to conceal things that were better concealed; sugar, upon which duty had not been paid and to the weight of a man, was one of them.

117 The way in which their well-nourished bodies had been able to react to

the physical demands made upon them surprised those few local Mayo men who had seen it.

118 Gladstone's historian has told the present author that Gladstone did not order Charles to leave Ireland for the simple reason that he had no power to do so.

Parts Three and Four

1 'Boycotting in the County of Cork'. Purcell & Co, Printers, Patrick St, Cork 1886.

2 Whilst the word 'boycott' is still, comparatively, new the offence the word describes is old (the idea of 'boycotting' was used in India many centuries ago). The surname 'Boycott' and the (new) verb to 'boycott' contains seven letters of which only the two O's are vowels. For this reason the word 'boycott', in itself, is hard and unyielding. The word matches its meaning. It may be for this reason that the word has travelled as far, and as fast, as it has. It performs a duty which is, almost always, unpleasant.

3 Medals are seldom presented to the members of expeditions which are thought to have failed. The Boycott Expedition had a strictly limited objective; and, in achieving this, it was successful.

4 Manning's medal is now in the National Museum in Dublin.

5 The brooch is now in the ownership of Mrs A.G. Evershed of Sevenoaks (one of Madeleine's descendants). Because they get caught up, so easily, in clothing a number of the brooch's tiny heads of corn are now either missing or broken.

6 On their outward journey to New York Charles was accompanied by his brother the Reverend Edmund Boycott.

7 Fighting had been severe. 204,000 men were killed in battle many as the result of hand-to-hand fighting. 510,000 men were wounded. 284,000 men died of disease. When, eventually, all the dead had been buried it was found that no less than 54% of all graves remembered only an 'unknown soldier'. For the most part Union soldiers were sufficiently fed. Confederate soldiers were not; many were forced to forage.

8 Most wars, between 'advanced' societies, are innovative. Several civil war developments threw their gaunt shadows on to the battlegrounds of France and the Atlantic fifty years later. The Gatling ten-barrelled gun, which, when powered externally, was capable of firing 3000 rounds per minute; the movement of troops by rail; the extensive use of trenches; the organised care of the wounded; reconnaissance from a manned balloon; land and naval mines; steps in the development of a reliable ocean-going submarine. (Barbed wire was not a civil war invention. It was, however, first used in America shortly after the Civil War.)

9 The following are known to have been amongst Murray's 'Colony' in Amelia County:
W.W. Astell (married Rosa M. Blacker); C. Beauclerk; A. St J Boycott; George Chapman; W.H. Clare; H.H.Clarke; M.S.Cottrell; W.F.G. Degacher (married Amelia E. Blacker); W.H. Handcock (married Theodosia V. Blacker); Thomas Hunter; Charles Le Coque (whose mother was Charlotte Blacker); Charles Middleton; E.H. de Morlegne; John Peter; Harry Sandys; G.B. Sloat; C.S. Trench; E.H. Tripp; R.L. Tritton; L.E.S.

Vidal. (The colonists also included Elizabeth A. Slack [who, later, married E.H. Tripp] and Bena Anderson [who, later, married Harry Sandys.])

(Murray and Frances Blacker had four daughters. The three eldest married members of their father's Virginian Colony as shown above; the youngest, Frances M. Blacker, did not marry.)

10 'Haw' means hawthorn. 'Branch' refers to a stream on the plantation which joins the Appomattox River. (A house has existed on the site, probably, since 1740.)

11 'Carpet baggers' were political adventurers from 'the North' who usurped power in the 'Southern', and defeated, states. They earned their – despised – name because their only 'property qualification' was their travelling 'carpet bags'. (Made, usually, from surplus runs of actual carpet.)

12 Mrs McConnaughey, in a letter to the present author, described the strong 'family outlook' which dominated life at Haw Branch before the Civil War. When her great-grandmother was given Haw Branch by her father sixty-eight slaves came with it; these included elderly Negroes and Negro children. Everyone did their best to keep 'family units' together; their slaves were treated well.

A caste system existed among the Negroes themselves. The children's Mammy – (Mammy Hodges) – sometimes took care of two or three generations and was dearly loved by the family. The butler had a place of honour in the system; as did the driver or coachman. The cook had her own kingdom (although daily supplies were meted out to her by the mistress of the house). 'Domestic servants' worked in the 'big house'. The lowest in the scale were the field hands; these, usually, were not qualified for anything but simple manual labour. In addition slaves provided the blacksmiths, gardeners and carpenters needed by a large plantation. (The carpenters carved the many tobacco leaves which still decorate the old house.)

13 Arthur St John Boycott (1863–1940) was the fourth child and eldest son of the Reverend Arthur William Boycott (who, had he not pre-deceased his own father, would have become the fourth Rector). A.W. Boycott died in 1865; his wife Isabella (née Blacker) in 1874. St John, together with three surviving and elder sisters and one younger brother then became Charles's wards. For various reasons, connected probably with the early death of both parents, St John's schooling had been disturbed; he went to Rugby when he was twelve but left when he was thirteen; later he went to Clifton; he never attended a University.

It seems certain that Uncle Murray offered the boy a home at Haw Branch. Later St John took out U.S. nationality. Horses were his life. He became a MFH in New York, Philadelphia and Virginia. He owned, and ran, a riding academy in New York. He became known, internationally, as a horseman. He died aged seventy-eight; and, literally, astride a horse as he was teaching a young man how to change a horse's step. He married Selina Marryat an Englishwoman. They had one (surviving) son and three daughters all of whom lived in America. St John gave a silver plate (still competed for annually) to the Amelia County Horse Show. Throughout his life St John remained devoted to Haw Branch. St John and his wife lie buried in Amelia County not far from Haw Branch.

As already stated St John (aged seventeen) was living with Charles at Lough Mask during October and November 1880. Some considerable time later he wrote his own account of 'the siege'; this included descriptions of

Charles and comments upon events. What he then wrote is valuable but he was young in 1880 and he left the writing of his remembrances too late; it is a pity he did not commit himself to paper earlier.

14 Epilepsy is the second most common neurological disorder after migraine. Its National Society was not founded until three years after William III died. The disorder becomes apparent when a message – within the brain – becomes blocked and so either is not further directed or is misdirected. Human beings may suffer from varying degrees of epilepsy. It is believed that Caesar, Alexander the Great, King Alfred and Napoleon all suffered from it.

15 There is one not far from where the present author lives.

16 The *Fermanagh Mail* and *Enniskillen Chronicle* of 29th October 1885 said that Charles 'of all men, was the man most free from danger . . .' Captain Boycott is 'very popular in his district.'

17 The ignorance that still dominated medicine is illustrated by an advertisement which appeared in the *Northampton Mercury* of 2nd June 1886.

'Perfect Health restored without medicine, purging, or Expense, by Du Barry's Delicious Rivalenta Ararica Food and Tonic and Salts, which repair the mucous membrane of Stomach and Bowels, the Blood, the Nerves, Lungs, Liver, Brain, Voice, and Breath – curing Dyspepsia, Indigestion, Constipation, Consumption, Diarrhoea, Dysentery, Acidity, Heartburn, Phlegm, Flatulency, Feverish Breath, Nervous (sic), Bilious, Pulmonary, Glandular, Kidney and Liver Complaints; Cough, Asthma, Typhoid, Scarlet, Gastric, Enteric and Bilious Fevers; Diphtheria, Spasms, Coughs, Measles, Cholera, Impurities and Poverty of the Blood; Ague; Nausea and Vomiting after Eating, during Pregnancy, and at sea; Eruptions, Sleeplessness, Dropsy, Paralysis, Noises in the Ears, Atrophy, Wasting in Adults & Children; 37 years invariable success with old and young, even in the most hopeless cases. 10,000 cures, including those of H.I.M. the late Emperor Nicholas of Russia, Mr H.M. Stanley, the African Explorer, the Marchioness of Brehán, Lord Stuart de Decies; of Dr Ure, Wurzer, Shorland, Routh etc. of London. Four times more nourishing than meat; and assimilated when no other food will keep in the stomach. It saves 50 times the cost of medicine. It rears successfully the most delicate children from their birth. Suitably packed for all climates. Sells – in tins of half lb at 2/-; 1lb 3/6; 2lbs 6/-; 5lbs 14/-; 12lbs 32/- or about 2d per meal. Also Revolenta Biscuits, 1lb 3/6; 2lbs 6/-. All tins carriage free on receipt of P.O.O. Du Barry and Co (Limited) No 77 Regent Street, London W; and at all Grocers and Chemists.'

18 30.0 to 40.0 million people could not, for long, attempt to rule the world. (The 1871 census showed that some 31.0 million people then lived in England.)

19 Lees became the Chief Constable of the Northamptonshire County Police in 1875 at the age of thirty-two. In 1890 he was appointed Chief Constable of the Isle of Wight; in which capacity he received the Queen's personal thanks for his handling of the Diamond Jubilee celebrations.

20 The male heir to the Flixton Estate was killed in the Second World War. The estate was broken up, and sold, in 1950. (Later the old Flixton Estate was found to be an immense source of gravel.)

21 Douglass's appeal for money for Upton Church is still preserved in the bibliography of Norfolk.

22 Douglass Boycott married Alice M. Godfrey – the daughter of the Reverend E. Godfrey – on 13th July 1887.

BIBLIOGRAPHY

DIVIDED INTO 'ENGLISH' AND 'IRISH' groups. (These form only part of a longer reading list)

England

Agricultural Revolution in Norfolk. Naomi Riches. 1967.

Boileau Letters (10 letters from C.S. Boileau to Lady A.M. Elliot in Brighton 1830). (Norfolk Record Office).

Captain Swing. Hobsbawn & Rudé.

Church Revival. S. Baring-Gould. Methuen 1914.

Coastguard: An Official History of H.M. Coastguard. William Webb. H.M.S.O. 1876.

Contentious Tithe. Eric J. Evans. Routledge & Kegan Paul.

Crowd in Hitory 1730-1848. George Rudé. Routledge & Kegan Paul 1976.

Various writings by Rear Admiral Sir Charles Cunningham R.N.

Englishman's Food. J.C. Drummond & Anne Wilbraham. Jonathan Cape 1939.

English Country Life 1780- 1930. E.W. Bovill. O.U.P. 1962.

English Landed Society in C. XIX. F.M.L. Thompson. Routledge & Kegan Paul 1963.

A Fiendish Outrage: A Study of Animal Maiming in E. Anglia 1830-1870. J.E. Archer.

Gentlemen and Poaching: English Game Laws 1671–1831. P.B. Munsche. Gladstone Diaries (Vol IX) (Ed. Dr H.C.G. Matthew).

Great Affray. Harry Hopkins.

Growth of British Civil Service 1780–1939. E.W. Cohen. Case 1965.

Harriette Wilson: Memoirs. Harriette Wilson. Folio Society 1964.

History of the English Clergy. C.K. Francis Brown. Faith Press 1953.

History of the Parson's Wife. Margaret H. Watt. Faber & Faber 1943.

Jacobin City: Norwich 1798–1802. C.B. Jewson. Blacker & Glasgow 1975.

King William IV. Philip Zeigler. Collins 1971.
Long Affray – The Poaching Wars 1760–1914. Harry Hopkins. Secker and Warburg 1985.
Life in God's Family. W.D. Boycott. Stockwell 1908.
Learning and Living 1790–1960. J.F.C. Harrison. Routledge & Kegan Paul 1961.
Man & Nature on Tidal Waters. A.H. Patterson. Methuen 1909.
Mid-Victorian Britain 1851–1875. G. Best. Fontana.
Mr Secretary Peel. Life to 1830. Norman Gash.
Nature in Norfolk; A Heritage in Trust. Norfolk Naturalist Trust.
Naval Mutinies of 1797. Conrad Gill. Manchester University Press 1913.
Norfolk Notebook. Lilian Rider Haggard. Faber & Faber 1946.
North Sea. George Morey. Frederick Muller, London 1968.
Notable British Trials; Trial of J.B. Rush. Ed. W.T. Shore.
19th Century Country Parson (c 1832–1900). A. Tindall Hart & Edward Carpenter. Shewsbury 1954.
Norfolk in Europe. Kenneth Hudson (Norfolk Museum Services 1980.)
Observations on the Fauna of Norfolk. Rev Richard Lubbock. Muscett, London 1845.
Peasants & Poachers; A Study of Rural Disorder in Norfolk. M.J. Carter. Boydell Press.
Perlustrations of Great Yarmouth (3 Vols). C.J. Palmer.
Private Lives, Public Spirit. José Harris. O.U.P. 1993.
Poor Man's Friend. William Cobbett. Dent, London 1956.
Report on the Fisheries of Norfolk. F.T. Buckland. 1875.
Dr Routh. R.D. Middleton. O.U.P. 1938.
Rural Rides. William Cobbett. Dent, London 1956.
Scott Papers. (Property of Donald Scott. W. Sussex.)
Suffer and be Still. Women in the Victorian Age. Ed. Martha Vicinus. Indiana University Press 1972.
Stress and Stability in Late 18th Century Britain. Ian R. Christie. O.U.P.
Victorian People and Ideas. R.D. Altick. Clarendon Press, Oxford 1984.
Victorian Shooting Days. East Anglia 1810–1910. Derek E. Johnson. Boydell Press 1981.
'Waveney Valley'. (E. Anglian Magazine.) D.R. Butler.
Wild Life on a Norfolk Estuary. A.H. Patterson. Methuen 1907.
Wherries and Waterways. Robert Maltster and Terence Dalton. Appletree 1970.

Ireland

Achill. Kenneth McNally. David and Charles 1973.
Advance of the Fungi. E.C. Large. Jonathan Cape 1940.

After Sixty Years. Shan F. Bullock. Simpson, Low and Marston c1930.
Dearth, Diet and Disease in Ireland 1850: A Case Study of Nutritional Deficiencies. E.M. Crawford. Queens University, Belfast.
Disturbed Ireland. Bernard H. Becker. Macmillan 1881.
Economic Thought on Irish Questions 1817–1870. R.D.C. Black. O.U.P. 1960.
Edward Nangle and the Achill Mission 1834–1852. Irene Weldon 1884.
Edward Nangle and the Achill Mission 1834–1852. Colonel F.E. Nangle. (published privately).
Lord Erne and his Lough Mask Tenantry. (Leaflet) Dublin 1880.
Gleanings in the West of Ireland. Honorable and Reverend S.G. Osborn. Boone, London 1850.
Great Famine. R. Dudley Edwards and T. Desmond Williams. Bourne & Nolan, Dublin 1956.
Great Hunger. Cecil Woodham-Smith. Hamish Hamilton 1962.
History of the Great Irish Famine of 1847. Reverend John O'Rourke. Duffy 1902.
History of Scurvy & Vitamin C. Kenneth J. Carpenter. O.U.P 1968.
History and Social Influence of the Potato. R.N. Salaman. O.U.P. 1949.
Ireland. Robert Kee. Wiedenfeld & Nicolson, Oxford 1950.
An Invasion That Failed. Commander E.H.S. Jones R.N.
Irish Administration 1801–1914. R.B. McDowell. Routledge & Kegan Paul 1964.
Ireland: After The Famine. R.B. McDowell.
Ireland: Before the Famine 1798–1848. O'Tuthaugh. Gill and Macmillan 1972.
Ireland from 1798–1898. William O'Connor Morris. Innes 1898.
Ireland: Its Scenery, Character etc. Mr & Mrs S.C. Hall. London 1841.
Ireland Sober, Ireland Free. Elizabeth Malcolm. Gill and Macmillan 1986.
An Irish Portrait. Paul Henry Batsford. London 1951.
The Incredible Mr Kavanagh. Donald McCormack. Macmillan.
Islands of Ireland. T.H. Mason. Mercier Press. Cork 1936.
Insanity and the Insane in Post-Famine Ireland. M. Finnane Croome Helm. London 1981.
Landlords and Tenants in Ireland. Dun Finlay 1881.
Land Question and the Irish Economy 1870–1903. Barbara Solow. Harvard University Press 1971.
James Finton Lalor: Patriot and Political Essayist. Talbot Press.
Modernisation of Irish Society 1848–1918. Joseph Lee. Gill and Macmillan 1973.
National Horse Racing Museum. Newmarket.
New History (of Ireland) 1801–1879. O.U.P
Paddy & Mr Punch. R.F. Foster. Allen Lane. Penguin Press 1993.

Origins & Development of Boycotting. Gerard Moran (Galway Archaelogical & Historical Society Journal 1985/86.)
Prose, Poems and Parodies of Percy French. Simpkins Marshall 1922.
Protestant Crusade in Ireland 1800–1870. Desmond Bowen. Gill & Macmillan 1978.
Realities of Irish Life. W. Steuart Trench. Longmans Green 1870.
Reflections on the Revolution in France (1790). Edmund Burke. Everyman 1910.
Reminiscences of My Irish Journey in 1849. Carlyle. London 1882.
Reminiscences of an Irish Land Agent. S.M. Hussey. Duckworth 1904.
Short History of Ireland. J.C. Beckett.
Sin, Sheep & Scotsmen. Dr W.E. Vaughan. Appletree Press, Belfast 1983.
Tour of Ireland: with Meditations and Reflections. James Johnson M.D.. Highley, London 1844.
Three Months Tour in Ireland. Madame de Bovet. Chapman Hall 1891.
Troubles of Captain Boycott. (Article.) T.H. Corfe.
Twilight of the Ascendancy. M. Bence Jones. Constable 1987.
World of the Irish R.M. Somerville & Ross. Viking 1985.
Wrecks (a) British Encyclopedia. (9th Editions 1888.)
(b) *The Life Boat*. (Research Publishing Co. London).
150 years of Irish Railways. Fergus Mulligan. Appletree Press 1971.
Valuation Office of Ireland (Valuation List 29). Mayo Electorial Division (Slievemore).
Voices in Ireland. P.J. Kavanagh. Murray 1994.

Index

NOTE: CB = Charles Cunningham Boycott